POLITICAL LANDSCAPES OF DONALD TRUMP

This book delves into the life and work of President Donald Trump, who is arguably the most famous and controversial person in the world today. While his administration has received enormous attention, few have studied the spatial dimensions of his policies.

Political Landscapes of Donald Trump explores the geographies of Trump from multiple conceptual standpoints. It contextualizes Donald and his rise to power within the geography of his victory in 2016. Several essays in the book are concerned with his white ethnonationalist political platform and social bases of support. Others focus on Trump's use of Twitter, his ties to professional wrestling, and his innumerable lies and deceits. Yet another set delves into the geopolitics of his foreign policies, notably in Cuba, Korea, the Middle East, and China. Finally, it covers how his administration has addressed – or failed to address – climate change and its treatment of undocumented immigrants.

This book will be of interest to anyone interested in the Trump administration, as well as social scientists and the informed lay public.

Barney Warf is a Professor of Geography at the University of Kansas. His research and teaching interests lie within the broad domain of human geography. Much of his research concerns producer services and telecommunications, particularly the geographies of the internet, including the digital divide, e-government, and internet censorship.

POLITICAL LANDSCAPES OF DONALD TRUMP

Edited by Barney Warf

LONDON AND NEW YORK

First published 2021
by Routledge
2 Park Square, Milton Park, Abingdon, Oxon OX14 4RN

and by Routledge
52 Vanderbilt Avenue, New York, NY 10017

Routledge is an imprint of the Taylor & Francis Group, an *informa* business

© 2021 selection and editorial matter, Barney Warf; individual chapters, the contributors

The rights of Barney Warf to be identified as the author of the editorial material, and of the authors for their individual chapters, has been asserted in accordance with sections 77 and 78 of the Copyright, Designs and Patents Act 1988.

All rights reserved. No part of this book may be reprinted or reproduced or utilised in any form or by any electronic, mechanical, or other means, now known or hereafter invented, including photocopying and recording, or in any information storage or retrieval system, without permission in writing from the publishers.

Trademark notice: Product or corporate names may be trademarks or registered trademarks, and are used only for identification and explanation without intent to infringe.

British Library Cataloguing-in-Publication Data
A catalogue record for this book is available from the British Library

Library of Congress Cataloging-in-Publication Data
Names: Warf, Barney, 1956- editor.
Title: Political landscapes of Donald Trump / edited by Barney Warf.
Description: Abingdon, Oxon : Routledge, 2020. | Includes bibliographical references and index.
Identifiers: LCCN 2019057980 (print) | LCCN 2019057981 (ebook) | ISBN
9780367196998 (hbk) | ISBN 9780367197001 (pbk) | ISBN 9780429242670
(ebk)
Subjects: LCSH: Trump, Donald, 1946- | Presidents--United
States--Election--2016. | Electoral geography--United States. | United
States--Politics and government--2017- | Nationalism--United
States--History--21st century.
Classification: LCC E912 .P65 2020 (print) | LCC E912 (ebook) | DDC
973.933092--dc23
LC record available at https://lccn.loc.gov/2019057980
LC ebook record available at https://lccn.loc.gov/2019057981

ISBN: 978-0-367-19699-8 (hbk)
ISBN: 978-0-367-19700-1 (pbk)
ISBN: 978-0-429-24267-0 (ebk)

Typeset in Bembo
by KnowledgeWorks Global Ltd.

This volume is dedicated to the very fine people of Lawrence Liberals.

CONTENTS

List of figures	*x*
List of tables	*xiii*
Notes on contributors	*xv*

1	Introduction	1
	Barney Warf	

PART I
Trump's history and biography   9

2	The Donald in context	11
	Barney Warf	
3	Three generations of Trump schemes: The private side of planning history	55
	Samuel Stein	

PART II
Trump's electoral victory and its aftermath   67

4	The geographies of Trump's electoral success	69
	Ron Johnston, Charles Pattie, Ryne Rohla, David Manley, and Kelvyn Jones	

viii Contents

5 The 2016 U.S. presidential election and Trump's populist
rhetoric: Wisconsin as a case study 92
Ryan Weichelt

6 The heart of whiteness: Patterns of race, class,
and prejudice in the divided Midwest 111
David Norman Smith and Eric Hanley

7 Postfascist (sub)urbanism: "Social cleansing"
in the age of Trump 129
Scott Markley and Coleman Allums

8 The five pillars of Trump's white ethnonationalist appeal 144
David H. Kaplan

9 "Standing with patriots"? Trump, Twitter,
and the silent majority 161
Lewis J. Dowle

10 Donald Trump and the potency of his assemblage 180
Sam Page

11 Smarks, marks, and the electorate: Trump, wrestling
rhetorics, and electoral politics 193
David Beard and John Heppen

12 Presidential lies and post-truth geographies 214
Barney Warf

PART III
The geopolitics of the Trump administration **233**

13 With friends like these: Trump's Middle East geopolitics
as the space of exception 235
Carl T. Dahlman and Nathan S. French

14 Trump in the tropics: Territorialities and the misdirection
of U.S. foreign policy toward Cuba 249
Richard N. Gioioso and Lisa A. Baglione

Contents ix

15 Peace for prosperity? The geopolitics
of the Korean peace process 265
Steven M. Radil and Jin-Soo Lee

16 The Trump effect in China: Social aspects
of the Sino-U.S. trade conflict and the
pro-Trump group in China 280
Xiang Zhang

17 Tangier Island for Trump: A geographic reconfiguring
of visibilities in American climate change displacement
discourse 298
Victoria Herrmann

18 The emotional regime of apathy, Trump, and climate
injustice 311
Nino Antadze

19 Undocumented youth and their unequal rights:
State responses to Trump's immigration policies 322
Marie Price and Nicole Prchal Svajlenka

Index 339

LIST OF FIGURES

2.1	Trump supporters at a rally in Arizona	15
4.1	The percentage of the two-party vote won by Romney in 2012 and Trump in 2016, by state	70
4.2	The percentage of the two-party vote won by Romney in 2012 and Trump in 2016, by congressional district	71
4.3	The percentage of the two-party vote won by Romney in 2012 and Trump in 2016, by county	73
4.4	The percentage of precincts won by a landslide in metropolitan areas by Romney in 2012 and Trump in 2016	78
4.5	The percentage of precincts won by a landslide in the rural portions of states by Romney in 2012 and Trump in 2016	79
4.6	The Republican Party candidate's percentage share of the two-party popular vote and the Electoral College votes at presidential elections, 1960-2016	86
4.7	Bias in the allocation of Electoral College votes at presidential elections, 1960-2016	87
4.8	The electorate and abstentions bias components at presidential elections, 1960–2016	88
4.9	The distribution efficiency bias component at presidential elections, 1960–2016	89
5.1	Percent voting Democrat at county level, 2016 United States presidential election	97
5.2	Percent voting Democrat at county level, 2012 United States presidential election	97
5.3	Plurality victory by county, 2016 United States presidential election	98
5.4	Percent change in Democratic vote in the presidential elections, at county level, 2012 to 2016	99

List of figures **xi**

5.5	Change in Republican votes in the presidential elections, at county level, 2012 to 2016	99
5.6	Counties where Trump performed better or worse in 2016 than Mitt Romney in the 2012 presidential election, by total votes cast	100
5.7	Primary election rallies held by Trump in Wisconsin, 2016	103
5.8	2016 Republican primary election results	104
5.9	Trump's general election rallies held in Wisconsin, 2016	106
5.10	Television markets for northern Wisconsin and Minneapolis	107
5.11	Percent voting for Hillary Clinton in the 2016 presidential election in Wisconsin at voting district level	108
6.1	Distribution of non-college educated voters, 2016.	113
7.1	Map of Marietta, Georgia	136
7.2	(A) Flagstone Village and Woodlands Park apartments, May 5, 2014 (B) After demolition, May 7, 2016. (C) Training complex for Atlanta United FC, March 31, 2017	137
7.3	Racial change in Marietta and Franklin Road, 1970–2013/17	137
8.1	Percent GOP vote level change, 2012–2016	149
8.2	Trump vote share by percent non-college educated whites	152
8.3	Percent of population reporting "American" as their only ancestry, 2017	155
9.1	The silent majority in the Republican primaries	165
9.2	Tweet #1	166
9.3	Tweet #2	167
9.4	Tweet #3	168
9.5	Tweet #4	169
9.6	Tweet #5	170
9.7	Tweet #6	171
9.8	Tweet #7	172
9.9	Tweet #8	173
9.10	Tweet #9	174
10.1	"Stupid" (Boot 2017)	186
10.2	"Deformed" (Dancyger 2018)	187
10.3	"Mad" (Chunn 2017)	187
10.4	"Illegitimate" (Solnit 2017)	187
10.5	"Usurper" (Singh 2016)	187
10.6	"Sin" (Klaas 2017)	187
11.1	Wrestling attendance ratio, 2015	202
11.2	Wrestling attendance ratio, 2016	205
11.3	2016 presidential election results at 2015 WWE event sites	208
11.4	2016 presidential election results at 2016 WWE event sites	208
11.5	Trump vote prediction, 2015	209

xii List of figures

11.6	Trump vote prediction, 2016	210
12.1	Cumulative number of lies told by Donald Trump, Jan. 2017–July 2020	215
12.2	Average number of lies told per month by Donald Trump, Jan. 2017–May 2020	216
15.1	Meeting in the DMZ in June 2019 between President Moon, Trump, and Kim Jong-Un	269
15.2	Destruction of a DMZ guard post	274
15.3	A version of the "new economic map" from the South Korea government's Ministry of Unification (2018a)	275
15.4	Dorasan Station map and sign – explaining the hoped-for outcomes of a lasting South-North peace	277
16.1	Total trade value and components of U.S.-China Trade, 1980–2016	284
16.2	Percentage of China's exports by sector, 2016	284
16.3	Export-to-import ratio in mainland China, 2017	285
16.4	Export-to-import ratio of U.S.-Sino trade among Chinese provinces, 2017	286
16.5	Exports to the U.S. from Chinese provinces, 2017 (as a percentage of total exports)	286
16.6	Exports to the U.S. from Chinese provinces, 2017 (as a percentage of GDP)	287
19.1	DACA recipients by state	327
19.2	State lawsuits with regard to DACA	328
19.3	Undocumented youth and access to higher education by state	330
19.4	Undocumented authorization to drive by state	332

LIST OF TABLES

4.1	The number of states, congressional districts, and counties according to whether Trump outperformed Romney or vice versa, by type of state, and the percentage of precincts won by landslides by each candidate	72
4.2	The number of counties where Trump outperformed Romney and vice versa, by type of state and type of county	73
4.3	The county mean change in the percentage point share of the two-party vote gained by Trump and Romney, by type of state and county	75
4.4	The Patchwork Nation's 12 community types	75
4.5	The Republican candidates' (county means) share of the votes cast by community type and type of state	76
4.6	The county mean change in the percentage point share of the two-party vote gained by Trump and Romney, by community type and type of state	77
4.7	The number of counties where Trump outperformed Romney and vice versa, by community type and type of state	77
4.8	Binomial logistic regressions of voting at the 2012 and 2016 presidential elections	81
4.9	The distribution of visits and events during the 2016 presidential campaign	84
4.10	The distribution of spending on booked advertisements by the presidential candidates and supporting PACS, October 21 – November 7, 2016	85
6.1	Percentages of voters in the 2016 electorate by race and region	114
6.2	Percentages of white voters in the 2016 electorate by region and education	114

xiv List of tables

6.3a	Percentages of white voters favoring Romney and Trump by region, election year, and education, excluding voters who favored third-party candidates	115
6.3b	Percentages of white voters favoring Romney and Trump by region, election year, and education, excluding voters who favored third-party candidates	115
6.4	Demographic variables relevant to voting for Trump among white voters	116
6.5	Logistic regression coefficients predicting presidential vote choice by year and region, white voters without college degrees only (voters favoring third-party candidates excluded)	117
6.6	Dispersion of attitudes toward leaders by education, white voters only (N=1883). High scores, on a 1–10 scale, indicate stronger support	118
6.7	Percentages of white voters favoring the Republican presidential candidates in 2012 and 2016 by education	119
6.8	Mean DL values by region and education, 2016, white voters only (N=1883)	119
6.9	Percentages scoring high (>0) on the Domineering Leader (DL) scale by region, education, and percentages voting for Trump, 2016, white voters only	120
11.1	Highest wrestling attendance ratios, 2015	203
11.2	Lowest wrestling attendance ratios, 2015	204
11.3	Lowest wrestling attendance ratios, 2016	206
11.4	Highest wrestling attendance ratios, 2016	207
11.5	Regression analysis results Trump vote and attendance ratio	209
11.6	Regression analysis results using best predicted metro areas	210
12.1	Lies Trump has told most frequently, as of May 2019	218
16.1	Numbers of registered users of the Baidu Trump discussion board	290
16.2	Frequently used neologisms on the pro-Trump discussion board	293
16.3	IP address based locations of frequent discussants on the pro-Trump discussion board	294

NOTES ON CONTRIBUTORS

Coleman Allums is a National Science Foundation Graduate Research Fellow in the Department of Geography at the University of Georgia. His research interests primarily cohere around urban and suburban geographies of racial capitalism in the U.S. South, while also intersecting matters of critical theory and of epistemology in qualitative and postqualitative inquiry.

Nino Antadze is an Assistant Professor of Environmental Studies at the University of Prince Edward Island, Canada. Her interdisciplinary work focuses on moral dimensions of environmental issues. In particular, Dr. Antadze studies environmental planning processes with an emphasis on environmental justice, and large-scale environmental change with a focus on climate justice, sustainability transitions, and social innovations.

Lisa A. Baglione is a Professor of Political Science and member of the International Relations Program at Saint Joseph's University. She has published works on, among other topics, American-Soviet arms control decision-making and the post-communist transformation of Russia, and she is the author of *Writing a Research Paper in Political Science: A Practical Guide to Inquiry, Structure, and Methods*, now in its fourth edition with CQ/Sage.

David Beard is Professor of Rhetoric in the Department of English, Linguistics, and Writing Studies at the University of Minnesota Duluth. He has published in journals like the *International Journal of Listening*, *Archival Science*, *Philosophy and Rhetoric*, *Southern Journal of Communication*, and *Enculturation*, among other venues. With Heather Graves, he co-edited *The Rhetoric of Oil* (Routledge). With John Heppen, he has published several articles and book chapters about professional wrestling.

xvi Notes on contributors

Carl T. Dahlman is Professor of Geography and International Studies at Miami University in Oxford, Ohio. His most recent publications have focused on borders, migration, and nationalism in Europe, the former Yugoslavia, and Kurdistan. He is currently writing a book on the temporal geopolitics of Kosovo, as well as studies of decentralization and ethnic identity in that region.

Lewis J. Dowle is a PhD student at the University of St Andrews, Scotland. His research interests within political geography include borders, migration, and emotional geopolitics, with a specific focus on theorising borders in the Nordic context. Supervised by Sharon Leahy, Mike Kesby, and David McCollum, Lewis received the American Association of Geographers' 2019 Political Geography Specialty Group's PhD Student Paper Award for a paper entitled "Toward a (Co) Relational Border? Order, Care and Chaos in a Nordic Context."

Nathan S. French is an Assistant Professor in the Department of Comparative Religion at Miami University in Oxford, Ohio where he is also an affiliate in International Studies. Recently, he has contributed to the *Routledge Handbook on Islam and Gender* and to *Teaching Islamic Studies in the Age of ISIS, Islamophobia, and the Internet*. His work has also appeared in the *Journal of Religion and Violence* and *Mizan*.

Richard N. Gioioso is an Assistant Professor of Political Science and Director of the Latin American and Latinx Studies Program at Saint Joseph's University in Philadelphia, PA. He researches various aspects of youth and young adulthood in Cuba, including socioeconomic mobility, political attitudes and behaviors, and time management and life planning.

Eric Hanley (PhD UCLA) specializes in economic, environmental, and political sociology. His recent research focuses on political behavior in the United States, specifically the rise of white nationalism. Other projects also include analyses of the anti-mining movement in Peru and the political and economic processes contributing to land degradation in western China. Recent publications include "State Corporatism and Environmental Harm: Tax Farming and Desertification in Northwestern China" (with KuoRay Mao, 2018, *Journal of Agrarian Change*) and "The Anger Games: Who Voted for Donald Trump in the 2016 Election, and Why?" (with David Smith, *Critical Sociology*, 2018).

John Heppen is Professor of Geography at the University of Wisconsin River Falls. His teaching and research interests are in political geography and the geography of the United States. He was one of the editors of the *Atlas of the 2016 Elections*.

Victoria Herrmann is the managing director of The Arctic Institute, a nonprofit dedicated to Arctic security research. As a National Geographic Explorer, she traveled across the country in 2016–2017 interviewing 350 community leaders to identify gaps in climate change adaptation support. Her current project, Rise Up to Rising Tides, is creating an online matchmaking platform that connects pro bono experts with climate-affected communities. Dr. Herrmann teaches sustainability management at American University and science communication at the University Centre of the Westfjords, Iceland.

Ron Johnston was a professor in the School of Geographical Sciences at the University of Bristol, UK. He published widely in the field of electoral studies including work on the spatial polarisation of voting patterns at recent United States elections. He passed away as this volume was in production.

Kelvyn Jones is Emeritus Professor of Geography at the University of Bristol, UK. He is a Fellow of the British Academy, being elected to both to Sociology, Demography and Social Statistics, and to Anthropology and Geography. Awarded the Murchison Award of the Royal Geographical Society in 2013 for his contribution to quantitative geography. His research focuses on the analysis of social science data with complex structures through the application of multilevel models; especially in relation to change and health outcomes.

David H. Kaplan is Professor of Geography at Kent State University. His research interests include nationalism, borderlands, ethnic and racial segregation, urban and regional development, housing finance, and sustainable transportation. Dr. Kaplan edits the *Geographical Review* and *National Identities*. He is the President of the American Association of Geographers (2019–2020) and Councilor for the American Geographical Society.

Jin-Soo Lee is a Ph.D. student in the Department of Geography and Geological Science at the University of Idaho. He is interested in the geopolitics and geoeconomics of East Asia. His research examines the role of capitalist development in the peace-making process between North and South Korea and the geopolitics of the U.S.–South Korean relationship.

David Manley is a Professor of Human Geography at the University of Bristol. His research spans the urban and political literatures and deals with understanding how neighbourhoods develop, how much segregation matters, how where you live influences your life course, and why people vote in the ways that they do. He uses advanced quantitative methods to explore these issues.

Scott Markley is a Ph.D. student in geography at the University of Georgia. His current research examines the multiple spatial expressions of racial capitalism, directing special attention toward the historically co-constructed geographies

xviii Notes on contributors

of race and economic value in metropolitan areas. His past research has focused on the uneven racial geographies of gentrification and displacement in the Atlanta suburbs, and it has appeared in *Urban Geography, Journal of Urban Affairs, Southeastern Geographer*, and *Atlanta Studies*.

Sam Page is a political geographer currently residing in Helsinki, Finland. His PhD research at University College London into the UK Labour Party's 2015 General Election campaign and the Deleuzo-Guattarian concepts of assemblage and affect, have contributed a novel approach to political parties and electoral geography. He has previously written on Donald Trump's rise to presidency in the U.S. with Professor Jason Dittmer (UCL), and the recent resurgence of London breweries with Dr Adam Dennett (UCL). He has taught political geography at the London School of Economics and Political Science.

Charles Pattie is Professor of Politics at the University of Sheffield. An electoral geographer, he researches contextual effects on voting, local campaign effects, and the influence of geography on electoral systems, and (with Ron Johnston and others) has published widely on those topics.

Marie Price is a Professor of Geography and International Affairs at the George Washington University where she has taught since 1990. A Latin American and migration specialist, her studies have explored human migration's impact on development and social change. She is President of the American Geographical Society and a non-resident fellow of the Migration Policy Institute. Since 2012 she has served on the Board of the Dream Project-VA, an organization that supports undocumented youth in their pursuit of higher education.

Steven M. Radil is an Assistant Professor of Geospatial Science at the U.S. Air Force Academy. As a political geographer, his research examines the geographical dimensions of international and domestic politics. He has regional expertise in sub-Saharan Africa and East Asia and is a co-author of *The Geography of Conflict in North and West Africa* (OECD, 2020).

Ryne Rohla is a postdoctoral scholar with UCLA's Anderson School of Management, having earned a PhD in economics from Washington State University. His research on the social, economic, and policy consequences of political polarization has been published in journals such as *Science*. His extensive political cartography work has been featured by the *New York Times* and other leading popular press.

David Norman Smith (Ph.D., Wisconsin) teaches sociology at the University of Kansas. He is the author of books on Orwell, the modern working class, and Marx's *Capital,* and his articles have appeared in journals including *Sociological Theory, Sociological Quarterly, The American Psychologist, Critical Sociology,* and *Current Perspectives in Social Theory*. With past support from the National Endowment for the Humanities, Smith is editing *Marx's World: Global Society and Capital Accumulation in Karl Marx's Late Manuscripts* for Yale University Press, forthcoming.

Samuel Stein is a housing policy analyst in New York City. He is the author of *Capital City: Gentrification and the Real Estate State* (Verso, 2019). His academic work has been published in *The Journal of Urban Affairs, International Planning Studies, New Labor Forum,* and *Metropolitics*, and his popular writing has appeared in *The Guardian, Jacobin Magazine, The Village Voice* (RIP), and many other publications.

Nicole Prchal Svajlenka is Associate Director of Research for Immigration Policy at the Center for American Progress, where she works on a diverse set of immigration issues with an emphasis on data and quantitative analysis. Svajlenka has spent a decade working in think tanks, including at the Brookings Institution and the Pew Charitable Trusts, researching the relationships between federal, state, and local immigration policies. She holds a Master of Arts in geography from George Washington University and a Bachelor of Arts in environmental geography from Colgate University.

Barney Warf is Professor of Geography at the University of Kansas. His research and teaching interests lie within the broad domain of human geography. Much of his research concerns the geographies of the internet, including the digital divide, e-government, and internet censorship. He views these topics through the lens of political economy and social theory. He also studies corruption and cosmopolitanism. He has authored numerous books and more than 110 journal articles. He is editor of *Geojournal* and co-editor of *Growth and Change*.

Ryan Weichelt is Associate Professor of Geography and Director of First Year Experiences at the University of Wisconsin – Eau Claire. His current research has been focused on electoral geography of Wisconsin and redistricting and gerrymandering studies. Highlighting these issues are recent publications of the *Atlas of the 2016 Elections* (contributor and co-editor) and a chapter in *The Handbook of the Changing World Language Map*, titled "The Language of Reorganizing Electoral Space" with co-author Gerald Webster.

Xiang Zhang is a Lecturer of International Development at Nottingham Trent University in Nottingham, UK. His principle area of specialization is the economic geography of the internet, social changes of digital economy, globalization, and geopolitical issues in the Global South. Currently he is working on the geopolitics of e-commerce in China and its impact on the global trade system. He also writes about the social change in developing countries driven by technological progress and globalization.

1

INTRODUCTION

Barney Warf

Donald J. Trump, 45th president of the United States, is arguably the most famous person in the world at this juncture in history. Brash, bombastic, flamboyant, and constantly in the limelight, he is at the center of enormous political and cultural controversies. He is the defining figure of American politics, generating strong views across the political spectrum, ranging from being a demigod to his supporters to a symbol of authoritarian neoliberalism for his detractors. Since his surprising electoral victory in 2016, Trump has generated wave after wave of publicity, often for his crass outbursts and Twitter storms. For many people, Trump embodies the worst of American culture: arrogance, ignorance, racism, xenophobia, and misogyny. For his followers, the famed "base," largely consisting of white working class voters that propelled him to victory, Trump speaks truth to power, undermines liberal coastal "elites," and is the only force between them and the horrors of the global economy.

Trump is in many ways an icon for those dispossessed by globalization and neoliberalism, the working class that has seen limited opportunities, declining fortunes, and stagnant wages for two generations. His outlook and behavior are often mirrored around the world by autocrats and dictators who rode similar waves of conservative populism to power.

Since he announced his presidential ambitions, it became abundantly clear that Trump was a candidate – and a president – unlike any other. Trump has systematically violated every norm of politics, hurling childish taunts and insults, boasting incessantly, and spewing forth vast numbers of lies. His aggression and pugnaciousness are unrivalled. Indeed, many mental health professionals have expressed concern about the dangers posed by his sadism and narcissism (Lee 2017). He has repeatedly said outrageous things that would have quickly ended the careers of other politicians, yet seems to pay no price. He has attacked the media and his own federal law enforcement agencies, expressed sympathy for white nationalists and neo-Nazis, slandered every political rival and opponent, and run an administration that has been continuously mired in scandal and blatant corruption. The shadow of collusion with Russia hung over Trump for the first two years of his presidency, although it was largely disavowed by the Mueller report. As president, he insulted and alienated allies, started trade wars, and rejected the long-standing internationalism that defined both major political parties, unapologetically advocating an "America First" agenda. Trump has violated numerous political norms, appointed family members as advisors, refused to release his tax forms, and used public office to enrich himself. As Representative Jamie Raskin (D-MI) said, "You have to think of the Trump phenomenon as a religious cult surrounding an organized crime family" (Goldberg 2019). There have been many demagogues in American political history, such as Huey Long of Louisiana, but Trump is the first demagogue to be elected president. Kakutani (2018, p. 4) notes that "If a novelist had concocted a villain like Trump – a larger-than-life, over-the-top avatar of narcissism, mendacity, ignorance, prejudice, boorishness, demagoguery, and tyrannical impulses ... she or he would likely be accused of extreme contrivance and implausibility."

The list of topics concerning Trump nears infinity: the racism, sexism, misogyny, and Islamophobia; the grifters, nepotism, and corruption of his administration; the mystery of his appeal among the white working class and evangelicals; his lies, insults, boasts, infantile behavior, and rank hypocrisy; his prolific use of Twitter and rallies; his disastrous environmental record; the undermining of the post-World War II global order; his trade wars and tariffs; the border wall with Mexico and mistreatment of immigrants; his celebration of dictators and autocrats and alienation of allies. No one volume can do justice to all these topics.

The Trump phenomenon exists simultaneously at many conceptual levels: it is economic, social, political, and psychological. But it is also geographical, a dimension mostly overlooked in the rapidly increasing libraries dedicated to the subject. Not surprisingly, Trump's visibility and policies have generated a growing body of literature in geography concerned with his racism, geopolitics, and immigration and environmental policies (e.g., Ingram 2017; Finn 2017; Pulido et al. 2019; Sparke and Bessner 2019). This volume is concerned with the political landscapes of Trump and Trumpism, i.e., how he and his administration are embedded within and in turn reshape multiple spatial scales. There is the geography of the 2016 presidential election, in which Trump won the Electoral College, including several "blue" or traditionally Democratic-leaning states in the Midwest such as Wisconsin, Michigan, and Pennsylvania, drawing unprecedented support from non-college educated whites. There are the spatial dimensions of his rhetoric and policies, notably concerning Muslims and immigrants, particularly those from Latin America, and his obsession with the border wall with Mexico. Trump has altered the international standing of the U.S., withdrawn from global agreements such as the Trans-Pacific Partnership, marginally revised NAFTA, and started trade wars with China, Canada, and the European Union. He has alienated allies and courted autocrats around the world, notably including Russia's Vladimir Putin. His foreign policy toward North Korea and Iran, among others, is, to put it mildly, unique. Trump is both a reflection and promoter of global authoritarian neoliberalism. And then there are the environmental dimensions of Trump, a long-standing geographical concern, including the reversal of many Obama-era policies and withdrawal from the Paris Climate Accord. All of these issues, and more, point to the need to examine Trump and his policies from a geographical standpoint.

Outline of chapters

The essays in this volume are grouped into three broad categories. The first puts Donald Trump into context, provides biographical details about his life, personality, and policies, and examines his real estate empire. The second concerns his upset electoral victory, the geography of votes, Trump's support among the white working class, the discourses that emanate from Trump and which, in turn, are used to view him and his administration, and his victims. The third part concerns the major foreign policy initiatives of the Trump administration, notably in Korea and the Middle East, and his actions and policies concerning climate change.

In Part I, Chapter 2, by Barney Warf, contextualizes Donald Trump in several ways. The chapter opens by outlining his essential biographical information. It then briefly explores the 2016 presidential campaign, including Trump's popularity with white working class voters and Russian collusion. It summarizes Trump's persona and rhetoric, including his racism, misogyny, anti-intellectualism, extreme narcissism, contradictions, boasts, insults, and lies, and questions about his mental health. The chapter then turns to Trump's relations with American institutions such as the media and law enforcement agencies. It offers a summary of the dynamics of the Trump administration, including its nepotism, corruption, and disastrous environmental policies. Finally, it addresses Trump's foreign policies, including the wall with Mexico, immigration, trade wars, and alienation of U.S. allies.

Samuel Stein writes in Chapter 3 of Trump as both embodiment and driver of the globalization of real estate. Far from being geniuses of the private market, the scions of the Trump Corporation benefited mightily from public policies. Stein traces the history of the family's relations with real estate, starting with Friedrich Trump's migration to the U.S. in the early 20th century and Fred Trump's empire in Queens. A racist slumlord, Fred provided the wherewithal to launch Donald into the business as a tycoon profiting from government-subsidized housing. The young Donald mastered the art of the public-private partnership, and globalized the empire.

The second major part of the book opens with Chapter 4, by Ron Johnston, Charles Pattie, Ryne Rohla, David Manley, and Kelvyn Jones. They chart the geographical dimensions of Trump's electoral success. They compare the 2016 and 2012 elections to probe the regions in which Trump enjoyed successes at multiple spatial scales, including states, congressional districts, counties, and precincts. They also deploy regression analyses to explore the demographic and spatial dimensions of votes for Trump and note campaign strategies and the allocation of advertising expenditures. Third, they turn to the dynamics of the Electoral College that propelled Trump to victory, even though he lost the popular vote by almost three million votes.

The 2016 election was shocking in part because Trump won many traditionally Democratic Rust Belt states. In Chapter 5, Ryan Weichelt offers an in-depth examination of Trump's victory in Wisconsin. Republicans, led by Governor Scott Walker, had been making steady gains in the state. After contextualizing Trump's victory within national voting results, Weichelt looks at the Republican primary contest in the state, in which Walker was another contender for the nomination, Trump's rallies, and television coverage. In the general election, the Trump campaign exploited Wisconsin's political geography to maximum effectiveness.

Sociologists David Norman Smith and Eric Hanley write in Chapter 6 about the intersections among race, class, and prejudice in the Midwest. As in the South, in the Midwest Trump captured the lion's share of votes from non-college educated white voters. Using data from the American National Election Studies on voter attitudes in 2016, they show that, despite their educational and regional differences, white voters tend to share a strong sense of racial prejudice. They compare the Trump and Romney campaigns, and find disturbing evidence of support for an authoritarian leader. Finally, they look at the social and spatial similarities between support for Trump and that for Andrew Jackson in the 19th century; Jackson is Trump's hero, and the similarities in terms of racism are striking.

Trump's victory provoked widespread fears of impending fascism and racial conflict. Scott Markley and Coleman Allums in Chapter 7 write of postfascist suburbanism, whose policies are manifested in ethnic cleansing. Grounded in white anxiety over demographic displacement and a mythologized past, Trumpian fascism, or at least the 21st century form of reactionary populism that it has assumed, is the latest manifestation of racialized neoliberalism. They examine how this revanchism plays out at the local scale through a case study of Marietta, Georgia, where rapid population growth was accompanied by growing economic distress and ethnic cleansing took the form of eliminating "urban blight" in areas populated by African Americans.

One of the most salient features of Trump's political victory was his widespread support among blue-collar whites. David H. Kaplan writes in Chapter 8 about white ethnonationalism's ties to Trump. He unpacks the multiple meanings ensconced in the term ethnonationalism, how it has changed in the U.S. over time, and how it feeds white identitarian politics. He then examines how this ideology gave Trump broad appeal among working class whites, less educated voters, white evangelicals, and those who ethnically identify as "American." Fear of ethnic diversity is a common thread that ties together these disparate groups.

Trump is the world's most famous user of Twitter, which he uses habitually to boast, assault antagonists, and mobilize followers. In Chapter 9, Lewis J. Dowle puts a microscope to Trump's use of this medium during the 2016 Republican primaries to install fear and humiliate rivals. Trump's tweets, he writes, reflect the constipated geographical imaginations of white racists and their imagined Other, i.e., immigrants and Muslims. In this way, right-wing identity politics is mobilized by a drumbeat to create fear and loathing.

The Trump phenomenon is ripe for theoretical analysis. In Chapter 10, Sam Page examines Donald Trump not as a singular individual, but as part of a Deleuzo-Guttarian "war machine" that generates and feeds off waves of affect and the emotional geographies of fear and hatred. As a rhizomatic assemblage that constantly mutates from one form to another, the Trumpian monstrosity directs its anger at "elites," the state, immigrants, liberals, and any others who stand in its way. So powerful is this war machine that it has irrevocably altered the political landscape, the Republican Party, and the U.S. government itself.

Trump's demagoguery has a parallel to the rhetoric of professional wrestling, a sport with which Trump has long had a curious relationship. David Beard and John Heppen argue in Chapter 11 that wrestling taught him the art of lowbrow populism, and illustrate how his choice of words and phrases mimics that of wrestling promoters, including boasting, insults, misogyny, and the glorification of violence. Trump's close ties to the World Wrestling Entertainment's Vince McMahon gave him insights into the world of what would later become some of his most ardent followers. From wrestling, Trump learned to pose as the hero for the common fan.

In Chapter 12, Barney Warf details the frequency and extent of Trump's lies (more than 20,000 to date), the reasons he uses them, and why he gets away with them. Contrary to the widespread idea that Trump suffers for his mendacity, much of the country actively enjoys it. Warf examines the geographic aspects of Trump's lies, including the border wall with Mexico, immigration and refugees, the environment, and international trade. The chapter then offers a brief contrast of theories of truth proposed by Habermas, Foucault, and Trump himself, who is an inadvertent philosopher given to a nihilistic, self-serving version of truth suited to the era of simulacra.

Part III begins with a study of the Middle East, a region to which the Trump administration has devoted considerable attention and where the administration's policies have generated waves of consternation. Carl T. Dahlman and Nathan S. French examine in Chapter 13 how the region became a laboratory for Trump's dismissal of conventional norms and policies, kowtowing to Israel, arms sales to Saudi Arabia and Qatar, and dismissal of human rights. They look at his speeches and tweets to decipher if the administration truly has the policy of principled realism that it claims, i.e., whether there is such a thing as the Trump Doctrine. They point out how Trumpian geopolitics in the region mirrors assaults on Muslims and others in the U.S. (e.g., with the proposed ban on Muslim

6 Barney Warf

immigrants). Trump's use of extrajudicial suspension of international legal norms creates a space of exception in the region in which the normal rules of international diplomacy and law fail to have their intended effects. The repercussions of this strategy are felt in the multiple tragedies underway in Syria, Iran, Iraq, Egypt, Yemen, and Lebanon, and among refugees in Turkey.

Chapter 14, by Richard N. Gioioso and Lisa Baglione, turns to Cuba, where the Trump administration largely reversed the Obama-era policy of engagement. Drawing on ethnographic data of younger Cubans, they reveal not only the widespread demoralization and cynicism on the island but also how Trump's neoconservative policies aimed at deterritorializing the country have failed. Hard power is not enough. Disillusionment with the Castro regime and the Cuban Communist Party has hardly laid the groundwork for the collapse of the Cuban government.

The examination of Trump's geopolitics is continued in Chapter 15, by Steven M. Radil and Jin-Soo Lee, who focus on the Korean peninsula. Trump's "love" of North Korean dictator "Rocket Man" Kim Jong-Un is well known, as it is with many autocrats around the world. The chapter contextualizes the long-term peace process in Korea, and then turns to popular discourses that have swirled around Trump's initiatives, which include two summit meetings. The legacy of the Korean War, the North's nuclear weapons initiatives, and the prospects for reunification all call for a critical geopolitical analysis. Radil and Lee scrutinize the South Korean media's coverage of recent U.S.-Korean relations, including representations of the country within the global geopolitical context.

The notion of Trump supporters in China may strike some observers as odd, given the trade war between the U.S. and China that the president initiated. In Chapter 16, Xiang Zhang starts by examining Sino-U.S. trade, which links the world's two largest economies. He examines how this relationship plays out unevenly among China's provinces. The chapter then offers an ethnographic account of pro-Trump Chinese internet users, roughly 15,000 participants in a discussion board on Baidu. Many argue that Trump's policies toward China will cause its government to slow down its export-oriented growth strategy in favor of one more oriented toward domestic priorities, implicitly rebuking the authoritarian regime. Some share Trump's anti-Muslim sentiments. As in the U.S., Trump has enabled racists and xenophobes in China.

Everyone today faces the existential threat of climate change, Trump supporters included. In Chapter 17, Victoria Herrmann explores the odd but important relationship between Trump voters and the effects of rising sea levels using a case study of Tangier Island, Virginia. Although the island is rapidly sinking beneath the ocean (and predicted to disappear within 50 years), its residents overwhelmingly voted for Trump and for the most part ignore the reality that his policies contribute to their plight. The chapter explores the emotional geographies that result from this contradiction, including the contempt and scorn of many liberals. The case study illuminates the broader dynamics through which news and opinion about Trump is generated and consumed by his followers.

Chapter 18, by Nino Antadze, concludes the volume by looking at Trump and climate change. A well-known denier of anthropogenic climate change, Trump has advanced numerous policies that have retarded earlier efforts to cope with a warming planet. The chapter argues that Trump does not simply embody apathy about the issue, but institutionalizes it by deliberately overlooking the suffering that it causes. Antadze illustrates this "emotional regime of apathy" by examining the aftermath of Hurricane Maria, which devastated Puerto Rico in 2017, and the Trump administration's decision to withdraw from the Paris Climate Accord. Reactionary policies toward climate change, in this reading, operate not only at the political and economic registers, but at the emotional, affective one as well.

Finally, Chapter 19, by Marie Price and Nicole Prchal Svajlenka, addresses the highly contentious issue of the Trump administration's treatment of undocumented immigrant youth. Of all the horror stories to emanate from this regime – and there are many – perhaps few captivated the public imagination as much as images of detained children locked in cages. Price and Svajlenka focus on the Deferred Action for Childhood Arrivals (DACA) program initiated by the Obama administration, which offered roughly 700,000 undocumented immigrants a path toward citizenship. They highlight differing state responses to Trump's immigration policy, which create a geography of precarity for these young people. These patterns of inclusion and exclusion point to the profound spatiality embedded within the administration's actions.

References

Finn, J. 2017. Implications of the Trump administration for Latin American geography. *Journal of Latin American Geography* 16(2): 163–165.

Goldberg, M. 2019. Trump's TV trial. *New York Times* (March 4). www.nytimes. com/2019/03/04/opinion/trump-investigation.html

Ingram, A. 2017. Geopolitical events and fascist machines: Trump, Brexit and the deterritorialisation of the West. *Political Geography* 57: 91–93.

Kakutani, M. 2018. *The Death of Truth: Notes on Falsehood in the Age of Trump*. New York: Crown Publishing.

Lee, B. (ed.) 2017. *The Dangerous Case of Donald Trump*. New York: St. Martin's Press.

Pulido, L., T. Bruno, C. Faiver-Serna, and C. Galentine. 2019. Environmental deregulation, spectacular racism, and white nationalism in the Trump era. *Annals of the American Association of Geographers* 109(2): 520–532.

Sparke, M., and D. Bessner. 2019. Reaction, resilience, and the Trumpist behemoth: Environmental risk management from "hoax" to technique of domination. *Annals of the American Association of Geographers* 109(2): 533–44.

PART I

Trump's history and biography

2

THE DONALD IN CONTEXT

Barney Warf

"Part of the beauty of me is that I'm very rich."
Donald Trump (quoted in B. Johnson 2015)

To understand Trump and his administration, it is useful to situate the man within the broader context of his life story, political style, and administration. This chapter does so in several steps. It first offers a brief biography of Trump, and then traces his rise to power in 2016. It dwells on his remarkable persona and the public rhetoric, including his boasts, insults, lies, racism, misogyny, Islamophobia, xenophobia, and anti-intellectualism. It notes his contentious relations with two major American institutions, the media and federal law enforcement agencies. The chapter summarizes the first two years of Trump's administration, which have been marked by repeated scandals, nepotism, and corruption in the service of corporatocracy. Finally, it turns to the foreign policies of the Trump administration, which have upended decades of Republican policy, including a faith in free trade, alliances, and immigration.

Trump's biography

Trump's background, personality, career, ascent, and notoriety have unleashed a storm of biographies (e.g., D'Antonio 2016; Kranish and Fisher 2016; Taibi 2017; O'Brien 2015; O'Donnell 2016; Robinson 2017). Indeed, Trumpology has become a cottage industry in its own right. Trump's grandfather, Friedrich Trump, immigrated from Germany in 1885, earning a fortune through various ventures in the American West and Canada before eventually settling in New York. Donald Trump was born in 1946 and raised in Queens. His domineering father, Fred Trump (1905-1999), was a wealthy and well-known real estate developer known for his harsh treatment of his children. In 1959, at age 13,

Trump enrolled in the New York Military Academy, where he remained until 1964. He attended Fordham University for two years, and then graduated with a bachelor's degree in economics from the Wharton School of Business at the University of Pennsylvania in 1968. One of his professors there, William T. Kelley, said "Donald Trump was the dumbest goddamn student I ever had" (Chapman 2017). Trump received several draft deferments in the 1960s for bone spurs in one foot (later earning him the sobriquet "Cadet Bone Spurs"), although later he said could not remember which one (Parker 2018). He never served in the military, claiming that avoiding sexually transmitted diseases in New York constituted "my personal Vietnam" (Blake 2019).

Donald Trump developed an aggressive, adversarial style of conducting business and politics at an early age. He developed a close symbiotic relationship with the infamous Roy Cohn, attorney and consigliere to the equally infamous Senator Joe McCarthy, in 1983 (Mahler and Flegenheimer 2016), which lasted until Cohn's death. From Cohn, Trump learned unrelenting aggression, never to apologize, back down, or admit wrongdoing, always be on the offensive, to bluster and smear opponents, and be as brutal and dishonest as necessary. Win at all costs become his personal ethos.

Trump's history as a cheater and con man has deep roots. His niece, Mary Trump, reports that he paid someone to take the SAT exam for him (Trump 2020). He even cheated at his favorite pastime, golf, by miscounting strokes, tossing aside opponents' balls, and even declaring himself the winner of tournaments in which he did not play (Bamberger 2019; Reilly 2020).

Trump has had three wives, Ivana (married 1977-1990) from the Czech Republic, Marla Maples (married 1993-1999), and his current one, Melania (married 2005), who is from Slovenia. He has five children: Donald Jr., Eric, Ivanka, Tiffany, and Barron. Ivanka married Jared Kushner and converted to Judaism; she also started commercial lines of clothing, shoes, and jewelry. Donald Jr., Eric, Ivanka, and Jared Kushner all play significant advisory roles in his family business and in his presidential administration. Trump, Melania, and Barron lived in Trump Tower in Manhattan before his inauguration in 2017.

Trump became the head of the family business, the Trump Organization, in 1971, when he was 35, and managed it until his inauguration in 2017. The firm was primarily involved in real estate, including hotels, office buildings, casinos, and golf courses, several of which bear his name. His portfolio includes a vast number of properties, including: Trump Winery in Virginia; Mar-a-Lago Club in Florida; Trump Tower in Hollywood Beach; Trump International Hotel in Las Vegas; Trump International Hotel and Tower in Chicago; Trump Taj Mahal Casino in Atlantic City, NJ (now closed); Trump Tower, Trump Palace, and Trump Parc in New York; Trump Plaza in New Rochelle; Trump National Doral Miami hotel and resort; and Trump International Hotels in Washington, D.C. and Waikiki, Hawaii. He also owns commercial properties in other countries, such as Trump Towers in Istanbul, the Philippines, Delhi, Kolkata, Mumbai, Pune, Uruguay, and Vancouver. Trump owns 16 golf courses, including ones in Bedminster (NJ);

Westchester and Ferry Point (NY); Miami, West Palm Beach, and Jupiter (FL); Los Angeles; Washington, D.C.; Philadelphia; Scotland; Ireland; and Dubai.

Beyond real estate, Trump ventured into other lines of business. Some included merchandise. Trump Steaks were sold through Sharper Image, starting in 2007, which soon discontinued them due to low sales. The Trump Organization has at various times sold Trump Fragrance, Trump Springwater, Trump Vodka, the Trump Collection of clothing and accessories, and Trump Home furnishings. From 1996 to 2015, Trump owned the Miss America and Miss Universe beauty pageants. The Trump Modelling Agency closed in 2017. Between 1996 and 2015 he produced and hosted the reality television show *The Apprentice*, during which time his catchphrase "you're fired" became famous; Trump became a well-known celebrity as a result. Trump University, a for-profit educational institution, opened in 2004 to offer classes on real estate, entrepreneurship, and wealth creation. It was closed in November 2016, following Trump's election, due to two class action lawsuits in federal court alleging fraud – Trump paid $25 million to the defrauded students.

Trump is without doubt a very wealthy man, the country's first billionaire president. It is impossible to know his net worth precisely as he will not release his tax returns, but most estimates place his fortune around $3 billion. Trump has been known to exaggerate his wealth, so it is difficult to be accurate: he often understates his wealth to minimize taxes and overstates it when applying for bank loans. He frequently touts his life story as that of a self-made, successful entrepreneur and master negotiator. He claims to have written 15 books touting his business acumen, all ghostwritten, the most famous of which is *The Art of the Deal* (1987), which was ghostwritten by Tony Schwartz. However, as Barstow et al. (2018) report, writing for *The New York Times* in an exhaustive survey, Trump's rise had little to do with his self-proclaimed bargaining skills and much to do with the $413 million loaned to him by his father, developer Fred Trump, as well as a long history of tax evasion. Donald was a millionaire by age eight. His record as a businessman is mixed, including six bankruptcies (three casinos, two casino holding companies, and a Manhattan hotel). He has long been plagued by allegations that he did not pay or underpaid his contractors and employees (Nguyen 2016; Kopan 2016). Because many U.S. banks refused to lend to him, Trump turned primarily to Deutsche Bank, from which he borrowed millions of dollars over several decades. Between 1985 and 1994, he lost $1.17 billion dollars, the largest amount by any American during that period (Buettner and Craig 2019).

In the 1980s, the man carefully cultivated an image as a wealthy playboy and womanizer, going as far as to telephone reporters under the pseudonyms John Barron, John Miller, and David Dennison to boast about the models who slept with Donald Trump (Douthat 2016; M. Walsh 2016; Farrow 2018). In 1990 he proudly graced the cover of *Playboy* (Wootson 2017). Trump dabbled in politics as well, giving campaign contributions to Republicans and Democrats alike. He changed his political positions frequently, moving, for example, from being pro-choice to pro-life as it suited the circumstances.

Trump's presidential campaign and election

On June 15, 2015, Trump announced his presidential campaign from Trump Tower in Manhattan; his audience contained a few paid actors (Bump 2017). Few observers thought he had a chance of winning. Trump faced a large number of rivals during the Republican primaries, including Jeb Bush, Rick Perry, Ted Cruz, Chris Christie, Lindsey Graham, Rand Paul, and Marco Rubio. Pundits predicted over and over again that Trump's inflammatory statements, crude insults, boasts, and lack of experience in government would be fatal flaws; instead, he converted them into assets, portraying himself as an "outsider" working for working men and women against liberals and pro-globalization "elites" (Taibi 2017). As Glynn (2019) puts it, "In the age of performative politics, Trump is king."

The stage was set with the earlier rise of the Tea Party and increasing hostility to the government relentlessly fueled by the conservative media. Trump's presidential campaign centered on a "Make America Great Again" slogan, evoking nostalgia for a mythologized golden past, a phrase that often adorned red baseball caps. He portrayed himself as the disruptor of a broken system, a dealmaker who could overcome Washington's gridlock. His campaign was strongly anti-immigrant in nature and opposed to foreign trade deals, which he blamed for stagnant or declining working class incomes. Trump excelled at channeling working class resentment at "elites," which he coupled with fears of demographic change and white cultural and political displacement (Chokshi 2018). He ran on a platform of bringing back industrial jobs, building a wall on the border with Mexico (which he repeatedly promised Mexico would pay for), combating Muslim terrorism, limiting immigration, revising international trade agreements, and reviving the coal industry, which faced a long-term decline in employment. Many voters liked the idea of a businessman in the White House. Others celebrated his unfettered machismo and alleged virility. During the campaign, the media gave him between $2 billion and $5 billion dollars of free coverage. Finally, Trump chose Indiana Governor Mike Pence as his running mate, a deeply religious man who appealed to religious conservatives.

Candidate and President Trump used Twitter to great effect, allowing him unfiltered contact with his fans. The world's most famous user of Twitter, his followers number roughly 60 million (although some are undoubtedly "fake" accounts). Twitter is Trump's weapon of choice, his cudgel to bludgeon and demean opponents, praise allies, and announce policy and staff decisions. He has repeatedly unleashed twitterstorms designed to draw attention to himself, change the subject when it suits him, and render his opinion about a vast array of topics.

Trump's election shocked the political world. Few saw it coming, given that Hillary Clinton enjoyed a consistent advantage in the polls. Even Trump may not have expected to win. Trump won all traditionally Republican states as well as several battleground ones such as Ohio, Iowa, Florida, and North Carolina. Moreover, Trump won Rust Belt states that traditionally voted Democratic, such as Pennsylvania, Michigan, and Wisconsin, albeit by small margins. His Electoral

College victory was procured by roughly 78,000 votes spread over these three states, roughly the crowd of a football stadium.

It is worth emphasizing that Trump did not win the popular vote, although he falsely claimed that "I won the popular vote if you deduct the millions of people who voted illegally" (Kessler 2016a). Rather, Hillary Clinton received 65,844,610 votes, or 48.2% of the total, whereas Trump received 62,979,636 votes, or 46.1% of the total, a difference of 2.86 million. Trump's victory was purely a product of the dynamics of the Electoral College, in which winners of the popular vote do not necessarily win the White House (as in Bush v. Gore in 2000), as well as decades of GOP-led voter suppression efforts that disenfranchised large numbers of minority voters. In the Electoral College, Trump won with 306 votes (270 are needed to win) versus Clinton's 227, although two "faithless electors" defected, leaving him with 304. Trump falsely claimed that his election was the "biggest Electoral College win since Ronald Reagan" (Dann 2017).

Perhaps the biggest surprise concerning Trump's victory was the strong support shown for him by white working class voters (Kivisto 2017; Walley 2017; Morgan and Lee 2018). Besieged by decades of neoliberalism, globalization, automation, and the offshoring of production, these voters had long been ignored by the Democratic Party, which took them for granted. As the U.S. economy shifted ever more into producer services, in which higher education is a necessity, those without college degrees found themselves increasingly left behind (Figure 2.1). Many blamed their declining fortunes on immigration,

FIGURE 2.1 Trump supporters at a rally in Arizona.

Source: Wikicommons, https://commons.wikimedia.org/wiki/File:Donald_Trump_supporters_(29829448390).jpg

and were highly receptive to Trump's xenophobic message. Trump's appeal to this group of voters was explicit: "I love the poorly educated," he proclaimed (Taranto 2016); while others scoffed, the poorly educated were listening. The billionaire from New York became a hero to financially stressed workers furious with "elites" (Decker 2017) whom they saw as indifferent to their plight. (However, others, e.g. Carnes and Lupu (2017), challenge this narrative, arguing his supporters were disproportionately wealthy Republicans.) Trump's attacks on elites included those that traditionally led the Republican Party, which soon fell under his control. His message resonated particularly well in rural areas and small towns, including many in the traditionally Democratic Rust Belt states. In this sense, Trump is part of a long tradition of American populism stretching back to the 19th century Know-Nothing Party (Kazin 2016). Trump's rise is indicative of the growth of right-wing populist nationalism globally, a phenomenon replicated in much of Europe and elsewhere, which exhibit a similar distrust of globalization, xenophobia, and fears of immigration.

Although he is very popular in the GOP, receiving 90% of their votes, not all Republicans supported Trump. Some, such as Marco Rubio (R-FL) and Lindsey Graham (R-SC), initially opposed Trump only to fall in line later. The Koch Brothers-backed Club for Growth spent $1 million trying to stop him. A small but vocal "Never Trump" movement, largely consisting of conservative intellectuals, held that he was unfit for office and not a true advocate of conservative principles but an opportunist. Leading voices in this movement include Max Boot, Erik Erickson, Steve Schmidt, George Will, Jonah Goldberg, Rick Wilson, Jennifer Rubin, and Joe Scarborough (whom Trump falsely accused of murdering an aide).

For a minority of voters – roughly 30% to 40% – Trump is infallible. Trump famously boasted during the 2016 campaign that "I could stand in the middle of Fifth Avenue, shoot somebody, and I wouldn't lose any voters" (Murdock 2016), and he is probably correct. The extreme tribal loyalty of his base provides him with political Teflon that has protected him from outrage about his many controversial statements and actions (e.g., paying off porn stars), any of which would have destroyed the careers of other politicians. As Zito (2016) put it, the press took Trump "literally, but not seriously," whereas Trump's supporters took him "seriously, but not literally." The personality cult that surrounds Trump includes a broad swath of conservatives and reactionaries, notably white non-college educated men. For them, Trump is the disruptor who challenges elites seeking to promote a globalized economy at their expense. For this group, Trump's bellicose behavior is a sign of combat on their behalf. Fears of demographic change in the country such as the growth of the non-white population, including outright racism and immigration, are another factor. Trump's statements and policies receive unswerving support from the lowbrow, right-wing infotainment media, notably Fox News commentators such as Sean Hannity and Tucker Carlson, and Breitbart, as well as *The National Enquirer*, which is owned by Trump's friend David Pecker. Trump is also highly popular among evangelicals (Gorski 2017), despite the fact that he is not particularly religious, thrice married, and committed adultery with pornography stars such as Stormy Daniels when his wife Melania was home with a newborn baby. Many evangelicals see him as anointed by God, and others hope he will abolish legal abortion. Yet others are white nationalists. Trump's base forms the core of his support, and he has rewarded them richly, at least in rhetoric if not with actual policies, just as they return the favor.

Unlike most presidents, Trump's political strategy as president has not attempted to expand his support beyond his base. As a result, he fares poorly in the polls. His approval rating has consistently hovered between 35% and 45%, while roughly 50% or more of the public expresses disapproval. He has never exceeded 50%. Few presidents have been more unpopular. Trump's poor standing in the polls is all the more remarkable given that the economy has prospered during his presidency, and may reflect the litany of lies, boasts, and insults that he has issued forth since announcing his candidacy, as well as his well-documented racism and sexism.

No account of Trump's election victory would be complete without mention of the role of secretive Russian support for him and his presidential campaign (Harding 2017; Miller 2018). More than a dozen intelligence agencies have confirmed that Russia attempted to sway the election in Trump's favor. The Russian military intelligence service GRU hacked thousands of emails from the servers of the Democratic National Committee, the Democratic National Campaign Committee, and Hillary Clinton's campaign manager, John Podesta. At one point the effort was explicitly abetted by Trump, who, during the presidential campaign, called on Russia to find Hillary Clinton's deleted emails as Secretary of State: "Russia, if you're listening, I hope you're able to find the 30,000 emails that are missing" (Schmidt 2018). Russian efforts were assisted by a secretive persona, Gucifer 2.0 (likely a group of intelligence agents), who was in touch with Trump's confidant Roger Stone, as well as WikiLeaks, which was hostile to Clinton. Moreover, the Russian Internet Research Agency created a "troll farm" in St. Petersburg that created hundreds of social media accounts that sought to sway voter opinions in the U.S. Russian officials reached out to the Trump campaign offering damaging information on Clinton, prompting Donald Jr. to reply "I love it" (Lavender 2017). Trump himself declared "I have nothing to do with Russia" (Durando 2017), which was patently untrue. Whether or not these efforts succeeded in tilting the outcome in Trump's favor is open to discussion, but the efforts cast a pall over Trump's victory, implying that he was a "Manchurian candidate" doing Moscow's bidding. Some of Trump's supporters are so endeared to him that they would still support him even if he openly acknowledged illegal Russian efforts to assist him in the campaign.

The issue of Russian meddling has been enormously contentious and hotly disputed by Trump, and gave rise to the investigation by Special Counsel Robert Mueller (about which more later). Certainly Trump has gone out of his way to lavish effusive praise on Russian President Vladimir Putin. He has a long history of admiration for the man, going back to when the Miss Universe contest was held in Moscow in 2013 (Porter 2017), when Trump said Putin "treated me unbelievably well" (Kaczynski, Massie, and McDermott 2017). He also said that Putin had done "a really great job outsmarting our country" (Sommerlad 2019), "he has very strong control over his country" (Smith 2016), he "gets an A for leadership" (Kaczynski, Massie, and McDermott 2017), and "I always knew he was very smart" (B. Walsh 2016). He defended Putin against charges the Russian government assassinated journalists and political opponents critical of it. When confronted with evidence of such murders, he replied "I think our country does plenty of killing also" (Waldman 2019). Trump boasted of his Moscow contacts as evidence of his ability to broker deals with Russia. Notably, Putin has returned the favor, repeatedly praising Trump in what has become the world's most famous bromance. At a summit meeting with Vladmir Putin in Helsinki in 2018, he explicitly took the word of the Russian president over that of his own intelligence agencies (Diamond 2018). His obeisance was widely condemned, even by some Republicans. Arizona Senator John McCain called it "one of the most disgraceful performances by an American president in memory" (Landler 2018). Trump's obsequiousness with the Russians even led his own FBI to instigate an investigation as to whether the president of the U.S. was working for Russia and thus constituted a national security threat (Goldman, Schmidt, and Fandos 2019).

Why Trump and company support Putin so resolutely has been open to debate. One unproven and explosive allegation is that the Russian government had "pee tapes" of prostitutes urinating in front of Trump at a Moscow hotel, and thus blackmailed him with *kompromat*. The claim is part of an infamous and salacious dossier on Trump compiled by British intelligence (MI6) officer Christopher Steele for the private research firm Fusion GPS. Trump's support may also have a financial dimension centered on his investments in Russia. Eric Trump boasted in 2014 that "we have all the funding we need out of Russia" (Firozi 2017). Trump lied about a proposed Trump Tower in Moscow, saying discussions about it ended in January 2016 when in fact they continued until election day. Trump's support for ending sanctions against the Russian government may thus constitute a conflict of interest. Finally, in warming to Russia, Trump broke with decades of Republican orthodoxy, which saw the country as an implacable opponent. Notably, most Republican voters now agree with Trump and view Russia and Putin favorably (Price 2018b).

Trump's persona and rhetoric

As candidate and president, Trump has demonstrated an outsized personality in which he consistently loves to be the center of attention. He is well known as a pugnacious and pugilistic person who adores combat, and is proud of his ability to "punch back" (McAdams 2016; Sherman 2017). He is overly self-confident, never apologizes, and places great emphasis on "being tough." As the leader of a political cult, his personality and ideology are seamlessly fused. Pertinent dimensions include his racism, misogyny, anti-intellectualism, narcissism, propensity to insult and boast, and pathological lying.

Trump has exhibited a long history of racism and sexism, tapping into a deep vein of white insecurity about the loss of privilege. His father, Fred Trump, was arrested at a Ku Klux Klan rally in 1927. In 1973, the Justice Department sued the Trump Management Corporation for racial discrimination, i.e., refusing to rent units to black people. The Trump Casino in Atlantic City was sued for removing black card dealers, including when Trump was on the floor. In 1989, he took out full-page ads in four New York City newspapers calling for the return of the death penalty in New York in response to the infamous case of a woman who was beaten and raped while jogging in Manhattan's Central Park. He has blamed blacks and Latinos for the bulk of violent crime. Michael Cohen, Trump's personal attorney, said that Trump told him, talking about blacks, that "they're too stupid to vote for me" (Kwong 2018). Trump was an early and enthusiastic proponent of "birtherism," the unfounded notion that President Obama was not born in the U.S., and continued to spout the notion long after it had been widely discredited (Blow 2016). Upon announcing his presidential campaign, he famously said:

> When Mexico sends its people, they're not sending their best. They're not sending you. They're sending people that have lots of problems, and they're bringing those problems with us. They're bringing drugs. They're bringing crime. They're rapists. And some, I assume, are good people. (Washington Post Staff 2015)

As a presidential candidate, he had Mexican-American journalist Jorge Ramos forcibly removed from his Iowa press conference (Foley 2015). Trump refused to renounce the support of white nationalist and KKK leader David Duke; not surprisingly, he is strongly supported by neoNazi websites such as the Daily Stormer. He disparaged federal district judge Gonzalo Curiel as "a Mexican" (he was born in Illinois) because he ruled against him in the case concerning the now-defunct Trump University, which bilked thousands of people. Following a march of white supremacists in Charlottesville, Virginia in 2017, Trump noted there were "some very fine people" among the neo-Nazis and KKK members (Gray 2017). Trump has justified the beating of Black Lives Matter protesters. He has repeatedly insulted black women politicians and journalists (Ryan 2018), such as Maxine Waters (D-CA). He lambasted African-American football players who kneeled during the national anthem as unpatriotic. He tweeted an anti-Semitic Hillary Clinton meme that featured a photo of her over a backdrop of $100 bills with a six-pointed Jewish Star of David next to her face. Trump repeatedly mocked Senator Elizabeth Warren (D-MA) as "Pocahontas" (Lee 2016), drawing the objections of Native Americans. He called Haiti and African nations "shithole countries" (Watkins and Philip 2018) and asked why the U.S. does not receive more immigrants from Norway. He claimed all immigrants from Haiti had AIDS and that Nigerians "should go back to their huts" (Marcin 2017). In 2019, he tweeted that four liberal minority Congresswomen should "go back" to the countries they came from (Sonmez and DeBonis 2019), even though three were born in the U.S. and one is a naturalized citizen, using an old racist trope to reinforce his narrative that the U.S. is a white Christian country in which all nonwhites are suspect. In 2019, he attacked Elijah E. Cummings (D-MD) of Baltimore, saying the city was "a disgusting, rat and rodent infested mess" where "no human being would want to live" (Stracqualursi 2019), terms he applies frequently to black-majority areas. In 2020, he retweeted a video of a supporter chanting "white power" (Shear 2020). Such comments were part of a carefully calculated strategy of amplifying racial animus that forms the core of his 2020 re-election strategy.

Trump's hatred of undocumented immigrants runs deep: he has called them "animals," "criminals," "rapists," "bad hombres," and "killers" (Davis 2018). Trump has moved to deport up to three million undocumented immigrants, the bulk of whom are Mexican, militarize the border, eliminate protections for 700,000 people covered by the Deferred Action on Childhood Arrivals (DACA) program, and revise the Constitution to eliminate birthright citizenship. His campaign against immigrants led to putting thousands of children in cages, separated from their parents (BBC News 2018).

In addition to racism, Trump exhibits sustained, intense Islamophobia. He insinuated that Barack Obama was secretly Muslim. As a candidate he called for a "complete and total shutdown" on Muslims entering the U.S. (J. Johnson 2015), and tried to enact such a ban as president. He said the U.S. needs to "watch and study the mosques" (Sargent 2015), "We're having problems with the Muslims" (Saul 2016), and "I think Islam hates us" (Schleifer 2016). When a supporter asked "When can we get rid of them?" he replied "We're going to be looking at that and plenty of other things" (Waldman 2017). He called for a national database to monitor Muslims in the country. He falsely claimed that Muslims in New Jersey cheered the fall of the World Trade Center in 2001. Trump has retweeted virulently anti-Muslim videos from British neofascist groups such as Britain First. Some of his advisors, such as Sebastian Gorka, were fired for their extreme, open Islamophobia.

Trump's sexism and misogyny are well known, although he claims "nobody respects women more than I do" (Blake 2017a). He has regularly referred to women as "fat," "slobs," "dogs," "pigs," and "disgusting animals" (Shear and Sullivan 2018; Walsh 2018). More than a dozen women have publicly alleged that he sexually molested them. In an interview with *Esquire* in 1991 he said "You know, it doesn't really matter what they [the media] write as long as you've got a young and beautiful piece of ass" (Hurt 1991). He called porn star Stormy Daniels "horseface" (Cillizza 2018), labelled Bette Midler a "washed up psycho" who is "an extremely unattractive woman" (Kurtz 2019), and said Rosie O'Donnell is "crude, rude, obnoxious and dumb" (Collins 2014). He said of former rival

Carly Fiorina "Look at that face. Would anyone vote for that?" (Geraghty 2015). After Fox News correspondent Megan Kelly strongly questioned him at a candidates' debate, he said it was because she had "blood coming out of her wherever" (Rucker 2015). About his opponent in the 2016 campaign, he said "If Hillary Clinton can't satisfy her husband what makes her think she can satisfy America?" (Blow 2015). Of Mika Brzezinski, co-host of MSNBC's *Morning Joe*, Trump said she "was bleeding badly from a face-lift" (Thrush and Haberman 2017). Of German gold-medal-winning Olympic skater Katarina Witt, he said in 1992 "she could only be described as attractive if you like a woman with a bad complexion who is built like a linebacker" (C. Cohen 2017). About sexual assaults in the military, he tweeted "What did these geniuses expect when they put men & women together?" (HuffPost Media 2013). He suggested that if there were a ban on abortion, he wanted "some form of punishment" meted out to women who violated it (Foley, Bobic, and Lachman 2016). During the 2016 campaign, he famously boasted that "when you're a celebrity, they let you do anything," which included grabbing women "by the pussy" in a notorious 2005 *Access Hollywood* tape (Farenthold 2016; *New York Times* 2016), for which he later apologized, but defended as "locker room talk." Nonetheless, 53% of white women voted for him. As Hesse (2020) puts it somewhat acidly, "his understanding of women voters is based on six reruns of "Happy Days" plus a vacuum cleaner ad from 1957." Given this history, however, it is little surprise that women tend to view him far more negatively than men do.

Calls to violence, either implicit or explicit, also form part of Trump's rhetoric, notably at his rallies, although he denies it. Of terrorists, he said "torture works" (Acosta, Sciotto, and Manchester 2016). About protestors, he has said "I'd like to punch him in the face" (Corasaniti and Haberman 2016); "Knock the crap out of them" (Reisman 2016); "Part of the problem ... is nobody wants to hurt each other anymore" (Gass 2016); "In the good old days this doesn't happen because they used to treat them very, very rough" (Mackey 2016); and "Try not to hurt him. If you do, I'll defend you in court, don't worry about it" (Sonmez 2018). During the 2016 campaign he speculated that "Second Amendment people" would stop Hillary Clinton from appointing liberal judges. He vowed to bring back waterboarding of captured terrorist suspects, "and worse." When a GOP congressional candidate, Greg Gianforte, body-slammed a reporter, Trump responded approvingly. In March 2019, he warned "I have the support of the police, the support of the military, the support of the Bikers for Trump – I have the tough people, but they don't play it tough until they go to a certain point, and then it would be very bad, very bad" (Sargent 2019b).

The cruelty that Trump and followers espouse is not incidental, but a core feature of political strategy. Whether it is mocking survivors of sexual abuse, suspects arrested by the police, school children who endured a mass shooting, immigrant children in cages, black athletes protesting police abuse, or disabled reporters, cruelty is the adhesive that unites political reactionaries. As Serwer (2018) points out, "The Trump era is such a whirlwind of cruelty that it can be hard to keep track." Cruelty to those they despise is a means of building community among his followers, a means of building intimacy, much like men who organized lynchings in an earlier era.

As a public figure, Trump's short attention span, anti-intellectualism, and ignorance have been unsurpassed. His refusal to read – even official daily intelligence briefs – is legendary, as is his unwillingness to consider evidence that does not mesh with his preconceived beliefs (Larison 2019). Rather than read or obtain advice from experts, he prefers to "trust his gut." As he puts it, "I have a gut and my gut tells me more sometimes than anybody else's brain can ever tell me" (Le Miere 2018). As a result, he has made a series of embarrassing mistakes. He vowed to protect all 12 Articles of the Constitution although there are only seven. He said President Andrew Jackson was "really angry" at "what was happening with regard to the Civil War," although Jackson died 16 years before it started; he also claimed "people don't ask the question, but why was there the Civil War?" (Bromwich 2017). At a meeting with the leaders of Estonia, Latvia, and Lithuania, Trump confused the Baltics with the Balkans, and accused the perplexed politicians of starting the 1990s Yugoslav wars (Porter 2018). Upon taking office, he did not understand the nuclear triad of missile silos, submarines, and jets. His refusal to consider evidence leads him to make grievous errors, such as accusing Iran of violating the nuclear deal when all data pointed to the contrary. He views NATO as a club in which members "pay dues." NBC News's Andrea Mitchell noted:

> On Iran he complained that Iran isn't buying our planes. It had to be pointed out to him that Iran is still under sanctions and cannot buy American planes. He thinks North Korea and Iran are the biggest trading partners when North Korea's biggest trading partner is China. He is completely uneducated about any part of the world. (Rubin 2016)

In denying anthropogenic climate change, he repeatedly confuses weather and climate. (At one point he falsified a map showing the trajectory of a hurricane). He called the Paris Climate Accord a "massive redistribution of United States wealth to other countries" (Halper and Zavis 2017). This is no surprise from someone who said "The concept of global warming was created by and for the Chinese in order to make U.S. manufacturing non-competitive" (Wong 2016). Trump also shows profound geographical ignorance. He once called Bhutan and Nepal "Button" and "Nipple," respectively, and did not know they were countries (Lippman 2018). He called Namibia "Nambia" (Papenfuss 2019).

Trump not only does not care that he is willfully ignorant, he appears to be proud of the fact, in keeping with a long tradition of American anti-intellectualism. Thus he has been called a "fucking moron" by his own Secretary of State, Rex Tillerson (Mackler 2017); "an idiot" who has "gone off the rails" by his Chief of Staff, John Kelly (Croucher 2018); a "dope" with the "intelligence of a kindergardener" by his own National Security Advisor, H.R. McMaster

The Donald in context **23**

(Woody 2017); and has the comprehension level of "a fifth- or sixth-grader" according to his own Secretary of Defense, James Mattis (Price 2018a). His dismissal of expertise is in keeping with the distrust of elites that pervades his political base. This ignorance is central to the alternative reality that he makes for himself and attempts to get others to adopt.

Trump is famous for his extreme, malignant narcissism (Lee 2017). He boasted that "I'm, like, a really smart person" and that he has a "very, very large brain." He said not paying much in taxes made him smart (Jordan 2016). In school, he was "always the best athlete" (Milbank 2018). About the multiple lawsuits that have erupted throughout his career, he said "Does anyone know more about litigation than Trump? I'm like a PhD in litigation" (Terris 2017). In his acceptance speech for the Republican nomination in 2016, he claimed that, in response to a broken political system, "I alone can fix it" (Marcus 2018). He noted "I am the least anti-Semitic person that you've ever seen in your entire life" (Scott 2018). For religious conservatives, he asserted "nobody reads the Bible more than I do" (Khazan 2016). Despite a history of divisiveness as candidate and president, "There's nobody that's done so much for equality as I have" (Campbell 2016). He stated "with the exception of the late, great Abraham Lincoln, I can be more presidential than any president that's ever held this office" (Baker 2017). "No president has ever worked harder than me" (Miller 2019). He uses "the best words" and has "one of the great memories of all time" (Blake 2017b). He described himself as "a very stable genius" (Diaz 2018). He knows "the details of taxes better than anybody. Better than the greatest C.P.A. I know the details of health care better than most, better than most" (Rubin 2017). He crowed that his studies at the Wharton School constituted "super genius stuff" (Kessler 2016b). In addition, according to Blake (2016):

> "I know more about renewables than any human being on Earth."
> "I think nobody knows more about taxes than I do, maybe in the history of the world."
> "Nobody knows more about taxes."
> "Nobody knows banking better than I do."
> "I understand money better than anybody."
> 'Nobody knows politicians better than Donald Trump."
> "Nobody knows more about trade than me."
> "I know more about ISIS [the Islamic State militant group] than the generals do."
> "There is nobody who understands the horror of nuclear [sic] more than me."

Trump's speech in Poland was "the greatest speech ever made on foreign soil by a president." (R. Cohen 2017). Fortunately, he understands legislation better "than any president that's ever been in office" (Milbank 2018).

The Donald is not modest about his accomplishments, real and imagined. He claimed credit for making NATO partners contribute more funds to the alliance

24 Barney Warf

although they simply lived up to previous spending commitments. He took credit for making the U.S. military the strongest in the world, which it has been for decades. In 2017, he credited himself for the "safest year on record" (Klapper 2018) in aviation although there had been no accidents since 2009. He has cited himself as the cause of a rising stock market (Wingrove 2020) and declining gasoline (Rainey 2019) and generic drug prices (Luthra 2019). He cited himself as the source of a veterans' healthcare law passed two years before he was elected. He also claimed to have invented the word "caravan" (first used in 1588) and the phrase "fake news." In 2019, he hailed his own "great and unmatched wisdom" (Sonmez 2019).

Trump loves, loves, loves to insult people. Often these take the forms of crude, childish labels and taunts, such as "Crooked Hillary," "Low Energy Jeb" Bush, "Lyin' Ted" Cruz, "Little Marco" Rubio, "Cryin' Chuck" Schumer, "Crazy Bernie" Sanders, and "Sleepy Joe" Biden (Flegenheimer 2018). During the 2016 primary election, he called Senator Rubio's wife ugly (Hopper 2016) and accused his father of participating in the assassination of JFK (MacCaskill 2016). On Twitter, he wrote "#JebBush has to like the Mexican Illegals because of his wife." He famously said Senator John McCain "was not a war hero because he was captured. I like people who weren't captured" (Martin and Rappeport 2015). He continued to attack McCain months after the senator had died. Former staffer Omarosa Maniguault is a "lowlife" after she was fired and then accused Trump of using the n-word (Blumberg 2018). Members of the media come in for special scorn. He tweeted that *National Review*'s Jonah Goldberg was "truly dumb as a rock" (Phillips 2015), *The Washington Post*'s Bob Woodward is "an idiot" (Bowden 2018), and conservative commentator Charles Krauthammer is "one of the worst and most boring political pundits on television" (Phillips 2015). Of rival candidate Rick Perry, now Trump's Secretary of Energy, he said "He should be forced to take an IQ test before being allowed to enter the GOP debate" (Byrnes 2015b). He called Republican strategist Karl Rove "a loser" and "a clown with zero credibility" (Krueger, Hardiman, and Kelly 2015). Jeff Bezos is "Jeff Bozo" (Hamilton 2019). Nor are foreign leaders immune to his insults. He called Canadian Prime Minister Justin Trudeau "very dishonest and weak" (Shear and Porter 2018). At a G-7 meeting with German Prime Minister Angela Merkel, Trump threw Starburst candy at her and said "Don't say I never give you anything" (Maza 2018). North Korea's Kim Jong Un (a.k.a. "Little Rocket Man") "is obviously a madman who doesn't mind starving or killing his people, who will be tested like never before" (Blake 2017c). Kim replied that Trump was a "mentally deranged U.S. dotard" (Sang-Hun 2017).

Publicity is to Trump as heroin is to an addict. He has long been known to cherish the limelight and dominate news cycles. His office in Trump Tower is decorated with numerous magazine covers with his photograph, including *Playboy* and *Time*. "I have so many that I can't put them up," he said (Katz 2017). At least one magazine cover – of *Time* magazine featuring Trump and his golf clubs at the Champions Sports Bar & Grill at the Trump National Doral Miami –

is fake (Farenthold 2017). *Time* requested that the Trump Organization take it down, to no avail. Trump's craving for attention reflects his narcissism, and explains his fondness for rallies in which his base enthusiastically idolizes him in what are essentially white power demonstrations. Trump often uses Twitter to insert himself into every national conversation, ranging from who won the Kentucky Derby to the fire at Notre Dame, fusing his tabloid personality with the most powerful political office in the world. Trump's inflammatory comments are designed to stoke the culture wars, keep his political base burning with white-hot resentment, and maintain his position in the media spotlight. He delights in provoking outrage among his opponents, and knows that each one will soon be displaced in the news cycle by a fresh outburst. Trump's admirers deeply appreciate his willingness to be outrageous, find his provocative behavior vastly entertaining, in the process confusing insulting liberals with "fighting."

No public figure has ever lied more than Trump, for whom it appears to be a compulsion. As Dowd (2019) puts it, "His motto might as well be: 'I cannot not tell a lie.'" According to *The Washington Post*, which keeps a tally of his lies, he lied more than 20,000 times in his first 3½ years days in office, an average of roughly 12 per day and sometimes up to 40 per day (Kessler et al. 2020b). The *Post*'s fact checker crew even published a book about Trump's assault on the truth (Kessler et al. 2020a). Trump lies even when he does not need to, and is blithely dismissive of any evidence to the contrary. He shows no sign of embarrassment of being caught lying, and moves quickly to the next falsehood. He may even believe some of his own lies. He uses lies as political weapons and as a means to enhance his public standing. Some of his greatest whoppers include the exaggeration of the size of the crowd at his inauguration, that Hillary Clinton won the popular vote only due to millions of undocumented immigrants engaging in voter fraud, that President Obama wiretapped his phones in Trump Tower, that thousands of New Jersey Muslims celebrated the fall of the Twin Towers in 2001 (Kessler 2015), that the wall with Mexico is under construction, that Californians were rioting in sanctuary cities, that U.S. Steel is "opening six new plants" (Tobias 2018), that "nobody knows" if Russia interfered in the 2016 election (Broniatowski and Crowley 2017), that he would release his tax returns as soon as the supposed "routine audit" into his finances is complete (Fang 2017), and that "Refugees are pouring into our great country from Syria" who could be agents of ISIS (Byrnes 2015a). Trump's own lawyers would not let him be deposed by the Mueller investigation because he is incapable of telling the truth. Much of the public believes his lies, or at least is not troubled by them (Carpenter 2018). His persistent prevarication has led much of the public to view him as untrustworthy and contributed to his low standing in the polls.

Consistency is not one of Trump's strong suits. Indeed, he has openly contradicted himself more than any other president. After admitting he would accept aid from a foreign power and not tell the FBI, he soon declared that "of course" he would inform the agency. He noted Robert Mueller's report declared "complete exoneration" (Landler and Haberman 2019), then denounced it as "total bullshit" and "pure, political garbage" (Stokols 2019). Despite having one of the "greatest memories of all time" (Petri 2017), he could not recall answers to Mueller's questions 37 times. After declaring an immigration "crisis" on the border with Mexico, he claimed "the border is tight." After boasting that "Mexico is paying for the wall" he complained that Democrats allocated "nothing" for it (Paletta and Werner 2019). After asserting that nuclear proliferation was the world's biggest problem, he argued Japan and South Korea should develop nuclear weapons. He said Russia had no reason to interfere in U.S. elections, then said he had no reason to think it didn't. He was "proud" to accept responsibility for a government shutdown (Haberkorn 2018), then argued "Democrats now own the shutdown" (Baker and Haberman 2019). After pushing House Republicans to pass an immigration bill, he tweeted "I never pushed the Republicans in the House to vote for the Immigration Bill" (Griffiths 2018).

President Trump has also engaged in a series of highly inappropriate, decidedly unpresidential behaviors. He called California Representative Adam Schiff "Adam Schitt" (Smith 2018) and said "Little pencil-neck Adam Schiff. He's got the smallest, thinnest neck I've ever seen" (Capehart 2019). About his then 16-year-old daughter Ivanka, he said "Don't you think my daughter's hot? She's hot, right?," described her as a "piece of ass," and that if they were not related "perhaps I'd be dating her" (Withnall 2016). After a speech to a Boy Scouts jamboree in which he talked about cocktail parties, he boasted that the head of the organization called him to say it was "the best speech ever," a flat-out lie (Blake 2017d). Trump has also used the rhetoric of a mafia boss, urging aides to "stay strong" and not turn into "rats" (Visoulis 2018).

Fearmongering is a time-honored Republican political tactic (communists, black men, gays, terrorists, immigrants). Throughout his campaign and his administration, Trump's style has centered on fear. His dystopian inaugural address warned of "American carnage." He plays on white fears of demographic change. He exaggerates the dangers posed by Muslim terrorism and engages in blatant Islamophobia. He fantasizes about the dangers posed by illegal immigration and whips up hysteria about "caravans" marching to the border with Mexico, which consist of exhausted people fleeing violence in Central America. He makes exaggerated claims about the gang MS-13, vowing to destroy "these animals" (Davis and Chokshi 2018).

Trump's rhetoric has been so extreme that it has raised concerns about whether he is a fascist (Tucker 2015; Kinsley 2016). Those who adhere to this view point to his hypernationalism, militarism, glorification of violence, fetishization of masculinity, theatricality, lost-golden-age syndrome, leadership cult, and emphasis on loyalty (McNeil 2016). Others note his mockery of the weak and promises to torture enemies but deny that he is a dyed-in-the-wool fascist (Douthat 2015). The fact that there is a debate as to whether the president of the U.S. is or is not a fascist is itself remarkable. At a minimum, Trump acts as a conduit to import extremist ideas from right-wing fringe groups into the political mainstream.

The Donald in context **27**

Finally, Trump has been imitated by autocrats around the world, such as Recep Tayyip Erdogan in Turkey ("getting very high marks") (McCaskill 2017a), Abdel Fattah Saeed Hussein Khalil al-Sisi in Egypt ("he's a fantastic guy") (Lima 2016), Rodrigo Duterte in the Philippines ("doing an unbelievable job") (Shabad 2017), Kim Jong Un of North Korea ("very open and terrific") (Lemire 2018), and Jair Bolsonaro in Brazil (in all respects doing a great job for the people of Brazil" (Sargent 2019a), precipitating concerns about a worldwide decline in democracy. Trump's fondness for autocrats is well known, and his counterparts adopt similar rhetorical strategies such as calling the media "the enemy of the people."

Trump's behavior has been so bizarre that it has generated a cottage industry of experts evaluating his mental health. For example, Lee (2017) offers a collection of insights by 27 psychiatrists, who explore his hedonism, pathological narcissism, trust deficit, delusional disorders, self-sabotage, sociopathy, bullying, sadism, deceitfulness, aggressiveness, cognitive impairment, dementia, lack of remorse, and incapacity to fulfill the demands of his office. Trump's famous malignant narcissism merits special attention, exhibiting as it does a toxic mixture of entitlement, exploitation, and lack of empathy. Tony Schwartz, ghost author of Trump's famous book *The Art of the Deal*, notes that "his development essentially ended in early childhood" (2017, p. 70). Trump never seems to sense guilt or contrition. Whereas mental health experts are normally very reluctant to diagnosis a public figure without a clinical evaluation, in Trump's case the "duty to warn" the public about the dangers of his presidency outweighs such considerations.

Trump and American institutions

As an iconoclast and self-described disruptor, Trump has had a contentious relationship with several major U.S. institutions that form the bedrock of the political order. Because more than any other president he is a creature of the media, particularly television, this relationship with is also worthy of consideration. He has criticized his own intelligence agencies far more than any other occupant of the White House.

Trump's relationship with the media has been highly unconventional. As a real estate and television celebrity in New York, he called reporters pretending to be "John Miller" or "John Barron" and boasted about the female celebrities who wanted to sleep with Trump (Borchers 2016). He has repeatedly attacked the press as "the enemy of the people" (Grynbaum and Sullivan 2019), employing a phrase commonly used by autocrats. Essentially, any outlet that does not report favorably on him is dismissed as "fake news." Trump famously mocked a disabled *New York Times* reporter, Serge Kovaleski, who suffers from arthrogryposis (Arkin 2016), then boasted "nobody's better to people with disabilities than me" (Milbank 2018). His favorite targets include CNN, MSNBC, the "failing" *New York Times*, and *The Washington Post*, which is owned by Jeff Bezos (who founded Amazon.com). Trump even proposed that the Post Office double its rates for packages delivered by Amazon as punishment for *The Post*'s coverage of him (Paletta and Dawsey 2018). He released a video showing himself at a wrestling match, punching and wrestling to the ground a reporter whose face was covered with the CNN logo. He banned CNN"s Jim Acosta after aggressive questioning at a press conference (Baker 2018), and apparently used anti-trust laws to stop a merger between AT&T and Time Warner, which owned CNN (Mayer 2019). He suggested that *Saturday Night Live* should be investigated for satirizing him (Cranley 2019).

On the other hand, Trump has a very intimate relationship with the right-wing mediasphere. Former advisor Steve Bannon was executive director of the conservative website Breitbart News before managing Trump's 2016 campaign (following the departure of Paul Manafort). Trump has appeared on the television show of well-known conspiracy monger Alex Jones. He is known to watch Fox News obsessively, often four to eight hours per day (Crilly 2017; Delkic 2017), particularly his favorite show, *Fox and Friends*, sometimes tweeting comments from the show in real time, and gives more interviews to the station than any other. The White House has been staffed by a considerable number of Fox News personnel, including former communications director Bill Shine, commentator John Bolton, now National Security Advisor, economic advisor Larry Kudlow, and former Fox anchor Heather Nauert, his nominee as ambassador to the United Nations (who withdrew). Trump is in frequent contact with Fox News commentators Sean Hannity and Laura Ingraham (Cranley 2018). Indeed, the boundaries between the White House and Fox News seem to have evaporated altogether, leaving them as a seamlessly merged entity. Finally, Trump is much beholden to other conservative voices such as Rush Limbaugh and Ann Coulter, who wrote an admiring volume, *In Trump We Trust* (2016), before becoming critical of him for his failure to build the border wall with Mexico.

Trump has often attacked U.S. intelligence agencies, with which he has long had a contentious relationship. He repeatedly dismissed assessments by the FBI about the dangers posed by Russian hacking, calling the agency and his own intelligence chiefs "wrong," "naïve," and "disgraceful," (Gearan and Barrett 2017). Nonetheless, "Nobody has been tougher on Russia than I have," he argued (Borchers 2018). He claimed the FBI planted an informant in his campaign (Abramson and Beckwith 2018). Trump attacked former director of the CIA, John Brennan, and took away his security clearance, sending a message about the costs of dissent. He has ignored agency advice about North Korea, Russia, Iran, and Syria. In 2019, when the intelligence agencies issued a national risk assessment, he called them "extremely passive and naïve" and said that they "should go back to school" (Maza 2019). Since Trump does not read his daily intelligence briefings, but obtains most of his information from Fox News, it is not altogether surprising that he would put such a low value on American intelligence agencies. Trump's refusal to accept expert opinion has led him, among other things, to claim that the threats from North Korea's nuclear missiles had ended, when in fact they have not (Baker and Sang-Hun 2018). His attacks on spy agencies have led several to call Trump a national security risk (Nicholas and Strobel 2019). At a minimum, such rhetoric suggests that Trump sees himself as above the law and accountable to no one.

Trump also attacked his own Justice Department, viewing it as part of a mythologized "deep state" of public bureaucrat's intent on undermining him (Bertrand 2019). He fired Attorney General Jeff Sessions (whom he called "a dumb Southerner"), the first senator to endorse him, for recusing himself from the investigation into Russian hacking and collusion. When the FBI raided the offices of his lawyer, Michael Cohen (who was later arrested and convicted to three years in prison), Trump ranted on Twitter that the Department's actions are "an attack on our country" (Shear 2018). Furious about the Mueller probe, he repeatedly claimed the FBI was engaging in the greatest "witch hunt" in American history (Chinoy, Ma, and Thompson 2018).

The Trump administration

The years of the Trump administration were largely characterized by chaos, high staff turnover, unfilled positions, numerous scandals and controversies, and the failure to pass much by way of meaningful policy. Many of its efforts appeared to be a concerted rollback of Obama-era legislation. The Trump administration is not known for inspirational policies. Despite two years of Republican control of both the House and the Senate, it did not repeal the Affordable Care Act or obtain funding for the wall with Mexico. The Senate did confirm two conservative Supreme Court justices – Neil Gorsuch and Brett Kavanaugh – and numerous federal judges. Its signature achievement was a massive income tax cut in December 2018 of $1.7 trillion over 10 years, the vast bulk of which went to corporations and households earning more than $500,000 annually (44% of the benefits went to those making $1 million or more). The tax cuts, unusual in a time of economic prosperity, fueled the long-standing economic expansion, at least temporarily. In addition, the GOP rolled back the estate tax, a favor to the wealthy, to the tune of $83 billion. Long justified on the basis of trickle-down economics, the cuts overwhelmingly favored a small group of the ultra-wealthy, many of whom are large donors to the GOP: as Lindsey Graham (R-SC) noted, "the financial contributions will stop" if they did not pass the legislation. The tax cuts and associated declines in federal government revenue propelled the budget deficit to new heights, adding roughly $4 trillion to the national debt in two years, even though candidate Trump promised to eliminate the federal debt in eight years.

Despite Trump's populist rhetoric, his administration has been a classic corporatocracy. About 70% of its senior personnel have corporate ties, and roughly 350 lobbyists or former lobbyists work for the administration. A former oil industry lobbyist runs the Department of the Interior, a pharmaceutical executive is head of Health and Human Services, and a coal lobbyist manages the Environmental Protection Agency. Trump's acting head of the Defense Department was a former Boeing executive, to be replaced by a Raytheon executive and lobbyist, and his nominee for the Federal Aviation Administration is a former Delta executive. Goldman Sachs veterans are pervasive, including Treasury Secretary Steve Mnuchin, Deputy Treasury Secretary James Donovan, and Gary Cohn, head of the White House Economic Council. The results are devastating. EPA officials, for instance, blocked NASA from monitoring pollution levels. The Interior Department has granted more than 1,700 waivers from workplace safety rules. The administration has also rolled back banking regulations such as Dodd-Frank.

From its inception, the Trump administration has been plagued by allegations that he and/or his collaborators colluded with Russian officials and hackers to sway the presidential election results (Harding 2017; Miller 2018). Led by Special Counsel Robert Mueller (a Republican), a prolonged, detailed, and extensive investigation inquired into whether the Trump campaign conspired with the Russian government and if it attempted to obstruct justice once the allegations surfaced (Burke, Bookbinder, and Eisen 2017), including the firing of FBI Director James Comey. After firing "nut job" Comey, Trump told the Russian Foreign Minister "I faced great pressure because of Russia. That's taken off" (Apuzzo, Haberman, and Rosenberg 2017). Mueller was meticulous and closed-lipped about the investigation, interviewing a wide variety of sources and subpoenaing records from the Trump Organization. The investigation made clear that a lengthy list of Trump's family members, advisors, and campaign operatives met with senior Russian figures before the election. Trump and associates met with Russian officials at least 100 times before the election. The most notable of these was a famous meeting at Trump Tower on June 9, 2016, which included Donald Jr., Jared Kushner, former campaign manager Paul Manafort, deputy campaign manager Rick Gates, Trump's close friend Roger Stone, Jeff Sessions, Michael Flynn, Carter Page, and George Papadopolous. The meeting clearly aimed to establish a clandestine back channel of communications with the Russians. Trump issued several proclamations about the meeting, stating at first that it only concerned adoptions, then that someone had written a clumsy denial, and that finally he himself had written it (Buchanan and Yourish 2018). Later the Mueller report indicated that Donald Trump Jr. went to the meeting expecting to get "dirt" on the Clinton campaign. Flynn and his son, Michael Jr., met with the Russian ambassador to the U.S., Sergey Kislyak, repeatedly before Trump assumed office. As might be expected, Trump and his allies strenuously deny any collusion whatsoever. Trump repeatedly called the investigation "the greatest witch hunt in American history," "presidential harassment" (Fabian 2017), and sought to undermine the probe's integrity. He argued "no politician in history … has been treated worse or more unfairly" (McCaskill 2017b). The accusations fit into the president's narrative of grievance and victimization. Indeed, Trump publicly attacked the Mueller probe more than 1,100 times. The investigation has led to grand jury indictments of 34 people and three companies, including 13 Russian nationals as well as former National Security Advisor Michael Flynn and Richard Gates. Flynn, then the National Security Advisor designate, secretly conferred with the Russian ambassador about undermining U.S. sanctions. To date, six people have been convicted and one jailed. Former campaign manager Paul Manafort and deputy campaign chair Rick Gates were indicted on 12 charges, including money laundering, tax evasion, bank fraud, and being unregistered agents of a foreign principal (Ukraine). Flynn and Gates pleaded guilty, and Cohen was sentenced to three years imprisonment; Manafort was sentenced to 7½ years. Trump advisor Roger Stone was arrested and indicted on seven felony charges in January 2018, including allegations that Stone knew that WikiLeaks had obtained hacked emails stolen from the Democratic National Committee and Hillary Clinton's campaign manager John Podesta. The Mueller investigation raised a host of constitutional issues, such as whether a president can pardon himself, and gave rise to discussions about impeachment.

Mueller submitted his report in March 2019; volume one concerned Russian interference with the 2016 election, and volume two addressed Trump's attempts to obstruct justice. The broad conclusion was that there was no overt conspiracy between Trump and Russia, although it documented more than 40 contacts between the Trump campaign and Russian officials, but left the question of obstruction of justice unanswered. The report carefully notes that Trump tried to fire Mueller, tried to limit the scope of the investigation, ordered White House counsel Donald McGahn to falsify records, fired James Comey because of "Comey's unwillingness to publicly state that the President was not personally under investigation," attempted to initiate investigations of political opponents (i.e., Hillary Clinton and Joe Biden), and refused to defend the U.S. against future Russian cyberattacks. The last sentence concludes "while this report does not conclude that the President committed a crime, it also does not exonerate him." Mueller held tightly to the Department of Justice dictum that sitting presidents cannot be indicted. After a redacted version of the report was released, Trump tweeted "No Collusion, No Obstruction, Complete and Total EXONERATION" (Marcin 2019), although the report explicitly did no such thing. Even without formal allegations of corruption, Trump's efforts to benefit from a foreign power's attempts to undermine a U.S. election are an enormous breach of public trust. Following the report, the administration defiantly refused to cooperate with 20 congressional committees and subpoenas by the House, prompting a constitutional crisis of sorts over the boundaries of executive power. Trump's aggressive defiance led to renewed calls for his impeachment. To add fuel to the fire, in June 2019 Trump publicly said he would welcome information from a foreign power peddling political dirt on an opponent (Itkowitz and Hamburger 2019), which is a violation of federal law, drawing protests from Democrats and, as usual, silence from Republicans.

The list of damaging environmental policies conducted by the Trump administration is long and depressing. Within days of taking office, information about climate change vanished from the White House website, replaced by text lauding fossil fuels. Trump has aided the fossil fuel industry at every turn and undermined renewable energy. Under director Scott Pruitt (who later resigned in disgrace) and then coal lobbyist Andrew Wheeler, the Environmental Protection Agency has initiated a flurry of disastrous changes (Greshko et al. 2019). It rolled back Obama-era attempts to combat climate change, such as coal power plant emissions (the Clean Power Plan), called for increased logging on public lands, reduced criminal enforcement of EPA laws, eased drilling on lands designed to protect the sage grouse, approved construction of the Keystone XL pipeline, approved the first offshore wells in the Arctic, disbanded the EPA's air pollution review panel, repealed rules on methane emissions, weakened automobile fuel economy rules, downsized Utah's Bears Ears and Grand Staircase-Escalante National Monuments, rolled back Endangered Species Act rules, overruled EPA scientists' plea to ban the insecticide chlorpyrifos (Lipton 2017), auctioned off 77 million acres in the Gulf of Mexico for oil and gas leases, canceled rules to protect whales from fishing nets, illegally tightened membership requirements for the EPA's 18-member Board of Science Advisors, and rolled back regulations on mercury emissions. The administration set about dismantling clean water rules under the Clean Water Act (Biesecker and Brown 2018). Climate change, which Trump dismissed as a hoax, has come in for special scrutiny. Trump withdrew from the Paris Climate Accord. His administration disbanded the federal climate advisory panel, cut NASA's climate monitoring program, censored the government's climate change websites, dropped climate change from the list of national security threats, and revoked federal flood-risk standards pertaining to sea level rise. By portraying environmental regulations as an unnecessary burden on the corporate sector, these changes essentially amount to giving extractive industries a green light to do as they wish.

The Trump administration exhibits over-the-top signs of corruption. Trump and colleagues display a contempt for the rule of law rarely seen in U.S. history. Despite claims that he would "drain the swamp," Trump has led what many observers believe to be the most corrupt administration in U.S. history. Indeed, their actions threaten the system of checks and balances that have long underpinned American governance (Zuckert 2018). A 2017 survey by Transparency International found that 44% of Americans believe the White House is corrupt, up from 36% the year before. Many of Trump's closest informal advisors are billionaires such as Rupert Murdoch and Carl Icahn, who stand to gain from his policies. The Trump family has benefited directly and enormously from his presidency. The appointment of his daughter Ivanka and son-in-law Jared Kushner as advisors was widely seen as morally questionable nepotism. Trump University was closed on charges it had defrauded students. Breaking with a half-century tradition of presidential candidates, Trump refused to divest himself of his business ventures or to release his tax returns. The Trump Inaugural Committee is being investigated by federal prosecutors on charges that it drew more than $107 million in donations, including from foreign donors (which is illegal), and spent $1.5 million at Trump International Hotel. Trump's charitable organization, the Donald J. Trump Foundation, which had no employees, was charged with sweeping violations of campaign finance laws during the 2016 election and forced to close in 2018, accused by the New York Attorney General of "functioning as little more than a checkbook to serve Mr. Trump's business and political interests" and of engaging in "a shocking pattern of illegality" (Goldmacher 2018).

The vast real estate holdings of the Trump Organization, managed by his sons Eric and Donald, Jr., such as the Trump International Hotel in Washington, D.C., have attracted foreign firms and dignitaries seeking favor with the president (Zibel 2018), potentially a violation of the Constitution's Emoluments clause (Article 1, Section 9, Clause 8), which prohibits foreign governments from bestowing gifts on American officials. Tax cuts on "pass through" companies saved his empire millions. Ivanka Trump promised U.S. visas to rich Chinese in exchange for $500,000 investments in Kushner properties, a violation of rules prohibiting conflicts of interest. Presidential counselor Kellyanne Conway touted Ivanka Trump's brand of shoes on television (Yglesias 2018). Ivanka Trump's apparel line sales increased 346% during the first month of her father's presidency. The White House website includes details of Melania Trump's jewelry line at QVC. Trump intimated that membership in his Mar-a-Lago resort in Florida and the Bedminster Golf Club in New Jersey offered front row seats to the inner workings of his presidency, and the State Department advertises Mar-a-Lago on its website (Global Anti-Corruption Blog 2018). The Trump Organization produces golf tees with the presidential seal. The Secret Service spends funds renting golf carts at Trump golf courses and renting two floors of Trump Tower in New York. Trump paid his lawyer Michael Cohen $130,000 to buy the silence of porn star Stormy Daniels (Feuer 2018) and the *National Enquirer* paid $150,000 to former Playboy bunny Karen McDougal (Palazzolo, Rothfeld, and Alpert 2016) to buy her silence shortly before the 2016 election, possible violations of campaign finance laws. In 2019, organizations related to the Trump administration were the subject of 12 different investigations; every single organization Trump has headed is under legal review, including the White House, the Trump Foundation, the Trump Organization, the Trump campaign, and the 58th Presidential Inaugural Committee. Numerous presidents have engaged in corrupt behavior; Trump, however, has blurred the once-sharp boundary between personal gain and public service in a way not seen since the Gilded Age.

Several of Trump's Cabinet officials have also been charged with corruption, including Veterans Affairs Secretary David Shulkin, EPA Administrator Scott Pruitt, Health and Human Services Secretary Tom Price, Interior Secretary Ryan Zinke, Housing and Urban Affairs Secretary Ben Carson, and Treasury Secretary Steve Mnuchin. Some, such as Pruitt, Zinke, and Price, were forced to resign for egregious abuse of office.

The policies of the Trump administration have likewise enabled corporate corruption of the state. It rescinded a Securities and Exchange Commission rule that required oil companies to disclose details of their payments to international governments in connection with oil and gas production. The Interior

34 Barney Warf

Department withdrew from a certification process of the Extractive Industries Transparency Initiative, which attempts to curb corruption in the oil and mining sectors that involves governments, corporations, and civil society groups (Coll 2017). While the administration cut funding for the Department of Housing and Urban Development, it left in place federal subsidies to private landlords, of which millions flow to the Trump Organization.

Trump's foreign policies

The Trump administration's foreign policy has been marked by marked departures from the norms of the international order, often depicting a world of ungrateful, parasitic allies that rely on the U.S. to defend them. Under the slogan "America First" (recycling the phrase adopted by 1930s isolationists), Trump enacted several steps that run contrary to the long-standing Republican Party's embrace of globalization and eroded the architecture of a world system created by the U.S. itself.

In 2017, Trump issued an executive order attempting to block immigrants from seven Muslim-majority countries (Iran, Iraq, Libya, Somalia, Sudan, Syria, and Yemen) until it was overturned by the courts. It led to the detention of 600 visitors and the revocation of 60,000 visas. It took effect for about a year until it was superseded by a milder version upheld by the Supreme Court.

The most famous and repeated claim that Trump made during his campaign was to build a "big, fat, beautiful wall" along the border with Mexico, which he claimed Mexico would pay for it. Mexican president Vicente Fox replied "I'm not gonna pay for that fucking wall" (Reilly 2016). Trump's estimates of the costs of the wall have varied between $12 billion and $21 billion. The wall is his signature promise, one he must keep to keep favor with his most ardent supporters. In the run-up to the 2018 midterm elections, he deployed U.S. troops to the border as a publicity stunt. Afterward, Trump insisted that Congress appropriate $5.7 billion for a wall, claiming that there was a national emergency resulting from a huge influx of undocumented immigrants. In fact, border apprehensions in 2018 were down 70% from 2000, and most people who enter the country illegally do so by overstaying tourist visas, not by crossing the border (McMinn 2019), so the wall would be useless even if built. The wall is actually more of a statement about white racism than an effective means to limit immigration. The Democrats' refusal to fund the wall led to a budget stand-off with the Democratic-controlled House, resulting in a 35-day partial closure of the federal government from mid-December 2018 to mid-January 2019. Upon failing to obtain funding, Trump declared a "national emergency" to divert funds from the military to build the wall, testing the boundaries of administrative action and congressional oversight and prompting lawsuits to stop the action.

The Immigration and Customs Enforcement Agency (ICE), part of the Department of Homeland Security, also initiated a family separation policy along the border with Mexico, in which thousands of children of undocumented immigrants were taken from their parents; some were locked in cages, and at least three died in the custody of ICE. Eventually the administration backed off of this tactic once it was pointed out that putting children in cages was a public relations disaster. These policies are the direct result of placing xenophobic officials such as Stephen Miller in charge of immigration policy.

Trump's trade relations have been marked by conflict. His protectionism and rejection of free trade are a major pivot in U.S. trade policy. On his first day in office, he withdrew the U.S. from the Trans-Pacific Partnership, the 12-nation agreement signed by President Obama, directing 40% of world trade toward China. The move is likely to raise the prices of imports, lower economic growth, and raise questions about the reliability of the U.S. as a trading partner. Trump also attempted to renegotiate NAFTA, the original of which he called "the worst trade deal ever made" (Davis and Rappeport 2017), leading to a slightly revised version (the U.S.-Mexico-Canada Pact) yet to be ratified. Trump imposed 25% tariffs on imports of steel and 10% tariffs on aluminum from several countries, including China, Canada, and the European Union, using the absurd pretext that they posed a national security threat. The president also initiated tariffs against imports China, saying that trade wars are "good, and easy to win" (Paletta 2018), provoking a sustained conflict between the world's two largest economies. Trump accused China of manipulating its currency and intellectual property theft, and imposed 25% tariffs on $200 billion of Chinese imports (Swanson 2018), prompting the Chinese to retaliate and raising the threat of a trade war between the world's two largest economies. China reciprocated with tariffs on U.S. automobiles, airplanes, and soybeans. With Chinese imports of U.S. farm products (notably soy beans) down drastically, Trump resorted to giving $12 billion in subsidies to help ease their pain. Finally, he has considered withdrawal of the U.S. from the World Trade Organization.

After denouncing the dictator of North Korea, Kim Jong Un, as "Little Rocket Man" (Le Miere 2017) and threatening to rain "fire and fury" upon him (Baker and Sang-Hun 2017), Trump met with him in Singapore, and later proclaimed that they "fell in love" (Rucker and Dawsey 2019). He proclaimed the threat from North Korea's nuclear missile program to be over, despite all evidence to the contrary (Baker and Sang-Hun 2018).

The administration made bellicose moves on a number of other fronts. He called the European Union a "foe." Trump withdrew from an accord with Iran negotiated by the Obama administration that lifted trade and investment sanctions in return for a suspension of that country's nuclear program. He moved the U.S. embassy to Israel from Tel Aviv to Jerusalem, placating Christian conservatives and many Jews. Without consulting his senior staff, Trump initiated the withdrawal of U.S. troops from Syria and Afghanistan (only later to reverse the decision), prompting the resignation of his Defense Secretary Jim Mattis. He inquired as to whether NATO was still necessary, calling it "obsolete," and discussed possible U.S. withdrawal from the organization, and chastised European leaders for failing to pay their "fair share." Trump signaled his intent to withdraw the U.S. from a 31-year old nuclear arms treaty with Russia, the Intermediate-Range Nuclear Forces (INF) Treaty signed by Reagan and Gorbachev in 1987, raising the possibility of a new nuclear arms race.

As Diehl (2019) notes, Trump's foreign policy follows the same strategy he used in his earlier real estate deals: target an adversary; make maximalist demands; when that fails, change targets and move on to a new one. Thus, Trump has at various time threatened North Korea, Venezuela, Iran, and Mexico, all without meaningful results.

Human rights and the environment have little room in this policy environment. Trump's transactional qualities rise to the fore in his foreign relations. When confronted with clear evidence that Saudi Arabia had murdered the journalist Jamal Khashoggi in Istanbul, he shrugged off the crime on the grounds that not doing so would jeopardize lucrative arms contracts to the country. Soon after his inauguration, he initiated the withdrawal of the U.S. from the Paris Accord to reduce greenhouse gas emissions that cause global warming.

Trump's lack of diplomacy and his isolationism have raised widespread concerns about the loss of U.S international leadership and the erosion of the post-WWII global liberal order (E. Cohen 2017; Stokes 2018). It has initiated a steady decomposition of the country's foreign policy and national security establishment. The administration's foreign policy has alienated many allies, notably in Europe and Australia, and left them distrustful of the U.S. Its actions have undermined the stability of the global system predicated on free trade and military alliances. The administration has shown no coherent strategy for dealing with Russia, has aggravated rather than resolved grievances in the Middle East, neglected to rally allies in the face of multiple threats to the multipolar world order, and abdicated the moral high ground. Many foreign leaders have sought to reshape alliances, bypassing the U.S., E. Cohen (2017) argues that "In almost every region of the world, the administration has already left a mark, by blunder, inattention, miscomprehension, or willfulness." His embrace of authoritarian figures has diminished the moral standing of the U.S. around the world. In the void left by the decline of U.S. leadership, China has stepped in vigorously. Perhaps the world will not mourn the decline of U.S. hegemony, but there are good reasons to suspect that those who celebrate the end of the American Century have odious intentions for doing so.

Trump in 2020

The year 2020 has been an *annus horribulus* for Trump. In December, 2019, the House of Representatives brought charges of impeachment against him, specifically for abuse of power and obstruction of justice (Fandos and Shear 2020). He thus became the third president to be impeached. The charges centered on Trump's attempts during an infamous July 2019 phone call to invoke the president of Ukraine, Volodymyr Zelensky, in a smear campaign against his likely

Democratic rival, Joe Biden, as well as a cover up. Trump threatened to withhold military aid to Ukraine unless it cooperated. The charges emanated after a whistle blower revealed the conspiracy. Trump's defense was to stonewall, ridicule and belittle his accusers, calling the impeachment a witch hunt and hoax, a strategy closely echoed by his sycophants on Fox News and other right-wing media outlets. The White House refused to allow key witnesses to testify at the House or subsequent Senate hearings, although Democrats persuaded some to do so anyway. One, Army Lt. Colonel Alexander Vindman, was fired from his position in the National Security Council after testifying in the House. In February 2020, the Republican-controlled Senate voted 52–48 to acquit Trump of both charges, a vote defined by party lines, with only one Republican, Mitt Romney, defecting to vote to convict on one charge (Kim 2020). The acquittal reflected the intense loyalty to Trump among Republican politicians, many of whom live in terror of his base of supporters.

In January and February, the novel coronavirus, which causes COVID-19, entered the United States. The pandemic had started in Wuhan, China and soon spread across the globe, starting the largest global health crisis in a century. Faced with growing numbers of cases and rising deaths, Trump essentially did nothing, abandoning even the pretense of leadership (Shear et al. 2020). Because the Trump administration effectively abandoned federal attempts to contain the virus, states were left on their own, desperately competing for limited medical supplies. The result was a patchwork of efforts that reflected local politics and priorities. Some locked down completely, others partially, and yet others not at all.

Compounding the problem was Trump's rhetoric of denial. "It's fading away. It's going to fade away," Trump told Sean Hannity on Fox News (Todisco 2020). He resorted to racist tropes, calling corona the "China virus" and "Kung flu." Milbank (2020) helpfully collected a number of Trump's sayings about the pandemic, which are worth quoting here:

> The coronavirus is very much under control in the USA. We have it totally under control. I'm not concerned at all. It's one person coming in from China. We pretty much shut it down. It will all work out well. We're in great shape. Doesn't spread widely at all in the United States because of the early actions that myself and my administration took. There's a chance it won't spread. It's something that we have tremendous control over.
>
> Looks like by April, you know, in theory, when it gets a little warmer, it miraculously goes away. One day it's like a miracle, it will disappear. Just stay calm. It will go away. The Democrats are politicizing the coronavirus. This is their new hoax.
>
> Whatever happens, we're totally prepared. Totally ready. We're rated number one for being prepared. We are so prepared like we never have been prepared. Taking early intense action, we have seen dramatically fewer cases of the virus in the United States. We're very much ahead of everything.

38 Barney Warf

For months, Trump refused to wear a face mask, becoming a model for right-wing science deniers who claimed the whole pandemic was a hoax. He repeatedly touted the drug hydroxychloroquine, even though medical studies showed it did not prevent or cure the virus and could cause serious side effects (Qiu 2020). At one point Trump even suggested that drinking or injecting bleach might help (Rogers et al. 2020), earning him widespread ridicule. He belittled testing for the virus, saying "I personally think testing is overrated, even though I created the greatest testing machine in history." At a rally in Tulsa, Trump proclaimed "when you do testing to that extent, you're going to find more people; you're going to find more cases. So I said to my people, slow the testing down please" (Abutaleb et al. 2020). When protests against quarantine orders arose in several states, Trump tweeted "LIBERATE MINNESOTA!," "LIBERATE MICHIGAN!" and "LIBERATE VIRGINIA, and save your great 2nd amendment. It is under siege!", thus conflating public health measures with gun confiscation. Trump and aides repeatedly ignored advice from health care professionals and epidemiologists, including his own advisor Dr. Anthony Fauci, at one point even leading a campaign to discredit him (Mindich 2020). Trump repeatedly called for state economies to reopen, students to return to school, and claimed that large gatherings were safe, all contrary to expert opinion (Baker 2020a).

The results of this mishandling and incompetence were catastrophic. By August, roughly 5.8 million Americans had become infected and 180,000 had died of the virus. With 4 percent of the world's population, the U.S. had almost a quarter of its cases. Daily new cases rose by more than 60,000, and more than 1,000 people per day died of the virus. Whereas European and East Asian countries had largely succeeded in "flattening the curve" and bringing the number of cases down dramatically, in the U.S. the pandemic continued to surge. Unsurprisingly, Trump's popularity declined in proportion to the rise in cases, with the majority of people disapproving how he handled it.

As the coronavirus took its toll, the economy went into meltdown. In the second quarter of 2020, U.S. GDP declined by 9.5%, the largest contraction in history (Caselman 2020), equivalent to a 32.9% annual decline. As states and cities went into a coronavirus-induced lockdown and consumer spending declined dramatically, scores of businesses went bankrupt, and unemployment rose to 14.9%. Waves of evictions raised the level of homelessness, and widespread desperation set in among the working poor. In response, Congress passed a multi-trillion dollar aid package, the effects of which soon wore off.

Simultaneously, a wave of protests erupted in American cities in response to police brutality against Black people, notably the murder of George Floyd. Trump's response was dismal. He staged a photo op in DC that involved clearing peaceful protestors with teargas so that he could have his picture taken holding a bible (upside down) in front of a church (Rogers 2020). He sent federal troops to quash peaceful protests in Portland, calling himself a "law and order" president while federal agents kidnapped people and put them in unmarked vans (Kumar 2020). He threatened to send federal troops to other cities, specifically those with Democratic mayors. He went out of his way to defend statues and military bases named after Confederate officers in the midst of an enormous upwelling of support for Black Lives Matter, even as the Pentagon and Nascar gave up such symbols. His race-baiting earned numerous comparisons to the Southern segregationist George Wallace (Baker 2020b).

Facing conjoined health, economic, and political crises, Trump became increasingly erratic in his behavior. He claimed Democratic nominee Joe Biden was a "radical left wing socialist" who was attempting to take people's windows (Parton 2020). Trump and his son, Donald Jr., retweeted bizarre claims by a Houston physician who justified hydroxychloroquine but added that gynecological problems were caused by dreams of sex with demons and that alien DNA was being used in medical experiments to create a vaccine that would make everyone an atheist (Andrews and Paquette 2020; von Drehle 2020). He rampaged against voting by mail (which he had done himself), without evidence, on the grounds that it would introduce fraud in the upcoming election, despite its popularity in the midst of the pandemic. The head of the Post Office, Louis DeJay, a major Trump campaign contributor, withheld overtime pay in an apparent effort to delay mailed ballots, anticipating enormous problems for the general election in November. The hysterics were widely seen as an attempt to discredit the results of the election if he lost, as seemed likely. In an interview with Fox News, when asked if he would accept the election's results, Trump replied "I have to see" (Mansoor 2020). In July, 2020, facing dismal poll numbers and diminishing prospects for re-election, he called for the presidential election to be postponed (Waldman and Ekeh 2020).

Conclusion

A president without any previous government experience, alleged to have won the election due to Russian interference, investigated by his own FBI as a possible Russian asset, and who generates fears of being a fascist, has violated almost every constitutional and diplomatic norm. Michiko Kakutani (2018, p. 159) summarizes his behavior beautifully:

> His tweets and offhand taunts are the very essence of trolling – the lies the scorn, the invective, the trash talk, and the rabid non sequiturs of an angry, aggrieved, isolated, and deeply self-absorbed adolescent who lives in a self-constructed bubble and gets the attention he craves from bashing his enemies and trailing clouds of outrage and dismay in his path.

This is the odd situation in which the United States finds itself since Trump's election in 2016. Trump's outsized personality has dominated the news on a daily basis, given his narcissism. A long list of unappetizing adjectives has been applied to the man in the White House: unhinged, insane, erratic, incompetent, undignified, cruel, immature, boorish, unpresidential, undignified, preposterous, abhorrent, ignorant, anti-intellectual, lazy, cowardly, weak, and so forth.

40 Barney Warf

Some of these are undoubtedly true, others the products of the intense political opposition that has mobilized against him. More importantly, Trump has initiated a series of disastrous policies concerning international trade, immigration, the environment, the economy, and foreign policy, all of which have severely damaged both American society and the global order.

References

Abramson, A., and R. Beckwith. 2018. President Trump claims his campaign was "spied" on. Here's what really happened. *Time* (May 23). https://time.com/5288607/donald-trump-fbi-spygate/

Abutaleb, Y., T. Telford, and J. Dawsey. 2020. Democrats, public health experts decry Trump for saying he asked officials to slow down coronavirus testing. *Washington Post* (June 21). www.washingtonpost.com/politics/2020/06/21/democrats-public-health-experts-decry-trump-saying-he-asked-officials-slow-down-coronavirus-testing/

Acosta, J., J. Sciotto, and J. Manchester. 2016. Donald Trump: "Torture works." *CNN Politics* (Feb. 17). www.cnn.com/2016/02/17/politics/donald-trump-torture-works/index.html

Andrews, T. and D. Paquette. 2020. Trump retweeted a video with false covid-19 claims. One doctor in it has said demons cause illnesses. *Washington Post* (July 29). www.washingtonpost.com/technology/2020/07/28/stella-immanuel-hydroxychloroquine-video-trump-americas-frontline-doctors/

Apuzzo, M., M. Haberman, and M. Rosenberg. 2017. Trump told Russians that firing "nut job" Comey eased pressure from investigation. *New York Times* (May 19). www.nytimes.com/2017/05/19/us/politics/trump-russia-comey.html

Arkin, D. 2016. Donald Trump criticized after he appears to mock reporter Serge Kovaleski. *NBC News* (Nov. 26). www.nbcnews.com/politics/2016-election/new-york-times-slams-donald-trump-after-he-appears-mock-n470016

Baker, P. 2017. "People love you": For Trump, a welcome escape from the capital. *New York Times* (July 25). www.nytimes.com/2017/07/25/us/politics/trump-ohio-rally.html

Baker, P. 2018. Trump bars CNN's Jim Acosta from the White House. *New York Times* (Nov. 7). www.nytimes.com/2018/11/07/us/politics/trump-cnn-acosta-white-house.html

Baker, P. 2020a. 'Mugged by reality,' Trump finds denial won't stop the pandemic. *New York Times* (July 24). www.nytimes.com/2020/07/24/us/politics/coronavirus-trump-denial.html

Baker, P. 2020b. A half-century after Wallace, Trump echoes the politics of division. *New York Times* (July 30). www.nytimes.com/2020/07/30/us/politics/trump-wallace.html

Baker, P., and C. Sang-Hun. 2017. Trump threatens "fire and fury" against North Korea if it endangers U.S. *New York Times* (Aug. 8). www.nytimes.com/2017/08/08/world/asia/north-korea-un-sanctions-nuclear-missile-united-nations.html

Baker, P., and C. Sang-Hun. 2018. Trump sees end to North Korea nuclear threat despite unclear path. *New York Times* (June 13). www.nytimes.com/2018/06/13/us/politics/trump-north-korea-denuclearization.html

Baker, P., and M. Haberman. 2019. Trump's wall, Trump's shutdown and Trump's side of the story. *New York Times* (Jan. 4). www.nytimes.com/2019/01/04/us/politics/trump-wall-shutdown.html

Bamberger, M. 2019. President Trump won a 2018 club championship — without actually playing in it! *Golf* (March 11). https://golf.com/lifestyle/celebrities/president-trump-club-championship-did-not-enter/

Barstow, D., S. Craig, and R. Buettner. 2018. Trump engaged in suspect tax schemes as he reaped riches from his father. *New York Times* (Oct. 2). www.nytimes.com/interactive/2018/10/02/us/politics/donald-trump-tax-schemes-fred-trump.html

BBC News. 2018 (June 18). Trump migrant separation policy: Children 'in cages' in Texas. www.bbc.com/news/world-us-canada-44518942

Bertrand, N. 2019. The President humiliates his own Department of Justice. *The Atlantic* (Jan. 13). www.theatlantic.com/politics/archive/2019/01/trumps-war-on-the-department-of-justice/580051/

Biesecker, M., and M. Brown. 2018. Trump EPA moves to roll back more clean air and water rules. *Washington Post* (March 1). www.washingtonpost.com/business/trump-epa-moves-to-roll-back-more-clean-air-and-water-rules/2018/03/01/6ac314d8-1dbf-11e8-98f5-ceecfa8741b6_story.html

Blake, A. 2016. 19 things Donald Trump knows better than anyone else, according to Donald Trump. *Washington Post* (Oct. 4). www.washingtonpost.com/news/the-fix/wp/2016/10/04/17-issues-that-donald-trump-knows-better-than-anyone-else-according-to-donald-trump/

Blake, A. 2017a. 21 times Donald Trump has assured us he respects women. *Washington Post* (March 8). www.washingtonpost.com/news/the-fix/wp/2017/03/08/21-times-donald-trump-has-assured-us-he-respects-women/

Blake, A. 2017b. 6 times Trump's allegedly unparalleled memory failed him at extremely convenient times. *Washington Post* (Nov. 3). www.washingtonpost.com/news/the-fix/wp/2017/11/03/trump-claims-one-of-the-great-memories-of-all-time-its-certainly-one-of-the-most-convenient/

Blake, A. 2017c. Trump is running out of Twitter tricks. *Washington Post* (Sept. 20). www.washingtonpost.com/news/the-fix/wp/2017/09/22/trump-is-running-out-of-twitter-tricks/

Blake, A. 2017d. Trump says the Boy Scouts called to tell him his speech was the 'greatest.' He appears to have imagined this. *Washington Post* (Aug. 2). www.washingtonpost.com/news/the-fix/wp/2017/08/02/trump-says-the-boy-scouts-head-told-him-his-speech-was-the-greatest-he-appears-to-have-exaggerated-or-imagined-this/

Blake, A. 2019. Trump's flippant talk about the Vietnam War. *Washington Post* (June 5). www.washingtonpost.com/politics/2019/06/05/trumps-flippant-talk-about-vietnam-war/

Blow, C. 2015. Enough is enough. *New York Times* (Aug. 27). www.nytimes.com/2015/08/27/opinion/enough-is-enough.html

Blow, C. 2016. Trump, grand wizard of birtherism. *New York Times* (Sept. 17). www.nytimes.com/2016/09/19/opinion/trump-grand-wizard-of-birtherism.html

Blumberg, A. 2018. Trump calls Omarosa 'a lowlife' after n-word claim surfaces. *HuffPost* (Aug. 11). www.huffpost.com/entry/trump-lashes-out-at-omarosa-over-claim-he-used-n-word_n_5b6de9e3e4b0530743c9d7c1

Borchers, C. 2016. The amazing story of Donald Trump's old spokesman, John Barron – who was actually Donald Trump himself. *Washington Post* (May 13). www.washingtonpost.com/news/the-fix/wp/2016/03/21/the-amazing-story-of-donald-trumps-old-spokesman-john-barron-who-was-actually-donald-trump-himself/

Borchers, C. 2018. White House: Trump has been tough on Russia because he said so. *Washington Post* (April 6). www.washingtonpost.com/news/the-fix/wp/2018/04/06/white-house-trump-has- Newbeen-tough-on-russia-because-he-said-so/

Bowden, J. 2018. Trump: Bob Woodward is an "idiot," his book "fiction." *The Hill* (Sept. 7). https://thehill.com/homenews/administration/405621-trump-bob-woodward-is-an-idiot-his-book-fiction

Bromwich, J. 2017. Trump on the Civil War: "Why could that one not have been worked out?" *New York Times* (May 1). www.nytimes.com/2017/05/01/us/politics/trump-andrew-jackson-fact-check.html

Broniatowski, M., and M. Crowley. 2017. Trump: "Nobody knows" if Russia interfered in US election. *Politico* (July 6). www.politico.eu/article/president-donald-trump-nobody-knows-if-russia-interfered-in-us-election/

Buchanan, L., and K. Yourish. 2018. The Russia meeting at Trump Tower was to discuss adoption. Then it wasn't. How accounts have shifted. *New York Times* (Aug. 6). www.nytimes.com/interactive/2018/08/06/us/politics/trump-tower-russia-meeting.html

Buettner, R., and S. Craig. 2019. *New York Times* (May 8). Decade in the red: Trump tax figures show over $1 billion in business losses. www.nytimes.com/interactive/2019/05/07/us/politics/donald-trump-taxes.html

Bump, P. 2017. Even the firm that hired actors to cheer Trump's campaign launch had to wait to be paid. *Washington Post* (Jan. 20). www.washingtonpost.com/news/the-fix/wp/2017/01/20/even-the-firm-that-hired-actors-to-cheer-trumps-campaign-launch-had-to-wait-to-be-paid/

Burke, B., N. Bookbinder, and N. Eisen. 2017. *Presidential Obstruction of Justice: The Case of Donald J. Trump*. Washington, D.C.: Brookings Institution. www.politicususa.com/wp-content/uploads/2017/10/presidential-obstruction-of-justice-the-case-of-donald-j-trump-final.pdf

Byrnes, J. 2015a. Trump: Refugees "pouring into" US could be ISIS. *The Hill* (Nov. 17). https://thehill.com/blogs/blog-briefing-room/news-campaigns-presidential-campaigns/260420-trump-refugees-pouring-into-us

Byrnes, J. 2015b. Trump: Rick Perry "should be forced to take an IQ test" before debate. *The Hill* (July 16). https://thehill.com/blogs/ballot-box/presidential-races/248260-trump-rick-perry-should-be-forced-to-take-an-iq-test

Campbell, C. 2016. Trump: "There's nobody that's done so much for equality as I have." *Business Insider* (March 1). www.businessinsider.com.au/donald-trump-equality-david-duke-kkk-2016-3

Capehart, J. 2019. What happened when "little pencil-necked Adam Schiff" took an eraser to Trump and his enablers. *Washington Post* (March 29). www.washingtonpost.com/opinions/2019/03/29/what-happened-when-little-pencil-necked-adam-schiff-took-an-eraser-trump-his-enablers/

Carnes, N., and N. Lupu. 2017. It's time to bust the myth: Most Trump voters were not working class. *New York Times* (June 5). www.washingtonpost.com/news/monkey-cage/wp/2017/06/05/its-time-to-bust-the-myth-most-trump-voters-were-not-working-class/

Carpenter, A. 2018. *Gaslighting America: Why We Love It When Trump Lies to Us*. New York: Broadside Books.

Caselman, B. 2020. A collapse that wiped out 5 years of growth, with no bounce in sight. *New York Times* (July 30). www.nytimes.com/2020/07/30/business/economy/q2-gdp-coronavirus-economy.html

Chapman, S. 2017. Donald Trump's biggest flaw: He's not that bright. *Chicago Tribune* (Nov. 3). www.chicagotribune.com/columns/steve-chapman/ct-perspec-chapman-donald-trump-dumb-20171103-story.html

Chinoy, S., J. Ma, and S. Thompson. 2018. Trump's growing obsession with the "witch hunt." *New York Times* (Aug. 22). www.nytimes.com/interactive/2018/08/22/opinion/trump-cohen-mueller-investigation.html

Chokshi, N. 2018. Trump voters driven by fear of losing status, not economic anxiety, study finds. *New York Times* (April 24). www.nytimes.com/2018/04/24/us/politics/trump-economic-anxiety.html

Cillizza, C. 2018. Donald Trump just called Stormy Daniels "horseface." Don't act surprised. *CNN Politics* (Oct. 16). www.cnn.com/2018/10/16/politics/donald-trump-stormy-daniels-horseface/index.html

Cohen, C. 2017. Donald Trump sexism tracker: Every offensive comment in one place. *The Telegraph* (July 14). www.telegraph.co.uk/women/politics/donald-trump-sexism-tracker-every-offensive-comment-in-one-place/

Cohen, E. 2017. How Trump is ending the American era. *The Atlantic* (Oct.) www.theatlantic.com/magazine/archive/2017/10/is-trump-ending-the-american-era/537888/

Cohen, R. 2017. Donald Trump's history lessons. *New York Times* (July 21). www.nytimes.com/2017/07/21/opinion/donald-trumps-history-lessons.html

Coll, S. 2017. The Trump administration rolls back anti-corruption efforts in the oil industry. *New Yorker* (Aug. 10). www.newyorker.com/news/daily-comment/the-trump-administration-rolls-back-anti-corruption-efforts-in-the-oil-industry

Collins, S. 2014. Donald Trump blasts "dumb," "desperate" Rosie O'Donnell return to "View." *Los Angeles Times* (July 11). www.latimes.com/entertainment/tv/showtracker/la-et-st-donald-trump-blasts-rosie-odonnell-view-20140711-story.html

Corasaniti, N., and M. Haberman. 2016. Donald Trump on protester: "I'd like to punch him in the face." *New York Times* (Feb. 23). www.nytimes.com/politics/first-draft/2016/02/23/donald-trump-on-protester-id-like-to-punch-him-in-the-face/

Coulter, A. 2016. *In Trump We Trust: E Pluribus Awesome!* New York: Sentinel.

Cranley, E. 2018. Trump reportedly talks to Sean Hannity most nights before bed. *Business Insider* (May 14). www.businessinsider.com/trump-sean-hannity-talk-before-bed-2018-5

Cranley, E. 2019. Trump seemingly threatens "SNL" with federal investigation over critical sketch. *Business Insider* (March 17). www.businessinsider.com/snl-sketch-trump-alec-baldwin-matt-damon-rerun-2019-3

Crilly, R. 2017. Donald Trump spends "up to eight hours a day watching TV" – report. *The Telegraph* (Dec. 10). www.telegraph.co.uk/news/2017/12/10/donald-trump-spends-eight-hours-day-watching-tv-report/

Croucher, S. 2018. Kelly called Trump an idiot: "He's gone off the rails. We're in crazytown." *Newsweek* (Sept. 5). www.newsweek.com/trump-kelly-white-house-fear-bob-woodward-book-1105477

D'Antonio, M. 2016. *The Truth about Trump.* New York: St. Martin's Griffin.

Dann, C. 2017. Trump's Electoral College win was not the biggest since Reagan. *NBC News* (Feb. 16). www.nbcnews.com/politics/donald-trump/trump-s-electoral-college-win-was-not-biggest-reagan-n722016

Davis, J. 2018. Trump calls some unauthorized immigrants "animals" in rant. *New York Times* (May 16). www.nytimes.com/2018/05/16/us/politics/trump-undocumented-immigrants-animals.html

Davis, J. and N. Chokshi. 2018. Trump defends 'animals' remark, saying it referred to MS-13 gang members. *New York Times* (May 17). www.nytimes.com/2018/05/17/us/trump-animals-ms-13-gangs.html

Davis, J., and A. Rappeport. 2017. After calling Nafta "worst trade deal," Trump appears to soften stance. *New York Times* (March 30). www.nytimes.com/2017/03/30/business/nafta-trade-deal-trump.html

Decker, C. 2017. Analysis: Trump's war against elites and expertise. *Los Angeles Times* (July 27). www.latimes.com/politics/la-na-pol-trump-elites-20170725-story.html

Delkic, M. 2017. President Donald Trump watches at least four hours of TV a day, associates say. *Newsweek* (Dec. 9). www.newsweek.com/president-trump-watches-four-hours-tv-743432

Diamond, J. 2018. Trump sides with Putin over US intelligence. *CNN Politics* (July 16). www.cnn.com/2018/07/16/politics/donald-trump-putin-helsinki-summit/index.html

Diaz, D. 2018. Trump: I'm a "very stable genius." *CNN Politics* (Jan. 6). www.cnn.com/2018/01/06/politics/donald-trump-white-house-fitness-very-stable-genius/index.html

Diehl, J. 2019. Trump's string of foreign policy bankruptcies *New York Times* (June 9). www.washingtonpost.com/opinions/global-opinions/trumps-foreign-policy-formula-bluster-bully-and-forget/2019/06/09/5c5c1bdc-8877-11e9-a870-b9c411dc4312_story.html

Douthat, R. 2015. Is Donald Trump a fascist? *New York Times* (Dec. 3). www.nytimes.com/2015/12/03/opinion/campaign-stops/is-donald-trump-a-fascist.html

Douthat, R. 2016. A playboy for president. *New York Times* (Aug. 13). www.nytimes.com/2016/08/14/opinion/sunday/a-playboy-for-president.html

Dowd, M. 2019. A down and dirty White House. *New York Times* (June 15). www.nytimes.com/2019/06/15/opinion/sunday/dowd-trump-.html

Durando, J. 2017. Trump says "I have nothing to do with Russia." That's not exactly true. *USA Today* (Jan. 11). www.usatoday.com/story/news/world/2017/01/11/donald-trump-russia-vladimir-putin/96444482/

Fabian, J. 2017. Trump: I'm victim of "single greatest witch hunt." *The Hill* (May 18). https://thehill.com/homenews/administration/trump-tweet-greatest-witch-hunt-in-history-special-councel

Fandos, N. and M. Shear. 2020. Trump impeached for abuse of power and obstruction of Congress. *New York Times* (Dec. 18). www.nytimes.com/2019/12/18/us/politics/trump-impeached.html

Fang, M. 2017. Donald Trump keeps up charade that he might release his tax returns. *Politico* (April 30). www.huffpost.com/entry/donald-trump-tax-returns_n_5905f439e4b0bb2d086f3982

Farenthold, D. 2016. Trump recorded having extremely lewd conversation about women in 2005. *Washington Post* (Oct. 8). www.washingtonpost.com/politics/trump-recorded-having-extremely-lewd-conversation-about-women-in-2005/2016/10/07/3b9ce776-8cb4-11e6-bf8a-3d26847eeed4_story.html

Farenthold, D. 2017. A *Time* magazine with Trump on the cover hangs in his golf clubs. It's fake. *Washington Post* (June 27). www.washingtonpost.com/politics/a-time-magazine-with-trump-on-the-cover-hangs-in-his-golf-clubs-its-fake/2017/06/27/0adf96de-5850-11e7-ba90-f5875b7d1876_story.html

Farrow, R. 2018. Donald Trump, a playboy model, and a system for concealing infidelity. *New Yorker* (Feb. 16). www.newyorker.com/news/news-desk/donald-trump-a-playboy-model-and-a-system-for-concealing-infidelity-national-enquirer-karen-mcdougal

Feuer, A. 2018. What we know about Trump's $130,000 payment to Stormy Daniels. *New York Times* (Aug. 27). www.nytimes.com/2018/08/27/nyregion/stormy-daniels-trump-payment.html

Firozi, P. 2017. Eric Trump in 2014: "We have all the funding we need out of Russia." *Business Insider* (May 7). https://thehill.com/homenews/news/332270-eric-trump-in-2014-we-dont-rely-on-american-banks-we-have-all-the-funding-we

Flegenheimer, M. 2018. Band of the insulted: The nicknames of Trump's adversaries. *New York Times* (Jan. 5). www.nytimes.com/2018/01/05/us/politics/trump-nicknames.html

Foley, E. 2015. Donald Trump kicks Jorge Ramos out of press conference. *Huffington Post* (Aug. 26). www.huffingtonpost.co.uk/entry/donald-trump-kicks-jorge-ramos-out-of-press-conference_n_55dcf2b1e4b0a40aa3aca654

Foley, E., I. Bobic, and S. Lachman 2016. Donald Trump goes full anti-woman, suggests "punishment" for women who abort. *Huffington Post* (March 30). www.huffpost.com/entry/donald-trump-abortion-women-punishment_n_56fc2a99e4b083f5c606880d

Gass, N. 2016. Trump: "There used to be consequences" for protesting. *Politico* (March 11). www.politico.com/blogs/2016-gop-primary-live-updates-and-results/2016/03/trump-defends-protest-violence-220638

Gearan, A., and D. Barrett. 2017. Trump calls conduct at the FBI "disgraceful" in latest criticism of bureau. *Washington Post* (Dec. 15). www.washingtonpost.com/world/national-security/trump-calls-conduct-at-fbi-disgraceful-before-appearing-at-quantico/2017/12/15/4f4a4fae-e1a7-11e7-bbd0-9dfb2e37492a_story.html

Geraghty, J. 2015. "Look at that face! Would anyone vote for that?" *National Review* (Sept. 10) www.nationalreview.com/corner/look-face-would-anyone-vote-jim-geraghty/

Global Anti-Corruption Blog. 2018 (May 2). Tracking corruption and conflicts in the Trump administration. https://globalanticorruptionblog.com/profiting-from-the-presidency-tracking-corruption-and-conflicts-in-the-trump-administration/#govtpayments

Glynn, J. 2019. The reelection of Donald Trump. *The American Spectator* (May 14). https://spectator.org/the-reelection-of-donald-trump/

Goldmacher, S. 2018. Trump Foundation will dissolve, accused of "shocking pattern of illegality." *New York Times* (Dec. 18). www.nytimes.com/2018/12/18/nyregion/ny-ag-underwood-trump-foundation.html

Goldman, A., M. Schmidt, and N. Fandos. 2019. F.B.I. opened inquiry into whether Trump was secretly working on behalf of Russia. *New York Times* (Jan. 11). www.nytimes.com/2019/01/11/us/politics/fbi-trump-russia-inquiry.html

Gorski, P. 2017. Why evangelicals voted for Trump: A critical cultural sociology. *American Journal of Cultural Sociology* 5(1): 338–354.

Gray, R. 2017. Trump defends white-nationalist protesters: "Some very fine people on both sides." *The Atlantic* (Aug. 15). www.theatlantic.com/politics/archive/2017/08/trump-defends-white-nationalist-protesters-some-very-fine-people-on-both-sides/537012/

Greshko, M., L Parker, B. Howard, D. Stone, A. Borunda, and S. Gibbens. 2019. A running list of how President Trump is changing environmental policy. *National Geographic* (Jan. 17). https://news.nationalgeographic.com/2017/03/how-trump-is-changing-science-environment/

Griffiths, B. 2018. Trump falsely claims he never told House Republicans to vote for immigration bill. *Politico* (June 30). www.politico.com/story/2018/06/30/donald-trump-immigration-vote-tweets-689501

Grynbaum, M., and E. Sullivan. 2019. Trump attacks the *Times*, in a week of unease for the American press. *New York Times* (Feb. 20). www.nytimes.com/2019/02/20/us/politics/new-york-times-trump.html

Haberkorn, J. 2018. Trump says he would be "proud" to shut down the government over border wall funding. *Los Angeles Times* (Dec. 11). www.latimes.com/politics/la-na-pol-congress-trump-shutdown-20181211-story.html

Halper, E., and A. Zavis. 2017. Trump quits the Paris Climate Accord, denouncing it as a violation of U.S. sovereignty. *Los Angeles Times* (June 1). www.latimes.com/politics/la-na-pol-trump-paris-20170601-story.html

Hamilton, I. 2019. Trump invented a new nickname for Jeff Bezos in a tweet mocking his divorce. *Business Insider* (Jan. 19). www.businessinsider.com/donald-trump-calls-jeff-bezos-jeff-bozo-in-mocking-tweet-2019-1

Harding, L. 2017. *Collusion: How Russia Helped Trump Win the White House*. London: Guardian Faber Publishing.

Hesse, M. 2020. All the president's 'suburban housewives'. *Washington Post* (July 31). www.washingtonpost.com/lifestyle/style/all-the-presidents-suburban-house-wives/2020/07/30/7b100624-d1d7-11ea-9038-af089b63ac21_story.html

Hopper, J. 2016. Donald Trump targets Ted Cruz's wife on Twitter again. *ABC News* (March 24). https://abcnews.go.com/Politics/donald-trump-targets-ted-cruzs-wife-twitter/story?id=37889421

HuffPost Media. 2013. Donald Trump's awful tweet about sexual assault in the military. *Huffington Post* (May 8). www.huffpost.com/entry/donald-trump-tweet-sexual-assault-military_n_3239781

Hurt, H. 1991. Donald Trump gets small. *Esquire* (May 1). http://archive.esquire.com/article/1991/5/1/donald-trump-gets-small

Itkowitz, C., and T. Hamburger. 2019. Trump says he'd consider accepting information from foreign governments on his opponents. *Washington Post* (June 12). www.washingtonpost.com/politics/trump-says-hed-consider-accepting-dirt-from-foreign-governments-on-his-opponents/2019/06/12/b84ba860-8d5c-11e9-8f69-a2795fca3343_story.html

Johnson, B. 2015. Donald Trump by Donald Trump. *Newsweek* (June 17). www.newsweek.com/donald-trump-donald-trump-343805

Johnson, J. 2015. Trump calls for "total and complete shutdown of Muslims entering the United States". *Washington Post* (Dec. 7). www.washingtonpost.com/news/post-politics/wp/2015/12/07/donald-trump-calls-for-total-and-complete-shutdown-of-muslims-entering-the-united-states/

Jordan, M. 2016. When Trump said that not paying taxes "makes me smart," undecided voters in N.C. gasped. *Washington Post* (Sept. 27). www.washingtonpost.com/politics/a-lean-toward-clinton-among-one-group-of-undecided-north-carolina-voters/2016/09/27/ff271b2e-8469-11e6-92c2-14b64f3d453f_story.html

Kaczynski, A., C. Massie, and N. McDermott. 2017. 80 times Trump talked about Putin. *CNN*. www.cnn.com/interactive/2017/03/politics/trump-putin-russia-timeline/

Kakutani, M. 2018. *The Death of Truth: Notes on Falsehood in the Age of Trump*. New York: Crown Publishing.

Katz, A. 2017. President Trump's no good, very bad week on magazine covers. *Time* (Feb. 3). https://time.com/4659951/donald-trump-magazine-covers-presidency/

Kazin, M. 2016. Trump and American populism: Old whine, new bottles. *Foreign Affairs* (Oct. 6). http://ouleft.sp-mesolite.tilted.net/?p=2183

Kessler, G. 2015. Trump's outrageous claim that "thousands" of New Jersey Muslims celebrated the 9/11 attacks. *Washington Post* (Nov. 22). www.washingtonpost.com/news/fact-checker/wp/2015/11/22/donald-trumps-outrageous-claim-that-thousands-of-new-jersey-muslims-celebrated-the-911-attacks/

Kessler, G. 2016a. Donald Trump's bogus claim that millions of people voted illegally for Hillary Clinton. *Washington Post* (Nov. 27). www.washingtonpost.com/news/fact-checker/wp/2016/11/27/trumps-bogus-claim-that-millions-of-people-voted-illegally-for-hillary-clinton/

Kessler, G. 2016b. Five myths Donald Trump tells about Donald Trump. *Washington Post* (Jan. 28). www.washingtonpost.com/opinions/five-myths-donald-trump-tells-about-donald-trump/2016/01/28/b7cead16-c46e-11e5-9693-933a4d31bcc8_story.html

Kessler, G., S. Rizzo, and M. Kelly. 2020a. *Donald Trump and His Assault on Truth: The President's Falsehoods, Misleading Claims and Flat-Out Lies*. New York Scribner.

Kessler, G., S. Rizzo, and M. Kelly. 2020b. President Trump has made more than 20,000 false or misleading claims. *Washington Post* (July 13). www.washingtonpost.com/politics/2020/07/13/president-trump-has-made-more-than-20000-false-or-misleading-claims/

Khazan, O. 2016. How to sound charismatic. *The Atlantic* (May 25). www.theatlantic.com/science/archive/2016/05/how-to-sound-charismatic/484307/

Kim, S. 2020. In historic vote, Trump acquitted of impeachment charges. *Washington Post* (Feb. 5). www.washingtonpost.com/politics/in-historic-vote-trump-acquitted-of-impeachment-charges/2020/02/05/8b7ea90e-4832-11ea-ab15-b5df3261b710_story.html

Kinsley, M. 2016. Donald Trump is actually a fascist. *Washington Post* (Dec. 9). www.washingtonpost.com/opinions/donald-trump-is-actually-a-fascist/2016/12/09/e193a2b6-bd77-11e6-94ac-3d324840106c_story.html

Kivisto, P. 2017. *The Trump Phenomenon: How the Politics of Populism Won in 2016.* Bingley, UK: Emerald Publishing.

Klapper, E. 2018. Trump takes credit for airline safety, despite slim record. *Huffington Post* (Jan. 2). www.huffpost.com/entry/trump-airline-safety-slim-record_n_5a4bbbf0e4b025f99e1df476

Kopan, T. 2016. Reports: Donald Trump stiffs contractors. *CNN* (June 11). www.cnn.com/2016/06/10/politics/donald-trump-unpaid-bills-reports/index.html

Kranish, M., and M. Fisher. 2016. *Trump Revealed: The Definitive Biography of the 45th President.* New York: Scribner.

Krueger, H., K. Hardiman, and C. Kelly. 2015. Trump's most notable insults. *The Hill* (July 26). https://thehill.com/blogs/ballot-box/249102-trumps-most-notable-insults

Kumar, A. 2020. Trump campaign gets its cue: Go all-in on 'law and order'. *Politico* (June 3). www.politico.com/news/2020/06/03/trump-campaign-protests-296864

Kurtz, J. 2019. Trump rips "washed-up psycho" Bette Midler for sharing fake quote. *MSN.com* (June 5). www.msn.com/en-ca/entertainment/celebrity/trump-rips-washed-up-psycho-bette-midler-for-sharing-fake-quote/ar-AACoXFM

Kwong, J. 2018. Michael Cohen claims Donald Trump said "black people are too stupid to vote for me," among other racist comments. *Newsweek* (Nov. 2). www.newsweek.com/michael-cohen-donald-trump-black-people-stupid-1199924

Landler, M. 2018. Trump sheds all notions of how a president should conduct himself abroad. *New York Times* (July 16). www.nytimes.com/2018/07/16/us/politics/trump-putin-summit.html

Landler, M., and M. Haberman. 2019. Trump declares exoneration, and a war on his enemies. *New York Times* (March 24). www.nytimes.com/2019/03/24/us/politics/trump-exonerated.html

Larison, D. 2019. Trump's invincible ignorance. *American Conservative* (Feb. 3). www.theamericanconservative.com/larison/trumps-invincible-ignorance/

Lavender, P. 2017. "I love it": Donald Trump Jr. knew he was meeting with Kremlin-linked lawyer. *Huffington Post* (July 11). www.huffpost.com/entry/donald-trump-jr-emails_n_5964e8b9e4b005b0fdc8815c

Le Miere, J. 2017. Trump called Kim Jong Un 'Little Rocket Man' because to the president, 'little' is the ultimate insult. *Newsweek* (Sept. 29). www.newsweek.com/trump-kim-jong-un-rocket-674536

Le Miere, J. 2018. Donald Trump says "my gut tells me more sometimes than anybody else's brain can ever tell me." *Newsweek* (Nov. 27). www.newsweek.com/donald-trump-gut-brain-climate-change-fed-1234540

Lee, B. (ed.) 2017. *The Dangerous Case of Donald Trump.* New York: St. Martin's Press.

Lee, M. 2016. Why Donald Trump calls Elizabeth Warren "Pocahontas." *Washington Post* (June 28). www.washingtonpost.com/news/fact-checker/wp/2016/06/28/why-donald-trump-calls-elizabeth-warren-pocahontas/

Lemire, J. 2018. From 'rocket man' to 'terrific': Trump lauds 'very open' Kim. *Sydney Morning Herald* (Sept. 25). www.smh.com.au/world/north-america/from-rocket-man-to-terrific-trump-lauds-very-open-kim-20180925-p505s9.html

Lima, C. 2016. Trump praises Egypt's al-Sisi: 'He's a fantastic guy'. *Politico* (June 22). www.politico.com/story/2016/09/trump-praises-egypts-al-sisi-hes-a-fantastic-guy-228560

Lippman, D. 2018. Trump's diplomatic learning curve: Time zones, "Nambia" and "Nipple." *Politico* (Aug. 13). www.politico.com/story/2018/08/13/trump-world-knowledge-diplomatic-774801

Lipton, E. 2017. E.P.A. chief, rejecting agency's science, chooses not to ban insecticide. *New York Times* (March 29). www.nytimes.com/2017/03/29/us/politics/epa-insecticide-chlorpyrifos.html

Luthra, S. 2019. Fact-checking Donald Trump's claim that drug prices are going down. *Politifact* (May 22). www.politifact.com/factchecks/2019/may/22/donald-trump/fact-checking-donald-trumps-claim-drug-prices-are-/

MacCaskill, N. 2016. Trump accuses Cruz's father of helping JFK's assassin. *Politico* (May3).www.politico.com/blogs/2016-gop-primary-live-updates-and-results/2016/05/trump-ted-cruz-father-222730

Mackey, R. 2016. Trump concerned his rallies are not violent enough. *The Intercept* (March 11). https://theintercept.com/2016/03/11/trumps-good-old-days-when-battering-protesters-was-celebrated-in-the-white-house/

Mackler, J. 2017. Is Trump a moron? *CounterPunch* (Oct. 17). www.counterpunch.org/2017/10/17/is-trump-a-moron/

Mahler, J., and M. Flegenheimer. 2016. What Donald Trump learned from Joseph McCarthy's right-hand man. *New York Times* (June 20). www.nytimes.com/2016/06/21/us/politics/donald-trump-roy-cohn.html

Mansoor, S. 2020. 'I have to see.' President Trump refuses to say if he will accept the 2020 election results. *Time* (July 19). https://time.com/5868739/trump-election-results-chris-wallace/

Marcin, T. 2017. Trump said Haitians have AIDS, Nigerians live in huts in Oval Office meeting, *New York Times* reports. *Newsweek* (Dec. 23). www.newsweek.com/trump-haitians-aids-nigerians-live-huts-oval-office-new-york-times-report-758000

Marcin, T. 2019. Donald Trump, White House say Mueller report "exonerated" president, but Attorney General says it didn't. *Time* (March 24). www.newsweek.com/donald-trump-white-house-mueller-report-exonerated-president-ag-no-1373490

Marcus, R. 2018. Trump said, "I alone can fix it." How wrong he was. *Washington Post* (Jan. 20). www.washingtonpost.com/opinions/trump-said-i-alone-can-fix-it-how-wrong-he-was/2018/01/20/c2802e1a-fe05-11e7-a46b-a3614530bd87_story.html

Martin, J., and A. Rappeport. 2015. Donald Trump says John McCain is no war hero, setting off another storm. *New York Times* (July 18). www.nytimes.com/2015/07/19/us/politics/trump-belittles-mccains-war-record.html

Mayer, J. 2019. The making of the Fox News White House. *The New Yorker* (March 11). www.newyorker.com/magazine/2019/03/11/the-making-of-the-fox-news-white-house

Maza, C. 2018. Donald Trump threw Starburst candies at Angela Merkel, said "don't say I never give you anything." *Newsweek* (June 20). www.newsweek.com/donald-trump-threw-starburst-candies-angela-merkel-dont-say-i-never-give-you-987178

Maza, C. 2019. Donald Trump tells his own intelligence chiefs to "go back to school" over "naïve" assessment of "dangers of Iran." *Newsweek* (Jan. 30). www.newsweek.com/donald-trump-intelligence-twitter-iran-school-1311429

McAdams, D. 2016. The mind of Donald Trump. *The Atlantic* (June). www.theatlantic.com/magazine/archive/2016/06/the-mind-of-donald-trump/480771/

McCaskill, N. 2017a. Trump says Turkish president gets 'very high marks'. *Politico* (Sept. 21). www.politico.com/story/2017/09/21/trump-erdogan-turkey-praise-242986

The Donald in context **49**

McCaskill, N. 2017b. Trump: No politician "has been treated worse or more unfairly." *Politico* (May 17). www.politico.com/story/2017/05/17/donald-trump-coast-guard-gradution-unfairly-treated-president-238505

McMinn, S. 2019. Where does illegal immigration mostly occur? Here's what the data tell us. *NPR* (Jan. 10). www.npr.org/2019/01/10/683662691/where-does-illegal-immigration-mostly-occur-heres-what-the-data-tell-us

McNeil, J. 2016. How fascist is Donald Trump? There's actually a formula for that. *Washington Post* (Oct. 21). www.washingtonpost.com/posteverything/wp/2016/10/21/how-fascist-is-donald-trump-theres-actually-a-formula-for-that/

Milbank, D. 2018. How Trump is transforming himself into the greatest president ever *Washington Post* (April 4). www.washingtonpost.com/opinions/nobody-is-humbler-than-trump/2018/04/04/f246044c-3840-11e8-acd5-35eac230e514_story.html

Milbank, D. 2020. A Trump fireside chat — in his own (unfortunate) words. *Washington Post* (March 31). www.washingtonpost.com/opinions/2020/03/31/fireside-chat-trump-should-deliver/

Miller, G. 2018. *The Apprentice: Trump, Russia and the Subversion of American Democracy*. New York: Custom House.

Miller, H. 2019. Donald Trump claims "no president ever worked harder." Twitter isn't buying it. *Huffington Post* (Feb. 11). www.huffpost.com/entry/donald-trump-claims-worked-harder_n_5c618068e4b0eec79b262c03

Mindich, D. 2020. Trump's campaign against Fauci ignores the proven path for defeating pandemics. *Washington Post* (July 22). www.washingtonpost.com/outlook/2020/07/22/trumps-campaign-against-fauci-ignores-proven-path-defeating-pandemics/

Morgan, S., and J. Lee. 2018. Trump voters and the white working class. *Sociological Science* 5: 234–245.

Murdock, S. 2016. Trump claims he could shoot someone and not lose voters. *Huffington Post* (Jan. 23). www.huffpost.com/entry/trump-could-shoot-someone_n_56a3ccbbe4b07 6aadcc6da93

New York Times. 2016 (Oct. 8). Transcript: Donald Trump's taped comments about women. www.nytimes.com/2016/10/08/us/donald-trump-tape-transcript.html

Nguyen, T. 2016. Trump accused of routinely stiffing his own employees. *Vanity Fair* (June 10). www.vanityfair.com/news/2016/06/donald-trump-lawsuit-contractors

Nicholas, P., and W. Strobel. 2019. Trump's attacks on spy agencies are called a national security risk. *Wall Street Journal* (Jan. 30). www.wsj.com/articles/trump-criticizes-u-s-intelligence-community-over-assessment-of-iran-nuclear-threat-11548862307

O'Brien, T. 2015. *TrumpNation: The Art of Being the Donald*. New York: Warner Books.

O'Donnell, J. 2016. *Trumped! The Inside Story of the Real Donald Trump – His Cunning Rise and Spectacular Fall*. Hertford, NC: Crossroads Press.

Palazzolo, J., M. Rothfeld, and L. Alpert. 2016. *National Enquirer* shielded Donald Trump from Playboy model's affair allegation. *Wall Street Journal* (Nov. 4). www.wsj.com/articles/national-enquirer-shielded-donald-trump-from-playboy-models-affair-allegation-1478309380

Paletta, D. 2018. Trump insists "trade wars are good, and easy to win" after vowing new tariffs. *Washington Post* (March 2). www.washingtonpost.com/news/business/wp/2018/03/02/trump-insists-trade-wars-are-good-and-easy-to-win-after-vowing-new-tariffs/

Paletta, D., and E. Werner. 2019. Trump falsely claims Mexico is paying for wall, demands taxpayer money for wall in meeting with Democrats. *Washington Post* (Jan. 2). www.washingtonpost.com/business/economy/trump-falsely-claims-mexico-is-paying-for-wall-demands-taxpayer-money-before-meeting-with-top-democrats/2019/01/02/408bf86e-0e97-11e9-8938-5898adc28fa2_story.html

Paletta, D., and J. Dawsey. 2018. Trump personally pushed postmaster general to double rates on Amazon, other firms. *Washington Post* (May 18). www.washingtonpost.com/business/economy/trump-personally-pushed-postmaster-general-to-double-rates-on-amazon-other-firms/2018/05/18/2b6438d2-5931-11e8-858f-12becb4d6067_story.html

Papenfuss, M. 2019. Trump called Nepal and Bhutan "Nipple" and "Button" in intel briefing. *Huffington Post* (Feb. 4). www.huffpost.com/entry/trump-called-bhutan-nepal-button-nipple-john-walcott_n_5c58c7b0e4b00187b5544631

Parker, A. 2018. Double amputee vet Duckworth: Trump can't even remember what foot the bone spur was in. *American Independent* (Jan. 28). https://americanindependent.com/sen-tammy-duckworth-trump-cant-even-remember-what-foot-the-bone-spur-was-in/

Parton, H. 2020. Trump's unhinged Rose Garden campaign rally: His sideshow act is getting truly pathetic. *Salon* (July 15). www.salon.com/2020/07/15/trumps-unhinged-rose-garden-campaign-rally-his-sideshow-act-is-getting-truly-pathetic/

Petri, A. 2017. President Trump has one of the greatest memories of all time. *Washington Post* (Oct. 27). www.washingtonpost.com/blogs/compost/wp/2017/10/27/president-trump-has-one-of-the-greatest-memories-of-all-time/

Phillips, A. 2015. Your next president, Donald Trump, basically tweets like a 12-year old. *Washington Post* (June 5). www.washingtonpost.com/news/the-fix/wp/2015/06/05/your-next-president-donald-trump-basically-tweets-like-a-12-year-old/

Porter, T. 2017. How do I love thee? A short history of Trump's praise for Putin. *Newsweek* (Nov. 11). www.newsweek.com/heres-all-times-trump-has-praised-putin-708859

Porter, T. 2018. Trump confused the Baltics with Balkans – and accused confused leaders of starting Yugoslav wars. *Newsweek* (Nov. 11). www.newsweek.com/trump-confused-baltics-balkans-and-accused-confused-leaders-starting-yugoslav-1210939

Price, G. 2018a. James Mattis said Donald Trump has the understanding of "a fifth- or sixth-grader," Bob Woodward book claims. *Newsweek* (Sept. 4). www.newsweek.com/mattis-trump-fifth-grader-woodward-book-1104417

Price, G. 2018b. Republicans, once the party of McCarthyism, now approve of Trump's Putin praise, new poll indicates. *Newsweek* (July 19). www.newsweek.com/republicans-apprve-trump-putin-mccarthyism-1032595

Qiu, L. 2020. Trump's inaccurate claims on hydroxychloroquine. *New York Times* (May 21). www.nytimes.com/2020/05/21/us/politics/trump-fact-check-hydroxychlo-roquine-coronavirus-.html

Rainey, J. 2019. Trump claims credit for cheap gas. Experts it's not so simple. *NBC News* (Jan. 1). www.nbcnews.com/politics/politics-news/trump-claims-credit-cheap-gas-experts-say-it-s-not-n953626

Reilly, M. 2016. Former Mexican President: "I'm not going to pay for that f**king wall." *Huffington Post* (Feb. 25). www.huffpost.com/entry/vicente-fox-donald-trump-mexico-wall_n_56cf5008e4b0bf0dab3132b5

Reilly, R. 2020. *Commander in Cheat: How Golf Explains Trump.* New York: Hachette Books.

Reisman, S. 2016. Trump tells crowd to "knock the crap out" of protesters, offers to pay legal fees. *Media ITE* (Feb. 1). www.mediaite.com/online/trump-tells-crowd-to-knock-the-crap-out-of-protesters-offers-to-pay-legal-fees/

Robinson, N. 2017. *Trump: Anatomy of a Monstrosity.* Atlanta: Demilune Press.

Rogers, K. 2020. Protesters dispersed with tear gas so Trump could pose at church. *New York Times* (June 1). www.nytimes.com/2020/06/01/us/politics/trump-st-johns-church-bible.html

Rogers, K., C. Hauser, A. Yuhas, and M. Haberman. 2020. Trump's suggestion that disinfectants could be used to treat coronavirus prompts aggressive pushback. *New York Times* (April 24). www.nytimes.com/2020/04/24/us/politics/trump-inject-disinfectant-bleach-coronavirus.html

Rubin, J. 2016. Trump's ignorance is shocking. *Washington Post* (March 31). www.chicagotribune.com/opinion/commentary/ct-donald-trump-abortion-women-punishment-20160331-story.html

Rubin, J. 2017. Trump is as unfit and ignorant as ever. *Washington Post* (Dec. 29). www.washingtonpost.com/blogs/right-turn/wp/2017/12/29/trump-is-as-unfit-and-ignorant-as-ever/

Rucker, P. 2015. Trump says Fox's Megyn Kelly had "blood coming out of her wherever." *Washington Post* (Aug. 8). www.washingtonpost.com/news/post-politics/wp/2015/08/07/trump-says-foxs-megyn-kelly-had-blood-coming-out-of-her-wherever/

Rucker, P., and J. Dawsey. 2019. "We fell in love": Trump and Kim shower praise, stroke egos on path to nuclear negotiations. *Washington Post* (Feb. 25). www.washingtonpost.com/politics/we-fell-in-love-trump-and-kim-shower-praise-stroke-egos-on-path-to-nuclear-negotiations/2019/02/24/46875188-3777-11e9-854a-7a14d7fec96a_story.html

Ryan, A. 2018. April Ryan: I'm a black woman. Trump loves insulting people like me. *Washington Post* (Nov. 10). www.washingtonpost.com/outlook/2018/11/10/im-black-woman-white-house-reporter-trump-loves-insulting-people-like-me/

Sang-Hun, C. 2017. Kim's rejoinder to Trump's Rocket Man: "Mentally deranged U.S. dotard." *New York Times* (Sept. 21). www.nytimes.com/2017/09/21/world/asia/kim-trump-rocketman-dotard.html

Sargent, G. 2015. Donald Trump on the Paris attacks: "Watch and study the mosques" here at home. *Washington Post* (Nov. 16). www.washingtonpost.com/blogs/plum-line/wp/2015/11/16/donald-trump-on-the-paris-attacks-watch-and-study-the-mosques-here-at-home/

Sargent, G. 2019a. Trump backs Bolsonaro on Amazon fires. Because of course he does. *Washington Post* (Aug. 27). www.washingtonpost.com/opinions/2019/08/27/trump-backs-bolsonaro-amazon-fires-because-course-he-does/

Sargent, G. 2019b. Trump: You wouldn't like my supporters in the military if they got angry. *Washington Post* (March 14). www.washingtonpost.com/opinions/2019/03/14/trump-you-wouldnt-like-my-supporters-military-if-they-got-angry/

Saul, H. 2016. Donald Trump claims "we're having problems with Muslims" after Brussels and calls for mosques to be studied. *The Independent* (March 22). www.independent.co.uk/news/people/brussels-attack-explosion-donald-trump-muslims-a6945891.html

Schleifer, T. 2016. Donald Trump: "I think Islam hates us." *CNN Politics* (March 10). www.cnn.com/2016/03/09/politics/donald-trump-islam-hates-us/index.html

Schmidt, M. 2018. Trump invited the Russians to hack Clinton. Were they listening? *New York Times* (July 13). www.nytimes.com/2018/07/13/us/politics/trump-russia-clinton-emails.html

Schwartz, T. 2017. I wrote *The Art of the Deal* with Donald Trump: His self-sabotage is rooted in his past. In B. Lee (ed.) *The Dangerous Case of Donald Trump.* pp. 69–74. New York: St. Martin's Press.

Scott, E. 2018. Six times President Trump said he is the least racist person. *Washington Post* (Jan. 17). www.washingtonpost.com/news/the-fix/wp/2018/01/17/six-times-president-trump-said-he-is-the-least-racist-person/

Serwer, A. 2018. The cruelty is the point. *The Atlantic* (Oct. 3). www.theatlantic.com/ideas/archive/2018/10/the-cruelty-is-the-point/572104/

Shabad, R. 2017. Trump praised Rodrigo Duterte for "unbelievable job on the drug problem" in Philippines. *CBS News* (May 24). www.cbsnews.com/news/trump-praised-rodrigo-duterte-for-unbelievable-job-on-the-drug-problem-in-philippines/

Shear, M. 2018. Trump denounces F.B.I. raid on his lawyer's office as "attack on our country." *New York Times* (April 9). www.nytimes.com/2018/04/09/us/politics/trump-fbi-raid-michael-cohen.html

Shear, M. 2020. Trump retweets racist video showing supporter yelling 'white power'. *New York Times* (June 28). www.nytimes.com/2020/06/28/us/politics/trump-white-power-video-racism.html

Shear, M., and C. Porter. 2018. Trump refuses to sign G-7 statement and calls Trudeau "weak." *New York Times* (June 9). www.nytimes.com/2018/06/09/world/americas/donald-trump-g7-nafta.html

Shear, M., and E. Sullivan. 2018. "Horseface," "lowlife," "fat, ugly": How the president demeans women. *New York Times* (Oct. 16). www.nytimes.com/2018/10/16/us/politics/trump-women-insults.html

Shear, M., N. Weiland, E. Lipton, M. Haberman, and D. Sanger. 2020. Inside Trump's failure: The rush to abandon leadership role on the virus. *New York Times* (July 20). www.nytimes.com/2020/07/18/us/politics/trump-coronavirus-response-failure-leadership.html

Sherman, J. 2017. *Donald Trump: Outspoken Personality and President*. Minneapolis: Lerner Publishing.

Smith, A. 2016. Donald Trump praised Vladimir Putin on the national stage again – here's what it all means. *Business Insider* (Sept. 10). www.businessinsider.com/donald-trump-vladimir-putin-strong-leader-obama-2016-9

Smith, A. 2018. Trump gives Rep. Adam Schiff a new and profane last name. *NBC News* (Nov. 18). www.nbcnews.com/politics/donald-trump/trump-calls-congressman-adam-schiff-little-adam-schitt-tweet-n937726

Sommerlad, J. 2019. Donald Trump's gushing praise of Vladimir Putin under fresh scrutiny after Michael Cohen allegations. *The Independent* (Jan. 18). www.independent.co.uk/news/world/americas/us-politics/trump-cohen-putin-russia-investigation-mueller-congress-fbi-a8734231.html

Sonmez, F. 2018. Reports: Trump warned evangelical leaders of "violence" from the left if Republicans lose the midterms. *Washington Post* (Aug. 28). www.washingtonpost.com/politics/reports-trump-warned-evangelical-leaders-of-violence-from-democrats-if-republicans-lose-the-midterms/2018/08/28/4f397bb6-ab0a-11e8-8a0c-70b618c98d3c_story.html

Sonmez, F. 2019. Trump hails his own "great and unmatched wisdom" in warning to Turkey. *Washington Post* (Oct. 7). www.washingtonpost.com/politics/trump-hails-his-own-great-and-unmatched-wisdom-in-warning-to-turkey/2019/10/07/13c65990-e935-11e9-9306-47cb0324fd44_story.html

Sonmez, F., and M. DeBonis. 2019. Trump tells four liberal congresswomen to "go back" to their countries, prompting Pelosi to defend them. *Washington Post* (July 14). www.washingtonpost.com/politics/trump-says-four-liberal-congresswomen-should-go-back-to-the-crime-infested-places-from-which-they-came/2019/07/14/b8bf140e-a638-11e9-a3a6-ab670962db05_story.html

Stokes, D. 2018. Trump, American hegemony and the future of the liberal international order. *International Affairs* 94(1): 133–150.

Stokols, E. 2019. Trump blasts Mueller report as Democrats demand unredacted version. *Los Angeles Times* (April 19). www.latimes.com/politics/la-na-pol-mueller-report-subpoena-judiciary-20190419-story.html

Stracqualursi, V. 2019. Trump attacks another African American lawmaker, and calls Baltimore a "disgusting, rat and rodent infested mess." *CNN Politics* (July 28). www.cnn.com/2019/07/27/politics/elijah-cummings-trump-baltimore/index.html

Swanson, A. 2018. Trump readies sweeping tariffs and investment restrictions on China. *New York Times* (March 15). www.nytimes.com/2018/03/15/us/politics/trump-china-trade-measures.html

Taibi, M. 2017. *Insane Clown President.* New York: Spiegel & Grau.

Taranto, J. 2016. "I love the poorly educated!" *Wall Street Journal* (Feb. 24). www.wsj.com/articles/i-love-the-poorly-educated-1456337093

Terris, B. 2017. Lawyers upon lawyers upon lawyers: In Trump World, everyone has an attorney. *Washington Post* (July 26). www.washingtonpost.com/lifestyle/style/lawyers-upon-lawyers-upon-lawyers-in-trump-world-everyone-has-an-attorney/2017/07/26/259e2c0c-70a0-11e7-8f39-eeb7d3a2d304_story.html

Thrush, G., and M. Haberman. 2017. Trump mocks Mika Brzezinski; says she was "bleeding badly from a face-lift." *New York Times* (June 29). www.nytimes.com/2017/06/29/business/media/trump-mika-brzezinski-facelift.html

Tobias, M. 2018. "U.S. Steel just announced that they are building six new steel mills." *Politifact* (Aug. 2). www.politifact.com/factchecks/2018/aug/02/donald-trump/us-steel-not-opening-six-new-mills-donald-trump/

Todisco, E. 2020. President Trump claims coronavirus will 'fade away' even without vaccine as cases rise in U.S. *New York Times* (June 18). https://people.com/politics/donald-trump-says-coronavirus-fade-away-without-vaccine/

Trump, D., and T. Schwartz. 1987. *The Art of the Deal.* New York: Ballantine Books.

Trump, M. 2020. *Too Much and Never Enough: How My Family Created the World's Most Dangerous Man.* New York: Simon and Schuster.

Tucker, J. 2015. Is Donald Trump a fascist? *Newsweek* (July 17). www.newsweek.com/donald-trump-fascist-354690

Visoulis, A. 2018. Trump's team keeps using Mafia-inspired language – to defend itself. *Time* (Aug. 1). https://time.com/5355482/donald-trump-rudy-giuliani-mafia/

von Drehle, D. 2020. Americans are suffering. Trump offers them a doctor who warns of sex with demons. *Washington Post* (July 28). www.washingtonpost.com/opinions/america-is-suffering-trump-offers-them-a-doctor-who-warns-of-sex-with-demons/2020/07/28/460fea3e-d0fb-11ea-8c55-61e7fa5e82ab_story.html

Waldman, M. and H. Ekeh. 2020. Trump's call to postpone elections is an outrageous break with American faith in democracy. *Washington Post* (July 30). www.washingtonpost.com/opinions/2020/07/30/trumps-call-postpone-elections-breaks-with-american-faith-democracy/

Waldman, P. 2017. Donald Trump looking at things. *The Week* (May 1). www.theweek.com/articles/695846/donald-trump-looking-things

Waldman, P. 2019. Trump sucks up to Putin, embarrassing us yet again. *Washington Post* (June 28). www.washingtonpost.com/opinions/2019/06/28/trump-sucks-up-putin-embarrassing-us-yet-again/

Walley, C. 2017. Trump's election and the "white working class": What we missed. *American Ethnologist* 44(2): 231–236.

Walsh, B. 2016. Donald Trump praises Vladimir Putin: "I always knew he was very smart!" *Huffington Post* (Dec. 30). www.huffpost.com/entry/donald-trump-vladimir-putin_n_5866b8e1e4b0eb58648952e0

Walsh, J. 2018. 11 insults Trump has hurled at women. *Business Insider* (Oct. 17). www.businessinsider.com/trumps-worst-insults-toward-women-2018-10

Walsh, M. 2016. Trump on '90s playboy image: "It's fortunate I don't have to run for political office." *Yahoo! News* (Oct. 11). https://news.yahoo.com/trump-on-90s-playboy-image-its-fortunate-i-dont-have-to-run-for-political-office-151754973.html

Washington Post Staff. 2015. Full text: Donald Trump announces a presidential bid. *Washington Post* (June 16). www.washingtonpost.com/news/post-politics/wp/2015/06/16/full-text-donald-trump-announces-a-presidential-bid

Watkins, E., and A. Philip. 2018. Trump decries immigrants from "shithole countries" coming to US. *CNN Politics* (Jan. 12). www.cnn.com/2018/01/11/politics/immigrants-shithole-countries-trump/index.html

Wingrove, J. 2020. Trump takes credit as markets rise, points finger when they fall. *Bloomberg* (Feb. 28). www.bloomberg.com/news/articles/2020-02-28/trump-takes-credit-as-markets-rise-points-finger-when-they-fall

Withnall, A. 2016. Donald Trump's unsettling record of comments about his daughter Ivanka. *The Independent* (Oct. 10). www.independent.co.uk/news/world/americas/us-elections/donald-trump-ivanka-trump-creepiest-most-unsettling-comments-a-roundup-a7353876.html

Wong, E. 2016. Trump has called climate change a Chinese hoax. Beijing says it is anything but. *New York Times* (Nov. 18). www.nytimes.com/2016/11/19/world/asia/china-trump-climate-change.html

Woody, C. 2017. Foreign policy journalists are questioning a report claiming Trump's national-security adviser said he has the intelligence of a "kindergartner." *Business Insider* (Nov. 20). www.businessinsider.com/hr-mcmaster-trump-intelligence-of-kindergartner-2017-11

Wootson, C. 2017. Donald Trump was proud of his 1990 Playboy cover. Hugh Hefner, not so much. *Washington Post* (Sept. 28). www.washingtonpost.com/news/arts-and-entertainment/wp/2017/09/28/donald-trump-was-proud-of-his-1990-playboy-cover-hugh-hefner-not-so-much/

Yglesias, M. 2018. Trump's corruption deserves to be a central issue in the 2018 midterms. *Vox* (March 1). www.vox.com/policy-and-politics/2018/3/1/17056562/trump-corruption-midterms

Zibel, A. 2018. Presidency for sale: 64 trade groups, companies, candidates, foreign governments and political groups spending money at Trump's properties. *PublicCitizen* (Jan. 18). https://corporatepresidency.org/presidencyforsale/

Zito, S. 2016. Taking Trump seriously, not literally. *The Atlantic* (Sept. 23). www.theatlantic.com/politics/archive/2016/09/trump-makes-his-case-in-pittsburgh/501335/

Zuckert, C. 2018. Trump as a Machiavellian prince? Reflections on corruption and American constitutionalism. In M. Sable and A. Torres (eds.) *Trump and Political Philosophy*. pp. 73–87. New York: Palgrave Macmillan.

3

THREE GENERATIONS OF TRUMP SCHEMES

The private side of planning history

Samuel Stein

Note: this chapter is excerpted from: Stein, Samuel. 2019. *Capital City: Gentrification and the Real Estate State*. New York: Verso.

Donald Trump's background as a developer is one of the most important factors in understanding the man and his mortally ludicrous presidency (Weber 2017).[1] While he may be more famous as a reality television host, celebrity endorser, and prosperity proselytizer, he made his fortune buying, building, managing, and licensing luxury apartments, clubs, casinos, office towers, hotels, and golf courses, first in New York and then around the world. He is a product and an embodiment of real estate's growing centrality to global capital's growth strategy.

Trump's rise was highly dependent on state action. A close look into the Trump family business demonstrates how real estate developers have historically benefitted from U.S. public policy, with each emerging pattern of planning creating opportunities for successive generations of Trumps to grasp and hold on to: as private property, personal profit, and generational wealth.

The Trumps were never quite leaders in their fields. There were always others who did what they did bigger and better (though never quite as loudly). Until recently, the Trumps were just a vulgar version of the completely normal capitalist developer. Their very ordinariness, however, is exactly what makes them a worthy case study. Taking a closer look at the Trumps allows us to see the flip side of planners' strategies in a private land market – the landowners who keep the public benefits that the state creates, manages, and distributes. In this sense, the Trumps are not just a real estate family, but emblems of the private side of U.S. planning history.

56 Samuel Stein

Friedrich Trump: Profiting off proto-planning

Friedrich Trump was born in 1869 in Kallstadt, a Bavarian winemaking village not yet incorporated into the German empire. At the age of 16, he fled conscription and immigrated to the United States. Sponsored by his older sister through an early version of "family reunification" immigration, Friedrich arrived in New York in 1885, the same year as the Statue of Liberty.

If he had come from many other parts of the world, he would have been turned away. The Naturalization Act of 1870, the Page Act of 1875, the Chinese Exclusion Act of 1882, the Alien Contract Labor Law of 1885, and many other laws severely restricted workers from most countries seeking to enter the United States (Kwong and Miščević 2005). Lawmakers classified Germans, however, as hardworking Whites, and largely encouraged their continued migration (Tichenor 2002).

Like many other German immigrants, Friedrich followed an established settlement pattern: first he lived on the Lower East Side of Manhattan; then what would become Murray Hill; then Harlem. For five years he was a barber, earning a modest living cutting other Germans' hair. This, however, is not how Friedrich Trump made his fortune.

Rumors were buzzing of opportunities out west: gold and silver to mine, cheap land to claim, new infrastructure, intentionally lax laws, and tons of finance capital. American proto-planners were helping to complete a genocidal westward expansion, and Friedrich wanted a part of it. He boarded a series of trains and headed to Seattle.

There, he established what family biographer Gwenda Blair (2001, p. 1–2) calls

> the Trump MO: scope out the best location (it tended to be in the red-light district); open a business (in this case, restaurants, at times on land to which he had no legal right); and offer customers (mostly rootless newcomers who had yet to see their first nugget) some right-now comfort in the form of booze and easy access to women.

In other words, Friedrich made his fortune buying and building brothels. He chased the routes of finance and railways, and set up shop – in Blair's phrase – "mining the miners" (2001, p. 61). Friedrich never mined a single ore, laid a single track of rail, or even put his money toward financing those projects. Instead, he profited off state and bank investments in land and industry, and skimmed money off workers – both the miners he charged and the sex workers, cooks, and bartenders he employed.

In 1891, with $600 from personal savings and family gifts, he bought his first brothel, the Dairy Restaurant. Two years later he sold it and, with extra money from his mother, bought 40 acres a dozen miles outside Seattle. He purchased this land from the Northern Pacific Railway, which had received it from the federal government in lieu of cash payments for building the railway. The first plot

Three generations of Trump schemes **57**

of Trump-owned land in the United States was therefore part of a complex plan to extend the railways and develop the American empire (Blair 2001, pp. 41–46).

Friedrich moved to nearby Monte Cristo and spotted a parcel by the site of a future train depot. He staked a mining claim on it without any intention to dig (Blair 2001, pp. 59–60). Instead, he built a hotel, restaurant, and brothel on that small patch of earth, even though he had no legal right to the land above ground. This kind of lax land use law was an early example of governing through informality, or the active process of looking the other way in order to enable a desired – if not quite legal – result (Roy 2005).

After a storm crushed his roof, Friedrich moved back to Seattle and opened a new brothel three blocks from the first. The place was so profitable he repaid his mortgage within a month. At the same time, however, Friedrich continued to play around with land use laws. He bought several mining claims on untapped land he did not own, then flipped the claims for a profit without ever digging a single hole. He did not even know if there was any metal to be mined; all he knew was that as long as the rails continued to be built and the desperate continued to flock, he could make easy money by commoditizing space plus time (Blair 2001, pp. 66, 70, 77).

Soon a major storm destroyed the town. Just before it hit, though, Friedrich sold his business and took off for the Yukon. In Bennett, British Columbia, he set up his most profitable businesses: the New Arctic Restaurant and Hotel, which featured scales on which miners could weigh their gold dust as payment for sex and booze; and the White Horse, the first business that new arrivals would see when they stepped off the train. He stayed a while and made a mint, but when a reformist mayoral candidate seemed likely to win, Friedrich sold the businesses. Once again he got out just in time—shortly after he skipped town, the brothel was busted and the town foundered (Blair 2001, pp. 85–93). That was the end of Friedrich's Western period, but it was not the last time he would profit off land and property made profitable by planners.

Fortune in hand, he went to Germany, where he met and married Elizabeth Christ. They moved back to the United States and settled in the Bronx, where he was a barber and hotel manager. They hated it, though, and returned to Kaiser Wilhelm II's Germany in 1904. Friedrich tried to regain citizenship, claiming "We are loyal Germans and stand behind the high Kaiser and the mighty German Reich" (Blair 2001, p. 101). It didn't work. They were refused for his past draft dodging and deported back to the United States in 1905, while Elizabeth was pregnant with their son Fred. Friedrich went back to barbering, this time at 60 Wall Street – a block away from a building his grandson Donald would come to own many years later (Blair 2001, p. 110).

Once again, however, Friedrich caught wind of a big investment opportunity, made possible by state planning and finance. Queens had recently been incorporated into the City of New York, along with the Bronx, Brooklyn, and Staten Island. He saw the Bronx changing all around him, and he suspected that Queens – then largely rural – would catch up fast. The city was about to build

58 Samuel Stein

the Queensboro Bridge, connecting the borough to Midtown Manhattan, and the Pennsylvania Railroad was building new rail lines.

In 1908, just before the bridge was completed, Friedrich and Elizabeth bought a two-story house in Woodhaven. Two years later they moved in to one half of the house and rented the other half out. Soon they bought another house and some vacant land nearby, and moved in while renting the first property (Blair 2001, pp. 111–112).

Between then and 1915, when the Interborough Rapid Transit Company opened the Queens subway, the borough's population grew by 40% and land values soared. Friedrich and Elizabeth capitalized off this urbanization and all the investments the city was making in the land – gridding streets, building pipes, enabling rail, and generally making the land buildable – and bought 14 properties and five vacant lots (Blair 2001, pp. 111–115).

In 1918, Friedrich died in the great flu pandemic that swept the country. Elizabeth and their son Fred, just 15 years old, took over the properties and began building on the vacant lots. In 1927, they incorporated as Elizabeth Trump & Son, and Fred took the reins of the family's burgeoning real estate business.

Fred Trump: The rational comprehensive builder

Fred Trump's real estate career began with single-family homes in Queens, financing one project with the sale of the last. The 1920s were booming times, both for Queens and the property racket in general, but it would all come crashing down in 1929. The Depression hit, and millions plunged into poverty, hunger, and homelessness.

The Depression, however, also prompted Fred's first big break: the fall of the Lehrenkrauss Corporation in 1934, and the foreclosure of thousands of Queens homes. Lehrenkrauss had issued $26 million in mortgages for 40,000 homes (Barrett 1992, p. 32). Due to fraud and debt, however, they were going out of business and auctioning off their properties. Through some clever self-inflation, Fred managed to place the winning bid on Lehrenkrauss's mortgage-servicing department, giving him a stream of income from debt-paying creditors as well as an inside scoop on homes that were about to fall into foreclosure and could be purchased cheaply (Blair 2001, pp. 126–34). Fred was back in the real estate game, with a great deal more firepower than his one-by-one projects had previously afforded him.

At the same time, the Roosevelt administration was searching for ways to jump-start the economy, and looked to mass homeownership as one key pathway. Congress passed the National Housing Act of 1934, which established the Federal Housing Administration (FHA) and its system of government-backed private mortgages. Under this program, the federal government would act as a backstop for banks against creditors who defaulted. This was an enormous boon to potential homeowners, who suddenly had access to capital; as well as to banks, whose lending risk fell dramatically; and to builders, who now had an enormous new pool of financiers and clients. It was also the beginning of institutionalized redlining, a long-term process of divestment from integrated and Black neighborhoods and investment in segregated White housing (Connolly 2014, pp. 93–99).

This enticed Fred Trump. In 1936 – nine years after being arrested at a Queens Ku Klux Klan rally (Bump 2016) – Fred got his first FHA contract to build a 450-home row housing project in East Flatbush, Brooklyn. The federal government provided about $750,000 dollars in mortgage insurance for what Trump described as an "exclusive development," which qualified him for even larger amounts of private loans (Kranish and Fisher 2016, p. 29). Soon he expanded to other parts of Flatbush and Crown Heights, and by 1937 had built over 2,000 government-financed homes for aspiring middle class Whites.

In 1941, with the Second World War in the air, Fred expanded his operation to Brighton Beach and told potential investors, "In the event of war, I believe that the profit will be quicker and larger" (Kranish and Fisher, p. 53). He was right. That year the federal government established the Office of Production Management (OPM). The OPM was mostly in the business of converting industrial sites to military production, but they also sponsored real estate projects in "defense housing areas." Because Brooklyn had a Navy yard, the entire borough counted as such an area, and the OPM paid Fred to build 700 homes in Bensonhurst (Blair 2001, pp. 155–156).

This led to an even bigger opportunity. Through Section 608 of the National Housing Act, which provided enormous subsidies to build apartment complexes for war workers, Fred extended the Trump family business to the mid-Atlantic and Midwest. In Norfolk, Virginia, Fred built his first rental complex, with over 1,300 apartments. Later he bought and managed the 500-unit Gregory Estates in Prince George's County and the 1,200-unit Swifton Village in Cincinnati.

In these places, Fred operated as a slumlord, denying basic services to his tenants. This sparked Norfolk's first documented rent strike, and a lawsuit alleging Fred's federally subsidized rentals suffered from "a lack of hot running water, sporadic or nonexistent air conditioning and elevator service, improper swimming facilities, and insect and rodent infestation" (Barrett 1992, pp. 78–79). He eventually showed up at Gregory Estates after years of tenant complaints and was swiftly arrested for running "a slum property," denied a license to operate in Maryland, and forced to promptly fix and sell the property (Barrett 1992).

In addition to being a slumlord, Fred was also a segregationist. Just as the FHA intended, his properties were designed to prevent what the government called "inharmonious" (i.e., integrated) development (Kranish and Fisher 2016, p. 53). In 1947, Fred built Shore Haven, a Bath Beach complex for White veterans composed of 32 six-story buildings with 1,344 apartments. It received $9 million in FHA-backed loans and would become Brooklyn's biggest private housing project. Soon after, with the help of both federal subsidies and mafia-connected contractors, he built the similarly segregated Beach Haven on Brighton Beach (Blair 2001, pp. 171–172).

60 Samuel Stein

Two years later, federal investigators accused Fred and many other Section 608 developers of being "real estate profiteers," or making enormous profits off loopholes in the wartime housing laws (Blair 2001, p. 176). Fred and other developers had realized that if their projects came up under budget or ahead of schedule, they could keep the extra subsidies they were paid and the higher rents they collected. This would allow them to pay off their mortgages quicker and call their extra earnings capital gains, which were (and are) taxed at a much lower rate than income. Fred also figured out that the subsidies were based on the number of units they built, not the number of rooms. He would therefore pack his buildings with studios and one-bedrooms, even though the subsidies were aimed to provide housing for veterans with families. He had to sit through some blistering hearings, but Fred prevailed without a charge. He was, however, blacklisted from future federal development and sued by his tenants (Blair 2001, p. 199).

This hardly slowed him down. Fred went back to building mansions in Queens and purchased another Section 608 complex in Staten Island. In 1963, he partnered with rational comprehensive city planners on a massive "urban renewal" project in Fort Greene, a largely African American and actively industrial area near Downtown Brooklyn. Along with three other private partners, Fred convinced the city to use Title I of the Federal Housing Act of 1949 to clear 20 acres for private hospital, university, and residential development, including his University Towers (Schwartz 1993, pp. 243–44). Against the protests of neighborhood residents and workers, the Brooklyn Civic Center urban renewal project razed 23 blocks, which had held 259 industrial and residential buildings, and 8,200 largely union jobs (Fitch 1993, pp. 46 and 99). At the time it was the largest condemnation in U.S. history (Curran 1998).

That same year, Fred embarked on the biggest project of his life: Trump Village in Coney Island. Using Title I yet again, he convinced the city to displace 900 working class families from the beach-adjacent land. Most of those households moved to fire-prone bungalows on the west side of Coney Island, which were never intended for winter residence (Denson 2002).

Trump Village was the first large-scale project to be completed under New York City's 1961 citywide rezoning, which encouraged intensive redevelopment and privately owned public spaces. With its seven 23-story buildings and 3,800 apartments laid out as "towers in a park," or high-rise buildings surrounded by privately built green space at odd angles, Trump Village was exactly the kind of program the city wanted to see. It also secured $60 million in state FHA funds from New York's Mitchell Lama subsidy program, which kept five of the buildings relatively affordable until 2007, when they were sold as market-rate apartments (Barrett 1992, p. 61). Fred made sure to work every possible angle and managed to overcharge New York State as well. This time he set up shell companies to purchase his own construction equipment, then rented the tools to himself at inflated prices and billed the state (Barrett 1992, p. 64).

Between the 1920s and 1970s, Fred made a fortune as the private builder of government-subsidized segregated housing. By the mid-1970s, when Fred's fourth child, Donald, had joined the business, a couple facts had changed. First, in those early years of the neoliberal era, both local and national governments were fast exiting the business of directly subsidizing affordable housing construction, and moving instead toward a system of tax breaks and vouchers. Second, many forms of outright racial discrimination in housing were formally outlawed in 1968 by the Fair Housing Act, which sought to punish landlords and realtors who enforced segregation and to stop the government from encouraging it through lending, land use, and tax policies. Both subsidies and segregation, however, were the basis of the Trump family business, and U.S. landlordism in general.

The Fair Housing Act immediately challenged Fred's business model. In 1969, a Black man named Haywood Cash tried to rent an apartment in Cincinnati's Swifton Village, but was told his income was too low and there no vacancies. Cash reported this to a local civil rights group called HOME, whose agents sent a White person to ask for an apartment. Though his income was the same as Cash's, Swifton management told the White tester there were plenty of apartments to choose from. When the tester revealed his rouse, management cursed him and threw him out. Cash then sued using the Fair Housing Act, and Fred settled quietly. Cash moved in victorious (Blair 2001, p. 247).

In 1971 and 1972, under suspicion that the Trumps were systematically violating the Fair Housing Act, the Justice Department sent several undercover testers to see how their agents responded to questions about vacancies in their New York properties. Over and over again, Black testers were quoted inflated prices and told there were no vacancies. Just like in Cincinnati, however, White testers were told there was plenty of room at reasonable rents. Out of all the buildings sampled, just one contained a large number of Black households – Patio Gardens, in the part of Flatbush now known as Prospect Lefferts Gardens. While that complex was 40% Black, every other building sampled was between 96.5% and 100% White. Black applicants were coded internally as "number nine," and their applications were placed in specially marked folders. With this evidence, the federal government filed *United States of America v. Fred C. Trump, Donald Trump and Trump Management, Inc.* in 1973 (Kranish and Fisher 2016, pp. 55–56).

The Trumps fired back with bluster, but they knew they had no case. In 1975, the Trumps settled and agreed to virtually everything the state wanted: they said they would advertise in Black newspapers, give the Urban League notice of vacancies, and stop discriminating against welfare recipients. The Trumps did none of this, however, and three years later the Justice Department hauled them back into court for contempt.

From that point on, Donald ran the family business. It was the late 1970s: the country was in a vicious recession and the city was emerging from a capital strike. Sensing these changing winds and indulging his own avarice, Donald followed the evolution of urban planning and public policy toward new heights of development, profitability, and malevolence. With millions of dollars in tax-sheltered

62 Samuel Stein

gifts from his father, Donald would move the family business across the river to Manhattan and pursue a strategy of glaringly gauche luxury development (Barstow, Craig, and Buettner 2018).

Donald Trump: The public-private partner

One of Donald's early pursuits was a complex development deal on Manhattan's West Side. Like his grandfather Friedrich before him, Donald was obsessed with the value of land in relation to infrastructure. But whereas Friedrich got rich speculating on rising land values along future rail routes, Donald profited from declining land values near current ones.

Donald had his eyes on the Pennsylvania and New York railroads. In 1968, struggling to survive amid automotive competition and declining industry, the Pennsylvania and New York railroads merged into the ill-fated Penn Central Transportation Company. As one of its first moves, the company sought to shed its less-profitable assets, including its rail yards at West 60th Street and West 34th Street. Together, they formed the largest piece of available land in Manhattan (Barrett 1992, p. 102). By 1974 Donald saw possibilities for profit and he pounced, putting in a bid to turn them into commercial and residential real estate developments. Building, though, would require some friendly actions from the state – particularly public financing and a significant rezoning.

Donald's proposal met some resistance. John Zuccotti, chair of the City Planning Commission and later First Deputy Mayor, was amenable to residential development on the 60th Street yards but wanted to keep 34th Street industrial. The Trumps, however, had a friend in the newly elected mayor, Abe Beame, who came out of the same Brooklyn Democratic Club as Fred. In a private meeting with Donald, Fred, Zuccotti and Penn Central's Ned Eichler, Beame proclaimed, "whatever my friends Fred and Donald want in this town, they get" (Blair 2001, p. 259).

Without Zuccotti's support, Beame could not make the changes Donald needed to do the deal. In the meantime, however, the mayor could make absolutely sure the yards were dead. In the mid-1970s, during a major oil crisis that caused many other cities to reinvest in rail, New York's West Side yards sat still. If the city had revived the yards during these years, it could have not only boosted New York manufacturers, but also cut back on the number of trucks that rolled through the city's highways and contributed to dramatic racial health disparities (Sze 2006). Instead, for most of the 1970s, the yards lay fallow (Barrett 1992, p. 102).

During those years, Mayor Beame successfully waited out Zuccotti, who stepped down in 1977. Shortly thereafter, in his final months in office, Beame approved Donald's plan (even though Donald had not yet bought all the land) and gave him an option to build. Soon thereafter Donald convinced the city to pay him $833,000 for permission to build a convention center on the 34th Street segment, further cementing the city's turn toward tourism over manufacturing (Barro 2015).

Trump then focused his sights on the Upper West Side yards. He finally bought that land – 74.6 acres, plus 18.6 more underground – in 1986 and claimed he would build on it the world's tallest building (Sorkin 1991, p. 141–147). This did not exactly pan out, and over the next ten years the plan went through a multitude of mutations. By 1992, Donald had struck a deal with local politicians and resident associations to build "Trump Place," also known as "Riverside South," a slightly smaller but still expansive strip of luxury glass condominiums along the Hudson River. After 20 years assembling the capital, land, subsidies, and zoning, he had finally won. Just a year and a half later, though – in a move recalling his grandfather Friedrich's mining claim speculation schemes – he sold the development rights to the Hong Kong-based New World Development Company for $88 million plus $250 million in debt repayment (Blair 2001, p. 449). Donald had essentially played a very long con on the city, its planners, manufacturers, workers, and community groups.

Along the way, Penn Central began shedding its Manhattan real estate holdings, which included an ailing hotel next to Grand Central Station. In 1975, Donald bought the Commodore Hotel with a plan to turn it into a shining glass high-rise known as the Grand Hyatt. The only way he could secure financing for the project, he claimed, was with a significant break on future property taxes. Given that 1975 was the year of the worst fiscal crisis in the city's history, it might not have been the best time to demand a tax cut – though he did go to the state legislature and try (Barrett 1992, p. 114). Behind the scenes, however, Donald – with Fred's help – negotiated one of the largest and most galling commercial tax breaks ever seen in New York City. It signaled a distinct turn away from the uneven Keynesianism of rational comprehensive planning and toward the neoliberal model (Phillips-Fein 2017, p. 267).

First, city and state planners had to call Trump's midtown hotel development an "industrial project" in order for it to be characterized as an economic development program. Then they had to declare the neighborhood – East 42nd Street and Park Avenue, just about the ritziest address in Manhattan – "blighted." The same terminology that rational comprehensive planners had earlier mobilized to justify "slum clearance" and "urban renewal" was now being used to validate corporate giveaways and luxury development.

Next, Trump would "sell" the land for $1 to the Urban Development Corporation (UDC). The UDC was the state's housing developer, created by Governor Nelson Rockefeller. The agency had the power to override local land use laws, building codes, and tax arrangements in order to encourage housing construction. Over the years, however, the agency took on far more debt than it could repay and faced an existential crisis. Later in the 1970s, it would be restructured into an "economic development" agency and become one of the state's leading prison builders (Norton 2015). In 1975, though, it needed a reason to exist, and developers like Trump could provide it.

With the UDC technically in possession of the Grand Hyatt, the state would pay taxes to itself and lease the building to Trump for a small fee (Blair 2001, p. 285).

The size and longevity of that fee would be decided by Trump family ally Mayor Beame. In terms of longevity, Beame stretched the abatement for the longest period ever granted in New York at that time: 40 years (Freeman 2001, p. 292). The fee's amount was linked to the building's profitability, but to ensure Donald's tab remained low, Beame had his people craft an unusually narrow definition of profits. For the purposes of this agreement, profit was defined as the "aggregate amount of monies actually received." The key words here are the last two. By pegging profit to "actually received" income, Donald was allowed to deduct any improvements he made to the building, as well as any money spent on upkeep and maintenance. The tax break would be worth about twice as much as the standard abatement, for which this project would not even have qualified (Barrett 1992, p. 134). Simply creating a new tax break for Donald Trump, however, would be a little too blatant. Instead, the UDC created the "Business Incentive Program" to provide public subsidies to commercial developments. To no one's surprise, Trump's Grand Hyatt Hotel was the program's first recipient (Barrett 1991, p. 119).

The West Side yards and Grand Hyatt experiences taught Donald a great deal about the neoliberal planning environment in which he was operating. In the 1930s through the 1960s, Fred figured out that the state was interested in subsidizing social reproduction for middle class Whites, and sought every opportunity to exploit that desire. In the 1970s and 1980s, Donald realized that the austerity state was unlikely to hand out cash for ordinary housing construction, but would gladly suspend taxes and provide land and airspace for luxury development that would increase land values and rebrand the city (Greenberg 2009). He took these lessons and applied them to his Manhattan magnum, Trump Tower. That building was constructed on the site of the former Bonwit Teller department store. To transform this stately store into a gigantic black box, Donald wanted two things: permission to build bigger than would otherwise be allowed, and an enormous tax break.

Donald played a couple of tricks to ensure he would be granted the maximum zoning capacity. First, he produced horrendously ugly depictions of what the building would look like if it did not receive a rezoning and had to be built without it. Next, he offered the Bonwit Teller Corporation a conditional lease that was premised on a larger floor size than the current zoning allowed. If the city wanted to keep Bonwit Teller in business and not end up with an architectural atrocity, it would have to give Donald his rezoning. The Planning Commission obliged, and the 12-story building could suddenly become 58 stories (Barrett 2001, pp. 172–173).

Donald also availed himself of a lucrative "density bonus" written into the 1961 citywide rezoning – a privately owned public space. By putting a "public atrium" in the entryway and two interior gardens on upper floors, Trump Tower was allowed to rise an additional 20 stories, worth an estimated $530 million (Elstein 2016).

With his rezoning and bonus in hand, Donald set out to grab as large a tax break as possible. In 1983, he applied for 421-a, the state's largest "geobribe"

(Smith 2002), but was denied by the city's department of Housing Preservation and Development. Undeterred, Donald sued the city and won a $20 million break on his tax bill (Gaiter 1983). Not only did he get to keep his money, Donald also recruited the Housing Commissioner, Anthony Gliedman, to leave city government and become one of his many political fixers (Frieden and Sagalyn 1991, p. 226). Trump Tower cost Donald roughly $200 million to build, but the initial condominium sales alone brought in $277 million. Since then, he has reaped tremendous profits, all the while paying precious little in property taxes.

This phase of Donald's career was characterized by schemes to secure generous land use exemptions, leverage public financing for private development, and profit off the city's deindustrialization. As city planning turned neoliberal, Donald turned a mighty profit. But in the late 1980s and early 1990s, a moment when Donald was holding on to an enormous amount of debt, the country faced a recession and he flew into a tailspin. Property values were dropping and some scholars were wondering if this was the end of gentrification (Smith and DeFilippis 1999). It was not, but it was the end of Donald's career as a straightforward developer.

Others went out of business, but Donald turned out all right. Most of his creditors renegotiated their interest rates instead of foreclosing on his properties (Blair 2001, p. 6). He used the corporate bankruptcy laws to his favor and mutated into a different kind of capitalist, becoming more of a brander than a builder.

Today, real estate capital is more powerful than ever, at every scale of U.S. government. Until recently, the Trumps were bit players in that transition, but their story was indicative of the transformation. As real estate rose in centrality to urban and national politics, developers, investors, and schemers like the Trumps made enormous profits off cities' development and eventual gentrification. The Trump family saga shows the progression of real estate in relation to planning over time: first from opportunists (like Friedrich) who capitalized on planners' work; then to builders (like Fred) who were directly financed by the state; and finally to tycoons (like Donald) who starved the state before seizing it. Like the larger class of real estate developers, the Trumps played planners for profit and walked away with the country.

Note

1 This account builds primarily from three Trump biographies: Blair (2001), Barrett (1992/2016), and Kranish and Fisher (2016).

References

Barrett, W. 1992/2016. *Trump: The Greatest Show on Earth: The Deals, the Downfall, the Reinvention*. New York: Simon and Schuster.

Barstow, D., S. Craig, and R. Buettner. 2018. Trump engaged in suspect tax schemes as he reaped riches from his father. *New York Times* (Oct. 2).

Barro, J. 2015. Donald Trump and the art of the public sector deal. *New York Times* (Sept. 18).

Blair, G. 2001. *The Trumps: Three Generations that Built an Empire*. New York: Simon and Schuster.

Bump, P. 2016. In 1927, Donald Trump's father was arrested after a Klan riot in Queens. *Washington Post* (Feb. 29).

Connolly, N. 2014. *A World More Concrete: Real Estate and the Remaking of Jim Crow South Florida*. Chicago: University of Chicago Press.

Curran, W. 1998. City policy and urban renewal: A case study of Fort Greene, Brooklyn. *Middle States Geographer* 31: 71–82.

Denson, C. 2002. *Coney Island: Lost and Found*. Oxford: Elsevier.

Elstein, A. 2016. Trump Tower fined over missing bench after the presumptive GOP nominee skips hearing. *Crain's New York Business* (June 23).

Fitch, R. 1993. *The Assassination of New York*. New York: Verso.

Freeman, J. 2001. *Working-Class New York: Life and Labor Since World War II*. New York: The New Press.

Frieden, B., and L. Sagalyn. 1991. *Downtown, Inc: How America Rebuilds Cities*. Boston: MIT Press.

Gaiter, D. 1983. City ordered to give abatement on taxes to the Trump Tower. *New York Times* (June 19).

Greenberg, M. 2009. *Branding New York: How a City in Crisis was Sold to the World*. London: Routledge.

Kranish, M., and M. Fisher. 2016. *Trump Revealed: An American Journey of Ambition, Ego, Money, and Power*. New York: Simon and Schuster.

Kwong, P., and D. Miščević. 2005. *Chinese America: The Untold Story of America's Oldest New Community*. New York: New Press.

Norton, J. 2015. Little Siberia, star of the north: The political economy of prison dreams in the Adirondacks. In K. Morin and D. Moran (eds.) *Historical Geographies of Prisons: Unlocking the Usable Carceral Past*. pp. 168–184. London: Routledge.

Phillips-Fein, K. 2017. *Fear City: New York's Fiscal Crisis and the Rise of Austerity Politics*. New York: Metropolitan Books.

Roy, A. 2005. Urban informality: Toward an epistemology of planning. *Journal of the American Planning Association* 71(2): 147–158.

Schwartz, J. 1993. *The New York Approach: Robert Moses, Urban Liberals, and Redevelopment of the Inner City*. Columbus, OH: Ohio State University Press.

Smith, N. 2002. New globalism, new urbanism: gentrification as global urban strategy. *Antipode* 34(3): 427–450.

Smith, N., and J. DeFilippis. 1999. The reassertion of economics: 1990s gentrification in the Lower East Side. *International Journal of Urban and Regional Research* 23(4): 638–653.

Sorkin, M. 1991. *Exquisite Corpse: Writing on Buildings*. New York: Verso.

Sze, J. 2006. *Noxious New York: The Racial Politics of Urban Health and Environmental Justice*. Boston: MIT Press.

Tichenor, D. 2002. *Dividing Lines: The Politics of Immigration Control in America*. Princeton, NJ: Princeton University Press.

Weber, R. 2017. Edifice rex: Egos, assets, and the financialization of property markets. *The Avery Review* 21 (Jan.).

PART II

Trump's electoral victory and its aftermath

4

THE GEOGRAPHIES OF TRUMP'S ELECTORAL SUCCESS

Ron Johnston, Charles Pattie, Ryne Rohla, David Manley, and Kelvyn Jones

The map of most election results usually closely resembles that of recent previous contests; major changes to the topography are relatively rare. Support for one party, or for presidential election candidates, varies between contests but although its level goes up and down, its relative variation across a territory remains quite stable. This is certainly the case with United States presidential elections, characterized – in Key's (1955) classic work, extended by Pomper (1967) – by sequences of maintaining elections in which the relative topography of a party's support changes very little (Archer and Taylor 1981; Darmofal and Strickler 2019): its highs and lows are in the same places each time, at a range of spatial scales. Those maintaining sequences – closely linked to the theory of the "normal vote" at the individual level (Converse 1966) – are occasionally interrupted by deviating elections when the map differs significantly, at least in parts of the territory involved, from that at preceding contests, perhaps reflecting the nature of a particular campaign or candidate (as in 1960 with Kennedy, the first Roman Catholic to win the presidency). The map may then return to its previous parameters. Alternatively, that deviation may turn out to be a realigning election, heralding a new map, which can take several contests to become fully crystallized – as with Nixon's 1968–1972 "Southern Strategy" which ended the Democratic Party's electoral predominance in the Southern states since the 1930s New Deal.

Was the 2016 presidential election such a deviating contest, with a map that differed markedly from the apparently settled pattern of the preceding three decades – characterised by: a substantial number of "red states" almost invariably won by the Republican Party candidates, usually with substantial majorities; a smaller number of "blue states" where Democrat candidates dominated; and a similar relatively small number of "swing (or purple) states" where the victorious party changed between elections? Cervas and Grofman (2017) show that outcome of the 2016 election depended more on the result in the swing states than at any previous election since 1868. Some commentators suggested that Trump's campaign – focused on the white working class for whom he promised to "Make America Great Again" (Abramowitz and McCoy 2019) – was such an election, at least in part (see Johnston et al. 2017). This chapter addresses whether that was so by exploring the voting patterns in 2012 and 2016 at a range of spatial scales, from the individual to the state, and their implications for the operation of the Electoral College.

From macro to micro: Comparing 2012 and 2016

These graphical analyses compare the geography of support for Donald Trump in 2016 to that for the 2012 Republican candidate, Mitt Romney. Trump lost the popular vote to Hillary Clinton by almost three million votes – 2.1 percentage points of the total cast – but prevailed in the Electoral College, by 304 votes to 227. He achieved the latter success by winning again all of the states where Romney was successful in 2012 plus six others where Barack Obama gained a plurality then, some by very small margins (three by less than one percentage point). Most of those swing states have relatively large populations, delivering Trump 99 Electoral College votes that had ensured Obama's 2012 victory. (Trump also gained a further College vote from Maine's Second Congressional District.)

Across the states

In relative terms, therefore, little apparently changed in the pattern of voting across the 50 states plus the District of Columbia, as shown Figure 4.1, which, like Figures 4.2 and 4.3, contrasts Romney's percentage of the two-party vote (i.e., of the total obtained by the Democratic and Republican Party candidates) with Trump's share four years later. The states are divided into red (won by the

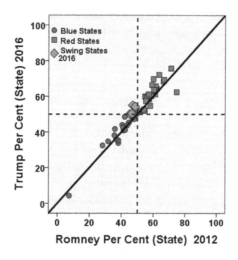

FIGURE 4.1 The percentage of the two-party vote won by Romney in 2012 and Trump in 2016, by state.

Republicans at both contests), blue (won by the Democrats at both), and swing (won by the Democrats in 2012 but the Republicans in 2016); the diagonal line represents the situation if the two Republican candidates had obtained the same share of the two-party vote in a state.

Trump outperformed Romney in most states (he gained 48.9% of the two-party vote compared to Romney's 48.0%), but those shifts were marginal. Most points on the graph are very close to the "equal shares" line; the main outlier is Utah, where an independent candidate, Evan McMullin, won 21.5% of the votes. (A former banker and CIA operative who strongly opposed Clinton's candidacy, McMullin believed Trump was unfit for the presidency.) Trump outvoted Clinton in Utah by 45.4% to 27.5%, whereas Romney's margin of victory there was 72.8% to 24.8%. The six swing states sit clearly in the middle of the graph: Romney lost there by small margins in 2012; Trump won there by smaller margins in 2016. (Of those six states, Romney lost in only one, Florida, by less than one percentage point to Obama.) On average, Trump's two-party vote share increased by 4.5 percentage points, compared to 2.2 points in the red states and only 1.2 points in the blue states. Trump attained the White House by increasing the Republicans' vote share more substantially in those six key states than elsewhere.

Congressional districts

The pattern across the states changed only marginally between 2012 and 2016, therefore, but was there more variety within states, reflecting differences in socio-economic and -demographic characteristics among their constituent places? Figure 4.2 replicates Figure 4.1 using data for the 435 congressional districts, showing another very close clustering of points around the "equal shares" line.

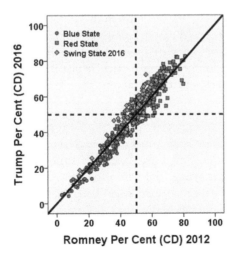

FIGURE 4.2 The percentage of the two-party vote won by Romney in 2012 and Trump in 2016, by congressional district.

TABLE 4.1 The number of states, congressional districts, and counties according to whether Trump outperformed Romney or vice versa, by type of state, and the percentage of precincts won by landslides by each candidate.

State Type	Blue	Red	Swing
States			
Romney outperformed Trump	7	5	0
Trump outperformed Romney	14	19	6
Congressional Districts			
Romney outperformed Trump	102	67	20
Trump outperformed Romney	88	92	67
Counties			
Romney outperformed Trump	165	143	34
Trump outperformed Romney	247	2052	442
Precincts: Metropolitan Areas (percentage won by landslide)			
Romney outperformed Trump	32	74	12
Trump outperformed Romney	82	103	73
Precincts: Rural Areas by State (percentage won by landslide)			
Romney outperformed Trump	1	0	0
Trump outperformed Romney	14	23	6

A stand-out feature of that graph is the variation in Trump's relative success compared to Romney's across the three state types. Table 4.1 shows the number of districts where Trump outperformed Romney and vice versa. Romney performed better than Trump in 102 of the blue state congressional districts, with the reverse situation in 88. Trump made relatively few advances in the Democratic strongholds, therefore, but he out-performed Romney in the red states, increasing the Republicans' vote share in 92 of the 159 districts. But on average he performed best overall in the six swing states' 87 districts, outperforming Romney in 67; across those 87 the mean difference between Trump's and Romney's vote shares was 3.4 percentage points, compared to 0.5 points in the 159 red state districts; in the 190 blue state districts Trump on average performed less well than Romney – the mean percentage change was -0.5 points. Targeted campaigning on particular population groups in particular places appears to have been the source of Trump's Electoral College success.

Counties

Congressional districts are large spatial units, with average populations exceeding 700,000; although in drawing district boundaries most states seek not to divide communities (Rossiter, Wong, and Delamater 2018), nevertheless many are far from homogeneous in their population characteristics. Counties are on average much smaller than congressional districts – the mean number of votes cast in the 3077 analyzed here was 44,021 in 2016 – but unlike districts they also vary greatly in size: 3.4 million votes were cast in the largest then but only 65 in the smallest.

Figure 4.3 shows the same general pattern of continuity in the electoral map as Figures 4.1 and 4.2, though with a much larger number of areas having a

Geographies of Trump's electoral success 73

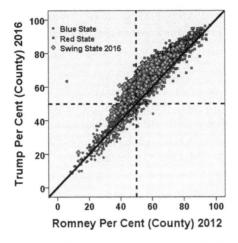

FIGURE 4.3 The percentage of the two-party vote won by Romney in 2012 and Trump in 2016, by county.

substantial shift towards Trump, almost entirely in counties where Romney won at least 40% in 2012. Trump outperformed Romney in all three types of state (Table 4.1), but less well in the blue states (where he gained a larger share of the two-party vote than Romney in 247 of the 412 counties) than in the red (he outperformed Romney in 2052 of the 2195). Crucial to his Electoral College success, he outperformed Romney in almost all 476 swing state counties. Indeed, Trump's largest gains in vote share were in "purple America," with a mean change of 9 percentage points in his favor, compared with 6.3 points in red state counties and only 0.8 points in blue states.

The concentration of a large number of both red and swing state counties with Republican majorities in both 2012 and 2016 reflects the party's predominance in much of rural America. This is clarified in Table 4.2, using a classification of

TABLE 4.2 The number of counties where Trump outperformed Romney and vice versa, by type of state and type of county.

	Blue		Red		Swing		All	
	R>T	T>R	R>T	T>R	R>T	T>R	R>T	T>R
Large Central Metro	35	11	7	2	8	4	50	17
Large Fringe Metro	45	34	45	179	14	39	104	252
Medium Metro	36	38	27	191	8	66	71	295
Small Metro	19	19	24	237	2	50	45	306
Micropolitan	20	58	15	431	1	111	36	600
Noncore (Rural)	10	87	24	1012	0	172	34	1271
All	165	247	142	2052	33	442	340	2471

Key: T>R – Trump had a higher percentage of the two-party popular vote in 2016 than Romney had in 2012; R>T – Romney had a higher percentage of the two-party popular vote than Trump.

counties along a central city/suburb/small city/rural continuum developed by the National Center for Health Statistics (Ingram and Franco 2013):

Metropolitan

1. *Large Central Metro* – these counties are parts of Metropolitan Statistical Areas (MSAs) with more than one million inhabitants: they either contain the entire population of the MSA's central cities; or have their entire population in the MSA's largest central city; or contain at least 250,000 of the population of one of the MSA's principal cities;
2. *Large Fringe Metro* – these are counties in MSAs with more than one million inhabitants that did not qualify as Large Central Metros (i.e., they are basically suburban areas of large metropolises);
3. *Medium Metro* – all of the counties in MSAs with populations between 250,000 and 999,999;
4. *Small Metro* – counties in MSAs with less than 250,000 inhabitants.

Non-Metropolitan

5. *Micropolitan* – counties in defined micropolitan urban areas (with populations of 10,000-49,999);
6. *Noncore* – all other counties (i.e., rural areas).

Romney outperformed Trump in the majority of central city counties in all three types of state, whereas at the other end of the continuum Trump outperformed Romney across the board. Between those extremes, in the suburbs and the counties comprising medium and small metropolitan areas, Trump did no better than Romney in about half of the counties in the blue states, but outperformed him in the great majority of red and, especially, swing states. As in the noncore (rural) counties, Trump won more votes than his Republican predecessor in over 94% of the micropolitan counties.

This urban-rural continuum is stressed by data showing the mean change, in percentage points, between Trump's and Romney's two-party vote shares (Table 4.3). Compared to his predecessor, Trump lost ground in the central city counties of the country's largest metropolitan areas, especially in the blue states. He also lost ground in the blue state suburban counties, but increased his party's share substantially in red and swing state suburban counties. Moving towards the rural end of the continuum (i.e., down the columns) the shift towards Trump increases in all three types of state, but much more in the red and, especially, swing than in the blue states. Those substantial shifts in the swing states were crucial in his capture of their Electoral College votes and victory over Hillary Clinton.

That conclusion regarding the importance of a few swing states is further stressed using a 12-category classification of counties according to their population characteristics – Patchwork Nation – developed using census data by the Knight Foundation (Table 4.4). On average, counties in all but two of those

TABLE 4.3 The county mean change in the percentage point share of the two-party vote gained by Trump and Romney, by type of state and county.

	Blue	Red	Swing	All
	T%-R%	T%-R%	T%-R%	T%-R%
Large Central Metro	-2.9	-1.3	-0.3	-2.3
Large Fringe Metro	-1.2	+4.6	+5.0	+3.3
Medium Metro	+0.4	+4.3	+6.3	+3.9
Small Metro	+0.4	+5.2	+6.3	+4.8
Micropolitan	+1.8	+6.3	+10.4	+6.4
Noncore (Rural)	+3.7	+7.4	+12.1	+7.8
All	+0.8	+6.3	+9.0	+6.0

Key: T%-R% – Trump's percentage share of the two-party vote in 2016 less Romney's share in 2012.

categories preferred Romney to Obama in 2012 and in all but one – the Industrial Metropolises – preferred Trump to Clinton in 2016, although on average they tied in the battle for support in the Campus and Careers places (Table 4.5). That national pattern concealed a great deal of interstate variation, however; Trump failed to average even 44% of the votes in all 12 categories in the blue states, but never less than 64% in the red states, and his mean percentage exceeded 50

TABLE 4.4 The Patchwork Nation's 12 community types.

Community Type	Description
Monied Burbs	Wealthier, highly educated communities with a median household income $15,000 above the national county average
Minorities Central	Large pockets of Black residents but below average percentages of Hispanics and Asians
Evangelical Epicenters	Communities with a high proportion of evangelical Christians, found mostly in small towns and suburbs; slightly older than the US average
Tractor County	Mostly rural and remote smaller towns with older populations and large agricultural sectors
Campus and Careers	Cities and towns with young educated populations; more secular than other communities
Immigration Nation	Communities with large Latino populations and lower-than-average incomes, typically clustered in the South and Southwest
Industrial Metropolis	Densely populated, highly diverse urban centres; incomes trend higher than the national average
Boom Towns	Fast growing communities with rapidly diversifying populations
Service Worker Centers	Midsize and small towns with economies fuelled by hotels, stores and restaurants and lower-than-average median incomes
Emptying Nests	Home to many retirees and aging baby boomer populations; less diverse than the nation at large
Military Bastions	High employment in the military or related to the presence of military and large veteran populations
Mormon Outposts	Large shares of members of the Church of Jesus Christ of Latter-day Saints and slightly higher median incomes

TABLE 4.5 The Republican candidates' (county means) share of the votes cast by community type and type of state.

	All		Blue		Red		Swing	
	R	T	R	T	R	T	R	T
Monied Burbs	55	57	38	36	64	68	54	58
Minorities Central	51	56	34	38	59	64	48	54
Evangelical Epicenters	72	79	44	42	72	79	71	78
Tractor Country	72	80	39	42	73	80	55	67
Campus and Careers	47	50	38	38	73	80	55	67
Immigration Nation	61	64	33	35	59	65	46	52
Industrial Metropolis	32	32	31	31	–	–	35	35
Boom Towns	60	61	43	41	65	68	55	59
Service Worker Centers	59	69	35	41	63	72	56	67
Emptying Nests	57	67	39	43	60	71	54	65
Military Bastions	59	63	39	39	65	71	54	57
Mormon Outposts	81	80	38	39	82	81	55	63
TOTAL	61	67	37	38	67	73	55	64

Key: R – mean percentage of the two-party vote won by Romney in 2012; T – mean percentage of the two-party vote won by Trump in 2016.

in all but the Industrial Metropolises – i.e., the big cities – in the all-important swing states. The Industrial Metropolises had a mean population of 1.3 million in 2010; of the 41 counties so classified, 32 were in the blue states and eight in the swing states.

Whereas on average Trump's support differed little from Romney's across all 12 categories in the blue states, it was several points greater in the red states and even more so – and from a smaller base – in the swing states. This is emphasized by the average difference between Trump's and Romney's vote shares (Table 4.6): less than one percentage point across all categories in the blue states – where it declined in four categories; but increases of 6.3 points in the red states and 9.0 in the swing states, with the largest differences in rural areas (Tractor Country), small towns (Service Worker Centers), and retirement areas (Emptying Nests). Indeed, Trump outscored Romney in virtually all swing state counties whatever their category (Table 4.7) – failing to do that in the great majority of cases only among their eight Industrial Metropolises. Trump also outperformed Romney across most red state categories, failing to do so only in the Mormon Outposts (where Romney, a Mormon, performed particularly well) and in around one-quarter of the Immigration Nation and Boom Town counties. In the blue states, on the other hand, he performed less well than Romney in around 40% of counties – his main successes coming in the small town communities (Service Worker Centers) and, especially, the counties with large Black populations (Minorities Central), the latter probably reflecting (as discussed below) lower turnout by Blacks for Clinton relative to Obama.

These analyses show that whether counties are categorized according to their size or their population characteristics – across each of which there were

Geographies of Trump's electoral success **77**

TABLE 4.6 The county mean change in the percentage point share of the two-party vote gained by Trump and Romney, by community type and type of state.

	Blue	Red	Swing	All
	T%-R%	T%-R%	T%-R%	T%-R%
Monied Blurbs	-2.4	3.8	4.1	2.1
Minorities Central	4.2	4.8	6.6	4.3
Evangelical Epicenters	-1.2	6.8	7.6	6.8
Tractor Country	3.4	7.3	11.4	7.4
Campus and Careers	-0.5	5.8	5.9	3.2
Immigration Nation	2.0	3.5	9.4	3.4
Industrial Metropolis	0.3	–	-0.1	0.2
Boom Towns	-1.8	2.7	3.5	1.9
Service Worker Centers	5.7	9.3	11.3	9.7
Emptying Nests	3.6	10.6	11.0	10.6
Military Bastions	0.1	5.5	2.3	4.1
Mormon Outposts	1.6	-1.3	–	-1.2
ALL	0.8	6.3	9.0	6.0

Key: T%-R% – the mean difference (percentage points) between Trump's and Romney's share of the two-party vote.

very substantial variations in support for Republican candidates – the main shifts towards Trump were in the red and swing states. He built on the party's strong electoral foundations in all but the large central cities and the Industrial Metropolises in the red states. In the swing states, he achieved Electoral College success by even more substantially enlarging his party's share of the votes cast,

TABLE 4.7 The number of counties where Trump outperformed Romney and vice versa, by community type and type of state.

	Blue		Red		Swing		All	
	R>T	T>R	R>T	T>R	R>T	T>R	R>T	T>R
Monied Burbs	58	16	16	133	11	46	85	195
Minorities Central	5	102	3	237	0	7	8	346
Evangelical Epicenters	1	0	2	445	0	15	3	460
Tractor Country	0	2	1	295	0	9	1	306
Campus and Careers	15	14	3	20	5	12	23	46
Immigration Nation	14	29	21	131	0	9	35	169
Industrial Metropolis	14	18	1	0	5	3	20	21
Boom Towns	52	23	63	184	8	33	123	240
Service Worker Centers	0	31	6	436	0	183	6	650
Emptying Nests	3	3	0	118	4	122	7	243
Military Bastions	3	8	2	34	0	3	5	45
Mormon Outposts	0	1	24	19	0	0	24	20
ALL	165	247	142	2052	33	442	340	2471

Key: T>R – Trump had a higher percentage of the two-party popular vote in 2016 than Romney had in 2012; R>T – Romney had a higher percentage of the two-party popular vote than Trump.

except in those same places. He changed the country's electoral map by tipping almost all community types in the red and swing states towards the Republicans, with little change in the blue states.

Precincts

Trump consolidated his party's hold over the red states at all scales but only advanced it – and to a much lesser extent – in the more rural parts of the blue states; his narrow Electoral College victory was achieved by increasing the Republicans' vote share in all but the inner cities and most of the community types of the six swing states. All of these findings refer to relatively coarse areal units, however; what happened in the country's neighborhoods?

To explore that question we use precinct scale data. These units, defined for electoral administration, are not fixed: many are redefined after each decennial redrawing of congressional district boundaries, and some are redrawn at other times. This precludes direct comparison of voting maps between 2012 and 2016 across a fixed set of precincts, so the focus here is on changes in the inter-election aggregate pattern using data on candidates' share of the two-party vote in 173,524 precincts with a mean of 712 votes cast at the 2012 election and for 173,526 precincts (many different from those deployed four years earlier) with a mean of 780 votes cast in 2016. Rather than compare whether Trump outpolled Romney or not in each precinct we contrast the number of precincts he won by 20 percentage points or more, what Bishop (2009) termed a "landslide" in his pioneering study of the growing spatial polarization of the American electorate, with the number won by Romney by the same margins (see also Darmofal and Strickler 2019).

Figure 4.4 graphs those two variables across 376 standard metropolitan statistical areas (SMSAs). The fit to the "equal shares" line is much weaker than

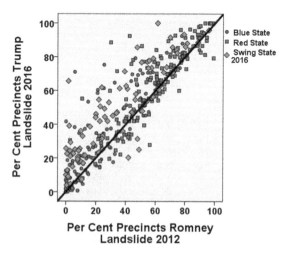

FIGURE 4.4 The percentage of precincts won by a landslide in metropolitan areas by Romney in 2012 and Trump in 2016.

Geographies of Trump's electoral success **79**

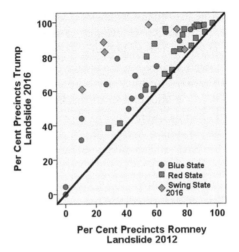

FIGURE 4.5 The percentage of precincts won by a landslide in the rural portions of states by Romney in 2012 and Trump in 2016.

at the larger scales, indicative of greater spatial variation in the two candidates' performances when the focus is on small-scale neighborhoods. Trump scored many more landslide victories than Romney in all three types of state but, as Table 4.1 shows, this was especially marked in the six swing states where 73 of the 85 SMSAs saw him win by more landslides than Romney. Most of those with the greatest increase in Republican landslides were Rust Belt metropolitan areas on whose white working class residents much of Trump's campaigning focused – places like Allentown-Bethlehem, Johnstown, and Scranton-Wilkes Barre in Pennsylvania; Jackson and Saginaw in Michigan; Eau Claire and Green Bay in Wisconsin; Dubuque in Iowa; and Springfield, Toledo, and Youngstown in Ohio (on Youngstown, see Gest 2016.)

In the non-metropolitan parts of 44 states where some counties are outside an SMSA Romney won by a landslide in a majority of precincts (Figure 4.5); Trump outperformed him virtually everywhere else, especially in the six swing states (Table 4.1). The number of landslide Republican victories increased by 17.8 percentage points in the blue states and 9.8 points in the red states (where most precincts had delivered Republican landslides in 2012), and 39.9 points in the six swing states. Almost everywhere, at every scale, Trump's largest gains were in those states that were vital to his Electoral College success.

The individual scale

Trump won in the Electoral College, therefore, if not the popular vote by sustaining the Republican base, winning again in almost every state, congressional district, and county where his predecessor prevailed. Indeed, he outperformed Romney in most places where he had performed well but, most importantly, he

80 Johnston, Pattie, Rohla, Manley, and Jones

did that sufficiently in six states that Obama won in 2012. So, which voters did he convince to vote for him and so achieve that needed switch?

Most studies of individual voting behavior in the United States focus on differences between people according to characteristics such as their age and sex, educational qualifications, income, race/ethnicity, and religious affiliations and commitments. There are also arguments, backed by empirical findings, of regional variations in attitudes additional to those associated with individual characteristics: see, for example, White (2018) and Balentine and Webster (2018). Data from the 2012 and 2016 Cooperative Congressional Election Surveys allow exploration of relationships between variables representing these characteristics, using binomial logistic regression equations: the dependent variable for the 2012 analysis is whether the respondent voted for Romney (coded 1) or Obama (coded 0 – those who did not vote or who voted for another candidate were excluded); for 2016 analysis it is whether they voted for Trump (coded 1) or Clinton (coded 0).

The regression equations, with the significant coefficients (at the 0.05 level or better) in bold, show few differences in voting behavior between the two elections (Table 4.8). Females were less likely than males to vote for the Republican candidates at both, for example, whereas higher income respondents were more likely to do so than those on low incomes; those with higher educational qualifications were less likely to vote Republican than those without high school qualifications; Blacks, Hispanics and Asians were less likely to vote Republican than Whites; born-again Christians were less likely to vote Republican; members of most religious groups were less likely to vote for the Republican candidates than Protestants (although Mormons were more likely than Protestants to vote for their co-religionist Romney, but not for Trump), as were those to whom religion was unimportant compared to those for whom it was important. The only substantial difference was that older people were less likely than those born since 1992 to vote for Romney whereas four years later the older the respondent the greater the probability of voting for Trump.

Apart from those age differences, therefore, Trump and Romney drew very much on the same sections of the electorate – unsurprisingly, given the continuity in voting geographies across the two elections outlined above. But Trump's campaign focused on the white working class, those most disillusioned with the economic effects of globalization on their employment prospects, incomes, and quality of life and increasingly distrustful of the "Washington elite" who favored the "liberal agenda" (hence Trump's claim that he would "drain the swamp"). Race is interrelated with many of the other variables, however – Blacks and Hispanics have fewer qualifications and lower incomes on average than Whites, for example, and are more likely to be unemployed and to be born-again Christians. In the 2016 sample of voters, 31% of Whites said they were born-again Christians, against 49% of Blacks; 19% of Whites compared to 33% of Blacks had incomes below $30,000; and 9% of Blacks were unemployed compared to 4% of Whites.

Geographies of Trump's electoral success 81

TABLE 4.8 Binomial logistic regressions of voting at the 2012 and 2016 presidential elections.

	2012: Obama-Romney			2016: Clinton-Trump		
	b	*se*	*exp*	*b*	*se*	*exp*
Constant	**-0.56**	**0.11**		-0.19	0.10	
Gender (comparator, Male)						
Female	**-0.41**	**0.07**	**0.67**	**-0.69**	**0.06**	**0.50**
Year of birth (comparator, born 1992–)						
1982–1991	**-0.49**	**0.08**	**0.61**	0.09	0.05	1.10
1972–1981	**-0.36**	**0.08**	**0.70**	0.33	0.06	1.39
1962–1971	**-0.16**	**0.08**	**0.85**	0.54	0.06	1.72
1952–1961	**-0.30**	**0.08**	**0.74**	0.44	0.05	1.56
–1951	-0.08	0.08	0.93	0.41	0.05	1.51
Income group (comparator, <$30,000)						
$30,000–59,999	**0.64**	**0.09**	**1.89**	0.76	0.07	2.13
$60,000–99,999	**0.81**	**0.09**	**2.24**	0.77	0.07	2.15
$100,000–149,999	**0.88**	**0.09**	**2.42**	0.80	0.08	2.23
$150,000–199,999	**0.97**	**0.11**	**2.65**	0.71	0.10	2.03
$200,000–	**0.78**	**0.12**	**2.12**	0.70	0.01	2.02
Education qualifications (comparator, no High School)						
High School Graduate	**0.44**	**0.14**	**1.55**	0.50	0.12	1.65
Some College	**0.48**	**0.14**	**1.62**	0.30	0.12	1.34
2-Year	**0.41**	**0.15**	**1.50**	0.26	0.12	1.30
4-Year	0.27	0.14	1.32	-0.06	0.12	0.94
Postgraduate	-0.05	0.15	0.95	-0.42	0.12	0.65
Race (comparator, White)						
Black	**-3.86**	**0.12**	**0.02**	-2.84	0.08	0.06
Hispanic	**-1.08**	**0.08**	**0.34**	-1.07	0.07	0.34
Asian	**-0.30**	**0.11**	**0.74**	-0.50	0.09	0.61
Native America	**0.40**	**0.16**	**1.50**	0.41	0.14	1.51
Mixed	**-0.66**	**0.11**	**0.52**	-0.32	0.10	0.73
Other	0.20	0.12	1.22	0.72	0.13	2.06
Middle Eastern	0.01	0.35	1.01	-0.89	-0.30	0.41
Religion (comparator, Protestant)						
Roman Catholic	-0.05	0.04	0.95	-0.27	0.03	0.77
Mormon	**1.59**	**0.12**	**4.90**	0.21	0.12	1.23
Orthodox	-0.03	0.18	0.97	0.23	0.16	1.26
Jewish	**-0.59**	**0.09**	**0.56**	-0.99	0.09	0.37

(Continued)

TABLE 4.8 Binomial logistic regressions of voting at the 2012 and 2016 presidential elections. *(Continued)*

	2012: Obama-Romney			2016: Clinton-Trump		
	b	*se*	*exp*	*b*	*se*	*exp*
Muslim	**-1.01**	**0.30**	**0.37**	**-1.44**	**0.22**	**0.24**
Buddhist	**-1.67**	**0.22**	**0.19**	**-1.08**	**0.16**	**0.34**
Hindu	**-1.78**	**0.48**	**0.17**	**-1.23**	**0.31**	**0.29**
Atheist	**-1.26**	**0.10**	**0.28**	**-1.43**	**0.08**	**0.24**
Agnostic	**-0.70**	**0.07**	**0.50**	**-0.78**	**0.06**	**0.46**
Nothing in particular	**-0.19**	**0.04**	**0.83**	**-0.18**	**0.04**	**0.64**
Something else	**-0.51**	**0.06**	**0.60**	**-0.48**	**0.06**	**0.62**
Importance of Religion (comparator, Very Important)						
Somewhat Important	**-0.52**	**0.03**	**0.59**	**-0.40**	**0.03**	**0.67**
Not Too Important	**-0.99**	**0.04**	**0.37**	**-0.69**	**0.04**	**0.50**
Not At All Important	**-1.45**	**0.06**	**0.24**	**-1.04**	**0.05**	**0.36**
Born Again (No:Yes)	**-0.70**	**0.08**	**0.50**	**-0.43**	**0.06**	**0.65**
Unemployed (No:Yes)	0.17	0.11	1.19	0.01	0.12	1.00
White Female (No:Yes)	-0.04	0.08	0.96	**0.23**	**0.06**	**1.25**
White No High School (No:Yes)	0.24	0.15	1.27	**0.38**	**0.12**	**1.46**
White Unemployed (No:Yes)	0.19	0.13	1.21	**0.29**	**0.13**	**1.46**
White Born Again (No:Yes)	0.07	0.08	1.07	**0.31**	**0.07**	**1.37**
White Low Income (No:Yes)	**0.46**	**0.09**	**1.59**	**0.59**	**0.08**	**1.81**
N	33,133			36,454		
Nagelkerke R2	0.36			0.36		
Per cent correct						
Null model	54.6			52.1		
Full model	73.3			72.9		

As a result, Trump's appeal to White low-income, poorly educated, unemployed, and born-again Christians may be concealed by the analysis – and his misogynist remarks may have alienated him from some females (on sexism and support for Clinton, see Knuckey 2019).

To explore the impact of Trump's focused campaign, five interaction variables were included to contrast White females, Whites with no high school qualifications, Whites who were unemployed, Whites who were born-again Christians, and Whites in the lowest income category with non-Whites having the same characteristics. Four of those five were statistically insignificant in 2012: only low-income Whites were more likely to vote for Romney than comparable non-Whites. But all five variables have statistically significant regression coefficients in 2016, all showing that members of the identified White groups were more likely to vote for Trump than their non-White counterparts. Overall, females were more likely to vote for Clinton, but White females were less likely to do so than non-White females; unemployed Whites were more likely to vote for Trump than unemployed non-Whites; born-again Christian Whites were more likely to vote Republican than comparable non-Whites; low income voters were in general less likely to vote for Trump than those with higher incomes, but Whites in the lowest income group were more likely to vote for him than similar non-Whites; and whereas those with no high school qualifications were less likely to vote for Trump than those with higher qualifications (though not those with degrees), Whites with no high school qualifications were more likely to vote for Trump than were non-Whites. In sum, Trump performed better among those groups clearly targeted in his campaign – the under-privileged Whites and born-again Christians – than Romney (see also Abramowitz and McCoy 2019).

This outcome could have resulted from a combination of three changes: more disadvantaged Whites switched from voting for Obama in 2012 to supporting Trump in 2016 than switched from Romney to Clinton; disadvantaged Whites who did not vote in 2012 turned out in 2016, with more voting for Trump than Clinton; and more disadvantaged non-Whites who voted from Obama in 2012 abstained in 2016 than did those who voted for Romney in 2012. Table 4.8 shows the behavior of different groups in 2016 compared to 2012, using respondents' recalled 2012 behavior in the 2016 Cooperative Congressional Election Survey.

Those who supported Obama were less likely to vote for Clinton four years later than was the case with former Romney voters supporting Trump and many more Obama than Romney voters abstained in 2016. Few switched parties, although relatively more switched from Obama to Trump than from Romney to Clinton. Most non-voters in 2012 abstained again in 2016; those who voted at the latter election were slightly more likely to choose Clinton than Trump.

Two clear patterns stand out among the five White groups: Obama supporters were much more likely to switch to Trump than were Romney supporters to switch to Clinton; and Obama's voters were much more likely to abstain four years later than Romney's supporters – Clinton retained much less support from Obama's voters than did Trump from Romney's. By way of contrast, very few disadvantaged Blacks switched from Obama to Trump, whereas substantial percentages (albeit of small absolute numbers) switched from Romney to Clinton. Her relative success among those groups was considerably weakened by the large percentages of Obama's 2012 supporters who then abstained in 2016, although of the disadvantaged Blacks – and Hispanics – who failed to turn out in 2012 but voted in 2016 many more supported Clinton than Trump.

Trump's victory rested on his greater ability to retain support from 2012 Republican supporters; Clinton not only lost many more disadvantaged Whites to Trump than she gained from Romney but also saw many more Obama supporters abstain in 2016 than did Romney's. In addition, many more disadvantaged Whites who abstained in 2012 but voted in 2016 chose Trump rather than Clinton.

84 Johnston, Pattie, Rohla, Manley, and Jones

Blacks and Hispanics who failed to vote in 2012 but did so in 2016 were more likely to vote for Clinton rather than Trump, but those gains were countered by many more Obama than Romney 2012 supporters not voting in 2016. Those net changes, especially among disadvantaged Whites, could well have cost Clinton the five Rust Belt states that swung to Trump, and her relative decline of support among Hispanics could have had the same impact in the other swing state – Florida.

How were those changes achieved? Campaigning is crucial to winning and losing electoral support and in 2016 it focused very much on swing states, both the six that supported Obama in 2012 but Trump in 2016 and another six that might have changed hands – five were won by Obama in 2012 with relatively small majorities; the other, North Carolina, was won by Romney by just two percentage points. Voters across the country received printed campaigning materials and telephone calls as well as contacts though social media, but the presidential candidates focused their personal campaigning efforts on those 12 states. Their visits, across the whole period after they gained their party's nomination and during the campaign's last month show that Trump made seven visits to Colorado, for example, including four in the last month (Table 4.9). There were a total of 399 events attended by a party's candidate for either president or vice president, of which 375 (94%) were confined to just 12 states – the six swing states, five of the possible swing states (the exception was Minnesota), and Arizona. The intensive candidate-focused search for votes was geographically very concentrated.

TABLE 4.9 The distribution of visits and events during the 2016 presidential campaign.

		Visit				*Events*	
		Trump		*Clinton*			
		All	*Last*	*All*	*Last*	*Rep.*	*Dem.*
Arizona	Red	4	1	1	1	7	3
Colorado	Possible Swing	7	4	3	1	16	3
Florida	Swing	19	10	15	8	35	36
Iowa	Swing	6	2	4	1	14	7
Michigan	Swing	7	3	4	3	14	8
Minnesota	Possible Swing	1	1	1	0	2	0
Nevada	Possible Swing	4	3	6	0	9	8
New Hampshire	Possible Swing	9	5	4	2	15	6
North Carolina	Possible Swing	15	6	11	4	31	24
Ohio	Swing	17	5	15	5	30	18
Pennsylvania	Swing	14	7	15	5	28	26
Virginia	Possible Swing	10	2	2	0	18	5
Wisconsin	Swing	5	0	0	0	9	5

Key: All –Visits by presidential candidates between the end of the primary elections and the presidential election; Last –Visits by presidential candidates during the last four weeks of the campaign.

Source: data on visits from https://abcnews.go.com/Politics/hillary-clinton-donald-trumps-campaigns-numbers/stGeorgiary?id=43356783; data on events from www.nationalpopularvote.com/campaign-events-2016

Geographies of Trump's electoral success **85**

TABLE 4.10 The distribution of spending on booked advertisements by the presidential candidates and supporting PACS, October 21 – November 7, 2016 ($m).

		Trump	*Clinton*
Arizona	Red		0.7
Colorado	Possible Swing	2.1	0.8
Florida	Swing	10.4	18.8
Iowa	Swing	0.9	2.6
Michigan	Swing	0.1	0
Minnesota	Possible Swing	0	0
Nevada	Possible Swing	2.3	4.2
New Hampshire	Possible Swing	2.0	3.8
North Carolina	Possible Swing	3.0	6.3
Ohio	Swing	4.0	8.0
Pennsylvania	Swing	3.5	8.5
Virginia	Possible Swing	2.1	0.2
Wisconsin	Swing	2.4	0
Swing States		21.3	37.9
All States		40.2	63.0

Source: https://adage.com/article/campaign-trail/states-where-trump-clinton-spending-most-on-advertising/306377/

Visits by the candidates to a state are largely undertaken to mobilize their supporters and gain airtime coverage of their reception. Those brief punctuation marks in the campaign occur within the matrix of intensive advertising. Data from AdAge.com shows the amount of advertising space/time booked by each candidate's campaign plus their supportive PACs in the last three weeks. Pro-Trump expenditures totaled $40.2 million compared to Clinton's $63.0 million, of which 53% and 60% respectively was spent in the six swing states – though for the latter that was confined to four of the states only since there was no booking in Michigan and Wisconsin (Table 4.10). The *Guardian* reports that the Trump campaign spent $5 million on "get-out-the-vote" targeted digital advertising in Florida, Michigan, Pennsylvania, and Wisconsin in the last few days of the campaign. Both candidates also spent heavily in Colorado, Nevada, New Hampshire, and North Carolina.

From votes to the Electoral College

Trump performed better against Clinton than Romney did against Obama, therefore, but still lost the popular vote – by 2.1 percentage points compared to Romney's defeat by 4.9 points. Yet Trump won in the Electoral College because, as in so many electoral contests where the winner takes all in each territory, he won votes in the right places – more than enough in all of the red states, plus just enough in the six states that swung from the Democrats to the Republicans, and also in one of Maine's congressional districts.

Why this uneven translation of popular votes into Electoral College votes? In a "fair" system each candidate's percentage share of the Electoral College votes

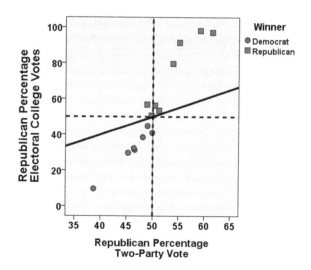

FIGURE 4.6 The Republican Party candidate's percentage share of the two-party popular vote and the Electoral College votes at presidential elections, 1960-2016.

should be commensurate with their popular vote share but, as Figure 4.6 shows, this has rarely been the case across the 15 elections since 1960, with very few showing the Republican candidates' vote shares being commensurate with the percentage share of the Electoral College votes (shown by the solid black line). On the three occasions when they gained 55% or more of the popular vote, those candidates gained at least 80% of the Electoral College total; the one candidate who gained less than 40% of the popular vote (Goldwater) only obtained 9% of the Electoral College votes.

Such disproportionality is typical of winner-take-all-elections such as the Electoral College, where the candidate with a plurality of the support in all but two (small) states gets all of its Electoral College votes. But in the operation of such disproportional systems, are the two parties equally treated? Analysts term any deviation from equal treatment bias (or partisan asymmetry): if both candidates received half of the popular votes they should both get half of the 538 Electoral College votes. (Analyses of bias, such as those of the UK (Johnston et al. 2001), derive from the pioneering work of Brookes (1959; 1960) in New Zealand; comparable analyses in the US, using the term partisan symmetry, build on the foundation laid by Grofman (1983) and King and Browning (1987; Browning and King 1987)). If one received more Electoral College votes than the other, that would be bias – measured here as the difference in the number of Electoral College votes that the two parties would have obtained if they had equal vote shares; a positive number indicates a bias favoring the Democratic Party and a negative figure a pro-Republican bias.

Bias was the norm at U.S. presidential elections between 1960 and 2012 (Pattie and Johnston 2014; Johnston, Pattie, and Rossiter 2001; Johnston, Rossiter, and

Geographies of Trump's electoral success 87

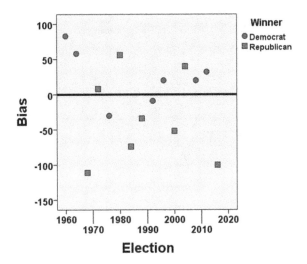

FIGURE 4.7 Bias in the allocation of Electoral College votes at presidential elections, 1960-2016.

Pattie 2005; see also Tamas 2019), only slightly in some contests (notably 1972, 1992, and 1996) but quite substantial in others (Figure 4.7): in 1960, if Kennedy and Nixon had shared the popular vote, Kennedy would have won by some 90 votes in the Electoral College, for example, whereas in 1968 Nixon would have gained about 120 more Electoral College votes than Humphrey. Over the 15 elections, the bias favored the Democratic Party's candidate in eight contests and the Republican Party's in seven. Several Republicans – Nixon in 1968, Reagan in 1984, and George W. Bush in 2000 – benefited from a bias in their favor of more than 50 College votes, with Donald Trump having a bias of 100 votes, a crucial feature of his campaign given that he lost the popular vote. (On the calculation of the bias components see Johnston Pattie, and Rossiter 2001; Johnston et al. 2001.)

Bias results from three main features of the country's electoral system and geography. The first is malapportionment. The number of each state's Electoral College votes is determined by its number of representatives and senators; because each has two senators and is guaranteed one representative irrespective of population, smaller states have lower ratios of population to Electoral College vote than larger. Wyoming and Vermont both had three Electoral College votes in 2016; their 2010 populations – when Electoral College votes were last redistributed – of 568,300 and 630,337 meant they had one Electoral College vote per every 189,433 and 210,112 residents respectively; New York (2010 population 19,421,055) and California (37,341,989), on the other hand, had one Electoral College vote per 669,692 and 698,945 residents respectively; and even middle-sized states like Kansas (2,863,813) and Minnesota (5,314,879) had substantially smaller populations per Electoral College vote (477,302 and

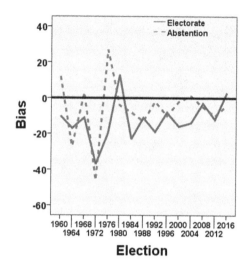

FIGURE 4.8 The electorate and abstentions bias components at presidential elections, 1960–2016.

531,488 respectively) than the largest. A party with support concentrated in the smaller states is thus substantially advantaged – it needs many fewer popular votes per Electoral College vote than one whose main strength is in the larger states.

The second major bias source relates to turnout: just as the more voters there are in a state the more votes a presidential candidate needs to gain its Electoral College votes so in states with the same number of registered voters the larger the proportion of those who turn out at the election, the larger the number of popular votes needed to gain the Electoral College votes. In a state with one million voters, if nobody abstains, 500,001 popular votes are needed to gain its Electoral College components; if 200,000 abstain, only 400,001 popular votes are needed, advantaging a party whose support is concentrated in the states with low turnout.

Figure 4.8 shows the trajectories of those two bias components at presidential elections since 1960. At all but two of those contests the electorate size component benefited Republican candidates, by between 10 and 20 Electoral College votes in most cases, indicative of the party's strength in the country's smaller states. The first exception was in 1980, when Reagan won all but six states and the District of Columbia; apart from his home state of Georgia, the other six that Carter won yielded only 37 Electoral College votes. And the other was Trump's victory in 2016; his victories in several swing states with ten or more Electoral College votes meant that although he also won in all of the smallest states, except Maine, New Hampshire, and Vermont, this component returned a net bias of three Electoral College votes to Clinton compared to Romney's 12-vote advantage on that component four years earlier.

The final major bias source relates to the geographical distribution of a party's support. If it wins 51% of the popular vote in every state, it wins all the Electoral

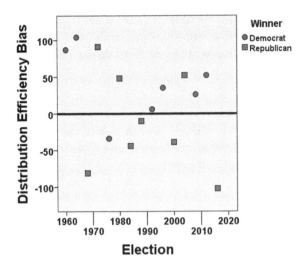

FIGURE 4.9 The distribution efficiency bias component at presidential elections, 1960–2016.

College votes; if it wins 49% everywhere (assuming only two candidates) it wins none. If it wins 51% of the votes in just the 12 states with most Electoral College votes, and none elsewhere, however, it would nevertheless get a College majority. The party that gains most Electoral College votes from the geographical distribution of its popular votes is the one that "wastes" fewest of those votes. In a state where it loses, all of its popular votes are wasted since they generate no Electoral College votes; and in a state where its votes exceed the number needed to win (i.e., more than 51% of the total in a two-candidate race) those "surplus to requirements" are also wasted. Thus, the party that is most advantaged by its popular vote distribution across the states is the one that best fits the adage – win small, lose big. Figure 4.9 shows that this bias component has favored the Democratic party's candidates more frequently than its opponent's, by as many as 100 Electoral College votes in the 1960, 1964, and 1972 elections and by as many as 50 votes in three subsequent contests. But in 2016 Donald Trump had an advantage over Hillary Clinton of 102 votes on this component – substantially larger than that gained by any of his party's other candidates.

In 2004, 2008, and 2012 there was an overall bias of 20–30 Electoral College votes favoring the Democratic candidates despite two of the sources – size and turnout – slightly favoring the Republicans whose strengths, relative to the Democrats', were in smaller states and those with lower than average turnout. The Democratic Party's candidates were favored overall because their support was better distributed – they wasted fewer popular votes – than their Republican opponents'. In 2004 and 2012 this source alone meant that the Democratic candidate would have won 50 more Electoral College votes than his opponent if they had shared the popular vote equally. But in 2016, thanks to those victories by very small majorities in several large swing states (Florida with 29 Electoral College votes, Pennsylvania with 20, Ohio with 18, Michigan with 16, and Wisconsin with 10), Trump wasted very few popular votes in gaining their 93 Electoral College votes.

Conclusions

Votes win elections, but where those votes are won is important in winner-take-all contests such as the Electoral College. At macro and mesoscales, the distribution of support for the Republican presidential candidates varied only slightly between 2012 and 2016, though where Trump outperformed Romney most was in the six crucial swing states that delivered his Electoral College victory despite losing to Hillary Clinton in the popular vote. The microscale of neighborhoods across metropolitan areas showed that differential even more clearly; Trump became president because he won over more voters – mainly disadvantaged Whites – in the Rust Belt swing states whereas Clinton lost support there among Blacks and voters who, after supporting Obama strongly in 2012, chose to abstain four years later. Those small shifts to Trump, largely unobserved in the larger-scale analyses, meant that the biases in the electoral system – in particular those resulting from the geographical distribution of his support – rewarded him with an Electoral College majority despite losing the popular vote.

Geography mattered in the 2016 election. Trump's campaign team recognized this in organizing where he expended most of his personal resources of time and energy, and he was rewarded by a victory that owed so much to geography.

References

Abramowitz, A., and J. McCoy. 2019. United States: Racial resentment, negative partisanship and polarization in Trump's America. *Annals of the American Academy of Political and Social Science* 681: 137–156.

Archer, J., and P. Taylor. 1981. *Section and Party: Political Geography of American Presidential Elections from Andrew Jackson to Ronald Reagan.* Chichester: Research Studies Press.

Balentine, M., and G. Webster. 2018. The changing electoral landscape of the western United States. *Professional Geographer* 70: 566–582.

Bishop, B. 2009. *The Big Sort: Why the Clustering of Like-Minded America is Tearing Us Apart.* Boston: First Mariner Books.

Brookes, R. 1959. Electoral distortion in New Zealand. *Australian Journal of Politics and History* 5: 218–233.

Brookes, R. 1960. The analysis of distorted representation in two-party, single-member electoral systems. *Political Science* 12: 158–167.

Browning, R.X., and G. King. 1987. Seats, votes and gerrymandering: Estimating representation and bias in state legislative redistricting. *Law and Policy* 9: 305–322.

Cervas, J., and B. Grofman. 2017. Why noncompetitive states are so important for understanding the outcomes of competitive elections: The Electoral College 1868–2016. *Public Choice* 170: 99–113.

Converse, P. 1966. The concept of a normal vote. In A. Campbell, P.E. Converse, W. Miller, and D. Stokes (eds.) *Elections and the Political Order.* pp. 9–39. New York: John Wiley.

Darmofal, D., and R. Strickler. 2019. *Demography, Politics, and Partisan Polarization in the United States, 1820–2016*. Cham, Switzerland: Springer.

Gest, J. 2016. *The New Minority: White Working Class Politics in an Age of Immigration and Inequality*. Oxford: Oxford University Press.

Grofman, B. 1983. Measures of bias and proportionality in seats-votes relationships. *Political Methodology* 9: 295–327.

Ingram, D., and S. Franco. 2013. *2013 NCHS Urban-Rural Classification Scheme for Counties*. Hyattsville, MD: U.S. Department of Health and Human services, Centers for Disease Control and Prevention, National Center for Health Statistics, DHHS Publication No.2014-1366.

Johnston, R.J., C. Pattie, D. Dorling, and D. Rossiter. 2001. *From Votes to Seats: The Operation of the UK Electoral System since 1945*. Manchester: Manchester University Press.

Johnston, R.J., C. Pattie, D. Manley, and K. Jones. 2017. Was the 2016 United States' presidential contest a deviating election? Continuity and change in the electoral map – or "Plus ca change, plus c'est la même géographie." *Journal of Elections, Public Opinion and Parties* 27: 369–388.

Johnston, R.J., C. Pattie, and D. Rossiter. 2001. He lost … but he won! Electoral bias and George W. Bush's victory in the US presidential election, 2000. *Representation* 38: 150–158.

Johnston, R.J., D. Rossiter, and C. Pattie. 2005. Disproportionality and bias in US presidential elections: How geography helped Bush defeat Gore but couldn't help Kerry beat Bush. *Political Geography* 24: 952–968.

Key, V. Jr. 1955. A theory of critical elections. *Journal of Politics* 17: 3–18.

King, G., and R. Browning. 1987. Democratic representation and partisan bias in congressional elections. *American Political Science Review* 81: 1251–1273.

Knuckey, J. 2019. "I just don't think she has a presidential look": Sexism and vote choice in the 2016 election. *Social Science Quarterly* 100(1): 342–358.

Pattie, C., and R. Johnston. 2014. "The electors shall meet in their respective states." Bias and the US presidential Electoral College, 1960–2012. *Political Geography* 40: 34–45.

Pomper, G. 1967. Classification of presidential elections. *Journal of Politics* 29: 535–566.

Rossiter, K., D.W. Wong, and P. Delamater. 2018. Congressional redistricting: keeping communities together? *Professional Geographer* 70: 609–623.

Tamas, B. 2019. American disproportionality: A historical analysis of partisan bias in elections to the U. S. House of Representatives. *Election Law Journal*. https://doi.org/10.1089/elj.2017.0464

White, S. 2019. Race, religion, and Obama in Appalachia. *Social Science Quarterly* 100(1): 38–59.

5

THE 2016 U.S. PRESIDENTIAL ELECTION AND TRUMP'S POPULIST RHETORIC

Wisconsin as a case study

Ryan Weichelt

A billionaire becomes a populist

In 2011, Donald Trump sat near the back of a crowded room at the annual White House Correspondents' Association dinner. Having been the loudest voice of the "birther movement" regarding Barack Obama, Trump was forced to listen to nearly five minutes of continuous barbs thrown at him by Obama himself. The barrage of insults did not stop, as the host, comedian Seth Myers, continued the assault. Myers said, "Donald Trump has been saying that he will run for president as a Republican – which is surprising, since I just assumed that he was running as a joke" (Wang 2017). Trump sat stoic, taking the jabs as they came. The *New York Times* would later report that evening accelerated Trump's ferocious efforts to gain stature within the political world (Haberman and Burns 2016). Born into a life of privilege, Donald Trump grew up among the wealthy of New York City. Given millions by his father, Trump developed a unique name for himself as a real estate mogul. In time Trump squandered billions as a mediocre real estate baron, but his charisma and charm in front of the camera made him appealing. "You're fired" became a national phrase as Trump turned the reality TV show, *The Apprentice*, into a ratings goldmine. Though Trump was a famous TV personality, his antics and temperament made him a mere sideshow in the eyes of many. Politically, Trump made attempts to run for president, but these were seen by some as mere publicity stunts. That night in 2011 clearly illustrated how Washington viewed the billionaire on Park Avenue as nothing more than a punching bag.

What Trump lacked in experience was more than made up for in bravado. After the 2011 dinner, Trump began positioning himself within the conservative limelight. He wrote millions in campaign contributions to conservative candidates and by 2012 he forced Republican candidate Mitt Romney to accept his endorsement. In that same year he cancelled *The Apprentice* and became a regular on Fox News (Haberman and Burns 2016). With a pulpit on which to preach, Trump began to craft his message of American economic decline and corruption in Washington. By June 16, 2015 in the building bearing his name, Trump Tower, he declared his intention to run for president. While many continued to believe this was a publicity stunt, Trump would surprise all as he proved, at least to himself, that he belonged.

Though Donald Trump always had a flare for the dramatic, his movement into the national political spotlight only intensified his rhetoric. Seemingly, Trump found the more outlandish his claims, the more his popularity swelled. As he stated in January 2016, "I could stand in the middle of Fifth Avenue and shoot somebody, and I wouldn't lose any voters" (Lacapria 2016). His unique and peculiar style contrasted with the political norms of Washington, as Trump fashioned himself as the anti-establishment candidate. Nevertheless, his message resonated with many rural white voters who felt Trump spoke for them. Pundits classified Trump and the other Democratic candidate, Bernie Sanders, as populists (Packer 2016). Yet, defining populism in the modern age of Trump, as Greven (2016) claims, "puts the proposition to the test" (p. 1). Barrack Obama agreed, challenging the media's crowning of Trump among the populist ranks as mere opportunity stating, "Candidates don't suddenly become populist because they say something controversial in order to win votes. That's not the measure of populism; that is nativism or xenophobia, or worse ... just cynicism" (Bonikowski 2016, p. 9).

The term "populism" emerged from the Great Plains in the 1890s when farmers became increasingly frustrated with the two-party system that they believed unjustly favored the economic interests of business and industry over that of the agrarian sector. Robert Durden (1965) wrote the Populist or People's Party sought to gain political power at the federal level as a response to the inherent and serious problems of American capitalism. Though authors such as Norman Pollack (1966) and George Tindall (1966) put a rather positive spin on the U.S. populist movement in the 1890s, J.F. Conway (1978) delivers a more critical approach, suggesting Richard Hofstadter (1955) provides the most consistent definition of populism as narrow, deeply nostalgic for the past, and racist in followers' responses to new immigrants flowing into the United States (p. 101). Thomas Greven (2016) proposes that modern-day populism has been generalized as a political message that attempts to resonate with concerns of "ordinary people." Though, he argues, as does Hofstadter, the identity and common interests of modern-day populists lie in contempt of the "other" (mainly minorities and immigrants), who they believe are "favored" by the elites of the establishment. Modern-day populist goals are accomplished through negativity in communications that are generally so outlandish that media outlets cannot ignore them, resulting in free media exposure.

Trump and his actions embody what both Hofstadter and Greven identify as the modern-day populist and, given Trump's privileged upbringing, are obviously ironic. Using phrases like "Make America Great Again" and "Drain the Swamp," Trump and his team constructed a message that appealed to many poor white Americans who felt minorities were given unfair advantages in hiring practices and government benefits. Moreover, Trump's overall tone focused on a promise to return to an America that once was. An America that dominated industry and manufacturing worldwide. An America that was not under constant threat from illegal immigrants who bring crime, drugs, and gangs with them. An America that was not under constant risk of both domestic and international Muslim terrorists. Finally, Trump also promised an America that would be free of Barack Obama by eliminating his signature legislation, Obamacare. As eccentric as Trump's message became, the media could not get enough. Throughout the campaign, Trump's rallies swelled, as thousands traveled great distances to simply see what Trump would say next.

By November 9, 2016, Trump pulled off one of the greatest upsets in modern political history. Trump combined his theatrics with a campaign centered on modern populist rhetoric. Polls did not account for the disdain for Hillary Clinton among large swaths of the American electorate. Likewise, polls also didn't account for the excitement Donald Trump generated across specific areas of the United States. It can be argued, one state, Wisconsin, was perhaps Trump's greatest upset.

Though Obama easily won Wisconsin in 2012, statewide, Democrats saw continued defeats leading up to and after the November 2016 election. Republicans' continued success at the ballot box provided a clear window into how to win the Badger State. Through legislation and campaign strategies, Wisconsin Republicans created an electorate polarized between rural, blue collar, and suburban Republicans and urban Democrats. Republicans laid the foundation of a modern-day populist agenda. Though many state Republicans hoped their candidate would not be Donald Trump, but rather popular Governor Scott Walker, who was running for president, Republican activities over the decade primed the Wisconsin electorate for the Trump campaign in 2016.

It is crucial to look to the social and economic geography both nationally and locally to understand how Trump was able to win this historic election. Nationally and in Wisconsin, Trump was able to tap into specific regional frustrations and craft tailored populist messages at different campaign sites. Furthermore, where he chose to visit was tied to his ability to reach voters who often felt ignored by Democrats and Washington in general.

This chapter is divided into two sections. The first provides a national overview of the geography of the November 9, 2016 presidential election with special attention to changing election patterns compared to the 2012 election. The second section provides a specific analysis of Trump's primary and general election strategies and results in Wisconsin. A detailed focus will be on how Trump used geography to moderate his modern-day populist message in key areas of Wisconsin giving Republicans their first win in the Badger State since 1984.

National analysis

On June 16, 2015, at the Trump Tower in New York City, Donald Trump officially declared he would run for president of the United States as a Republican. In his first speech as a candidate Trump would make the first of his many populist claims. He declared, if he were elected as president, he would build a large wall and have Mexico pay for it. Furthermore, Trump continued his attack on Mexico by saying:

> When Mexico sends its people, they're not sending their best. They're not sending you. They're not sending you. They're sending people that have lots of problems and they're bringing those problems with us. They're bringing drugs, they're bringing crime, they're rapists, and some, I assume, are good people. (Stracqualursi 2016)

Comments about border walls, criminals, and corruption placed Trump at the center of attention leading up to the first Republican primary debate on August 6, 2015. Trump elicited boos from the crowed when he refused to rule out running as a third-party candidate and gained further attention for his interaction with Fox News host, Megyn Kelly, when he verbally attacked her for posing a question about his treatment of women. After the debate Trump continued his controversial statements garnering plenty of free media airtime. In a press release on December 7, 2015, Trump's campaign stated, "Donald J. Trump is calling for a total and complete shutdown of Muslims entering the United States until our county's representatives can figure out what is going on" (Diamond 2015). Response to the comment was immediate and bipartisan. Republican Senator Lindsey Graham asked all candidates to condemn Trump's statement and candidate Jeb Bush tweeted Trump was "unhinged." Hillary Clinton was quick to call the statement "reprehensible, prejudiced, and divisive" (Diamond 2015). This clearly defined Trump to many of his supports as a true anti-establishment candidate.

By the Iowa caucus on February 2, 2016, Trump continued to be the focus of the primary season. Though he would lose the caucus to Marco Rubio, Trump finished a surprising second with his greatest support coming from the many rural counties of Iowa. Trump would quickly follow his second-place finish with a first-place finish on February 9 in New Hampshire. Both he and Democrat Bernie Sanders easily won the election, suggesting that voters were not interested in establishment candidates like Hillary Clinton or Jeb Bush. Trump reveled in the victory, but at the same time the Republican Party was left stunned. Former New Hampshire Republican governor, John Sununu stated, after Trump's victory, "By name, I only know five people supporting Donald Trump. So, I say I cannot understand this electorate" (Bidgood 2016). This similar mindset would continue as Trump slowly won key delegates on his way to securing the nomination.

On May 26, 2016, Trump won enough delegates to secure the Republican nomination. Republicans struggled with the fact that Trump would indeed be their party's presidential nominee. Obviously reckless, some believed Trump would tone down his antics after he won. Colorado Republican Party Chairmen Steve House said, "If he can surround himself with the political talent, I think he will be fine" (Collins 2016). Not all Republicans felt the same. Former Presidents George H.W. and George W. Bush, along with 2012 nominee, Mitt Romney, skipped the Republican Convention in Cleveland in protest of Trump. Second place finisher Ted Cruz spoke at the convention and refused to endorse Trump, who had insulted his wife during the primary. Pro-Trump delegates booed Cruz as he left the stage. The establishment protests only provided Trump and his supporters with fuel and in the end Trump was officially nominated as the Republican candidate for the president of the United States.

From June to November, Trump held 137 campaign rallies across the United States with an estimated 600,000 spectators (Wikipedia 2019). Rallies would sometimes resemble rock concerts. Peddlers sold "Lock Her Up" shirts, MAGA hats, and other rather offensive items. Hecklers of Trump were sometimes beaten by spectators. Trump visited Florida 25 times, North Carolina 18 times, Ohio 15 times, and Pennsylvania 14 times. His largest rally was held on October 24 in Tampa, Florida with an estimated crowd of between 15,000 and 28,000 people. In many of his rallies thousands were often left standing outside after the doors were closed. In states where Trump visited multiple times, he was keen to campaign in different areas of the state and seemed to avoid large urban areas when possible. This was especially true in the final week leading up to the election as he held rallies across the United States in smaller urban areas like Eau Claire, Wisconsin, Moon Township, Pennsylvania, and Grand Rapids, Michigan. Overall, it was obvious Trump was trying to reach his base: white, rural, and poor voters.

Trump's campaign strategy bore fruit. For the first time since 2000, a president was elected by losing the popular vote, but winning the Electoral College. Trump lost by over 2.8 million votes (2.09%), but defeated Clinton by 77 Electoral College votes. Both candidates' Electoral College votes would have been higher had it not been for faithless electors in Washington, Hawaii, and Texas. Trump boasted his election victory was the "Biggest Electoral College win since Ronald Reagan," despite Obama in 2012 and George H.W. Bush in 1988 having larger electoral victories (Cummings 2017).

Figures 5.1 and 5.2 provide county-level election results as a percentage of the total vote for the 2016 and 2012 presidential elections. Comparisons between the two maps clearly show Trump's support, nationally, was higher than Romney's in 2012. These two maps also show a more polarized electorate compared to 2012. Counties falling in the two middle classes (35–49.99% and 50–64.99%) were much less prevalent in 2016 compared to 2012. The most pronounced differences can be found throughout states like Minnesota in the Upper Midwest and the many Rust

The election and Trump's populist rhetoric 97

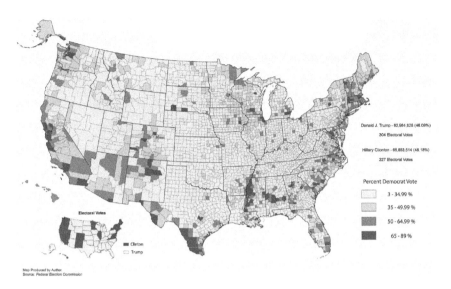

FIGURE 5.1 Percent voting Democrat at county level, 2016 United States presidential election.

Belt states bordering the Great Lakes. Two other states, Florida and North Carolina also show stronger support for Trump compared to Romney. In Florida, increases were greatest along the coasts and in North Carolina, Trump increased support along the Atlantic coast and in Appalachia. These differences clearly demonstrate Trump's appeal and vigorous campaigning had an impact.

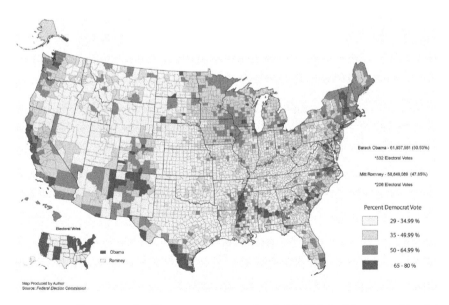

FIGURE 5.2 Percent voting Democrat at county level, 2012 United States presidential election.

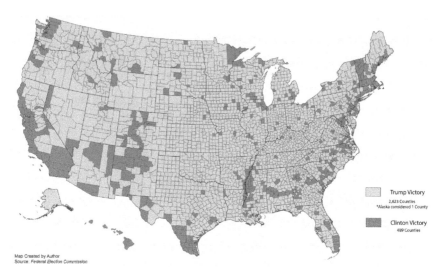

FIGURE 5.3 Plurality victory by county, 2016 United States presidential election.

Across the nation, exit polls illustrated how voting preferences cut along lines of race, gender, class, and age. Trump's support was highest among white males, voters aged 40 and older, and those without a college degree. On the other hand, Clinton's support was highest among non-white voters, women, voters younger than 40, and those with at least a college degree (CNN 2016). Figure 5.3 shows Trump's support was mainly in rural and suburban areas, with Clinton dominating large urban areas as well as areas with higher proportions of Hispanic voters, the traditional "Black Belt" in the South, and counties with higher proportions of Native Americans (i.e., Oglala Lakota County, SD and Menominee County, WI).

Beyond voter demographics, the 2016 election was also about comparisons to the candidates from 2012. Hillary Clinton attempted to ride the coattails of Barak Obama, while Trump was distinctly different from Romney in viewpoints and temperament. Figures 5.4 and 5.5 provide spatial evidence for both. By viewing these maps, it is clear Clinton lost two main sets of Obama voters: northern rural voters and northern urban African American voters (i.e., Milwaukee and Detroit). She lost African American support in the South as well, but not to the same degree. However, Democrats did make gains in the large metro areas of the southern United States such as Atlanta, Dallas, Houston, Phoenix, and Los Angeles. Trump's largest gains could be found throughout the Great Lakes, especially Ohio, Pennsylvania, and Michigan as well as central Florida. For places like Wisconsin, where increases aren't as pronounced, Trump was able to squeeze out just enough votes across rural counties to win the state.

The election and Trump's populist rhetoric 99

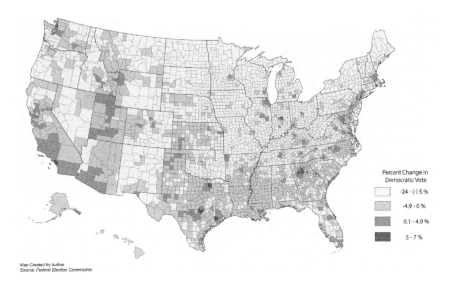

FIGURE 5.4 Percent change in Democratic vote in the presidential elections, at county level, 2012 to 2016.

Figure 5.6 illustrates that Trump outperformed Romney in most of the country but struggled in urban areas, suburban areas, and other areas with larger proportions of minority populations, especially the South among African Americans and Hispanics throughout Texas and New Mexico.

Trump's victory was closely tied to electoral upsets in three states: Wisconsin, Michigan, and Pennsylvania. These states share common characteristics in that

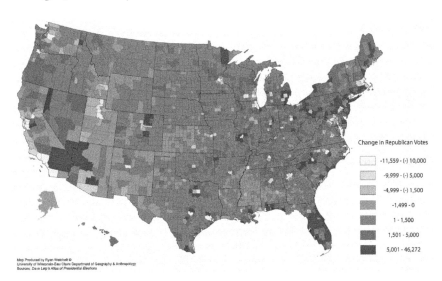

FIGURE 5.5 Change in Republican votes in the presidential elections, at county level, 2012 to 2016.

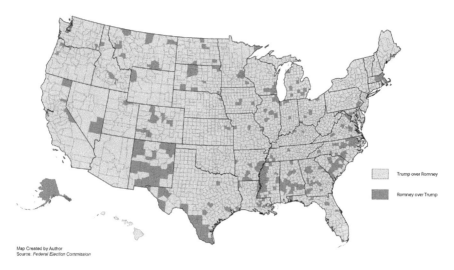

FIGURE 5.6 Counties where Trump performed better or worse in the 2016 presidential election than Mitt Romney in the 2012 presidential election, by total votes cast.

they are heavily dependent on manufacturing and agriculture, contain large, aging, rural white populations, and have all seen recent upsurges in Hispanic populations working in industry and agriculture, though to suggest all rural voters are the same would be an exaggeration. Rural areas are complex and voters in these areas face a variety of challenges that are not uniform across any statewide landscape.

Therefore, crafting distinct messages to voters would yield precious votes for Trump. Trump's use of a modern-day populist rhetoric was vital for his eventual victories in these states. Of these states, Trump's most narrow victory was Wisconsin, in which he won by just over 22,000 votes. The next section in this chapter will dive deeper into Trump's campaign in Wisconsin and how his team strategically targeted populations across the state to accomplish something a Republican had not done since 1984.

Wisconsin

Grooming a Republican victory

Wisconsin's recent elections show declining Democratic support in the many rural areas of the state and steady or increasing Democratic support in urban areas. Since 2010, Republicans have slowly but steadily gained support throughout much of rural Wisconsin through strategic legislation and messaging. Rural Wisconsin can be organized into two economic regions. The largest of these consists of fragmented dairying areas that dot the landscape across the central and southern areas of the state. The other can be found mainly in the northern section with large tracts of forestland and lakes dominated by tourist-based industries.

The election and Trump's populist rhetoric **101**

Additionally, throughout the rural areas of Wisconsin, there can also be found small manufacturing-based industries such as window manufacturers, transportation industries, and sand mining. However, rising operation costs coupled with increased competition both domestically and internationally, have forced many manufacturing facilities to close. As economic decline continued, rural communities began to lose their identities and are now confronted with new economic and social realities. Alcoholism and drug use, especially methamphetamine, is highest in Wisconsin's most rural counties (WI DOJ 2019). Rising healthcare costs and declining school funding exacerbated these problems. These hardships in Wisconsin's rural communities are important in understanding Trump's victory, as is the state's recent political history.

The 2010 midterm election was a watershed for Wisconsin as Republicans took control of the state legislature and governorship. Inspired by the ideas of the Tea Party, newly elected Governor Scott Walker initiated legislation to drive wedges between Wisconsin voters. As the decade progressed, there was increased polarization between rural and suburban Republicans and urban Democrats. Walker and his allies in the state government initiated legislation with modern-era populist tendencies. Legislation focused on curtailing unions and lowering taxes in hopes of expanding the manufacturing base. Other bills also tapped into rural and urban social divides by allowing the first grey wolf hunt and examining Wisconsin's whitetail deer populations to increase hunting. Furthermore, Walker made it a point to consistently visit rural areas across the state on a regular basis. No matter the true nature of these strategies, it connected Republicans with voters throughout the state.

As these actions progressed, Democrats did little to stem the tide and took refuge in the major urban areas, believing they could still win elections based on obvious population advantages in places like Madison and Milwaukee. For example, the 2014 Democratic gubernatorial candidate Mary Burke made only a handful of appearances in rural areas of Wisconsin during her campaign, focusing much of her campaign on Madison, Milwaukee, and the Fox River Valley. This strategy backfired. John Andrews, a longtime Democrat turned Republican in Pepin County, Wisconsin, felt Democrats were overemphasizing a social agenda and ignoring rural voters. He explained why he switched parties during the 2010s, stating:

> When the city people came in – and the things that they were trying to push on the rest of us –that's why I left. I didn't want to deal with these people. I didn't want to be a part of what they were a part of. You're talking about people from the cities who are very progressive. I call them tree-huggers, a bunch of tree-huggers. They referred to us, meaning the people who've lived here and worked here all our lives, as a bunch of hicks. They just think they're a little bit better than everybody else, and that we're not as smart. (Kruse 2017)

Madison Professor Kathy Cramer found a similar sense of anger among rural Wisconsin voters in her book *Politics of Resentment* (2016) as she traveled across

The Wisconsin primary election

By Wisconsin's primary election on April 5, 2016, it was obvious the Republican nomination was a battle between Donald Trump and Texas Senator Ted Cruz. Trump held an early advantage and as Super Tuesday (March 3) approached, the map began showing Republicans in the South and in typically Democratic-leaning states like Massachusetts and Vermont were favoring Trump, but traditional Republican states like Oklahoma and Kansas favored Cruz. Though Cruz was behind Trump he was picking up key delegates and a strong win in Wisconsin could potentially give Cruz much needed momentum. In the end Cruz comfortably won Wisconsin, but it never gave him the bump his campaign needed. It allowed Trump to introduce himself to Wisconsin voters as he engaged in a vigorous campaign schedule in the week leading up to the April 5 vote.

Trump's primary election campaign message focused on three main components: increase jobs through manufacturing, xenophobia, and corruption in Washington. While nationally manufacturing jobs decreased 28.3% between 2000 and 2017, Wisconsin fared somewhat better, dropping only 21.4% (132,100 jobs) (Wisconsin Newspaper Association 2019). These losses were more pronounced in the eastern areas of the state. In terms of migration, between 2000 and 2015, the state's Hispanic population doubled and increased faster than any other, accounting for nearly 46% of Wisconsin's population growth (NBC 2016). While this growth was largest in cities like Milwaukee and Madison, rural communities saw increased Hispanic populations, especially in western and southwestern Wisconsin. Currently, foreign-born populations engaged in manufacturing and agriculture are higher than native born (Jones 2017). This change has been difficult for not only Hispanics in terms of integration into communities, but also for the white populations who perceive Hispanics as competitors. In a 2017 NPR study, over 3,400 Hispanics were surveyed throughout the Midwest and "a third or more say they have personally experienced racial or ethnic slurs and people making negative assumptions or insensitive comments about their race or ethnicity. Roughly one in five say they have experienced violence or threats because they are Latino" (p. 20).

Trump made his debut Wisconsin appearance on March 29, 2016 at a town hall meeting in Janesville, a community reeling from the closure of the GM plant in 2008 that at one time employed over 7,000. Trump wasted little time in attacking Governor Scott Walker, who had just endorsed Ted Cruz, by tying Walker and Cruz to the Trans-Pacific Partnership (TPP) and Wisconsin's poor economic climate. Always the showman, Trump was able to draw boos toward Scott Walker by reframing Janesville as "a blue-collar town that has suffered the consequences of manufacturing decline" (Diamond 2016). A similar message was applied to his speeches in Appleton, De Pere, and Racine. Yet, when traveling to the cities of Eau Claire, Rothschild, and La Crosse, Trump would pivot and infuse more discussion regarding immigration into his speeches, only to eliminate that language almost completely when he visited Superior in the northwest region of the state. Trump used a similar approach, tapping into a modern-day populist rhetoric based on local geography, in his 10 speeches across the Badger State leading up to the April 5 primary election (Figure 5.7).

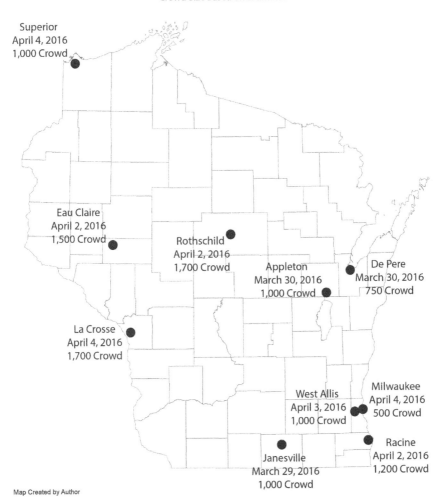

FIGURE 5.7 Primary election rallies held by Trump in Wisconsin, 2016.

Wisconsin is an open primary state, meaning people do not register for a specific party before they vote. Voters can choose whom they want on the day of the election. As the polls closed on April 5, Donald Trump ultimately lost Wisconsin to Ted Cruz by over 144,000 votes. Figure 5.8 shows the county-level results for the primary election. Trump dominated the rural counties of northern and western Wisconsin, but fared poorly in the urban areas, the traditional manufacturing sectors of eastern Wisconsin, and the suburban counties around Milwaukee. As with other primaries, Trump would find it difficult to connect with traditional conservative voters in suburban areas. For Wisconsin, this was clear in Waukesha, Ozaukee, and Washington counties. These counties are largely white wealthy suburban counties of the Milwaukee metro area and are the most ardent supporters of Scott Walker. Though Trump lost Wisconsin, a *New York Times* exit poll of Wisconsin voters hinted at Trump's appeal when asking respondents, the following question: If Donald Trump is elected president, which best describes your feelings about what he would do in office? Eighty-nine percent of Trump voters indicated they were excited (9% of Cruz votes said they would be excited for Trump), while 0% interviewees indicated they would be excited for Cruz or Kasich (2016).

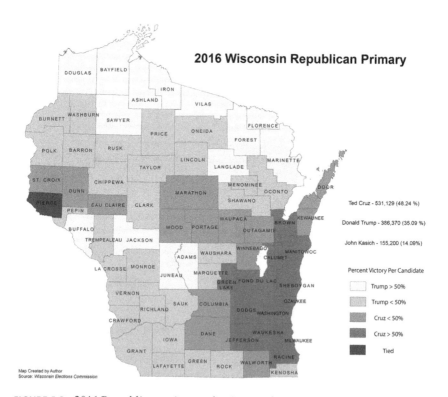

FIGURE 5.8 2016 Republican primary election results.

By the end of the primary season, Donald Trump bucked many pundits and won the Republican nomination. As the presidential election ramped up, Democrats were confident the United States would elect its first female president, though the electorate seemed rather unexcited by Clinton. Trump continued to draw thousands to his rallies where he played the crowd like a modern-day P.T. Barnum.

2016 Wisconsin general election

Scott Walker embodies the modern-day Wisconsin Republican. A devoted Christian, college dropout, and the self-proclaimed greatest fan of Ronald Reagan, Walker rose through the ranks to win the governor's seat in 2010. After his successful assault on unions and surviving a recall election victory in 2012, Walker headed into the 2016 election cycle as one of the favorites to win the Republican nomination. Seemingly untouchable, Walker was the first to clash with Trump and lose. Walker not only lost; he was embarrassed. After a Walker staffer was overheard calling Trump a "DumbDumb," Trump unleashed on the governor (Epstein 2015). Walker was the first major candidate to drop out of the race after only two months of campaigning.

Any Republican hoping to win Wisconsin would need Walker's support. Walker's support of Ted Cruz during the primary was a major reason for Cruz's relatively easy victory in Wisconsin. As with many in the Republican Party and based on Walker's embarrassments in 2015 due to Trump, Walker unwillingly wanted Trump on the ticket. After Trump secured the nomination in early May, Congressman Paul Ryan was the first major Wisconsin Republican to support him. A week later, in an interview with *USA TODAY*, Walker was asked if he supported Trump. Walker's response was tepid at best. Using Hillary Clinton as the reason why he supported Trump, he made it clear Trump was not his first choice, but would support him, nonetheless. In the coming months, both Ryan and Walker took a slow approach with Donald Trump. Neither provided overwhelming support and neither would be seen with Trump on the campaign trail until October 6, 2016 at a fall festival in Elkhorn, Wisconsin.

Though it can be argued Trump would not have won Wisconsin without either Walker's or Ryan's support, he was not expected to win the state. Polls in the Badger State remained consistent from July to November. The final Marquette Poll released on November 1 showed Clinton with a six-point lead. No poll during the presidential cycle in Wisconsin gave Trump more than 42% of the vote. The average according to the *RealClear Politics* showed Clinton at 46.8% to Trump's 40.3% (2016). Based on these comfortable leads, Hillary Clinton made the decision to not campaign in Wisconsin, instead sending her husband, daughter, Bernie Sanders, and Barrack Obama to campaign for her. On the other hand, Trump's campaign consistently visited Wisconsin during the election, adding an Eau Claire rally late in the game.

FIGURE 5.9 Trump's general election rallies held in Wisconsin, 2016.

As in the primary campaign, geography played a pivotal role in dictating Trump's speech themes and how the message was delivered. Trump would hold five campaign rallies throughout Wisconsin from August to November and one on the border in Minneapolis (Figure 5.9). In analyzing Trump's campaign speeches in Wisconsin, five main themes developed: Hilary Clinton as corrupt; immigration and safety; anti-free trade; Obamacare; and "draining the swamp" (Factbase 2019). Due to West Bend and Waukesha voters' proclivity to more traditional Republican issues, Trump's speeches focused on jobs, cutting taxes, and healthcare. In Green Bay and Eau Claire, the speeches focused on specific examples of struggling manufacturing sectors, loss of jobs, and promotion of a border wall to stem immigration from Mexico. In his Eau Claire speech, Trump spent over nine minutes on the topic, more than any other during his nearly one-hour speech. Similarly, in Green Bay, illegal immigration was mentioned

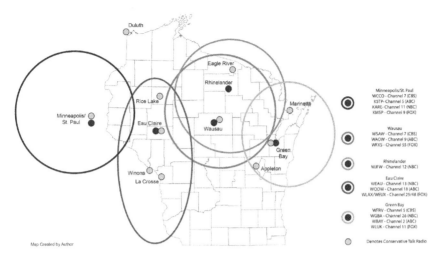

FIGURE 5.10 Television markets for northern Wisconsin and Minneapolis.

the most out of any of the topics. Speaking to his largest crowd in Minneapolis, Trump changed his rhetoric to focus on Obamacare, Syrian refugees, and for the first time in any of his speeches, spoke directly to farmers. He spoke very little on illegal immigration and only briefly mentioned building a wall twice.

Trump's primary results clearly identified in Wisconsin where his greatest support might be as well as the places he might struggle. The question was whether enough votes could be gleaned out of these areas to win the needed electoral votes. For rural voters, messages are received much differently than in the highly urbanized south. Wisconsin's rural populations lack access to broadband internet. Television, radio, newspapers, and speaking with friends and family are how voters receive their information. Figure 5.10 shows general media markets for local television and news stations as well as conservative talk radio stations across north and central Wisconsin. Both Green Bay and Eau Claire TV stations cover large geographic areas across mainly rural areas. As for newspapers, a vast majority of Wisconsin's newspapers are connected to the Gannet News Service. Cities like Wausau, Green Bay, Appleton, Marshfield, Wisconsin Rapids, La Crosse, and Milwaukee all share common stories. Finally, 11 conservative talk radio stations dot the rural landscape playing shows like Rush Limbaugh and Sean Hannity. Trump's campaign understood the importance of selecting campaign sites with the greatest traditional media reach into rural regions.

As November 9 approached, Clinton seemed cautiously optimistic. In Wisconsin, last minute polls showed her up by five to six points. Yet, very few could predict what the evening would have in store. Not called until the early morning of November 10, to the shock of many, Trump narrowly won Wisconsin by an estimated 22,000 votes. Adding to the dismay for Democrats, former Senator Democrat Russ Feingold also lost in a surprising manor to

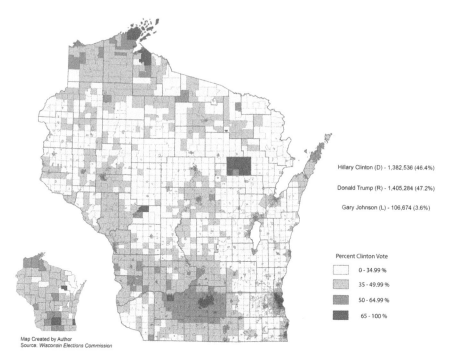

FIGURE 5.11 Percent voting for Hillary Clinton in the 2016 presidential election in Wisconsin at voting district level.

incumbent Republican Senator Ron Johnson. As can be seen in Figure 5.11, Trump's greatest support could be found throughout the rural areas of north and central Wisconsin as well as the mixed rural, manufacturing, and suburban areas along Lake Michigan.

Therefore, was it Trump's modern-era populist message or was it simply a lack of excitement and perhaps arrogance on the part of the Clinton campaign that cost her the election? The data suggest Clinton's loss can be attributed more to the large decline of support in the Milwaukee area, due to a lack of enthusiasm for her candidacy, and the spoiler effect of Libertarian, Gary Johnson, and Green Party candidate, Jill Stein, on the ballot. Compared to 2012, the 2016 election saw 96,788 fewer voters in Wisconsin. The Milwaukee area alone saw a decline of nearly 52,000 votes from 2012, with Clinton losing 43,514 votes compared to Obama. Gary Johnson's garnering of over 102,000 votes, mainly in college towns across the state, added to her loss as well. However, Hillary Clinton gained support, compared to Obama, in the traditionally Republican suburban counties around Milwaukee, highlighting a weakness for Trump. Yet, Trump was still able to inspire just enough votes in rural areas. Analysis at the voting district level finds in many rural areas Trump was able to gain an average of 20 extra votes compared to Romney in 2012. These small numbers, coupled with declines in traditional Democratic areas like Milwaukee, provided just enough for Trump to secure the victory.

Conclusions

Trump is a political enigma. Born of privilege and power, he ironically evolved to embody a new era of populism in the United States. With a flair for the dramatic, Trump was able to capture the moment using his stagecraft to appeal to a wide spectrum of voters. While the election itself was a convoluted mixture of intrigue, deceit, and malice from both parties, the resulting election map clearly identified how Trump won. The campaign masterfully crafted a modern-era populist message meant for individual voters in specific states. Nationally Trump's strategy for the winning the election was clearly Florida, Ohio, North Carolina, Michigan, Pennsylvania, and Wisconsin. This was a tall order based on the polls, but Trump tapped rural areas in each to win slim victories in all. In Wisconsin, Trump selected, catered, and altered his campaign to specific areas of the state relying on already established political connections and traditional forms of media to deliver his messages. Yet Trump's victory was also tied to Clinton's lack of appeal to many voters. He was able to garner just enough excitement among his supporters compared to Hillary Clinton. It was clear nationally and in places like Wisconsin, geography played a vital role in Trump's success.

After the election Trump would continue with his populist slant. In the coming years he would institute a Muslim ban, initiate tariffs against places like China, insist on a border wall, and will not stop talking about Hillary Clinton. As 2020 approaches, geography will again play a vital role in Trump's campaign strategies. Unlike his first election, this time Trump will have to run on his own record. Trump's Chinese tariffs are being felt by rural farming communities and economic development in traditional manufacturing areas has been slow and declining, but will this have an impact? Undoubtedly Trump will follow a similar approach to 2020. He already holds campaign style rallies across the nation in generally small communities in key states and still packs the buildings. Always a showman, Trump will certainly put on a show in 2020.

References

Bidgood, Jess. 2016. Donald Trump and Bernie Sanders win in New Hampshire primary. *New York Times* (Feb. 10). www.nytimes.com/2016/02/10/us/politics/new-hampshire-primary.html

Bonikowski, B. 2016. Three lessons of contemporary populism in Europe and the United States. *Brown Journal of World Affairs* XXIII (1): 9–24.

CNN. 2016. 2016 election results: National exit polls. www.cnn.com/election/2016/results/exit-polls/national/president

Collins, E. 2016. AP says Trump has hit magic number of delegates to clinch GOP nomination. *USA Today* (May 26). www.usatoday.com/story/news/politics/elections/2016/05/26/donald-trump-delegates-nomination/84968566/

Conway, J.F. 1978. Populism in the United States, Russia, and Canada: Explaining the roots of Canada's third parties. *Canadian Journal of Political Science* 11(1): 99–124.

Cramer, K. 2016. *The Politics of Resentment.* Chicago: University of Chicago Press.

Cummings, W. 2017. Trump falsely claims biggest electoral win since Reagan. *USA Today* (Feb. 16). www.usatoday.com/story/news/politics/onpolitics/2017/02/16/trump-falsely-claims-biggest-electoral-win-since-reagan/98002648/

Diamond, J. 2015. Donald Trump: Ban all Muslim travel to U.S. *CNN* (Dec. 8). www.cnn.com/2015/12/07/politics/donald-trump-muslim-ban-immigration/index.html

Diamond, J. 2016. Trump knocks Walker in Wisconsin. *CNN* (March 30). www.cnn.com/2016/03/29/politics/donald-trump-scott-walker-wisconsin/index.html

Durden, R. 2015. *The Climax of Populism*. Lexington: University Press of Kentucky.

Epstein, R. 2015. Top Scott Walker fundraiser calls Donald Trump "DumbDumb." *Wall Street Journal* (July 24). https://blogs.wsj.com/washwire/2015/07/24/top-scott-walker-fundraiser-calls-donald-trump-dumbdumb/

Factbase. 2019. Donald Trump unabridged – Speeches, tweets, interviews. https://factba.se/trump

Federal Elections Commission. 2019. Election results. https://transition.fec.gov/pubrec/electionresults.shtml

Greven, T. 2016. The rise of right-wing populism in Europe and the United States. *Library. Fes.De.* https://library.fes.de/pdf-files/id/12892.pdf

Haberman, M., and A. Burns. 2016. Donald Trump's presidential run began in an effort to gain stature. *NYTimes.Com* (March 12). www.nytimes.com/2016/03/13/us/politics/donald-trump-campaign.html

Hofstadter, R. 1955. *The Age of Reform: From Bryan to F.D.R.* New York: Vintage Books.

Jones, M. 2017. The changing faces of Wisconsin's foreign-born residents. *WisContext.* www.wiscontext.org/changing-faces-wisconsins-foreign-born-residents

Kruse, M. 2017. What do you do if a red state moves to you? *POLITICO Magazine* (January/February). www.politico.com/magazine/story/2017/01/blue-red-state-democrats-trump-country-214647

Lacapria, K. 2016. Fact Check: Donald Trump's "Fifth Avenue" comment. *Snopes.Com* (Jan. 24). www.snopes.com/fact-check/donald-trump-fifth-avenue-comment/

NBC. 2016. Hispanic population doubles in Wisconsin from 2000-2015. NBC15.Com. www.nbc15.com/content/news/Hispanic-population-doubles-in-Wisconsin-from-2000-2015-405026675.html

New York Times. 2016. Wisconsin exit polls. www.nytimes.com/interactive/2016/04/05/us/elections/wisconsin-republican-primary-exit-polls.html

NPR. 2017. NPR choice page. www.npr.org/documents/2017/oct/discrimination-latinos-final.pdf

Packer, G. 2015. The populists. *The New Yorker* (Aug. 30). www.newyorker.com/magazine/2015/09/07/the-populists

Pollack, N. 1966. *The Populist Response to Industrial America*. New York: Norton.

RealClearPolitics. 2016. Election 2016 – Wisconsin: Trump Vs. Clinton. www.realclearpolitics.com/epolls/2016/president/wi/wisconsin_trump_vs_clinton-5659.html

Stracqualursi, V. 2016. Key moments of the 2016 election. *ABC News* (Nov. 4). https://abcnews.go.com/Politics/key-moments-2016-election/story?id=43289663

Tindall, G. 1966. *A Populist Reader: Selection from the Works of American Populist Leaders*. New York: Harper.

Wang, A. 2017. Did the 2011 White House Correspondents' Dinner inspire Trump to run for president? *Chicago Tribune* (Feb. 26). www.chicagotribune.com/nation-world/ct-white-house-correspondents-dinner-trump-20170226-story.html

WI DOJ. 2019. Methamphetamine in Wisconsin: An overview. www.doj.state.wi.us/dci/drugs-wi

Wikipedia. 2019. List of rallies for the 2016 Donald Trump presidential campaign. https://en.wikipedia.org/wiki/List_of_rallies_for_the_2016_Donald_Trump_presidential_campaign

Wisconsin Elections Commission. 2019. Wisconsin elections results. *Elections.Wi.Gov.* https://elections.wi.gov/elections-voting/results

Wisconsin Newspaper Association. 2019. Manufacturing declining as share of Wisconsin's economy. www.wnanews.com/2019/01/14/manufacturing-declining-wisconsin-economy/

6

THE HEART OF WHITENESS

Patterns of race, class, and prejudice in the divided Midwest

David Norman Smith and Eric Hanley

In July 2012, in an unguarded moment at the Republican National Convention, Senator Lindsay Graham of South Carolina spoke plaintively about the future prospects of his party: "The demographics race we're losing badly. We're not generating enough angry white guys to stay in business for the long term" (Helderman and Cohen 2016). He had good reason to worry. Just 20 years earlier, the nonwhite share of presidential voters had been 13%. But now, on the eve of Barack Obama's reelection, that share had more than doubled, rising to 28%. Among Democratic voters the absolute increase was greater, as nonwhites went from 21% of the party in 1992 to 45% in 2012 (Abramowitz and Webster 2018). And whites without college degrees, who were increasingly seen as a crucial swing constituency, were a steadily declining part of the electorate. As recently as 1980, voters with that profile had comprised over two-thirds of eligible voters, but by 2010 they were no longer the majority (Griffin, Teixeira, and Halpin 2017a).

Fast forward to February 2016. As Donald Trump's successes in the primaries accumulated, the seasoned right-wing publicist Pat Buchanan sounded a triumphal note:

> Trump is winning because, on immigration, amnesty, securing our border and staying out of any new crusades for democracy, he has tapped into the most powerful currents in politics: economic populism and "America First" nationalism. Look at the crowds Trump draws. … If Beltway Republicans think they can stop Trump … they will be swept into the same dustbin of history as the Rockefeller Republicans. America is saying, "Goodbye to all that." For Trump is not only a candidate. He is a messenger from Middle America. And the message he is delivering to the establishment is: We want an end to your policies and we want an end to you. (Buchanan 2016)

112 David Norman Smith and Eric Hanley

What had happened? Was Donald Trump, in fact, a messenger from Middle America? Many pundits now say *yes*. They credit his victory to his surging popularity among less educated white voters, above all in the key battleground states of Michigan, Wisconsin, and Pennsylvania. Our research shows that this interpretation is substantially accurate but that it must be qualified in several respects.

Black votes matter

It is essential, first, not to overlook the nonwhite vote. Concern about the swing potential of less educated white voters has been so obsessive that it's easy to neglect the part played by minority voters – but that role was decisive. Whites and blacks voted at nearly equal rates in 2008 and 2012, but the white vote in 2016 exceeded the black vote by 5.7%. That reflected a seven-point decline in black turnout, from 66.6% to 59.6%. And Clinton also won a reduced share of the Latino vote (Aldrich et al. 2019). These shifts mattered, not least in the Midwestern battleground states, where, if turnout among black voters had remained unchanged, Clinton would have won both Michigan and Wisconsin. And if the level of white voting had remained constant in Pennsylvania, Clinton would have won that state too (Griffin, Teixeira, and Halpin 2017b). A victory for Clinton in Pennsylvania, coupled with wins in Michigan and Wisconsin, would have entirely reversed the outcome of the election (Shelley, Heppen, and Morrill 2018). Trump won those states by 77,744 votes: 44,292 in Pennsylvania, 10,704 in Michigan, and 22,748 in Wisconsin. That gave him 46 Electoral College votes and the election. So clearly, white votes and black votes both mattered a great deal – and nowhere was that more fateful than in the Midwest.

In what follows we will keep the spotlight on white voters, with particular attention to the "white working class."[1] Our aim is to complicate the conventional discussion about the 2016 election by showing the limitations of many widely held assumptions about white voters, the Midwest, and the electoral effects of education. White voters differ greatly from one another, not just educationally but regionally and attitudinally. And, in fact, the effects of college education differ regionally too. Closely inspected, the differences within and between regions prove to be complex, in ways that defy easy generalization. White voters in some regions, it seems, are whiter than others. They identify as white *culturally,* across class lines, and they vote accordingly. And that isn't simply true of the South, as people might think. It applies to the Midwest as well.

White polarities

Donald Trump was not the darling of less educated white voters in quite the way that standard narratives usually suggest. Many, many millions of voters with that profile opposed him, and in some places Trump was less popular with less educated white voters than Mitt Romney had been in 2012. Those facts cannot be ignored, and we will develop them fully below. But it remains true that Trump drew an unprecedented level of support from white voters without college degrees. The *Wall Street Journal* observed on the eve of the election that Lindsay Graham's favorite demographic still had untapped potential. Forty-seven million white adults without college degrees had not voted in 2012; that fact was most consequential in Ohio and Iowa, which, of all the battleground states, had the highest concentrations of white voters over the age of 24 without college diplomas, 72% each (Zitner and Chinni 2016). States like these were golden opportunities for the "messenger from Middle America."

A month later, the election proved the strength of this observation. Of the 206 counties that pivoted to Trump after voting for Obama in 2012 and 2008, 59% were in six Midwestern states: Iowa, Wisconsin, Minnesota, Michigan, Illinois, and Ohio. And four of those same states (Ohio, Wisconsin, Michigan, and Iowa) were among the half-dozen states that flipped from Obama to Trump nationally (Krier, Oberhauser, and Kusow 2019).

Why was Clinton vulnerable in those particular states? One reason, according to Alan Abramowitz, "was that all of the battleground states in the Midwest and Northeast – Michigan, Wisconsin, Pennsylvania, Ohio, and Iowa – have less racially diverse and less educated electorates" than the U.S. average (Abramowitz 2018). In some respects, that statement is clearly true. As Shelley, Heppen, and Morrill (2018) note "the Midwestern states that flipped from Obama to Trump … are at the core of a large swath of counties in which" Trump eclipsed Romney – a swath we see depicted in Figure 6.1 which shows that less educated white voters

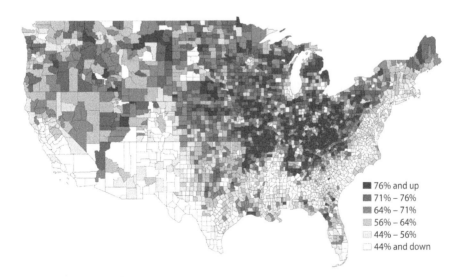

FIGURE 6.1 Distribution of non-college educated voters, 2016.

Source: Reprinted with permission from Griffin, Teixeira, and Halpin 2017a.

114 David Norman Smith and Eric Hanley

TABLE 6.1 Percentages of voters in the 2016 electorate by race and region.

Voters in 2016	Midwest	Northeast	West	South	Non-Midwest
White	79.0	72.1	63.8	63.4	66.4
Nonwhite	21.0	27.9	36.2	36.6	33.6

are most densely concentrated in the Midwest and in adjacent area in the Plains and Great Lakes.

That concentration is also apparent in the tables presented. In Table 6.1, we see that white voters made up nearly four-fifths of the Midwestern electorate in 2016, a percentage far beyond the average (66.4%) found in the other three regions. In Table 6.2, we see that less educated white voters made up an absolute majority of the Midwestern voting public (55.6%) (see Appendix for definitions of regions). That figure, too, differs sharply from the averages in the other three regions, where their counterparts comprised just 41.4% of the overall electorate.[2]

These numbers lend intuitive support to the thesis that key Midwestern states pivoted to Trump because they have high populations of white voters and, among white voters, high concentrations of the less educated. But a moment's reflection shows that the South poses a problem for this premise, since Southern voters also favored Trump over Romney, even though the white share of the Southern electorate was 15.6 points smaller than in the Midwest. What are we to make of this?

A tale of four regions

Our analysis of the 2012 and 2016 American National Election Studies shows that regional identities matter, and that those identities complicate the standard narrative about Trump's debt to less educated white voters. What we learn, from Table 6.3a, is that white voters differ strikingly from region to region. In both the South and the Midwest, less educated white voters performed as most people would have predicted, rallying to Trump's siren song by margins significantly exceeding their support for Romney four years earlier. But their peers in the West and Northeast did not emulate them. In the Northeast, flying in the face of conventional expectations, less educated white voters actually tilted *away* from Trump. Where Romney had won 60% of the less educated white vote in the Northeast, Trump won only 54.3%.

TABLE 6.2 Percentages of white voters in the 2016 electorate by region and education.

White voters in 2016	Midwest	Northeast	West	South	Non-Midwest
Without college degrees	55.6	41.8	39.4	43.1	41.4
With college degrees	23.4	30.3	24.4	20.3	27.6
Total	79.0	72.1	63.8	63.4	69.0

The heart of whiteness 115

TABLE 6.3A Percentages of white voters favoring Romney and Trump by region, election year, and education, excluding voters who favored third-party candidates.

White voters	2012	2016	Difference
Without college degrees			
South	69.8	80.3	10.5**
Midwest	51.8	64.6	12.8**
West	49.0	57.4	8.4
Northeast	60.0	54.3	-5.7
U.S.	59.7	66.4	6.7**
With college degrees			
South	61.6	61.2	-0.4
Midwest	45.7	46.6	0.9
West	50.6	36.0	-14.6*
Northeast	50.2	32.7	-17.5**
U.S.	53.1	44.6	-8.5**

* p < .05   ** p < .01   *** p < .001 (two-tailed test)
Source: ANES data, 2012 and 2016.

That shift was not statistically significant in itself, but it was large enough to sharply reduce the overall and highly significant shift from Romney to Trump among less educated voters nationally.

No less remarkable is the unexpected fact that, while college educated white Romney voters abandoned Trump in droves in the West and Northeast, they did nothing of the kind in the South and Midwest. In fact, Trump's share of the educated white vote in the Midwest actually exceeded the share Romney had won in the prior election.

In all, three distinct patterns emerged among white voters in 2016. As we see in Table 6.3b, Western voters stood pat, but Northeastern voters diverged sharply from those in the South and Midwest. In the Northeast, Trump was less popular

TABLE 6.3B Percentages of white voters favoring Romney and Trump by region, election year, and education, excluding voters who favored third-party candidates.

All white voters	2012	2016	Difference
Pattern 1			
West	49.4	48.3	-1.1
Pattern 2			
Northeast	56.1	44.2	-11.9**
Pattern 3			
South	66.7	73.1	6.4*
Midwest	49.7	58.6	8.9*
Aggregate patterns			
U.S.	57.2	57.7	0.5

* p < .05   ** p < .01   *** p < .001 (two-tailed test)

Source: ANES data, 2012 and 2016.

116 David Norman Smith and Eric Hanley

than Romney across the board, by wide margins. In the South and Midwest, in contrast, Trump held his own among college graduates while winning massive new support from the less educated.

If we had looked only at aggregate figures, we could easily have concluded that Romney and Trump drew upon similar reserves of white support. But the disaggregated data speak to a different register. We discover that both region and education play vital roles, and that they interpenetrate in entangling, complicating ways. Similar aggregate outcomes issue from contrasting regional and educational patterns. Evidently, what it means to be white or educated differs, electorally at least, from region to region.

Divided by degrees

Not all of this is new. Our prior research, like similar research by others, has demonstrated the reality of what is often called "the diploma divide" (Harris 2018). In "The Anger Games," we showed that, of five often-cited demographic variables, education was associated with Trump voting to a unique extent (Smith and Hanley 2018). In Table 6.4, we see that, while older age and marriage also predicted support for Trump, education had much larger effects.

We now know that this education effect is unevenly distributed across regions. But why? Why did white voters without college degrees flock to Trump in the South and Midwest but tilt away from him in the Northeast? Why did white college degree holders differ so significantly across regions? Here too "The Anger Games" suggests a possibility. We showed there that, when the attitudes reported in the 2016 American National Election Study (ANES) were examined alongside the demographic variables, those attitudes proved decisive. White voters only favored Trump when they shared his prejudices. Less educated voters supported Trump in exceptionally large numbers because they were likely to share his prejudices – against immigrants, minorities, Muslims, women, and authority figures who defended those groups. The same was true for white college

TABLE 6.4 Demographic variables relevant to voting for Trump among white voters.

Voting for Trump	Impact
Education (some college or less = 1)	.834***
Marital status (married = 1)	.402**
Age (years)	.012***
Gender (male = 1)	.097
Income (in tens of thousands USD$)	−.013

* p < .05   ** p < .01   *** p < .001

Source: 2016 American National Election Study (N = 1883)[3]

TABLE 6.5 Logistic regression coefficients predicting presidential vote choice by year and region, white voters without college degrees only (voters favoring third-party candidates excluded).

	South	Midwest	West	Northeast	U.S.
2012:					
• Anti-immigration scale	1.68***	1.90***	1.65***	2.31***	1.72***
• Activist government scale	-2.07***	-2.01***	-2.10***	-1.66***	-1.93***
• Restrictions on imports	.00	-.55*	-.15	.11	-.07
2016:					
• Anti-immigration scale	3.16***	3.22***	3.56***	3.22***	3.33***
• Activist government scale	-.99**	-.75*	-1.82***	-1.39***	-1.05***
• Restrictions on imports	.50*	.38	-.02	.87**	.35**
Difference:					
• Anti-immigration scale	1.48*	1.33[+]	1.90*	.91	1.61***
• Activist government scale	1.08*	1.25*	.28	.27	.88***
• Restrictions on imports	.50	.93**	.13	.76[+]	.42*

* p < .05   ** p < .01   *** p < .001 (two-tailed test)

graduates, who were only less visible in this respect because they were less likely (on average, in the aggregate) to share Trump's biases.

Later, when we extended the analysis to compare 2016 to 2012, we found that two attitudes in particular had increased in strength by statistically significant margins: bias against immigrants, and the wish to have an intolerant, domineering leader. Other biases were also influential, but they had not grown stronger in the intervening years.[4]

In Table 6.5, we find something similar when we examine the degree to which the preferences of less educated white voters evolved after 2012 with respect to three of Trump's signature themes (restrictions on immigrants and imports and support for government activism).

For present purposes, what this table shows us is threefold: that in the interval from 2012 to 2016 nativist opposition to immigration became much stronger than either support for government activism or trade protectionism among less educated white voters; that this sentiment was the only attitude that voters in all four of the regions shared; and, finally, that anti–immigrant sentiment was nearly uniform across all four regions, in strength, valence, and significance.[5]

The latter point raises a question. If voters in the South and Midwest were not unique in their nativist sentiments, what did they have in common? What did make them likelier to vote for Trump than white voters elsewhere? This returns us to the wish for a domineering leader. As we reported in "The Anger Games," we found that this wish – expressed as the wish for a strong leader who would "crush evil" and "get rid of the 'rotten apples' who are ruining everything" – was one of the most powerful attitude variables in the ANES.

118 David Norman Smith and Eric Hanley

Voicing that wish was strongly associated with a preference for Trump over his rivals, and it was most widespread among voters who called themselves his strong supporters.[6]

Mapping authoritarianism

In 2016, the wish for a domineering leader was strongest among white voters without college degrees. That wish was expressed by agreement with the ANES items which comprise what we call the Domineering Leader or DL scale. As Table 6.6 shows, the wish for a domineering leader was significantly stronger among less educated voters in every quartile than among college educated voters. The score for less educated voters at the midpoint of the range (7.5 out of 10) was double the score of college graduates at that same midpoint (3.7).

This vividly illustrates the dispersion of attitudes toward authority across educational lines. But not until we derive DL scores per region does the bigger picture come into focus. We see then that white Southern and Midwestern voters do have something in common – distinctively higher Domineering Leader scores. And those DL scores are higher in both regions not only for less educated voters but also for college graduates. Among white voters with some college or less, the regional difference here is statistically significant only for the contrast between the South (.343) and the West (.160). But among college graduates white voters in the South and Midwest differ markedly from their peers in the West and Northeast, and all of those differences are significant at the p < .001 level.

What we see here, in other words, is that white college graduates are an essential part of the 2016 story. The "white working class," so called, is not by itself the secret to Trump's success. Trump profited from the wish for an intolerant leader among college graduates as well as among less educated voters, especially in the South and Midwest.

The South and Midwest, in other words, are Donald Trump's heartland. White voters in these regions are likelier than average to wish for a domineering leader *whether or not* they hold college degrees. That clashes with the conventional wisdom about 2016 and raises fresh questions. Was Trump borne aloft on a flood tide of white working class support? Does he owe his election, as so many say, to "working class populism"?

TABLE 6.6 Dispersion of attitudes toward leaders by education, white voters only (N=1883). High scores, on a 1–10 scale, indicate stronger support.

	Some college or less			BA degree or higher		
Percentiles	25th	50th	75th	25th	50th	75th
DL scores (1=low, 10=high)	5.0	7.5	8.7	1.2	3.7	7.5
Number of cases		975			908	

The heart of whiteness **119**

TABLE 6.7 Percentages of white voters favoring the Republican presidential candidates in 2012 and 2016 by education.

White voters	2012	2016
• Some college or less	58.6	61.4
• BA degree or higher	50.0	42.4
Range	8.6	19.0

Further evidence bearing on these questions appears in Table 6.7. What we see here is that, though Trump did outstrip Romney by 2.8 points among less educated white voters, that gain was exceeded by a 7.6-point decline in voting among college graduates. In other words, the widening diploma divide – rising to 19.0 points from just 8.6 points four years earlier – was largely the result of disaffection among college graduates. Also, as we see in Table 6.8 below, the divide between less educated and college educated voters was smaller with respect to Domineering Leader attitudes in the Midwest (.221) than in any of the other three regions.

This loss of support among college educated voters is not quite as dramatic as it might seem, since, as we saw above, the absolute number of less educated white voters exceeds the number of white college graduates. Hence a 2.8 point increase among less educated voters is larger than it would have been for college graduates, and a 7.6 point decline among college graduates is not as large as it would have been for less educated voters. But that decline is still remarkably large – and it would have hurt Trump very badly, if millions of Obama voters had not stayed home on election day.[7]

The divided Midwest

In many respects, white voters in the Midwest resemble their peers in the South. Unlike white voters elsewhere, they were solidly pro-Trump in 2016. In striking contrast to their Northeastern counterparts, whose support for the GOP presidential ticket sagged when Trump became the nominee, less educated white voters in the Midwest and South favored Trump over Romney by 12.8% and 10.5%, respectively; and even white college graduates in the South and Midwest remained faithful to the GOP ticket. Southern and Midwestern voters also

TABLE 6.8 Mean DL values by region and education, 2016, white voters only (N=1883).

	All	Some college or less	BA degree or higher	Difference
South	.243	.343	.021	.322***
Midwest	.177	.246	.025	.221***
West	–.009	.160	–.264	.424***
Northeast	.015	.205	–.259	.464***

$\star$ p < .05 $\star\star$ p < .01 $\star\star\star$ p < .001 (two-tailed test)

120 David Norman Smith and Eric Hanley

showed exceptional levels of enthusiasm for the prospect of an authoritarian leader who would "crush evil" and get rid of "rotten apples."[8] For college graduates, that preference was out of step with the preferences of their peers elsewhere.

Why then is the Midwest so divided? Considering its electoral centrality, the region has been surprising little studied by political scientists.[9] But some observations seem pertinent. The Midwest is whiter than the South, and it has a higher proportion of white voters without college degrees – and yet, while the South is solidly Republican, the Midwest remains a battleground. Earl Black and Merle Black (2007, p. 157), in their book on the 2004 election, called the Midwest "the hardest American region to nail down." Frank Munger (1966), 40 years earlier, had called the Midwest "a puzzle; ... the most difficult [region] to define and to characterize." But one fact has long been obvious. As early as 1908, Frederick Jackson Turner called the "middle region ... a buffer area, a fighting ground." A century later, Black and Black (2007) echoed that remark: "The divided Midwest is America's swing region. ... It is the most volatile, evenly balanced, and reliably competitive geographical area" in the country. Each of the major parties won 39% of the Midwestern vote in 2004, and the gap dividing them was under 5% in six states, including Wisconsin, Michigan, and Ohio. The GOP's biggest problem in the Midwest, they conclude, is "relatively weak support from white voters" (Black and Black 2007).

Why have white voters been less reliably Republican in the Midwest than in the South? A partial answer to that question emerges from Table 6.9, which shows the results of a granular look at the regional voting habits of white voters who scored either high or low on the Domineering Leader scale in the 2016 American National Election Study.

What we see here is twofold: on the one hand, the South and Midwest continue to stand apart from the other regions. Southern and Midwestern white voters were much likelier than white voters elsewhere to score high on the wish for a domineering leader in 2016. But at the same time, a major difference appears when we ask whether those high scorers also voted for Donald Trump. The answer is that high scorers in the South stood alone in their pro-Trump ardor. High scorers in the Midwest were 14.5% less likely to vote for him – a gap that was nearly twice the size of the gap that separated them from high scorers in the Northeast. A related pattern appears when we examine low scorers. We find,

TABLE 6.9 Percentages scoring high (>0) on the Domineering Leader (DL) scale by region, education, and percentages voting for Trump, 2016, white voters only.

	% high on DL	% of high DL scorers voting for Trump	% of low DL scorers voting for Trump	Difference
South	63.6	92.3	39.2	53.1★★★
Midwest	58.0	77.8	28.0	49.8★★★
West	44.3	80.7	20.5	60.2★★★
Northeast	40.5	70.3	22.2	48.1★★★

again, that the South stands alone. Nearly two-fifths of Southern *low* scorers supported Trump – a fact worthy of investigation in its own right.

We know in aggregate, from our analysis of 17 variables in "The Anger Games," that the wish for a domineering leader was strongly predictive of Trump support. But we now know that this wish differed in its effects from one region to the next. That does not alter the underlying point – that, all else being equal, wishing for an authoritarian leader was far more common among Trump voters than among other white voters in 2016. But regional differences complicate that discovery. Can we account for those differences?

Andrew Jackson's America

In their new book, Darmofal and Strickler (2019, p. 130) report a striking finding – that "support for Andrew Jackson in a county in 1828 was significantly associated ... with support for Donald Trump in the [same] county 188 years later." While the correlation coefficient for this association is fairly modest (just .270), the association is nonetheless highly significant (p < .001). And a series of other facts attest to its robustness. In counties that Jackson won by 82% or more, Trump's victory margin was 43.3%. In other pro-Jackson counties, which made up 90% of the total, Trump's margin of victory was 17% lower. The difference between those outcomes was significant at the p < .001 level. In counties that Jackson won by at least 60%, Trump won by 37%, which was 11.9% above his margin in the remaining three-fourths of pro-Jackson counties. That difference in Trump's victory margins also proved to be significant at the p < .001 level.

For insight into what this finding might mean, Darmofal and Strickler steer us to Walter Russell Mead (2001), whose accounts of a very Trump-like Jackson, and the tradition he personifies, date back to the last century. Mead is unstinting in his praise for Jackson, whom he regards as one of "the greatest of American presidents," and he is almost as positive about the Jacksonian "folk community" which, in his estimation, remains at the heart of the American electorate (Mead 2001, p. 223, pp. 226f.). Though he concedes "the deeply regrettable Jacksonian record of racism," Mead does not hesitate to extol features of Jacksonian America which, he cheerfully admits, "right-thinking" liberals abhor (Mead 2001, p. 260, p. 229). Jacksonians draw an "absolute and even brutal distinction" between insiders and outsiders (Mead 2001, p. 236). They have no qualms about the use of lethal violence (legal or extralegal, with or without harm to bystanders, on just about any scale) which would serve their interests or satisfy their moral impulses.

Well into the 20th century, Mead says, the Jacksonian folk community was ethnically bounded. He treats Hiram Wesley Evans, the Imperial Wizard of the Ku Klux Klan, as a representative Jacksonian figure in the 1920s, and he includes George Wallace and Pat Buchanan among latter-day Jacksonians (Mead 2001, pp. 228–230). But over time, the concept of the "folk" who belong to the folk community has democratized. Mead even attempts, awkwardly, to claim Martin Luther King, Jr. for Jacksonian America, on the ground that, though

King espoused a pacifism antithetical to Jacksonian values and "elicited bloody and violent resistance from Jacksonian America," he nonetheless "touched it as well" (Mead 2001, p. 237). The happy result is that most "northern and southern Jacksonian opinion is steadily, if not always rapidly," moving towards tolerance for anyone who abides by the Jacksonian "honor code" (Mead 2001, p. 237, pp. 231f.). That code may have changed little since Andrew Jackson's time, but it is no longer the private property, the monopoly, of "old stock Americans" (Mead 2001, p. 228).

Where do we find Jackson's America today? Not, evidently, in every region: "It is more strongly entrenched in the heartland than in either of the two coasts. It has been historically associated with white Protestant males of the lower and middle classes, the least fashionable element in the American political mix" (Mead 2001, p. 244). But fashions come and go, and Jackson's America is not passé. Writing at the turn of this century, Mead said that, "Jacksonian America produced, and looks likely to continue to produce, one political leader or movement after another. … The Jacksonian hero dares to say what the people feel and defies the entrenched elites" (Mead 2001, p. 226). That daring, that defiance, enables the latter-day hero to "tap into … the populist energy that Old Hickory rode into the White House" (Mead 2001, p. 230).

In January 2016, Mead found Andrew Jackson's undead "revenant" in the mortal form of Donald J. Trump.

> It is Jacksonians who most resent illegal immigration, don't want to subsidize the urban poor, support aggressive policing and long prison sentences for violent offenders, and who are the slowest to 'evolve' on issues like gay marriage …. Trump, for now, is serving as a kind of blank screen on which Jacksonians project their hopes. (Mead 2016)

Branding himself as an indomitable winner "who 'gets' America but is above party, Trump appeals to Jacksonian ideas about leadership" (Mead 2016).

Those undead Jacksonian ideas about leadership are not far from what we have characterized as the wish for a domineering leader – and they are found in purest form, Mead affirms, in "the heartland." But he would probably be reluctant to call this wish intolerant: "as folk cultures go, Jacksonian American is actually open and liberal" (Mead 2001, p. 260).

Where does the truth lie? A few final reflections will address that question.

Andrew Jackson's heartland

Mead's clear implication is that Jacksonian America has a core and a periphery. The core is the "heartland," which is effectively a romantic nickname for small town and rural America – that is, the Midwest, the Plains, the peri-agrarian South. The periphery is urban America, whether that is found on the coasts or in the interior, in "flyover country." This dichotomy is a stereotype, but it also

The heart of whiteness **123**

contains elements of truth. Rural and suburban areas clearly do stand opposed to urban America in some major respects. But the reason, we learn from recent research by sociologists at Iowa State University, has less to do with rurality *per se* or with economic disadvantage than with ethnicity and education. Careful analysis of data for the whole Midwestern census region yields the finding that rural and semi-rural areas are most likely to back Trump when they are densely populated by white voters and, especially, by white voters without college degrees. Income and poverty also have relevant effects but, typically, the Midwestern counties that flipped from Obama to Trump were "high income counties with growing job opportunities and high levels of employment," not enclaves of "workers left behind by globalization" (Krier, Oberhauser, and Kusow 2019; see also Oberhauser, Krier, and Kusow 2019).

The strength of Mead's notion of Jacksonian America, once we get past his apologetic intent, lies in his emphasis on culture. The Midwest is culturally, regionally distinct. Like every other region it is a patchwork of norms, habits, and ideas inherited from the past. Those norms change, but they also have inertial powers. Change can be slow. Counties that voted for Jackson in 1828 and Trump nearly two centuries later are, in a sense, messengers from the Middle American past. But when we examine that past closely, what we find is not simply Jacksonian. The Midwest is divided, a battleground, because it embodies contradictory tendencies. We have shown that the authoritarian wish for a domineering leader is strong and widespread in the Midwest. That is the Jacksonian side of the coin. But democratic and inclusive sentiments are also indelibly Midwestern. Here, uniquely, racial prejudice and tolerance balance in a kind of equipoise. The South tilts red, the coasts tilt blue. Divisions run deep there, too. But only in the Midwest is division a defining, existential trait.

Historically, the decade leading up to the Civil War was the point of origin for today's divisions. An astute contemporary observed, in 1861, that the Midwest – then called "the Northwest" and now known by historians as "the Old Northwest" – had been reliably pro-Southern until the 1850s. But in that decade, lured by land grants issued to the railroads for distribution among homesteaders, a flood of Yankee and German immigrants arrived, most of whom opposed slavery.

> It did not escape the slaveholders that a new power had arisen, the Northwest, whose population, having almost doubled between 1850 and 1860, was already pretty well equal to the white population of the slave states – a power that was not inclined either by tradition, temperament or mode of life to let itself be dragged from compromise to compromise. (Marx 1861, p. 42)

The Northwest had indeed become a power to be reckoned with. In 1860, the seven states of Indiana, Illinois, Iowa, Michigan, Minnesota, Ohio, and Wisconsin had a population of 7,773,820, which was just fractionally smaller than the white

124 David Norman Smith and Eric Hanley

population of the Southern slave states (8,036,940). That demographic shift was reflected in politics as well. Conflict over Kansas, Karl Marx wrote,

> called the Republican Party into being ... The Republican Party put forward its first platform for the presidential election in 1856. Although its candidate, John Frémont, was not victorious, the huge number of votes that were cast for him ... proved the rapid growth of the Party, particularly in the Northwest. (Marx 1861, p. 39)

Frémont, who was famously unsympathetic to slavery, received 41.7% of his total vote from Ohio, Michigan, Indiana, Illinois, Iowa, Wisconsin, and Iowa.

Subsequently, during the Civil War, divisions in the Old Northwest became increasingly marked. Unrepentant Democrats, many of whom had migrated from the South, became dissenting "Copperheads" who campaigned against slave emancipation (Voegeli 1963). From that point forward, the divisions in the region were not only obvious but remarkable for their stability. Before long, as Frederick Jackson Turner later noted, the Midwest was divided between a "Whig-Republican northern zone" occupied by "descendants of New England stock" and a prairie zone, marked "the persistence of feelings aroused by ... the Civil War" (Turner 1914, p. 593). To explore the political significance of this division, Turner developed maps showing county-level voting trends in Ohio, Indiana, and Illinois in four elections. What those maps showed, Shelley and Archer explain, was that most of the counties that Frémont carried in 1856 were also won by Republicans in 1868, 1888, and 1900, while counties carried by the Southern Democrat Buchanan in 1856 also voted for Democrats in 1868, 1888, and 1900 (Shelley and Archer 1989, p. 228). Key and Munger, who examined voting trends in Indiana from 1868 until 1952, found "an astonishing parallelism ... in the county-by-county division of party strength" (Key and Munger 1959, p. 283).

South by Midwest

What explains these astonishing patterns? Why has the Midwest oscillated so consistently between the South – which, in the period from Turner to Key, was still very much in thrall to Jim Crow – and the other regions? Part of the answer lies in the affinity between the South and some parts of the Midwest. A national county-by-county study of Trump's supporters in early 2016 showed a correlation of 0.61 with the presence of white voters with no more than high school diplomas. That was the single strongest predictor. But fifth on the list, above evangelical Christianity and problems in the sphere of labor force activity, was a county's history of voting for George Wallace in 1968. Counties with that profile, which correlated 0.47 with a preference for Donald Trump (Irwin and Katz 2016), are often found in the Midwest.

In 1964, looking for support outside the South, Wallace entered Democratic primaries in Wisconsin and Indiana, where he won 34% and 30% of the vote. In 1968, running as an independent, Wallace won 14% of the national vote, almost half of which came from outside the original 11 states of the Confederacy (Kliman 2017). United Auto Workers Local 326 in Michigan endorsed Wallace by a wide margin. "A secret poll conducted by the AFL-CIO in ... September 1968 discovered that one-third of union members supported Wallace" (Devinatz 2017, p. 234). Another poll showed that Wallace was highly popular among autoworkers in Illinois, and still another poll showed that Chicago steelworkers were also in Wallace's camp (Devinatz 2017, pp. 234–235). In 1972, Wallace entered 17 Democratic primaries, winning five (including the Michigan primary) while placing second in Wisconsin, Indiana, Pennsylvania, and three other states. In 1972, in other words, George Wallace either won or placed second in all three of the Midwestern states that flipped from Obama to Trump. He won Michigan with 51% of the vote while winning 22% of the Wisconsin vote and 21% of the Pennsylvania vote (Kliman 2017). That, it seems fair to conclude, is unlikely to have been a coincidence.

With these facts in mind, Andrew Kliman (2017) poses a reasonable question. "What were these voters enraged about? Globalization, neoliberalism, and financialization" – the usual suspects in attempts to explain the Trump vote – "had not yet arrived on the scene."

It would take us too far afield to explore this question in the depth it warrants.[10] But interestingly, F-scale scores in the American National Election Study in 1952 – the endpoint of the cycle of elections studied by Key and Munger – resembled what we saw 64 years later with Domineering Leader scores. In that earlier election, the South and the Midwest registered the highest F scores and the Midwest was separated by a gap from the two lower-scoring regions. But in 1952 the South had outscored the Midwest by a wide margin. In this century, in contrast, the Southern and Midwestern DL scores converged, while the gap between the Midwest and the two lower-scoring regions remained roughly the same as before.[11]

The F-scale, like the DL scale, was devised to tap authoritarian attitudes.[12] Attitudes of that kind now appear to have been relatively invariant over nearly seven decades, for each major region. The South and Midwest stand apart from the West and Northeast, now as before. That invariance, that regional consistency, seems relevant, at the very least, to the other continuities we have considered. If the Midwest is a cultural hybrid – half-Jacksonian, and half-egalitarian – it seems likely that this duality reflects tendencies inherited from the past, not simply conjunctural responses to current crises.

We have shown in the past that DL attitudes co-vary strongly and significantly with racial prejudice, homophobia, and the disposition to vote for Donald Trump. We now know that these attitudes vary regionally, while, it seems, remaining relatively stable over time. We look forward to future studies, in the hope that they will test these points more definitively.

Appendix: How we define the regions

Since the ANES has no standard regional taxonomy, we emulated the approach taken by Black and Black in their analysis of the 2000 and 2004 elections.[13] We then altered that map to make the states in the region conform more closely to the results in 2016. That yielded the following breakdown:[14]

1. **Midwest**: Illinois, Indiana, Iowa, Michigan, Minnesota, Ohio, Wisconsin, Pennsylvania;[15]
2. **South**: Alabama, Arkansas, Florida, Georgia, Kentucky, Louisiana, Mississippi, Missouri, North Carolina, South Carolina, Tennessee, Texas, Virginia, West Virginia;
3. **Northeast**: Connecticut, Delaware, District of Columbia Maine, Maryland, Massachusetts, New Hampshire, New Jersey, New York, Rhode Island, Vermont;
4. **West**: Arizona, California, Colorado, Nevada, New Mexico, Oregon, Washington.

Notes

1 That phrase in conventional usage normally refers to non-Hispanic white voters without four-year college degrees. Though, as explained elsewhere (Smith 2021), we find this usage problematic, we too want to understand that population, which we will often designate with various shorthand phrases, such as "less educated white voters."

2 For a nuanced account of the significance of recent Midwestern trends, see Hopkins (2017) – The effects of local geographic polarization in the Midwest. In *Red Fighting Blue*, p. 208ff. Griffin, Teixeira, and Halpin report similar figures for the key states that flipped to Trump in 2016. In Michigan, white voters were divided between the less educated (54%) and degree holders (28%); in Pennsylvania the figures were 54% and 30%; and in Wisconsin the split was a bit narrower, 47% to 39% (2017b, pp. 7-10).

3 More complete regression data for this table in particular (with standard errors, constants, and pseudo-r square figures) appear at http://criticalsociology.org/the-anger-games-who-voted-for-donald-trump-in-the-2016-election-and-why/

4 A fuller account of this finding will appear in David Smith, "Nativism, populism, and the white working class," *Critical Sociology*, 2021, forthcoming.

5 Further information about this finding, bringing to bear details about a range of other coefficients (age, gender, and income), is available in Eric Hanley's 2019 manuscript, *Racial Backlash or Economic Nationalism*.

6 The pair of items that measure this attitude were first included by the American National Election Study (at our suggestion) in the 2013 internet follow-up to the 2012 survey. Both were drawn from scales which Bob Altemeyer had devised many years before. For details, see again Smith and Hanley (2018).

7 Philip Bump says that 4.4 million Obama voters did not vote in 2016 – "What we're talking about when we talk about the white working class in the Midwest," *Washington Post*, May 20, 2019. Griffin, Teixeira, and Halpin (2017b, p. 19) report that Clinton lost college graduates in Michigan by two points, 46% to 48%.

8 The 2018 ANES pilot study included the following item, which resembles our DL items: "Having a strong leader in government is good for the United States even if the leader bends the rules to get things done." Analysis of the responses shows that Midwestern Republicans had the highest mean score on this item and that the gulf between Midwestern Republicans and Democrats exceeded that in any other region. We owe this point to Dr. Brock Ternes.

9 The ANES Bibliography 2010–2019 lists over a thousand publications reporting ANES results but not one includes the words "Midwest," "heartland," or even "battleground" in its title – or Iowa, Michigan, Wisconsin, Ohio, or Pennsylvania. In contrast, the words "South" and "Southern" occur 18 times. https://electionstudies.org/project/bibliography_2010-2019/

10 One of the many pertinent issues that deserve further consideration is the degree to which the nation as a whole can be said to have been "Southernized" in recent decades. That issue is addressed well by Bateman, Katznelson, and Lapinski (2018) and Adorf (2016).

11 Further details about these findings will appear in a paper on the 1952 survey by Smith and Altamura, forthcoming. Most immediately relevant, here, is the fact that the marked differences between the high F and low F regions are statistically significant, while the difference between the South and Midwest is insignificant.

12 The F-scale first appeared in 1950 in Adorno et al., *The Authoritarian Personality*. Designed to capture "prefascist tendencies," the F-scale appeared in many studies in the ensuing decade, including the 1952 and 1956 Election Studies. Preliminary analysis shows a meaningful correlation between the F and DL scales.

13 https://adriankavanaghelections.org/2017/01/06/the-geography-of-the-2016-usa-presidential-election/

14 Given sample size limitations we omitted Hawaii and included, from the Mountain-Plains region, only Nevada, Arizona, Colorado, and New Mexico.

15 We moved Pennsylvania from the Northeast to the Midwest on the grounds that it was demographically similar and that it broke toward Trump in a manner that was typical of many of the Midwestern states.

References

Abramowitz, A. 2018. *The Great Alignment: Race, Party Transformation, and the Rise of Donald Trump*. New Haven & London: Yale University Press.

Abramowitz, A., and S. Webster. 2018. Negative partisanship: Why Americans dislike parties but behave like rabid partisans. *Advances in Political Psychology* 39 (Supplement 1): 119–135.

Adorf, P. 2016. *How the South Was Won and the Nation Lost: The Roots and Repercussions of the Republican Party's Southernization and Evangelicalization*. Bonn: Bonn University Press.

Adorno, T., E. Frenkel-Brunswik, R.N. Sanford, and D. Levinson. 1950. *The Authoritarian Personality*. New York: Harper & Bros.

Aldrich, J., J. Carson, B. Gomez, and D. Rohde. 2019. *Change and Continuity in the 2016 Elections*. Thousand Oaks, CA: Sage Publishers.

Bateman, D., I. Katznelson, and J.S. Lapinski. 2018. *Southern Nation: Congress and White Supremacy after Reconstruction*. Princeton and Oxford: Princeton University Press.

Black, E., and M. Black. 2007. *Divided America: The Ferocious Power Struggle in American Politics*. New York: Simon & Schuster.

Buchanan, P. 2016. Nationalism and populism propel Trump. *Real Clear Politics* (Feb. 23).

Bump, P. 2019. What we're talking about when we talk about the white working class in the Midwest. *Washington Post* (May 20). www.washingtonpost.com/politics/2019/05/20/what-were-talking-about-when-we-talk-about-white-working-class-midwest/

Darmofal, D., and R. Strickler. 2019. *Demography, Politics, and Partisan Polarization in the United States, 1828–2016*. New York: Springer.

Devinatz, V. 2017. Donald Trump, George Wallace, and the white working class. *Labor Studies Journal* 42(3): 233–238.

Griffin, R., R. Teixeira, and J. Halpin. 2017a. Democrats need to be the party of and for working people – of all races. *American Prospect* (June 1) https://prospect.org/article/democrats-need-be-party-and-working-people—-all-races

Griffin, R., R. Teixeira, and J. Halpin. 2017b. *Voter Trends in 2016: A Final Examination.* Center for American Progress. November. www.americanprogress.org/issues/democracy/reports/2017/11/01/441926/voter-trends-in-2016/

Hanley, E. 2019. *Racial Backlash or Economic Nationalism? Support for Trump among White Americans.* Unpublished manuscript.

Harris, A. 2018. America is divided by education. *The Atlantic* (Nov. 7). www.theatlantic.com/education/archive/2018/11/education-gap-explains-american-politics/575113/

Helderman, R., and J. Cohen. 2012. As Republican convention emphasizes diversity, racial incidents intrude. *Washington Post* (Aug. 29). www.washingtonpost.com/politics/as-republican-convention-emphasizes-diversity-racial-incidentsintrude/2012/08/29/b9023a52-f1ec-11e1-892d-bc92fee603a7_story.html

Hopkins, D. 2017. *Red Fighting Blue: How Geography and Electoral Rules Polarize American Politics.* New York: Cambridge University Press.

Irwin, N., and J. Katz. 2016. The geography of Trumpism. *New York Times* (March 12). www.nytimes.com/2016/03/13/upshot/the-geography-of-trumpism.html

Key, V.O., and F. Munger. 1959. Social determinism and electoral decision: The case of Indiana. In E. Burdick and A. Brodbeck (eds.) *American Voting Behavior.* Glencoe, IL: Praeger.

Kliman, A. 2017. *Combatting White Nationalism.* www.researchgate.net/publication/320237973_Combatting_White_Nationalism_Lessons_from_Marx

Krier, D., A. Oberhauser, and A. Kusow. 2019. *Political Sociology and Place: Shifting Patterns in the American Heartland.* Paper presented at the annual meeting of the Midwest Sociological Society.

Marx, K. 1861. The North American Civil War. *Die Presse,* October 25. Reprinted in Karl Marx and Frederick Engels. 1984. *Collected Works, Vol. 19.* New York: International.

Mead, W.R. 2001. *Special Providence: American Foreign Policy and How It Changed the World.* New York: Routledge.

Mead, W.R. 2016. Andrew Jackson, Revenant. *The American Interest* (Jan. 17). www.the-american-interest.com/2016/01/17/andrew-jackson-revenant/

Munger, F. 1966. The Midwest. In F. Munger (ed.) *American State Politics.* New York: Crowell.

Oberhauser, A., D. Krier, and A. Kusow. 2019. Political moderation and polarization in the Heartland: Economics, rurality, and social identity in the 2016 U.S. presidential election. *Sociological Quarterly* 60(2): 224–244.

Shelley, F., and J. Archer. 1989. Sectionalism and presidential politics: Voting patterns in Illinois, Indiana, and Ohio. *Journal of Interdisciplinary History* 20(2): 227–255.

Shelley, F., J. Heppen, and R. Morrill. 2018. Results of the 2016 presidential election at the state and county levels. In R. Watrel, R. Weichelt, F. Davidson, J. Heppen, E. Fouberg, J. Archer, R. Morrill, F Shelley, and K. Martis (eds.) *Atlas of the 2016 Elections.* pp. 58–75. Lanham, MD: Rowman & Littlefield.

Smith, D.N., and E. Hanley. 2018. The anger games: Who voted for Donald Trump in the 2016 election, and why? *Critical Sociology* 44: 195–212.

Smith, D.N. 2021. Nativism, populism, and the white working class. *Critical Sociology* 45, forthcoming.

Turner, F.J. 1908. Is sectionalism in America dying away? *American Journal of Sociology* 13(5): 661–675.

Turner, F.J. 1914. Geographical influences in American political history. *Bulletin of the American Geographical Society* 46(8): 591–595.

Voegeli, J. 1963. The Northwest and the race issue, 1861–1862. *Mississippi Valley Historical Review* 50(2): 235–251.

Zitner, A., and D. Chinni. 2016. Voters' education level a driving force. *Wall Street Journal* (Oct. 14). www.wsj.com/articles/voters-education-level-a-driving-force-this-election-1476401440

7

POSTFASCIST (SUB)URBANISM

"Social cleansing" in the age of Trump

Scott Markley and Coleman Allums

On June 16, 2015, real estate magnate and reality television personality Donald Trump announced his candidacy for president of the United States. At the campaign launch, Trump set the tone for the rest of his unusual run, proclaiming, "The US has become a dumping ground for everybody else's problems." He continued:

> When Mexico sends its people, they're not sending their best. They're not sending you …They're sending people that have lots of problems … They're bringing drugs. They're bringing crime. They're rapists. And some, I assume, are good people. (*Washington Post* 2015)

Such outward contempt for immigrants was atypical for presidential politics, as it violated the norms of colorblindness that had long governed mainstream discourses. Trump's disregard for this convention in addition to his bombastic and inflammatory style earned him dismissive ridicule from observers the world over. His reactionary campaign was roundly derided as unserious, uncouth, and unlikely to result in much of anything, especially as "alt-right" and white identity groups started publicly arraying around him. Eighteen months later, Donald Trump took the oath of office.

Throughout Trump's campaign, Democrats and self-styled Never-Trump Republicans (many of whom have since returned to the fold) cast Trump as an historically aberrative candidate. Nearing the end of Trump's first term, this conclusion remains dominant among a broad swath of liberal political actors and mainstream journalists. The nativist populism of Trump and his high-profile supporters – distilled in such slogans as *America First* and *Make America Great Again* – has been characterized in the media as opposed to neoliberalism, an enemy of liberal democracy, and un-American (Gopnik 2016; Seidelman and Watkins 2019; Wolffe 2018).

Our argument in this chapter is that Trumpism is a uniquely American phenomenon that represents not a coarse rupture with an otherwise sedate, liberal political tradition. Rather, we contend, the reactionary backlash politics embodied by Trump – succinctly described by Enzo Traverso (2019) as Trumpian "postfascism" – emerge from and respond to a specific set of historical conditions structured by decades of neoliberal hegemony. This argument implies that the Trumpian postfascism observed at the national level manifests at other scales as well. At the local level, we argue, it precedes Trump and is realized in increased displacement and surveillance of racially marginalized residents, who are discursively constructed as interloping scapegoats for local crises of neoliberal capitalism and whose removal is positioned as a step toward reclaiming a mythic, prosperous past. In the prescient words of Neil Smith (2001), postfascist policy manifests locally as a "social cleansing strategy."

In the following section, we pursue an account of white anxiety as foundational to the reactionary politics of our contemporary conjuncture. We demonstrate how property, as an incubator of racialized material advantage, is a central vector for the post-crisis inflammation of white nationalist anxiety which feeds a postfascist turn in local politics. Next, we argue that this reactionary localism constitutes a multi-scalar, revanchist counterrevolution of whiteness which, in its "accidental" (Lennard 2019; Virilio 1999) development, emerges from and sublates the neoliberal urbanism of prior decades. Finally, we analyze recent events of displacement and surveillance in Marietta, Georgia – a northern suburb of Atlanta – to show how postfascist localism functions as a stabilizing project of racial expulsion at the suburban scale and works in relation to broader geographies of postfascism of which Trumpism is both symptomatic and constitutive.

A counterrevolution of whiteness

Trump's ascent would seem to signal a decisive break from colorblind neoliberal hegemony. However, a growing body of work from critical scholars contends that this break is not so clean. For instance, Lennard (2019, p. 3), building upon the formula developed by the late theorist Paul Virilio (1999), maintains that Trumpian fascism is not distinct from neoliberalism. It is, rather, an *accident* of neoliberalism that was "baked into" liberal capitalism. Virilio (1999, p. 89) summarizes the broader concept in more visceral terms: "When you invent the ship, you also invent the shipwreck." Fascism, in this rendering, is a latent, parasitic germ, already residing within the body of liberalism.

Lennard's assessment is not so strange as it might appear at first blush. We see a parallel argument from the Frankfurt School (Marcuse 2009; Horkheimer and Adorno 2002), as they theorized 20th century European fascism as failure and sublation of Enlightenment reason and capitalist democracy. Similarly, focusing on the U.S., Inwood (2019) argues that despite the apparent rhetorical departure, "Trump's political playbook is time-worn politics in the US." To Inwood, the

Postfascist (sub)urbanism **131**

Trump phenomenon is but the most recent manifestation of the "white backlash" acting as a "counter-revolutionary bulwark against progressive and even radical change in the United States" (ibid.). As the eminent writings of many attest (e.g., Du Bois 1935; Gilmore 2002; Robinson 1983), this is nothing new. On the contrary, it is an essential feature of U.S. politics.

Whiteness acts as property (Harris 1993), and as such, whiteness is, or may be perceived to be, under threat from those who do not possess it. Hence, when nonwhites or other marginalized groups make material, social, and/or political gains, there is a widespread perception that these advances must come at the expense of whites (Inwood 2019). An interest in safeguarding the property of whiteness in the face of these perceived threats – from the Obama presidency to the groundswell of anti-racist, anti-capitalist, feminist, and LGBTQ movements to the growing visible presence of people of color in positions of cultural and political significance and in the neighborhood – mobilized Trump's base, as similar anxieties mobilized those of Reagan, Nixon, Wallace, and Goldwater. In this reading, Trump's brand of reactionary populism is consonant with conservatism writ large. As Corey Robin (2018, p. 56) writes:

> Conservativism really does speak to and for people who have lost something. It may be a landed estate or the privileges of white skin, the unquestioned authority of a husband or the untrammeled rights of a factory owner. The loss may be as material as money or as ethereal as a sense of standing. It may be a loss of something that was never legitimately owned in the first place; it may, when compared to what the conservative retains, be small. Even so, it is a loss, and nothing is ever so cherished as that which we no longer possess.

Moreover, the growth of these perceived threats to whiteness coincided with the so-called jobless recovery to the capitalist crisis that erupted in the late 2000s. Hence, in his incendiary rhetoric, Trump managed something that his opponent, Hillary Clinton, did not: he acknowledged a problem with the existing order. He did not, however, identify the problem's actual cause, neoliberal capitalism. Rather, he emphasized an already existing discursive link connecting the growing precarity with the racialized Other (Inwood 2019).

Trump and his allies portray Hispanic and Muslim populations as menacing foreigners who threaten not only national prosperity and safety but also, importantly, the existence of the U.S. nation itself. Nonwhite immigrants, they insist, represent an existential threat to U.S. culture, the West, and to the very concept of America – the claim is then repeated and recycled by Trump media allies like Tucker Carlson, Breitbart News, and countless radio and YouTube personalities (Inwood 2019; Maza 2017). The purported danger that continued immigration promised, in other words, is about *survival*, thus providing a ready-made justification for virtually any action or policy, so long as it was marshalled in the name of cultural, national, or racial preservation.

Here, it is impossible to ignore the parallels with past fascist movements. A bombastic paternal figure campaigning to revive a mythic white past while painting people of color as criminal threats to the upstanding, true (read "white") Americans would certainly seem to check many of the boxes (Stanley 2018). Yet many commentators are reticent to ascribe the fascist label to Trump or to other contemporary reactionary populist movements across the globe (Chotiner 2016). On one level, this is understandable. Fascism can be a deeply ambiguous concept, and there is a danger that it may add more confusion than clarity. What's more, several significant characteristics of this Trumpian rendition clearly separate it from its antecedents, especially its professed adoration of neoliberal mainstays like the free market and a limited state. Nevertheless, we maintain that continuing to kick this particular can down the road only muddies the waters in a moment when precisely naming and contesting the forces of reaction is more urgent than ever.

Postfascism: Scales of reaction and revanchism

Fascism, like all nameable political phenomena, articulates to a particular set of places and times. We thus recognize that there will always be tension when applying such a term to an emergent configuration. Rather than seeking to avoid the messiness that such transposition invariably produces, it is our intent to use this tension, to press the contradictions of fascism in the current moment. As Enzo Traverso (2019, p. 4) contends, "the concept of fascism seems both inappropriate and indispensable for grasping this new reality." He thus proposes the term "postfascism" to capture this 21st century version of reactionary populism that spans continents. This term, according to Traverso (2019, p. 4), emphasizes a "chronological distinctiveness" and implies, much like Virilio's concept of the accident and the dialectical account of the Frankfurt School, both "continuity and transformation." It also suggests "a phenomenon in transition," one that "has not yet crystallised" and that remains "heterogenous and composite" and that expresses itself differently across geographies (p. 6). While "postfascism" does not carry the same historiographical weight as "fascism," it does concisely capture this moment of reactionary backlash, a fascist-like response specific to the crises of neoliberalism.

Conceptualizing the Trumpian moment as a postfascist backlash to the neoliberal order crucially situates it within a longer historical trajectory. Robin (2018) and Inwood (2019) provide critically important temporal context for Trumpism, helping to demystify the moment amidst popular media accounts that have too often fixated on the grandiose personality of Trump the man. But this temporal context advances a further question: in what ways has this backlash manifested at scales other than the national? For if Trump is but an embodiment of a political development larger than himself, then it follows that this development should manifest in some form across spatial scales. Traverso and others have made headway on this point by emphasizing the global dimensions of postfascism. Situating

Trump/ism within this much more expansive, transnational network of reactionary populists provides critical spatial context. Examining the geographies of Trumpian backlash politics, like examining its history, is thus necessary for demystifying the moment.

While attention has been paid to postfascism's international reach, much less has been directed toward its subnational articulations. Ugo Rossi (2018, p. 1426) offers one important exception, positing the post-recession rise in anti-refugee, "ethnic-majority revanchism" in Italy's urban outskirts as a reactionary response to neoliberalism's urban housing crisis. Neoliberal cutbacks led to a real shortage in council-owned flats, especially after the late 2000s financial crisis. As refugees were flowing into Italy in large numbers after 2010, reactionary opportunists could blame the shortage on them. Italy's ultranationalist revival, Rossi shows, has therefore been deeply rooted in a politics of the local.

A similar dynamic has no doubt existed in the U.S. As urban scholars have long highlighted, the so-called New Right – which gained national prominence in the 1970s before cementing neoliberal hegemony at the federal level – built its political base from local backlash movements (Kruse 2005; Lassiter 2006; Inwood 2015). These movements coalesced in resistance to hyper-local phenomena like racial integration, school busing, affordable housing construction, municipal incorporation, and the like. New Right luminaries from Richard Nixon to Newt Gingrich signaled their support for these local causes by advocating for "states' rights" and "local autonomy" (Kruse 2005; Lassiter 2006). Ronald Reagan then expanded the tactic by strategically exploiting white localized fears about urban decline and white-to-Black neighborhood transition to build his coalition of white voters (Hackworth 2019). Trump, in his own way, followed suit. During the 2016 presidential debates, amid a period of historically low crime rates, he said, "Our inner cities are a disaster. You get shot walking to the store" (Covert 2016).

As Stanley (2018) argues, emphasizing the supposed contrast between cities as dens of crime and degeneracy and the countryside (or suburbs) as homes to the righteous and hard-working, "real" citizens is a long-standing rhetorical feature of fascist politics. Thus, a particular brand of discursive localism is inherent to (post)fascism and reactionary thought in general. But this is not the only role for the local. In the U.S., local displays of state-sanctioned xenophobia preceded the 2016 presidential election. Despite Trump's electoral victory, the most intransigent reactionaries still enjoy their most immediate and decisive legislative successes in state capitols and city halls rather than in Washington, D.C. Years before Trump announced his candidacy, for instance, states like Arizona, Alabama, and Georgia were working to further criminalize and encage unauthorized immigrants (Lacayo 2011). And municipalities across the country were using their local powers to defund immigrant resource centers, enforce English-only rules, restrict non-nuclear family cohabitation, crack down on day laborers, and pass other regressive policies targeting Hispanic and immigrant residents (Odem 2008; Vitiello 2014; Hanlon and

Vicino 2015; Markley 2018a; 2018b). Thus, as in Italy, the nativist backlash in the U.S. was largely forged in local fires.

There is another key way that Trumpian postfascism articulates with the local. If, following Lennard (2019), we theorize postfascism as an "accident" of neoliberal capitalism, we must also consider how postfascist urbanism emerges as an "accident" of neoliberal urbanism. Fortunately, an existing framework already makes this connection: Neil Smith's revanchist city thesis. Developed in the context of Rudy Giuliani's 1990s New York City, Smith's account (1996) posited revanchism as a violent, revengeful reaction by privileged groups against those they perceived to have stolen the city from them. Overlapping Robin's (2018) characterization of conservatism, Smith (1996, p. 211) explained that the "revanchist antiurbanism" represented, in part, "a desperate defense of a challenged phalanx of privileges, cloaked in the populist language of civic morality, family values and neighborhood security." Presaging Inwood's (2019) account of Trumpian postfascism, Smith continued:

> More than anything the revanchist city expresses a race/class/gender terror felt by middle- and ruling-class whites who are suddenly stuck in place by a ravaged property market, the threat and reality of unemployment, the decimation of social services, and the emergence of minority and immigrant groups, as well as women, as powerful urban actors. It portends a vicious reaction against minorities, the working class, homeless people, the unemployed, women, gays and lesbians, immigrants. (1996, p. 211)

Thus, according to Smith, a revanchist discourse was constructed to frame the urban decline and sense of insecurity wrought by decades of neoliberal policy as products of the "major enemies of public order and decency" (Smith 1998, p. 3). For Giuliani and his police chief, William Bratton, internal enemies were explicitly named in their ominously titled memorandum, "Police Strategy No. 5: Reclaiming the Public Spaces of New York." They included panhandlers, "squeegee cleaners," sex workers, drivers of "boombox cars," "reckless bicyclists," and graffiti artists (Giuliani and Bratton 1994, p. 4). This discursive separation between the supposedly decent, law-abiding folks from those who threaten them produced its own set of repressive solutions. These included broken windows policing and zero tolerance policies, which Smith (2001, p. 69) provocatively referred to as a "social cleansing strategy." Their goal was to physically remove the internal "threats" from public space.

It should be no surprise that, in the U.S., the revanchist hammer fell hardest on Black and Brown urban residents. As Gordon MacLeod (2002) suggests, the violent politics of revanchism is the sinister underbelly of neoliberal urbanism, one of its "accidents." The heightened inter-urban competition for investment, tourists, and wealthy residents necessitated by neoliberalism impels city boosters to manufacture an idealized image of their cities, which, MacLeod (2002, p. 254) argues, must "not [be] compromised by the visible presence of ... marginalized groups." Where urban decline is believed to be delivered to a place by racialized bodies who bring it with them, the objective becomes achieving a "purification of urban space" (p. 255) via removing those bodies. Identifying, expunging, and replacing the alleged "culprits of urban decline" (Smith 1998, p. 3) are precisely the revanchist aims. Thus, when understood as part of a racial project, revanchism in action can be read as a local version of white nationalist policy, a postfascist localism responding to the crises of neoliberal urbanism. Smith, however, restricts his use of "social cleansing" to specifically describe zero tolerance policies. We argue that the contemporary conjuncture warrants broadening this metaphor to include other state-led efforts that stigmatize and expel marginalized residents from the locality. To make this case, we turn to the suburbs of Atlanta.

Postfacist (sub)urbanism: Social cleansing in Marietta, Georgia

> "If you remove the blight, you quadruple your chances of something coming right. A good developer can buy land still in metropolitan Atlanta and not have to worry what to do with 400 families. We basically took that step out of it."
>
> Mayor of Marietta, Steve "Thunder" Tumlin (MDJ Staff 2015a)

On November 5, 2013, voters in the Atlanta suburb of Marietta narrowly passed a referendum to fund a $68 million redevelopment bond (MDJ Staff 2013a). Four million dollars would upgrade the streetscape on one of Marietta's major roads near its downtown. But the lion's share would go toward purchasing and demolishing a set of aging apartments along Franklin Road, a one-and-a-half mile strip tucked away in the city's southeastern corner (see Figure 7.1). The city wasted little time. By 2016, they had flattened 1,134 units across three complexes, displacing around 1,700 residents. Of those displaced, about 38% were Black and 51% were Hispanic (Markley 2018a).

The bond's most avid public support came from the incumbent Republican mayor, Steve "Thunder" Tumlin, a steadfast conservative. Another major endorsement came from former Republican U.S. Senator and Cobb County resident, Johnny Isakson (MDJ Staff 2013b). Behind the scenes, the biggest funder of the pro-redevelopment campaign – raising $14,000 (MDJ Staff 2013a) – was the organization, Vote Yes! Marietta (VYM). Its co-founders, Heath Garrett and Mitch Hunter, are each deeply involved in Georgia Republican politics. According to his profile on the website of the lobbying firm, GMHC360, Hunter served as chief of staff for conservative Congressman Phil Gingrey and worked closely with several other top Georgia Republican lawmakers (http://gmhc360.com). Garrett, the "G" in GMHC360, was chief of staff for Johnny Isakson for a decade before managing campaign strategies for other top state GOP officials, including Georgia's Trump-endorsed governor, Brian Kemp. Viewed through

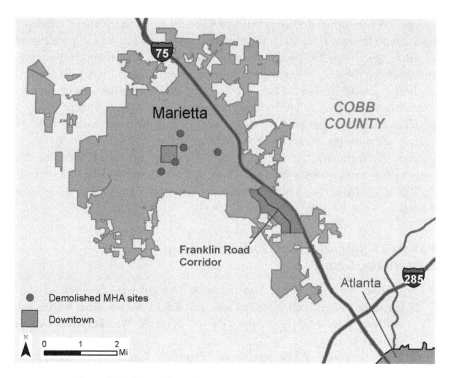

FIGURE 7.1 Map of Marietta, Georgia.
Source: Author.

the lens typical of conventional political discourses in the U.S., this would seem to be a conundrum. Conservatives, we are told, are supposed to be opposed to higher taxes and government intervention. But, as Robin (2018) reminds us, such an account is incomplete. Understood as part of a revanchist backlash to the localized crises of neoliberalism – a local manifestation of Trumpian reaction against loss – the apparent contradiction resolves itself.

At the time of the 2013 vote, city officials had no specific plans for the cleared lots. Rather, as the quote by Mayor Tumlin above suggests, they believed that bulldozing the apartments and expelling the tenants would make the area more attractive for private developers. Chillingly, they seem to have been correct. Since demolishing the apartments, razing a shopping center, repaving the streets and sidewalks, establishing a Community Improvement District (currently headed by seven white property owners), and changing the road's name to "Franklin Gateway," the area has received a new Hampton Inn and an Ikea, offices for Home Depot and WellStar, and a training complex for Major League Soccer's Atlanta United FC (Figure 7.2). In addition, rents in remaining multifamily units have reportedly skyrocketed, displacing others (*On Second Thought* 2015). Reversing a trend that had persisted since at least 1970, the number of white residents on Franklin Road increased by over 1,100 between the 2010 decennial

Postfascist (sub)urbanism 137

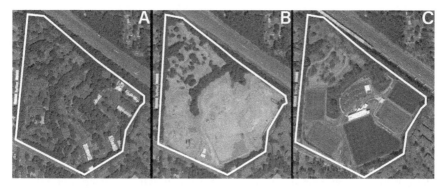

FIGURE 7.2 (A) Flagstone Village and Woodlands Park apartments, May 5, 2014. (B) After demolition, May 7, 2016. (C) Training complex for Atlanta United FC, March 31, 2017. Imagery from Google Earth. Marietta, GA. 33°56′06.14″N 84°29′54.72″W, Eye alt 4122 feet. Image Landsat/Copernicus. www.earth.google.com (February 18, 2018). Boundary added by first author.

census and the 2013–17 American Community Survey, while the number of Hispanic residents dropped by over 1,100 (Figure 7.3). "Social cleansing" would seem an apt characterization.

On the surface, the redevelopment efforts on Franklin Road appear as a pretty standard, if more outwardly callous, example of how an entrepreneurial local government might jump-start gentrification in one of its devalorized corridors. Indeed, many familiar tropes about the need for economic development and increasing property values appear in the statements made by the plan's

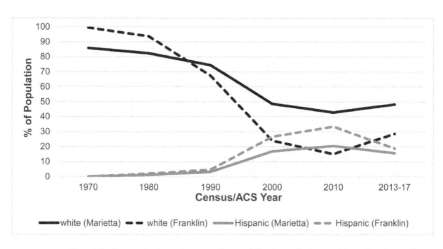

FIGURE 7.3 Racial change in Marietta and Franklin Road, 1970–2013/17. Data from Longitudinal Tract Database (Logan, Xu, Stults 2014) and American Community Survey (ACS).

Source: Author.

most ardent boosters. Upon closer inspection, however, it becomes apparent that these tropes are imbricated into a different sort of narrative, one that conveys deep-seated anxieties about racial change and community decline evocative of Trumpian postfascism. This narrative, which has been constructed primarily by the white and politically powerful supporters of redevelopment, tells a tidy, three-act story.

First, in line with fascist ideology more broadly (see Stanley 2018), the Marietta story romanticizes a mythic white past – the 1970s – when Franklin Road was a thriving spot for young white professionals. As Franklin became majority-minority by the 1990s, the story continues, it descended into an irredeemably dangerous warehouse for morally depraved criminals who threatened not only the upright, decent citizens of the city but the very existence of Marietta as a place. In its final act, redevelopment is recast as a palingenetic project that will not only remove Franklin's criminal element and boost the local economy but will also reclaim Franklin for its rightful occupants, restoring its golden age, and saving the city. Critically assessing this redemptive narrative arc as a hegemonic postfascist discourse requires a more careful reading of Marietta's local history.

During the mid-20th century, Marietta was transformed from a small southern town to a major node in a sprawling metropolis. In 1939, an internal survey revealed that the city had a population only slightly above 8,000 people, about 70% of whom were white and about 30% who were Black (Drummond, Green, and Buday 2014). Over the following three decades, the population tripled as the city received tens of thousands of jobs from a major warplane manufacturer and as Cobb County was swallowed by the burgeoning Atlanta behemoth. This economic and population boom was matched by a changing racial composition. Like many of the surrounding northern suburbs, Marietta became overwhelmingly white (86%) by 1970. However, that would soon change. Over the ensuing decades, Marietta's population continued to rise, but the white population share slumped back toward pre-boom levels, reaching 74% in 1990. Changes during the 1990s accelerated. There was an absolute decline of 4,000 white residents, while the Black population nearly doubled, and the Hispanic population grew by 600%. In 2000, whites comprised less than 50% of Marietta's population for the first time in its history.[1]

Marietta's changing racial character paralleled growing signs of financial distress. In 1970, Marietta's per capita income was about 96% of Cobb's. By 2000, it had dropped to 84%, and by 2010, 81%. This was matched by a consistent rise in the poverty rate, ballooning from 11% in 1970 to 15.7% in 2000 and 18.5% in 2015.[1] With Marietta in the throes of neoliberalism's unforgiving competition for investment, the situation was ripe for a vicious reaction against the alleged culprits of decline. Early indications of a revanchist backlash appeared in the 1990s when the Marietta Housing Authority (MHA) ramped up police patrols at their buildings, instituted a "one strike" policy for all MHA residents, and even built a concrete barricade to separate one of its complexes from neighboring homes (Drummond, Green, and Buday 2014). These drastic measures were purportedly adopted to deter crime; in the end, they helped ossify the image of Marietta's public housing as irredeemable dens of delinquency. This image no doubt came into play in 2003, when the MHA – citing budgetary concerns and persistent crime – began bulldozing its properties (Drummond, Green, and Buday 2014). By 2013, every one of MHA's 627 non-senior public housing units across five sites had been razed, and their prime lots had been subsequently sold to private, luxury developers (Markley 2018a). Most displaced residents – who were predominantly Black – were given Housing Choice Vouchers and scattered throughout the county. Those replacing them have been overwhelmingly white and much more affluent (Markley 2018b).

Demolishing public housing was the city's first major step toward gentrifying its town center. But public housing made up only a tiny fraction of Marietta's total housing stock. City leaders soon shifted their gaze toward Franklin Road, which, to some, represented the epicenter of Marietta's racial change and economic decline. While the housing stock along the corridor was entirely privately owned, Franklin's redevelopment followed a similar script to Marietta's destruction of its public housing. In 2006, Marietta officials implemented a five-year crime-fighting initiative along Franklin with the help of federal grant money. As part of the Department of Justice's "Weed and Seed" program, police surveillance and stops were increased, zero tolerance policies were enforced, and arrests for non-violent misdemeanors went up (Dobies 2010; Simmons 2010). Then, in circular fashion, Franklin's boosters used the reputation this program helped create to pursue apartment demolition. Invoking other racialized urban places, the VYM website warned:

> Is Franklin Road really that bad? YES! ... The Franklin Corridor qualified for a federal grant from the ATF and the FBI called Weed & Seed which is reserved for the most dangerous places in the country – inner city Chicago, L.A., New Orleans, etc... (Vote Yes! Marietta 2013)

Shortly before the bond referendum vote, Heath Garrett, the co-founder of VYM, embellished this line in the *Marietta Daily Journal*, saying, "The U.S. Department of Justice and *all the major federal law enforcement agencies* (!) have designated Franklin Road as one the highest concentrations of poverty and crime ... in all of Metro Atlanta" (emphasis added; MDJ Staff 2013a). He dubiously added that there were over 1,700 drug-related and violent crimes along Franklin over the previous three years, failing to mention that arrests had been inflated due to police sweeps and a zero tolerance policy implemented by the city (MDJ Staff 2013a). Even though the VYM website lists four main reasons to support the bond – to "reduce crime, encourage new business investment, improve schools, and increase property values" (Vote Yes! Marietta 2013) – crime is the fulcrum upon which the other three rotate. On its "Why Vote Yes?" page, VYM claims that Franklin's "high concentration of crime" has "driven employers and jobs out of the city" and "hindered the recruitment of new businesses." Further, VYM asserts, "Reducing crime in Marietta through revitalization of our most troubled corridor will benefit schools and increase property values" (Vote Yes! Marietta 2013).

The broad, postfascist revanchism of Marietta's response to neoliberal crises is condensed most succinctly in the words of one redevelopment advocate – Mary Southerland, owner of W.D. Little Mortgage Corporation – who urged support for the bond by stressing that the city needed redevelopment on Franklin Road "desperately" in order to "keep Marietta from dying on the vine and continuing to decline" (MDJ Staff 2013b). In this framing, the city's frustrations and anxieties have been displaced onto Franklin and, by extension, its predominantly Black and Hispanic residents. Franklin Road is located – spatially, culturally, politically – as the site of Marietta's infection, and the only solution can be to "remove the blight." Displacing Franklin's residents, then, is recast as a tough decision but one that nonetheless must be made for the good of the larger body:

> We see communities that are willing to admit they have problems and do something about those problems, and then we see communities that ignore problems and eventually suffer the loss of identity and the loss of economic activity and the loss of the middle class, and we saw that happening in Marietta. (Heath Garrett quoted in MDJ Staff 2013b)

Thus, amid apartment demolitions, Mayor Tumlin's wife fondly recalled the time she lived on Franklin in the 1970s. Contrasting it with the more recent Franklin Road, she remarked:

> It was a very nice area. Lots of nice single complexes. Very safe. And it was mostly young professionals. Everybody I lived around either worked in Atlanta or taught – (or were) nurses. It's just the way it was. You never thought about it not being safe because all the complexes were good. (MDJ Staff 2015a)

Her husband expressed similar sentiments when, in response to demolition, he exclaimed, "It's almost like a dream. It's almost like it's 1970 again" (MDJ Staff 2015b). Here: the racial myth, the criminal Other, the redemptive rise. The postfascist simulacrum rests, as it must, upon the accidents of neoliberalism.

Conclusion

Conventional narratives about US liberal democracy extol its supposedly inherent trajectory toward progress. The election of Donald Trump threw this comforting story into disarray. While many of U.S. liberalism's most committed adherents have attempted to rescue it by painting the 2016 presidential election as aberrant, critical observers have located the historical threads that prefigured Trump's ascent. The latter have convincingly shown that Trump is not an aberration but an embodiment of reaction to crisis and perceived loss. Trumpian postfascism, in other words, emerged as an "accident" specific to U.S. neoliberal capitalism.

As we aimed to demonstrate in our case study, Smith's theorization of revanchism has proven to be a prescient heuristic for distilling what lies at the heart of postfascism. Smith's (1998) pithy description of revanchism as a reaction against the perceived "culprits of urban decline" cogently captures the key relationship between postfascism's local and national expressions. Although postfascist ideology acknowledges there is a problem with the status quo, it misdiagnoses its causes, blaming perceived economic and/or cultural decline on a set of racialized Others. Since postfascism's adherents believe this decline to be embodied by these Others – a belief that emanates from the ontological co-constitution of race and value under racial capitalism – they have only one answer to neoliberalism's crises: social cleansing. On the national level, this is exemplified by nativist policies that ban Muslims and deport nonwhite immigrants. At the local level, revanchist policies that expel Black and Hispanic residents from the locality accomplish an analogous goal for municipalities undergoing their own racial transitions and economic hardships. Thus, for those of us who study cities, it may be useful to treat postfascism in (sub)urban space as more continuous than discrete vis-à-vis the recent hegemony of colorblind neoliberalism. The accidental shipwreck of reactionary localism is, after all, made possible only in the turbulent wake of the neoliberal ship.

Note

1 Figures estimated using National Historical GIS (Manson et al. 2018).

References

Chotiner, I. 2016. Is Donald Trump fascist? *Slate* (Feb. 10). https://slate.com/news-and-politics/2016/02/is-donald-trump-a-fascist-an-expert-on-fascism-weighs-in.html

Covert, B. 2016. Donald Trump's imaginary inner cities. *The Nation* (Nov. 7). www.thenation.com/article/donald-trumps-imaginary-inner-cities/

Dobies, K. 2010. Police: High-crime area patrol a success. *Marietta Daily Journal* (April 8). www.mdjonline.com/news/police-high-crime-area-patrol-a-success/article_1711e3c2-568a-5943-8664-b9fb2ad5bb8d.html

Drummond, L., G. Green, and R. Buday. 2014. *From Holland Town to the Renaissance on Henderson: A Social and Developmental History of the Marietta Housing Authority*. Marietta, GA: Marietta Housing Authority.

Du Bois, W.E.B. 1935/1992. *Black Reconstruction in America, 1860-1880*. New York: The Free Press.

Gilmore, R.W. 2002. Fatal couplings of power and difference: Notes on racism and geography. *Professional Geographer* 54(1): 15–24.

Giuliani, R., and W. Bratton. 1994. *Police Strategy No. 5: Reclaiming the Public Spaces of New York*. City of New York.

Gopnik, A. 2016. Why Trump is different – and must be repelled. *New Yorker* (Nov. 3). www.newyorker.com/culture/cultural-comment/why-trump-is-different-and-must-be-repelled

Hackworth, J. 2019. Urban crisis as conservative bonding capital. *City* 23(1). https://doi.org/10.1080/13604813.2019.1575116

Hanlon, B., and T. Vicino. 2015. Local immigration legislation in two suburbs: An examination of immigration policies in Farmers Branch, Texas and Carpentersville, Illinois. In K. Anacker (ed.) *The New American Suburb: Poverty, Race and the Economic Crisis*. pp. 113–133. Burlington, VT: Ashgate.

Harris, Cl. 1993. Whiteness as property. *Harvard Law Review* 106(8): 1707–1791.

Horkheimer, M., and T. Adorno. 2002. *Dialectic of Enlightenment: Philosophical Fragments*. G.S. Noerr (ed.) Trans. E. Jephcott. Stanford, CA: Stanford University Press.

Inwood, J. 2015. Neoliberal racism: The "Southern Strategy" and the expanding geographies of white supremacy. *Social and Cultural Geography* 16(4): 407–423.

Inwood, J. 2019. White supremacy, white counter-revolutionary politics, and the rise of Donald Trump. *Environment and Planning C* 37(4). https://doi.org/10.1177/2399654418789949

Kruse, K. 2005. *White Flight: Atlanta and the Making of Modern Conservatism*. Princeton: Princeton University Press.

Lacayo, A. 2011. *One Year Later: A Look at SB 1070 and Copycat Legislation*. Washington, D.C.: UnidosUS. http://publications.unidosus.org/bitstream/handle/123456789/666/A_look_at_SB_1070.pdf

Lassiter, M. 2006. *Suburban Politics in the Sunbelt South: The Silent Majority*. Princeton: Princeton University Press.

Lennard, N. 2019. *Being Numerous: Essays on Non-Fascist Life*. London: Verso Books.

Logan, J., Z. Xu, and B. Stults. 2014. Interpolating US decennial census tract data from as early as 1970 to 2010: A longitudinal tract database. *Professional Geographer* 66(3): 412–420.

MacLeod, G. 2002. From urban entrepreneurialism to a "revanchist city"? On the spatial injustices of Glasgow's renaissance. In N. Brenner and N. Theodore (eds.) *Spaces of Neoliberalism: Urban Restructuring in North American and Western Europe*. pp. 254–276. Malden, MA: Blackwell.

Manson, S., J. Schroeder, D. Van Riper, and S. Ruggles. 2018. *IPUMS National Historical Geographic Information System*: Version 13.0 [Database]. Minneapolis: University of Minnesota. http://doi.org/10.18128/D050.V13.0

Marcuse, H. 2009. *Negations: Essays in Critical Theory*. S. Bohm (ed.) Trans. J.J. Shapiro. London: MayFlyBooks.

Markley, S. 2018a. Suburban gentrification? Examining the geographies of New Urbanism in Atlanta's inner suburbs. *Urban Geography* 39(4): 606–630.

Markley, S. 2018b. New urbanism and race: An analysis of neighborhood racial change in suburban Atlanta. *Journal of Urban Affairs* 40(8): 1115–1131.

Maza, C. 2017. Why white supremacists love Tucker Carlson. *Vox* (July 21). www.vox.com/videos/2017/7/21/16008190/strikethrough-white-supremacists-love-tucker-carlson

MDJ Staff. 2013a. *Marietta Daily Journal* (Nov. 6). $68M redevelopment bond passes. www.mdjonline.com/news/m-redevelopment-bond-passes/article_ee8879d7-7d85-5807-bb0c-f5088be7f278.html

MDJ Staff. 2013b. *Marietta Daily Journal* (Sept. 17). Sen. Isakson endorses Franklin Road. www.mdjonline.com/news/sen-isakson-endorses-franklin-road-bond/article_974e036a-64f9-5d0c-8b8c-305b3eb1d783.html

MDJ Staff. 2015a. *Marietta Daily Journal* (June 28). Mayor: We're on schedule for success: Tumlin confident in Franklin Road redevelopment bond. www.mdjonline.com/news/mayor-we-re-on-schedule-for-success-tumlin-confident-in/article_3f75b84a-50a4-5276-8eaf-96d28bb96502.html

MDJ Staff. 2015b *Marietta Daily Journal* (June 6). Franklin falls, hopes rise as talks heat up. www.mdjonline.com/opinion/mdj_editorials/franklin-falls-hopes-rise-as-talks-heat-up/article_cafc61fc-bbb3-508f-a19f-8c0b8fbe3819.html

Odem, M. 2008. Unsettled in the suburbs: Latino immigrants and ethnic diversity in metro Atlanta. In A. Singer, S. Hardwick, and C. Brettel (eds.) *Twenty-First Century Gateways: Immigrant Incorporation in Suburban America*. pp. 105–136. Washington, D.C.: Brookings Institution Press.

On Second Thought. 2015. A gentrification battle brews in an Atlanta suburb. *Medium*. https://medium.com/on-second-thought/a-gentrification-battle-brews-in-an-atlanta-suburb-e3383a8aa028

Robin, C. 2018. *The Reactionary Mind: Conservatism from Edmund Burke to Donald Trump*. New York: Oxford University Press.

Robinson, C. 1983/2000. *Black Marxism: The Making of the Black Radical Tradition*. Chapel Hill, NC: University of North Carolina Press.

Rossi, U. 2018. The populist eruption and the urban question. *Urban Geography* 39(9): 1425–1430.

Seidelman, J., and J. Watkins. 2019. Commentary: Trump meant the end of neoliberalism. What comes next? *The Salt Lake Tribune* (May 25). www.sltrib.com/opinion/commentary/2019/05/26/commentary-trump-meant/

Simmons, A. 2010. Big efforts pay off: Franklin Road area revived. *Atlanta Journal-Constitution* (Aug. 11). www.ajc.com/news/local/big-efforts-pay-off-franklin-road-area-revived/DbGv5bam1WsQdmLJSB3KWL/

Smith, N. 1996. *The New Urban Frontier*. New York: Routledge.

Smith, N. 1998. Giuliani time: The revanchist 1990s. *Social Text* 57(Winter): 1–20.

Smith, N. 2001. Global social cleansing: Postliberal revanchism and the export of zero tolerance. *Social Justice* 28(3): 68–74.

Stanley, J. 2018. *How Fascism Works*. New York: Penguin Random House.

Traverso, E. 2019. *The New Faces of Fascism: Populism and the Far Right*. Brooklyn: Verso.

Virilio, P. 1999. *Politics of the Very Worst: An Interview by Philippe Petit*. New York: Semiotext(e).

Vitiello, D. 2014. The politics of immigration and suburban revitalization: Divergent responses in adjacent Pennsylvania towns. *Journal of Urban Affairs* 36(3): 519–533.

Vote Yes! Marietta. 2013. https://voteyesmarietta.wordpress.com/

Washington Post. 2015 (June 16). Donald Trump announces a presidential bid. www.washingtonpost.com/news/post-politics/wp/2015/06/16/full-text-donald-trump-announces-a-presidential-bid/

Wolffe, R. 2018. Donald Trump is the most un-American president in living memory. *The Guardian* (June 26). www.theguardian.com/commentisfree/2018/jun/26/donald-trump-immigration-most-un-american-president

8

THE FIVE PILLARS OF TRUMP'S WHITE ETHNONATIONALIST APPEAL

David H. Kaplan

Donald J. Trump began his presidential run as something of a marketing stunt, thinking his candidacy would enhance the quality of his brand. While not long a Republican, he stood out from a fairly strong crowd of Republican contenders in the primaries. He then triumphed in the Electoral College against Hillary Clinton, with big assists from WikiLeaks and an election-eve James Comey letter, even as many voters held their noses while casting their ballots.

In both contests, Trump added two elements to the standard Republican repertoire. The first was a more populist approach to issues like healthcare and social security. He appealed to those who believed the system had been unfair to them, indicting both big government and big business. Trump promised to maintain and even increase existing levels of government support to those disaffected and to root out the systemic corruption that was holding them back. The second element was a strongly racialized antagonism to immigration and diversity. Trump quickly sloughed off his populist positions, but he has doubled down on the anti-immigration/anti-diversity aspect of his appeal. He has twisted the more subtle "dog whistles" of previous Republican contenders into clarion calls of racism and xenophobia, grafting ethnonationalist thinking onto orthodox anti-government and socially conservative Republicanism.

The electoral geography of any political contest depicts the territorial bases of support for each candidate. Territory is particularly entrenched in the voting systems of the U.S. where we adopt a "first past the post" protocol for determining the winner of each electoral district (as opposed to other systems that use lists or proportional voting). The Electoral College turns the presidential election into a series of state-based contests where the goal is not to win the overall popular vote but to prevail in enough states to win a majority of electors. There have been two instances since 2000 where the winner of the overall popular vote did not win the Electoral College: George W. Bush vs. Al Gore and Donald Trump vs.

Hillary Clinton. In 2016, Trump won a majority of electors despite being three million votes behind Clinton in the popular vote.

Research has repeatedly demonstrated contextual effects to voting preference (Forest 2018). Just as political attitudes and candidate selection is related to gender, race, income, education, occupation, and other variables, so it is also related to where one lives. People talk to other people in a community. They see visible signs of candidate support in yard signs and bumper stickers. They listen to local radio and read local news. All of these signals can move opinion. People living in liberal areas are likely to have their liberalism reinforced and make conservatism harder to maintain. And the same is true for people living in conservative areas. Place also figures into attitudes towards immigrants, racial minorities, or other groups. In certain places, people may be less afraid to voice racist opinions or jokes, betting that they will not be shamed for these. More frequent articulation of these ideas spurs others to voice them as people now have "permission" to express what they view as anti-politically correct views. Social media has opened up dark corners where all manner of noxious opinions may be aired. But physical communities also provide some of this cover, reinforcing the importance of place.

This chapter examines the county-level geography of Donald Trump's support as it relates to various markers of ethnonationalism. Trump's appeal was uniquely suited to the nature of the Electoral College in 2016. We do not have a "white ethnonational" variable at our disposal but we do have some variables that correspond with white ethnonationalism and help track the geographical appeal of Trump.

The meaning of ethnonationalism

The phrase "white ethnonationalism" so often describes the basis of Trump's support that it can be tricky to know what it really signifies. This is particularly true since ethnonationalism is found throughout the world in one form or another, and has been a mainstay throughout history. Ethnonationalist appeals have festered during many periods, sometimes exploding into virulent political movements. While associated at times with fascism, it springs from separate ideological motivations. Fascism involves the exercise of political and economic power – it entails the "creation of a new nationalist authoritarian state" and "the organization of some new kind of regulated, multiclass, integrated national economic structure" (Payne 1980, p. 12). Ethnonationalism is tied to a nationalist political project. Since emerging in the 19th century, nationalism has become the key driver for state formation and consolidation (Eriksen 2002). Ethnonationalism is a particular variant of how the nation is perceived.

Nationalism relies on the conception of a shared community, even if that community is fictional. There must be something that binds together a group of strangers. Often characteristics like language, or religion, or a shared heritage apply but there are many instances, in fact most instances, in which a self-described nation includes members who do not easily fit into those boxes. When nations aspire to embody a political state, which after all is the entire rationale of nationalism, residents of a state's territory will be claimed as also belonging to the nation even if they differ in some particulars. This broader conception of a nation has been variously described as "civic" nationalism (Breton 1988) or "Western" nationalism (Hayes 1931). It conveys nationalism as a unifying force under circumstances where the given nation includes a diversity of cultures and religions.

The key factor involves where to draw the boundaries. The boundary of a nation consists of an internal boundary which is delineated by members of the group itself, and an external boundary determined by those outside the group (Royce 1982; Triandafyllidou 1998). Rarely do these boundaries coincide: people may feel membership within a nation that otherwise excludes them, or they may feel separate from a nation that otherwise claims them. Upon closer resolution, a national identity fractures into several national identities – identities which are emphasized by the members themselves or by the national state (Herb and Kaplan 2018). The German nation is comprised of diverse peoples, many of whom in other eras or in other circumstances would consider themselves to be a distinct nation in their own right. The development of the German state necessitated unification of the German nation, as disparate peoples were bound together (Johnson 2018). This messy process was somewhat successful but also left people behind. Most notoriously, the German state decided under the Nazi regime that certain Germans – most notably Jews and Gypsies – no longer belonged in the nation, propagating the horrors that followed.

The Nazi case is the extreme version of what happens when national identity excludes some groups from the national fabric. The nation ties itself to a particular cultural community – based on some criteria – and rejects those who do not fit into that narrower definition. According to Conversi (2004), this process underlies "ethnonationalism." Ethnonationalists insist that the nation has an impermeable cultural identity (and culture can mean whatever the ethnonationalists decide it will mean) and that those outside of this can either completely assimilate, leave, or be granted fewer rights. Political parties that practice ethnonationalism have offered variants of this philosophy. Francisco Franco and Benito Mussolini demanded that culturally distinct peoples inside the state drop their differences and completely adopt the culture of the dominant nation. For more recent ethnonationalist parties, the choices are often to prevent culturally distinct immigrants from entering and to exclude those who already reside within the national territory. The debates over immigration plays out in ethnonationalist terms as the issue becomes where the immigrants are coming from and what they represent. To strong ethnonationalists, culturally or racially distinct immigrants represent an unacceptable broadening of the nation and a threat to their version of national identity.

Many societies contain some version of ethnonationalism. Many would argue that the version of nationalism expressed most commonly in Korea and Japan is in fact racialized ethnonationalism. Both societies are resistant to expanding the nation to include people who are different and still think of themselves as homogeneous (Yonezawa 2005; Shin 2006). India contains a form of strident Hindu nationalism that is antagonistic to Muslims, Sikhs, and others who are considered outsiders (Bannerji 2006). In European societies or in societies settled predominantly by Europeans, the ethnonationalism expressed could be considered "white" ethnonationalism. This is the view that each nation is defined first and foremost by its native European residents, that this population represents the national norm to which non-Europeans can never truly belong. Kaufmann's (2018) idea of "whiteshift" describes when "whiteness" shifts from something that assumed to be the existing national template to where white majorities fret about losing their demographic, cultural, and political advantages to nonwhite minorities. This is a phenomenon animating politics in many countries. While it may not be known as "white nationalism" – in Sweden, whiteness is often implicitly associated with non-foreignness and with activities likely to only attract whites (Teitelbaum 2017) – the implications are generally the same.

In the case of the U.S., specifically "white" ethnonationalism – even if not called by this term – has a long provenance and relies on shifting how whiteness is bounded. The United States began with a view of itself as a Protestant nation – this was a conception that specifically excluded Catholics, Jews, Muslims, the African Americans who had been forcibly settled here, and the Native American who had been forcibly removed (Trautsch 2016). This narrow conception of the American nation was zealously guarded by such movements as the "Know Nothing Party" of the 1850s which railed against Catholic immigration, the Ku Klux Klan which persecuted blacks and also targeted Jews and Catholics, and other nativist organizations often disguised by some other purpose. Nineteenth century cartoonist Thomas Nast was particularly nasty in his anti-Catholic depictions (Zeitz 2015).

Over the course of the 20th century, these exclusionary ideals of whiteness were tested and the boundaries were gradually extended. Each wave of immigration brought with it distinct religions and cultural practices. At first, immigrants from places like Poland, Italy, and Ireland were considered nonwhite, even referred to as different "races" (Brodkin 1998). Later these immigrants were provided with entry into this white identity – in a slow, fitful way. In mid-century Kennedy (1944) spoke of a "triple melting pot" where the children of immigrants assimilated into three religious groups: Protestants, Catholics, and Jews – a categorization that explicitly rejected African Americans. This showed that "America" was no longer just defined by Protestantism but included a larger Judeo-Christian tradition (Herberg 1955) and was accompanied by a growing racial consciousness among immigrants as they sought to move from a position of "in-betweenness" to the "white" side of the color line (Roediger 2006). By the end of the 20th century, the sons and daughters of European immigrant groups could be safely assured entry into a white national identity (Alba 1981).

148 David H. Kaplan

During the 1960s and 1970s, the dominance of white American nationalism was challenged on several fronts. On one hand, the civil rights movement began the long, arduous, and incomplete process by which African Americans were permitted full citizenship rights. A growing awareness about the injustices suffered by Native Americans instigated the acknowledgement and accommodation of those peoples who had been first on the continent. And the nature of immigration changed – away from a predominantly European stream to one that originated in Latin American and Asian countries. This newer immigration configuration has altered the composition of the United States population, bringing in many more people of color, changing the linguistic landscape (especially with the expansion of Spanish in many parts of the country), and introduced several more faiths into the mix. The growth of Islam, while still small in proportion to the population, has had an outsized impact on the American consciousness. Islamophobia has infected much of the national discourse, leading to the sort of distrust not seen since the anti-Catholicism of the 19th century (Beydoun 2018). Ridiculous measures, such as local statutes banning the exercise of Sharia law or restrictions on the construction of mosques, show how far some Americans will go to disassociate themselves from this religion and to stamp Islam's place outside the boundaries of American national identity.

These are the sorts of signaling measures that can be used to develop a particular vision of American nationalism. Connor (1993), who has written more than any other scholar on ethnonationalism, has argued that ethnonationalism is inherent to all nationalisms, since each national identity is built around a common culture. Yet the more expansive view of American nationalism has developed a common culture around a set of ideas, of guiding principles. In its most tolerant form, all members of the society – whether here from the earliest days or newly arrived – have been invited to share in this idea, but this has been a fitful process (Bush and Bush 2008). Countering this vision is an ethnonationalism that restricts legitimate American identity to a subset of Americans. In this instance, certain members of society cannot be considered true Americans. Or alternatively, there are proposals to separate the country along explicitly racial lines (Swain 2002). The description of this as "white" ethnonationalism is potentially confusing but it hearkens back to a white dominant culture – and looks fearfully towards a future when whites will no longer belong to the demographic majority.

The pillars of Trump's victory

There are a number of ways to illustrate the 2016 election. Figure 8.1 shows how Trump performed by county relative to Mitt Romney in 2012. This was enough to counteract the improvements Hillary Clinton made compared to Barack Obama in 2012. Aside from Florida, this victory was consolidated by changes in voting patterns concentrated in the American Midwest and Appalachian counties.

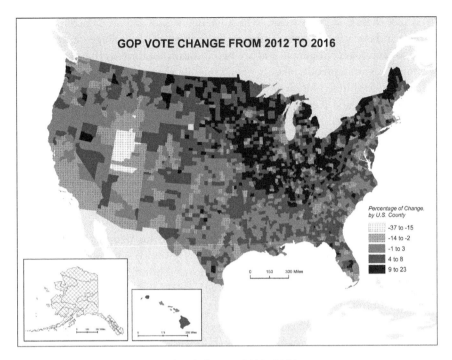

FIGURE 8.1 Percent GOP vote level change, 2012–2016.
Note: County level data on Alaska unavailable.
Source: Author, with assistance of Jessica Reese.

The surgical precision of Donald Trump's victory in the Electoral College allowed him to obtain just the right number of votes in specific states. Most notably, Trump won by mere thousands of votes in Michigan, Wisconsin, and Pennsylvania (accounting for well under 1% of the margin). He also flipped Iowa, Ohio, and Florida. Clinton's support deepened in large metropolitan areas, marked as small urban blotches of blue amid rural swaths of red. Nearly every state shows the same pattern, even deep red states like Tennessee, Kentucky, and Arkansas. Texas displays many such patches which explain how the state's increased metropolitanization has progressively increased the Democratic vote share.

Within this general geography, there are some pillars of Trump's success – places where he did consistently well, and improved on the last two Republican standard bearers. These places had a higher than average proportions of:

- Whites
- The less educated
- Evangelical Christians
- People who claim an "American" ethnicity
- People uncomfortable with diversity

150 David H. Kaplan

Of course these categories are quite broad in many cases and overlap considerably. Whites and the less educated (as measured in the lack of a college degree) comprise large numbers of people and are by no means uniform in their support for Trump. The more precise measure – and the one most supportive of Trump – is less educated whites. The category evangelical Christians corresponds with support for Trump and Republicans in general. The last two categories are related and cover people who claim no additional ethnic attribute, beyond "American," along with and including those who have little to do with diversity. Each of these pillars contributes in large part to Trump's base of support and each relates to white ethnonationalism, sometimes directly and sometimes indirectly.

Whites and the less educated

Trump's ethnonationalist appeal came largely from his denigration of immigrants and people who live in certain countries. "Mexico is not sending its 'best people'" (Lee 2015); describing some countries as "shithole" countries (Watkins and Philip 2018); equating immigration with crime and dehumanizing undocumented immigrants: "These aren't people; they're animals" (Davis 2018); and his remarks that certain people cannot be trusted based on their ethnicity: "I've had horrible rulings, I've been treated very unfairly by this judge. Now, this judge is of Mexican heritage" (CNN 2016). He has also denigrated African Americans – "You're living in poverty; your schools are no good; you have no jobs" (Wegmann 2019); questioned President Obama's citizenship, and complained that prominent African Americans were unpatriotic.

From this it would make sense that the broadest alignment with Trump's appeal comes from the sector of the population that considers itself "white." In fact, it seems difficult to imagine – given the above comments and gestures – how those Americans who do not consider themselves white would provide any support for Trump. Trump *does* command a proportion of nonwhite support, but he is overwhelmingly underwater with nonwhites as a whole. This is more pronounced than had been the case with George W. Bush, who fared much better with Asian and Hispanic populations though equally badly with African Americans (Suro, Fry, and Passel 2005; Ramakrishnan 2016).

Non-Hispanic whites are used as a proxy for "whites" in this analysis. In census classification, "white" is a race, as is African American, Asian, and American Indian. Hispanic/Latinx is a crosscutting ethnic category. Most Hispanics list their race as white, though the range of identification runs the gamut between clearly Latinx to a number of Hispanic whites who have increasingly strong affiliations with the white majority (Cohn 2014). It also explains why Latinx support for Trump and other Republicans, despite anti-immigrant rhetoric, will never fall to the low levels of support among African Americans.

The correlation between non-Hispanic white and support for Trump is quite strong with a correlation coefficient of 0.545. Clearly there are some exceptions. Several predominately white counties displayed low support for Trump. These would be more liberal counties in New England or the Pacific Northwest, as well as counties ringing larger universities such as Douglas County, Kansas. There were also counties with less than half the population as non-Hispanic white but strong support for Trump. Most of these counties were in Texas or New Mexico. It could be argued that this merely continues a long running trend for whiter districts to align more with the GOP nominee. But this is a much stronger association than took place four years prior, when Mitt Romney ran against Barack Obama. Despite Obama's identification as black, the association between whiteness and voting share for Romney was 0.44, still meaningful but significantly weaker. So Trump's appeal to white racial identity went further than previous GOP candidates, forcing a much sharper racial divide in political support.

Another pillar of Trump's appeal came from Americans with lower levels of education. This backing helped Trump in the GOP primaries and especially in the general election – so much so that Trump famously blurted out "I love the poorly educated!" (Hafner 2016). Education does not necessarily have any direct relationship to ethnonationalism though the nature of his appeal did bleed into it. Trump centered his pitch to working class people who felt upended in a globalizing economy. He promised to bring coal jobs back. He promised to bring manufacturing jobs back. He railed against the unfair practices of the Chinese. He complained bitterly about immigrants stealing jobs from hard-working Americans. In these last two plaints especially Trump conjured xenophobia and nativism, both ingredients of ethnonationalism.

The relationship between education and ethnonationalism has been confirmed in other countries' support for far-right racist parties. It is not an ironclad law – some of the most tolerant people in the world are less educated and education is no barrier to bigotry – but there is a tendency for schooling to breed greater cosmopolitanism, at least as shown in a European study (Hainmueller and Hiscox 2007). After all, a college's pitch is that a liberal education will expand people's minds, making them worldlier in their outlook. Trump, despite being an extremely wealthy resident of Manhattan, used his platform to attack the "globalist" elite. Steve Bannon, his ideological Svengali, shaped a viewpoint that was explicitly anti-intellectual and intended to appeal to the less educated.

The education gap only applied to whites. College educated and non-college educated minorities disliked Trump pretty much equally, though there was a small tendency for better educated nonwhites to vote for Trump (Pew Research Center 2018b). But among whites, the divide was stark. Altogether 55% of white college graduates voted for Hillary Clinton but fully two-thirds of whites without a college degree voted for Trump. This split has a strong geographical basis as well. Education, and not income, predicted county-level support for Trump, as higher educated counties were more likely to shift towards Clinton whereas lower educated counties would shift more towards Trump (Silver 2016).

We can see this when examining levels of education and support for Trump at a county by county level (Figure 8.2). The correlation coefficient between the county share of non-Hispanic whites without a bachelor's degree and the

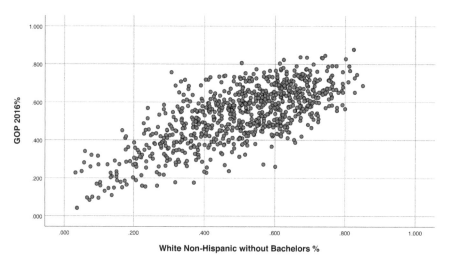

FIGURE 8.2 Trump vote share by percent non-college educated whites.

Note: Only counties with data on proportion of non-Hispanic whites without a college degree are included.
Source: Author, with assistance of Jessica Reese.

percentage voting for Trump is about 0.72, an extraordinarily powerful association. It strips away many of those heavily white counties that shun Trump since those mostly sport high educational attainment levels. Among all counties, about 50% of the population is made up of non-Hispanic whites without a bachelor's degree. Trump gained the majority in every single county where 75% of the population was made up of whites without a college degree. The obverse was largely true as well. Overall, for every unit increase in the proportion of white non-Hispanics without a college degree, the level of Trump support rose 0.65 units.

Significantly, this correlation is much higher than 2012. The correlation of non-college educated non-Hispanic whites with Romney's share of the vote was 0.54. This displays a steady trend where GOP candidates have attracted fewer college graduates. It was not so long ago that education levels were positively correlated with Republican support (Pew Research Center 2016). That began to flip in the 2000s, and is likely to remain this way long after Trump is gone

Evangelical Christians

The population of evangelical Christians has not always been identified with a political ideology or party. Billy Graham – the most famous evangelical – was studiously non-partisan. And the first self-identified evangelical Christian to win the presidency was Jimmy Carter. But over the past several decades, evangelical Christians have become more conservative. Jerry Falwell's Moral Majority emerged in the late 1970s to tether religion to conservative politics, strengthening the influence of the so-called Christian Right. This shows up in identification. In 1997, white evangelicals constituted almost a fifth of Democratic voters and about a third of Republican voters. Today the share of Democrats has plummeted to 7%, while the share of the GOP has remained the same. Over three-quarters of Evangelicals are Republican or Republican leaning (Pew Research Center 2018a).

A well-known playboy, Trump seems to embody almost every attribute that fundamentalist Christians disdain. Unlike George W. Bush, who was wayward in his youth, Trump never went through a redemption phase and he certainly never made a show of practicing any faith. He is unapologetic about what he is. Yet at the same time, Trump's most consistent core of support lies with the evangelical Christian community. And this embrace, a bit wary at first, has become more full throated with well-known figures like Franklin Graham (son of Billy Graham) and Jerry Falwell Jr. offering Trump absolution for every misdeed.

We could consider this support partly transactional. From a lifetime of favoring abortion rights, Trump emerged as a stalwart opponent of abortion. Defying a common taboo, he pledged to appoint judges who would overturn Roe v. Wade. Before this, GOP presidents would use "strict constructionist" as a principle they sought for judicial nominees. This appointment of socially conservative, anti-abortion judges – including Neil Gorsuch and Brett Kavanaugh – has been the single most successful aspect of Trump's presidency and one that Christian conservatives cheer. These judges have been skeptical of other socially tolerant issues, such as LGBT and women's rights, and have controverted environmental protection, labor rights, and voting protections. These views also jibe with that of many conservative Christians.

Yet there is another element of Trump's appeal to many fundamentalist or evangelical Christians beyond the transactional. It is rooted in their relationship with many aspects of ethnonationalism. First, many of these churches are overwhelmingly white, and approve of policies, such as voting restrictions, that tend to marginalize many minority groups. Second, many – not all – evangelical churches claim that the United States is a "Christian nation" or sometimes a variant that it is rooted in the "Judeo-Christian" tradition (Fea 2016; Jeffress 2019). Mark Silk (Winters 2019) shows how coming from a position of inclusion and tolerance earlier in the 20th century, now "'Judeo-Christian values' became, and remains, the shibboleth of the conservative side of that clash of civilization we call the culture war." This allows the inclusion of Jews, at least orthodox Jews, into the American community. But it does not allow other faiths to fully claim the mantle of American identity. In this respect, much fundamentalist Christianity is ethnonationalist. This Christian nationalism is embraced by a number of people but considered a threat by many others – more than half according to one poll (Piacenza 2019).

Evangelical Christianity is not tied to a particular denomination. It is a way of approaching the practice of religion and is dispersed among a variety of denominations. Yet, there are a few churches where it is most prevalent (Pew Research

Center 2015). Chief among these is the white Southern Baptist tradition, followed by nondenominational churches (including many mega-churches), and then Pentecostal denominations. Evangelical Christians also tend to be mostly white and skew towards lower levels of education. Evangelicals are found everywhere but, driven especially by Southern Baptists, predominate in the South.

Trump won in every state where Southern Baptists represent the largest religious group. He also prevailed in many places that report higher levels of "religiosity," the overall percentage of religious adherents, though this was less clear cut. However, while the link is strong between Trump support, Southern Baptists, and evangelicals, it is more of a continuation of GOP support in general. Since 1980, the Republican presidential candidate has done well in the South as an outcome of the "Southern Strategy" that flipped these states from reliably Democratic to reliably Republican. Counties with a higher African American and/or urban population tend to be less evangelical and Southern Baptist.

The correlations are moderately strong between Trump support and Southern Baptists and evangelicals (0.29 and 0.38 respectively). However, these are almost the same as the religious associations with Romney support in 2012. So it appears as if this is more of a generic GOP association than one especially targeted to Trump. These results beg the question as to whether there is some additional pillar of support among evangelicals that transcends Republicans as a whole. There *is* probably some independent effect: evangelicals are more likely to support Trump than non-evangelicals after controlling for political party (Bump 2019). But it is fairly small. Still the steadfast vocalization of support among leading evangelicals, and the ready forgiveness of Trump's various sins, makes me think that evangelical support is stronger and it is the ethnonationalist aspect that partly explains why.

Ethnicity and diversity

It is almost a cliché to say that the United States is a nation of immigrants. The hyphenated American is part of our national mythos. Many celebrate their heritage with festivals, religious services, camps, and the like. Several have established strong ethnic economies and used ethnic capital to help along their fellow ethnics. Yet the other strain of American ideology is a suspicion of outsiders, those who do not belong. Because this is the strain that accords so well with ethnonationalism, it helps to see who decides not to hyphenate.

Fortunately, the census asks a question regarding people's ancestry. This is a self-selected response and could include recent immigrants as well as people several generations removed from the immigrant experience. But the self-selection shows what is on people's minds. Among the possible choices, "German" ancestry has consistently ranked first, followed by "Irish," "Mexican," and "English" (African American, Asian, and Hispanic ancestries are covered under separate race and Hispanic categories). People are also allowed to put down either single or multiple ancestries, and about 60% of all respondents list only a single ancestry.

One telling response is for those who put down "American" as their single ancestry. This never overlaps with "Native American" or American Indian, but instead is found among people who either have no clear record of their ancestry or message that they do not identify with any ethnic group but just with the "American" national group. Stanley Lieberson (1985) described them as "unhyphenated Americans" who identify as white, but have no affinity with any European group. In fact, most people who claim "American" could likely trace some of their ancestry, possibly to Scots-Irish or English, but they have made a conscious choice not to do so.

Three things are important about this particular population of unhyphenated Americans. The first is that there is a distinct geography corresponding with middle and southern Appalachia with some outliers, all of them in the South (Figure 8.3). The second has been the lack of racial diversity within most such places. Very few recent immigrants and small numbers of African Americans occupy such counties, in contrast to the lowland South. The third is the political movement of these counties from Democratic strongholds to bastions of Republicanism.

It is easy to see the ethnonationalist appeal in places where "American" is a moniker. The racial resentments are strong here and residents see little benefit to globalization and immigration. Disdain for coastal and urban elites is also a major political driver where liberalism is a dirty word. Oddly, these are often places

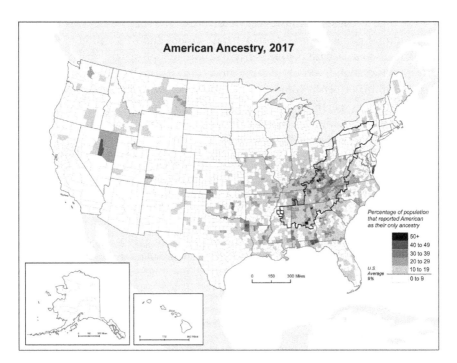

FIGURE 8.3 Percent of population reporting "American" as their only ancestry, 2017.

Source: Author, with assistance of Jessica Reese.

that benefit most from social welfare policies; usage of food stamps is just as high as in the poorest urban neighborhoods. But the formation of ideology hinges on race and resentments.

Given this, it was to be expected that Trump would do well in these "American" counties, far better than in nearly everywhere else in the country. This was not just true of the general election, but in the primaries as well, "where white identity mixes with long-simmering economic dysfunctions" (Irwin and Katz 2016). Trump's appeal to a greater past combined with distrust of immigrants resonated with voters and provided him with fantastic primary support; in fact, Irwin and Katz found that the "American" percentage in a county was a close second behind less educated whites in predicting Trump's success in the primaries.

In the general election, Trump extended the GOP winning streak in these counties by even greater margins (Arbour 2018). The counties that did not like Barack Obama really loved Donald Trump. The correlations between support for Trump and the percent unhyphenated Americans was 0.33. This was higher than the correlation between support for Romney and "American" ancestry – 0.28. There was even a significant positive correlation between the change in the Republican share between 2012 and 2016 and the proportion of "Americans" (0.18). Arbour sees this as more of a continuation of a GOP trend rather than something unique to Trump himself. But there is no denying how Trump's ethnonationalist appeal would resonate so powerfully here.

The final variable lies in the relative diversity of each county. This contrasts multicultural places where different ethnic groups and nationalities come into continuous contact with counties that are more homogeneous. The geographic pattern shows high levels of diversity along the coasts, along the southern border, and in major urban counties like Chicago – owing much to higher levels of immigration. There are also high levels of diversity in the lowland South, with higher African American populations, and in much of the West, with a higher Latinx population. Low levels of diversity are correspondingly found in Appalachia, much of the Midwest, Northern New England, non-coastal Northeast, and northern Mountain states.

Highly diverse communities sharply contrast with what many white ethnonationalists desire, since so much of their energy is devoted to preventing or avoiding such places. How close people are to difference can itself make a difference. As so much social science research has shown, diversity does not always equal tolerance. While diversity *in situ* can reduce intolerance, diversity in the general vicinity might aggravate it (Oliver and Wong 2003). Kaufmann and Harris (2014) have found that heterogeneous neighborhoods tend to be more accepting, perhaps due to self-selection, but that places within hailing distance of diversity are driven by prejudice. Even if the diversity is found throughout, the reaction of residents is unclear. Multicultural communities can provoke a range of sentiments, from engagement to hostility (Kaplan and Le Moigne 2019).

The relation between the level of diversity at the county level and support for Trump is clear cut. Some diverse counties were highly supportive of Trump as a whole, and less diverse counties, such as in the whole of Vermont, were decidedly not supportive of Trump. But the overall relationship between Trump support and levels of diversity was -.041. This was quite a bit lower than the relationship in 2012, which was only -0.26. If we consider this diversity index compared to GOP share change between 2012 and 2016, it is a very robust -0.46. This shows conclusively how much diversity mattered in the election of Trump. Of course people had many motivations for voting for Trump in the 2016 election, but I maintain that diversity and diverse communities are values shared largely among non-supporters of Trump – either because they are not part of the white majority or they are whites who welcome living within multicultural places. In fact, one study showed that as people became more negative towards diversity they were more likely to make the switch from having voted for Obama to voting for Trump (McElwee and McDaniel 2017).

Implications

Donald Trump is not a garden variety Republican. Sure, he benefitted from votes most Republicans get from die-hard partisans. But Trump augmented this with additional support among white ethnonationalists. Whether Trump himself is an ethnonationalist has been subject of many essays; what is significant is how he expanded the five pillars of his appeal, each of which can fit directly or indirectly into the ethnonationalist framework. Compared to Mitt Romney, the geography of Trump support was more strongly associated with counties that were whiter, had a higher proportion of less educated whites, contained more "Americans," and were less diverse. On an electoral geographic basis, Trump's association with evangelicals and Southern Baptists was no greater than Romney's, but he has since developed powerful connections among both leadership and rank and file.

Trump has remained a remarkably unpopular president since taking office, with approval never going above 45% (immediately after inauguration) and staying largely in the 40–42% band (FiveThirtyEight 2019). He has also been fairly unsuccessful in getting many of his policies approved, even when Republicans controlled Congress. But he maintains deep support among the minority of the electorate that overlaps with these five pillars.

The ethnonationalist attitudes of many Trump supporters are reflected in their views of American society and the world at large. There are several attitudes which have been reported especially in Pew Research Center Reports. Trump supporters tend to be much more suspicious of expertise. They have less education and distrust universities. This may be because they feel that cosmopolitan culture is too elitist, too politically correct, and too prescriptive in terms of what people are supposed to think and how they should behave.

Trump's foreign attacks – even on allies – resonate deeply. Trump supporters feel that the U.S. is getting ripped off by international agreements, that it pays too much to defend other countries, and has not been tough enough on the world stage. Many Trump supporters are leery of immigrants (even legal immigrants) and are

158 David H. Kaplan

especially suspicious of Muslims. Close to a majority of Republicans strongly supported banning Muslims from entering the U.S. before Trump was elected and that percentage has likely increased as more of Trump's views have been adopted by his party. More than eight out of ten favor building a wall along the Mexican border. Domestic diversity is shunned. Most Republicans in 2016 displayed some level of racial resentment and twice as many Republicans as Democrats showed levels of animosity towards blacks (McDaniel and McElwee 2016). Also, strong Trump supporters are against the idea of America as a melting pot (Kaufmann 2018).

The jury is out as to whether Trumps ethnonationalist appeal reflects an emerging American attitude or the dying embers of white male hegemony (Hobbes 2019; Brooks 2019). Certainly the geography of his support would suggest the latter. It is focused on places that languish in the rearguard, rather than the vanguard, of postindustrial American society. Yet such places have exhibited an extraordinary ability to steer American politics and the triumph of Donald Trump was a reminder to all of us that, no matter how cosmopolitan our aspirations may be, ethnonationalism remains a potent inspiration to many Americans.

References

Alba, R. 1981. The twilight of ethnicity among American Catholics of European ancestry. *Annals AAPSS* 454: 86–97.

Arbour, B. 2018. This is Trump Country: Donald Trump's base and partisan change in unhyphenated America. In C. Rackaway and L. Rice (eds.) *American Political Parties Under Pressure*. New York: Palgrave Macmillan.

Bannerji, H. 2006. Making India Hindu and male: Cultural nationalism and the emergence of the ethnic citizen in contemporary India. *Ethnicities* 6(3): 362–390.

Beydoun, K. 2018. *American Islamophobia: Understanding the Roots and Rise of Fear*. Berkeley: University of California Press.

Breton, R. 1988. From ethnic to civic nationalism: English Canada and Quebec. *Ethnic and Racial Studies* 11(1): 85–102.

Brodkin, K. 1998. *How Jews became White Folks and what that Says about Race in America*. New Brunswick, NJ: Rutgers University Press.

Brooks, D. 2019. The coming GOP apocalypse. *New York Times* (June 3). www.nytimes.com/2019/06/03/opinion/republicans-generation-gap.html

Bump, P. 2019. Why are evangelical Americans so loyal to Trump? Because they're heavily Republican. *Washington Post* (April 10). www.washingtonpost.com/politics/2019/04/10/why-are-evangelical-americans-so-loyal-trump-because-theyre-heavily-republican/

Bush, M., and R. Bush. 2008. United States nationalism and nationalism post World War II. In D. Kaplan and G. Herb (eds.) *Nations and Nationalisms in Global Perspective: An Encyclopedia of Origins, Development, and Contemporary Transitions*. pp. 1299–1312. Oxford: ABC-CLIO.

CNN. 2016. The lead with Jake Tapper. *CNN Transcripts* (June 3). http://transcripts.cnn.com/TRANSCRIPTS/1606/03/cg.02.html

Cohn, N. 2014. More Hispanics declaring themselves white. *New York Times* (May 21). www.nytimes.com/2014/05/22/upshot/more-hispanics-declaring-themselves-white.html

Connor, W. 1993. Beyond reason: the nature of the ethnonational bond. *Ethnic and Racial Studies* 16(3): 373–389.

Conversi, D. 2004. *Ethnonationalism in the Contemporary World: Walker Connor and the Study of Nationalism*. London: Routledge.

Davis, J. 2018. Trump calls some unauthorized immigrants "animals" in rant. *New York Times* (May 16). www.nytimes.com/2018/05/16/us/politics/trump-undocumented-immigrants-animals.html

Eriksen, T. 2002. *Ethnicity and Nationalism: Anthropological Perspectives*. London: Pluto Press.

Fea, J. 2016. *Was America Founded as a Christian Nation? A Historical Introduction*. Louisville, KY: Westminster John Knox Press.

FiveThirtyEight. 2019. How popular is Donald Trump? https://projects.fivethirtyeight.com/trump-approval-ratings/?ex_cid=rrpromo

Forest, B. 2018. Electoral geography: From mapping votes to representing power. *Geography Compass* 12(1): e12352.

Hafner, J. 2016. Donald Trump loves the "poorly educated" – and they love him. *USA Today* (Feb. 24). www.usatoday.com/story/news/politics/onpolitics/2016/02/24/donald-trump-nevada-poorly-educated/80860078/

Hainmueller, J., and M. Hiscox. 2007. Educated preferences: Explaining attitudes toward immigration in Europe. *International Organization* 61(2): 399–442.

Hayes, C. 1931. *The Historical Evolution of Modern Nationalism*. New York: Richard R. Smith.

Herb, G., and D. Kaplan (eds.) 2018. *Scaling Identities: Nationalism and Territoriality*. Lanham, MD: Rowman & Littlefield.

Herberg, W. 1955. *Protestant – Catholic – Jew: An Essay in American Religious Sociology*. Chicago: University of Chicago Press.

Hobbes, M. 2019. Turns out white millennials are just as conservative as their parents. *Huffington Post* (June 2). www.huffpost.com/entry/turns-out-white-millennials-are-just-as-conservative-as-their-parents_n_5ce856fee4b0512156f16939

Irwin, N., and J. Katz. 2016. The geography of Trumpism. *New York Times* (March 12). www.nytimes.com/2016/03/13/upshot/the-geography-of-trumpism.html?ref=politics&_r=2

Jeffress, R. 2019. America is a Christian nation. *Pathway to Victory*. https://ptv.org/america-is-a-christian-nation/

Johnson, C. 2018. The changing context of German nationhood. In G. Herb and D. Kaplan (eds.) *Scaling Identities: Nationalism and Territoriality*. Lanham, MD: Rowman & Littlefield.

Kaplan, D., and Y. Le Moigne. 2019. Multicultural engagements in lived spaces: How cultural communities intersect in Belleville, *Paris. City & Community* 18(1): 392–413.

Kaufmann, E. 2018. *Whiteshift: Populism, Immigration and the Future of White Majorities*. London: Penguin UK.

Kaufmann, E., and G. Harris. 2014. *Changing Places: Mapping the White British Response to Ethnic Change*. London: Demos.

Kennedy, R. 1944. Single or triple melting-pot? Intermarriage trends in New Haven, 1870-1940. *American Journal of Sociology* 49(4): 331–339.

Lee, M. 2015. Donald Trump's false comments connecting Mexican immigrants and crime. *Washington Post* (July 8). www.washingtonpost.com/news/fact-checker/wp/2015/07/08/donald-trumps-false-comments-connecting-mexican-immigrants-and-crime/

Lieberson, S. 1985. Unhyphenated whites in the United States. *Ethnic and Racial Studies* 8(1): 159–180.

McDaniel, J., and S. McElwee. 2016. Yes, Trump's biggest asset is racism: Why bigotry (not the economy) is the biggest factor driving his rise. *Salon* (March 22). www.salon.com/2016/03/22/yes_trumps_secret_weapon_is_racism_why_bigotry_not_the_economy_is_the_biggest_factor_driving_his_rise/

McElwee, S., and J. McDaniel. 2017. Fear of diversity made people more likely to vote Trump. *The Nation* (March 14). www.thenation.com/article/fear-of-diversity-made-people-more-likely-to-vote-trump/

Oliver, J., and J. Wong. 2003. Intergroup prejudice in multiethnic settings. *American Journal of Political Science* 47(4): 567–82.

Payne, S. 1983. *Fascism: Comparison and Definition.* Madison, WI: University of Wisconsin Press.

Pew Research Center. 2015. *America's Changing Religious Landscape.* www.pewforum. org/2015/05/12/americas-changing-religious-landscape/

Pew Research Center. 2016. *The Parties on the Eve of the 2016 Election: Two Coalitions, Moving Further Apart.* www.people-press.org/2016/09/13/the-parties-on-the-eve-of-the-2016-election-two-coalitions-moving-further-apart/

Pew Research Center. 2018a. *Wide Gender Gap, Growing Educational Divide in Voters' Party Identification.* www.people-press.org/2018/03/20/wide-gender-gap-growing-educational-divide-in-voters-party-identification/

Pew Research Center. 2018b. *An Examination of the 2016 Electorate, Based on Validated Voters.* www.people-press.org/2018/08/09/an-examination-of-the-2016-electorate-based-on-validated-voters/

Piacenza, J. 2019. Roughly half the electorate views Christian nationalism as a threat: Affinity toward the ideology was best predictor of Trump's support, per study. *Morning Consult* (April 2). https://morningconsult.com/2019/04/02/roughly-half-the-electorate-views-christian-nationalism-as-a-threat/

Ramakrishnan, K. 2016. How Asian Americans became Democrats. *American Prospect* (July 26). https://prospect.org/article/how-asian-americans-became-democrats-0

Roediger, D. 2006. *Working toward Whiteness: How America's Immigrants became White: The Strange Journey from Ellis Island to the Suburbs.* London: Hachette UK.

Royce, A. 1982. *Ethnic identity: Strategies of Diversity.* Bloomington, IN: Indiana University Press.

Shin, G.-W. 2006. *Ethnic Nationalism in Korea: Genealogy, Politics, and Legacy.* Palo Alto, CA: Stanford University Press.

Silver, N. 2016. Education, not income, predicted who would vote for Trump. *FiveThirtyEight* (Nov. 22). https://fivethirtyeight.com/features/education-not-income-predicted-who-would-vote-for-trump/

Suro, R., R. Fry, and J. Passel. 2005. *Hispanics and the 2004 Election: Population, Electorate and Voters.* Pew Research Center Reports June 27.

Swain, C. 2002. *The New White Nationalism in America: Its Challenge to Integration.* Cambridge: Cambridge University Press.

Teitelbaum, B. 2017. Implicitly white: Right-wing nihilism and the politicizing of ethnocentrism in multiracial Sweden. *Scandinavian Studies* 89(2): 159–178.

Trautsch, J. 2016. The origins and nature of American nationalism. *National Identities* 18(3): 289–312.

Triandafyllidou, A. 1998. National identity and the "other.æ *Ethnic and Racial Studies* 21(4): 593–612.

Watkins, E., and A. Philip. 2018. Trump decries immigrants from "shithole countries" coming to US. *CNN Politics* (Jan. 12). www.cnn.com/2018/01/11/politics/immigrants-shithole-countries-trump/index.html

Wegmann, P. 2019. Trump bets on more black support in 2020. (He might need it.) *RealClearPolitics* (June 7). www.realclearpolitics.com/articles/2019/06/07/trump_bets_on_more_black_support_in_2020_he_might_need_it.html

Winters, M. 2019. Mark silk on the history of the term "Judeo-Christian." *National Catholic Reporter* (April 15).

Yonezawa, M. 2005. Memories of Japanese identity and racial hierarchy. In P. Spiackard (ed.) *Race and Nation: Ethnic Systems in the Modern World.* pp. 115–132. New York: Routledge.

Zeitz, J. 2015. When America hated Catholics. *Politico* (Sept. 23). www.politico.com/magazine/story/2015/09/when-america-hated-catholics-213177

9

"STANDING WITH PATRIOTS"? TRUMP, TWITTER, AND THE SILENT MAJORITY

Lewis J. Dowle

A land of liberty

The playbook of politics has been rewritten. Its authors have been repealed and its style replaced. The words that remain are now caustically engraved into the fabric of the American political system for years to come. Donald Trump's successful campaign to become the Republican nominee and subsequent 45th president of the United States of America has changed politics as we know it. From when he announced his candidacy in June 2015, Trump received 13 million votes, enough to secure for him the Republican nomination amidst 16 other competitors. Trump's rise to political fame defied traditional demographics of prior elections such as education, religion, income, and age (Taub 2016). For many, Trump provided a hopeful change from the existing political establishment; for others, Trump represented a plutocratic and inexperienced demagogue (Gallagher 2017). When Trump began his campaign, before his very eyes lay a stirring Republican Party, desperate for a figurehead to restore the "American Dream" after two terms of Obama in office: someone to Make America Great Again (Anderson 2017).

Trump's success is framed against the backdrop of a fearful and threatened nation living in the colonial present following the horrors of the 9/11 terror attacks (Gregory 2004; *National Review* 2016). Trump's burst onto the political scene coincided serendipitously with social media's political revolution. Such was the homology of Trump and Twitter, scholars have begun to question the role Twitter played in the U.S. election of 2016 and its accompanying primaries (Ott 2017; for an overview, see Lee and Lim 2016; Wang, Li, and Luo 2016). However, these quantitative studies have failed to address qualitatively the discursive construction of Trump's tweets (Gonawela et al. 2018; Watt et al. 2017). This chapter therefore contributes to such novel scholarship, seeking to unravel the enigmatic performance of Donald Trump on Twitter during the Republican primaries through qualitative analysis. Particular attention is directed towards the formation of identity, fear, and emotion in Trump's successful campaign for the GOP nomination. To address this aim, the following research questions were explored. Firstly, to what extent did geographical themes such as place, space, identity, and power, both shape and serve Donald Trump's GOP Twitter campaign? Secondly, how did Trump (re)construct an exterior "Other" through fear and identity, specifically the "impending threat" pertaining to immigration and terror? Finally, to what extent did Twitter serve as a medium through which Trump performed his identity and empowered the "silent majority"?

A brief grounding in literature will be provided in relation to three key topics, namely: notions of discourse, emotional geopolitics, and social media. In order to address the aforementioned research questions, a total of 3,252 tweets were hand-coded and assorted into analytical themes before critical discourse analysis was undertaken in order to unlock the dataset further. The identity of American patriots will then be discussed in relation to an exterior "Other," before wrestling with Trump's expressions of "Americanism" and "globalism." After this, authoritarianism among voters and Trump's communicative style on Twitter will be expounded upon. The "wall" along the southern border will then be discussed in relation to discourses of fear. This fear will be explored in relation to acts of terror and the imminent "threat" Trump constructs regarding Islam and America. Following this, Trump's foreign policy of "America First" will be examined pertaining to the culmination of fear and identity before conclusions are drawn.

The power of discourse

Discourse is a contested term (Müller 2008). Van Dijk's (1985; 2008a) notion of discourse reveals the manifold manifestations of text (and spoken word) in a "semiotic" understanding conceived by its immediate cultural and social milieu, including the analysis of body language, imagery, and sound. Though distinct entities, the espousal of knowledge and power shape and serve the reception and fabrication of discourse (Flynn 2007; Van Dijk 2008a). Discourse is indivisible from power; a discursive medium through which power is sustained and control is made possible (Flynn 2007; Van Dijk 2008b). Indeed, both Foucault (2002) and Van Dijk (2008a) stress the importance of *context* when analyzing discourse through "situated knowledges" (Haraway 1988).

Geographical themes permeate discussions of discourse. Van Dijk (2008b) reveals the construction of distance through linguistic constructions such as "them" or "the Mexicans," where individuals bring into representation the myriad forces that determine and shape discourse (Foucault 2002). Prominent political discourses of nationalism and populism (two frequently employed tools adopted by Trump) are rooted in discursive processes of othering,

"Standing with patriots"? **163**

inseparable from factional control and domination through manipulation (Van Dijk 1997; 2008b). Throughout the primaries, Trump tweeted with authority, an issue raised by Foucault concerning the socially constructed infrastructure of the political system, challenging what is "true" or quite simply "fake news" (Flynn 2007).

Emotional geopolitics

Ó Tuathail and Agnew (1992, p. 190) proffered the "reconceptualization of geopolitics using the concept of discourse," seeking to liberate and refine geography and politics through "critical geopolitics" (Ó Tuathail 1994). Indeed, scholars sought the problematization of this affair within a poststructuralist lens, striving to situate political discourses within their cultural and historical place (Dalby 1996; Ó Tuathail 1994). Despite its progress, Hyndman (2004) argued that critical geopolitics failed to account for the embodiment of geopolitics prevalent at numerous scales. Therefore, Dowler and Sharp (2001), alongside Hyndman (2001), created the blueprint for a "feminist geopolitics." Central to this lens is the feminist adage of "the personal is political," usurping critical geopolitics' presumptive centering of state-level discourse and focusing instead on the mundane, the everyday, and the corporeal (Dowler and Sharp 2001).

Pain (2009) proposed the merging of the political with the banal and emotional, calling for an "emotional geopolitics" across a variety of scales, analyzing how power and resistance are made manifest in emotions. Individuals, across public and private spaces, are thereby bound by the ebb and flow of emotion, constrained, encouraged, and liberated by its presence (Pain 2009). An emotional geopolitics therefore calls for a "commitment to praxis," a lens centered on the "emotional grounding of one's life to a particular place" (Tyner and Henkin 2014, p. 294; Pain 2010; see also Benwell 2019; Seitz 2017). Great emphasis is ascribed to fear, an emotional reaction that Pain (2009) understands to carry within it both the seeds of oppression and despair, but also of hope and resistance. Much of Trump's Twitter feed plays to such fears within the electorate in order to garner support for his movement in opposition to the establishment. Determining how to "deploy," dissipate, and disseminate emotions between and within geopolitical narratives serves as emotional geopolitics' foundational pillar and will be utilized in this chapter (Pain 2009; 2010).

Rallying support through social media

The development of social networking sites (SNS), particularly Twitter, has provided a bridge between conventional (material) and novel (digital) media, particularly in the political realm (Alashri et al. 2016; Gross and Johnson 2016). Digital technologies "are creating complex arrays of *new* geographies," providing opportunities and challenges for geographical scholarship (Zook et al. 2004, p. 155, emphasis added). Due to its informality and simplicity, Twitter has bred

164 Lewis J. Dowle

malevolent discourse for the "sound-bite media age" of recent years (Gross and Johnson 2016, p. 749; Ott 2017).

Twitter has been instrumental in modern politics, culminating in the 2016 election which has been termed the "Twitter Election" (Coyne 2016). Twitter differs from other social media platforms primarily in four ways. First, Twitter is inherently *public*. Unlike Facebook, Snapchat, and other SNS, Twitter encourages individuals to share openly without the "limitations" of personal privacy (Chaudhry 2015). Connected to this feature is the use of hashtags. Hashtags draw together a collection of tweets that share a specific focal point (Kjeldsen 2016). Second, Twitter provides a platform for individuals to form communities and networks through the *following* of other individuals (Chaudhry 2015). Third, for every tweet, individuals are able to *favorite* or *retweet* it. Users can share tweets from other individuals in solidarity, interest, or irony, allowing tweets to gain momentum spatially across the world (Segesten and Bossetta 2016). Finally, Twitter encourages *brevity*, with a character limit per tweet (Gross and Johnson 2016).

Enli (2017) observed the ample opportunities Twitter provided for Trump, a medium which developed tangentially from the previous monopoly of the mainstream media. Trump adopted an "amateurish," yet crucially "authentic," social media profile, juxtaposed with a wooden and controlled performance by the Democrat nominee, Hillary Clinton (Lee and Lim 2016). Wang et al. (2016) brought to light the numerical advantage tweets would have when Trump launched tirades of abuse directed at Obama and Clinton. Despite the insight this and other similar papers provide, *what* was written, concerning both content and context, was overlooked. Once more, the communicative construction of Trump's attacks on his opponents is absent, resting on numerical values in its place (cf. Gonawela et al. 2018; Watt et al. 2017). Therefore, this chapter seeks to problematize existing scholarship on Trump and Twitter, concomitant with developing novel insights pertaining to the qualitative and discursive content of Twitter within contemporary political geography.

Methods

The primary data produced through Trump's tweets are stored online in Twitter's archive. Both Donald Trump (@RealDonaldTrump) and Twitter themselves have "control" over the archive and what is presented to the public, with Twitter randomly omitting various tweets per search (see Segesten and Bossetta 2016). The data period started with Trump's announcement to run for the presidency on June 16, 2015 and finished on the final day of the Republican National Convention (RNC) on July 21, 2016. The data was collected manually through Twitter's official website. The number of tweets analyzed totaled 3,252 and nine are presented here for in-depth analysis. Thematic analysis and critical discourse analysis were undertaken to analyze Trump's tweets as "manifestations" of power, where such power "does not necessarily derive from language, but language can be used to *challenge* [and manipulate] power" (Attride-Stirling 2001; Wodak and Meyer 2009, p. 10, emphasis added).

"Standing with patriots"

In the analysis of how Trump constructed identity, fear, and emotion through his use of Twitter, it is paramount to situate tweets in their broader context throughout the 13-month period. Figure 9.1 visualizes the weekly number of retweets and favorites from Trump's Twitter feed. Set against this backdrop are five Western terror attacks: Paris, San Bernardino, Brussels, Orlando, and Nice. The total number of both favorites and retweets increased throughout the timeframe, with favorites increasing at a particularly fast rate. Throughout the campaign, Trump adopted the term "silent majority" to encourage and communicate directly to the "forgotten" men and women of America (Burston 2017; Lieven 2016). Due to the often contentious hyperbole of Trump, his supporters faced many hostilities from media coverage and academia, being labelled irrational, racist, and sexist (Mead 2017; Wells 2017). The public act of a retweet can be done as much in awe as in affirmation, whereas favorites are solely positive. Further, though it is possible to trace who has favorited a tweet, when the numbers are in the thousands, individuals are enshrouded in secrecy. Trump's followers would thereby affirm his tweets through an instantaneous affectual response that required little forethought or subsequent consequences, causing a widening disparity between private favorites and public retweets, culminating in the growth of the "silent majority."

The graph also reveals a factor likely to have influenced the Republican primaries, namely that of terror. Bitter criticism of the West's dealings with Islamic

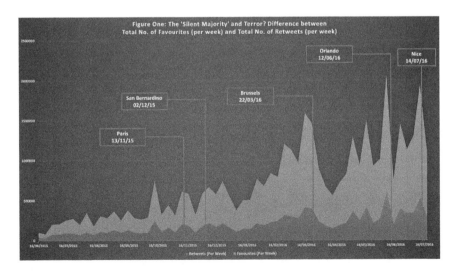

FIGURE 9.1 The silent majority in the Republican primaries.

extremism gave Trump an opportunity to reach out to voters who still felt the psychological burden of the events of 9/11. Where other politicians seemed to eschew blame and offence, Trump was quick to tweet and lambast the politicians, perpetrators, and religious sentiment behind the attacks. These tweets correspond to notable peaks throughout the primaries, with wide discrepancies once more between favorites and retweets, forming an essential backdrop to the dramaturgical performance of Trump's Twitter feed.

Trump's republic

Trump began his campaign in June 2015 with the now infamous words that Mexicans are "bringing drugs. They're bringing crime. They're rapists. And some, I assume, are good people" (*Time* 2015, np). Ben Anderson (2017) argues that this seemingly rash and affectual hyperbole was rooted in a dwindling of white hegemony and rising levels of fear and anger. At the time of Tweet #1 (Figure 9.2), Trump was sixth in the Republican primary polling, gaining just 6% of the potential vote (RealClearPolitics 2017).

Trump begins by separating the Mexican people from the nation itself. Note the simplicity through which Trump constructs the sentences, adopting lucent and evocative words such as "love" and "friend." Ott (2017) reveals that Trump's rhetorical performance publicly was that of an approximately 9-year-old's reading ability. This is transferred over into Trump's tweets. Trump speaks how he tweets, and he tweets how he speaks. Trump adopts the word "killing" to carry a double meaning, both figuratively and literally. Concomitant to this, he translates deaths on the ground, to death of the nation and the economy. Indeed, Trump continues in this tweet and issues the ambiguous imperative of "FIGHT!" to rally his supporters and encourage them to act. Whether fighting

FIGURE 9.2 Tweet #1.

"Standing with patriots"?   167

the Mexican economy or Mexicans themselves is left to the interpretation of the Twitter follower.

Americanism and globalism

Li and Brewer (2004, p. 728) note the psychological distinction between patriotism as a "pride and love for [one's] country," and nationalism as the "chauvinistic arrogance and desire for dominance in international relations." They also note that the two are not mutually exclusive, but rather conflate to reject diversity and those who challenge existing social norms. Since 2001, the Muslim community has been particularly marginalized in the U.S. as seen in Tweet #2 (Lalami 2016). Islamophobia is witnessed in the grouping and (re)creating of a new social category in which anyone who appears Arab, Muslim, or Middle Eastern is deemed a potential terrorist (Lal 2015).

This tweet (Figure 9.3) from Trump comes in the immediate aftermath of the Brussels terror attack. The Islamic State (ISIS) claimed the killing of 32 individuals in Brussels' airport and metro station in March 2016 (BBC 2016a). Trump uses "Incompetent Hillary" to turn the Brussels attack into support for an increasingly bordered America. Anderson (2017) captures the affectual atmosphere apparent in American psyches as the visual media relayed terror attacks, fostering an enmity towards Muslims, a discourse that Trump draws heavily on. However, it is important to note that Trump's "views" are not out of the ordinary within the Republican Party, but rather it is his rhetoric and style that singles him out (Lalami 2016). Trump's authority is also apparent: "No way!" he concludes the tweet. Though unelected at the time, Trump envisages future "Twiplomacy" on behalf of the American people *before* winning the Republican primaries (Šimunjak and Caliandro 2019). The authority through which Trump speaks is again evident in Tweet #3 (Figure 9.4), in which he once more contrasts himself with Clinton. At this time in the campaign, the importance of rallying

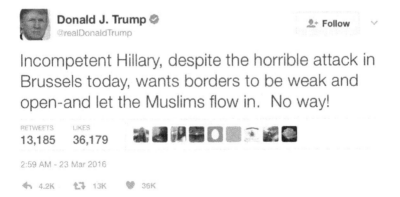

FIGURE 9.3   Tweet #2.

168 Lewis J. Dowle

FIGURE 9.4 Tweet #3.

the Republican Party together was paramount, and just about the only thing the party could agree on was their dislike for Hillary Clinton (Zakaria 2016). Trump proffers two options for voters: "Americanism" or "her corrupt globalism."

Americanism can be understood here as the deployment, imposition, and contagion of American principles, cultures, beliefs, and practices (Ciftci and Tezcür 2015; Rinke, Willnat, and Quandt 2015). Billig (1995) paints Americanism, exhibited in the banal, as the most significant form of nationalism. This has been met by great resistance in the Middle East and the Islamic world causing a "clash of civilizations" (Ciftci and Tezcür 2015; Huntington 1993). This is juxtaposed with Clinton's "corrupt globalism." In the aftermath of the USSR's collapse, globalism spread throughout the world, hinged on structures and forces shaping its interconnectivity (Dirlik 1999; Epstein 2009). Trump's "America First" approach to foreign policy is in direct opposition to a globalism that seeks the development of all nations in commonality (Epstein 2009).

Throughout the Clinton campaign, though trying several different hashtags, including #StrongerTogether and #HillYes, her principle hashtag was #ImWithHer to promote the first ever female Democrat nominee (McLevy 2016). Trump responded with what became a prominent expression for his own Twitter account: #ImWithYou. Other hashtags used by Trump included #MakeAmericaGreatAgain, #MAGA, #TeamTrump, and #AmericaFirst. The Republican used this hashtag to encapsulate the tweet, to at once condemn Clinton and her "corruption," but to also solidify the patriotic vote, presenting himself as the blue-collar billionaire who reaches out to voters directly, in contrast to Clinton's appeal for loyalty to the political elite.

Authoritarianism and the establishment

The anti-elite and "tactical populism" in Trump's rhetoric was ubiquitous throughout the Republican primaries (Blankenship 2019; Lacatus 2019). Trump's arrival onto the political platform sent shockwaves throughout the

FIGURE 9.5 Tweet #4.

"establishment" as he sought to address the resentment of many "forgotten" Americans across the country (Burston 2017; *National Review* 2016). Many voters sought the end of "politics as usual," exemplified not just in the Trump phenomenon shown in Tweet #4 (Figure 9.5), but also in the rise of Bernie Sanders on the political left (Baumgartner 2016, p. 775). Purdy (2016) paints Trump as an "anti-Obama," the insurgent seeking to overthrow the existing political infrastructure and dispense with all forms of political correctness (Fisher 2016).

Trump used such political capital and "affective solidarity" to nurture a specific identity, a solidarity and hope that their cause can triumph (Anderson 2017). Cohen et al. (2016) noted that never before had a candidate been so successful in the race to the White House with as little support from elites as Trump had. "Let's Trump the Establishment," Trump writes, at once inviting followers to partake in a movement, but equally to perform an identity in contrast to the "corrupt" political system (MacWilliams 2016). Weiler and MacWilliams (2016) assert authoritarianism as the key determinant for Trump's success, transcending social class and levels of education. When Trump declares that "We are no longer silent," not only does he unite himself with his Twitter followers as equals, but he is actualizing and vocalizing a deeply rooted, anti-elite sentiment within the electorate, immediately (re)constructing an American identity, captured in Trump's now trademark words: Make America Great Again.

During the Vietnam War, President Nixon (1969, np, emphasis added) uttered the poignant words, "[and] so tonight – to you, the great *silent majority* of my fellow Americans – I ask for your support." Noam Chomsky (2016, np) questions what Trump "has brought forth – not created, but brought forth" through the sudden surge in popularity and support embodied in the "silent majority" as seen in Tweet #5 (Figure 9.6). Through Twitter, Trump is able to provide a platform for the individuals who have seen declining incomes, as well as those who were "abandoned"

170 Lewis J. Dowle

FIGURE 9.6 Tweet #5.

by the Democrats, to believe that they are not alone and that a change is possible (Burston 2017; Lieven 2016). Trump declares his "LOVE" for those who followed him "despite so many media lies." Enli (2017) reveals the effects of capital letters as a simple technical device that enables Trump to appear more intimate and sincere. Though the mainstream media dismissed the voices of the many, Trump, through his Twitter account, was able to flip such tactics to serve his growing followers and instill a belief in a "silent majority" (Wells 2017).

"Stop the invasion"

The Paris terror attacks served as a defining moment in Trump's GOP campaign. The deaths of 129 people by Islamic State renewed a deeply rooted fear in America, causing a surge in Trump's popularity (BBC 2015). As seen in Tweet #6 (Figure 9.7), Trump associates Syrian refugees with Islamic State (ISIS), a conflation consistent with American right-leaning news sources such as FOX and Breitbart. Trump escalated the extremity of his views towards Islam following the attacks, even considering the closure of mosques on U.S. soil (Lal 2015). Trump raises the provocative question of "ISIS maybe?" in relation to the eight Syrian refugees found along the border. The question arouses suspicion, disquietude, and anxiety with his followers. Trump does not support his bold statement, before or afterwards, with any source, though it is likely he saw the story from Breitbart (2015) the day before. Yet the followers of Trump on Twitter are likely to treat the tweet as legitimate and harbor the "xenophobic bellicosity and the resurgence of nationalism" Trump is attempting to sow (Anderson 2017, np).

Trump stirred a fear in the electorate. Taub (2016) notes that the power of perceived risks and fears is particularly dangerous for *non*-authoritarians, as external situations can awaken a previously latent authoritarian desire. This is consistent with the understanding of emotional geopolitics. Pain (2009) discusses the emotional reactions an individual has to the geopolitical situation surrounding them,

FIGURE 9.7 Tweet #6.

the visceral experiences of hope, fear, and everything in between. As fear burgeons through the medium of Twitter, Trump then drives home the underlying intention for the tweet: to build a "BIG & BEAUTIFUL WALL" along the southern border. Obama is said to have been the president responsible for more deportations of undocumented migrants than any other, but it is Trump's *modus operandi* that distinguishes him from his peers (Taub 2016; Wells 2017). Trump is unashamedly forthright and vociferously clear in each message. His use of capital letters here for a prolonged time drives home an emphatic and memorable message. The wall, both materially and metaphorically, serves to strengthen the identity of Trump's followers, concomitant with the creation of an image of fear and terror ever-encroaching on the U.S. borders, both ideologically and physically.

The imminent threat

In early December 2015, American fears of terrorism reached their highest peak since 9/11 (Gallup 2015). The day of Tweet #7 (Figure 9.8) was a week after the San Bernardino shootings by American residents pledging allegiance to Islamic State, and just two days after Trump's provocative call to ban Islamic migration into America (CNN 2015b). To many neo-conservatives, radical Islam is perceived as a source of tyranny in the world, resounding in Trump's persistent rhetoric addressed towards the threat of Islam and terror (Anderson 2017). Trump lucidly declares the threat America faces from Islamic fundamentalists, requiring "smart," "tough," and "FAST" responses by the Capitol. MacWilliams (2016, p. 720) notes how Trump "electrified Americans disposed to authoritarianism" through such a stimulus of fear.

Our country is facing a major threat from radical Islamic terrorism. We better get very smart, and very tough, FAST, before it is too late!

RETWEETS 7,594   LIKES 14,727

2:56 AM - 9 Dec 2015

↩ 2.4K   ⟲ 7.6K   ♥ 15K

FIGURE 9.8 Tweet #7.

The impetus of a perceived threat within an environment draws forth what Feldman and Stenner (1997) state are "predispositions" within the electorate, a latency that requires a spark to energize and enable it (Barrett, Tugade, and Engle 2004). The urgency through which Trump exclaims, "FAST, before it is too late" seeks to tap into this susceptibility that many individuals face with respect to authoritarianism (Hetherington and Suhay 2011). The urgency and fear-filled discourse through which Trump tweets invites the electorate to rally behind him as the only one to solve the issue of terror. The technique that Trump adopts is geographically significant too. Trump scales the threat of terrorism from a localized attack in San Bernardino, to a nationwide assault; the transition from a *place* to a *space*. Temporally, the exigency of Trump's tweet implies that without effective governance, an act of terror could occur at any time.

Trump and the ban

Certain moments of the Republican primaries defined Trump's campaign, but what perhaps divided the nation more than any other policy was his declaration on December 7, 2015 to ban all Muslims from entering the United States (Trump 2015). Trump began that month polling at 28.7% yet finished the month at 35% (RealClearPolitics 2017). Such was the significance of the ban (and attachment Trump felt to it), he continued to refer to it in June 2016 in the aftermath of the Orlando terror attack, as shown in Tweet #8 (Figure 9.9). A gay nightclub in Florida was the target of Islamic terrorism and the site of the death of 49 predominantly Hispanic people, becoming the biggest mass shooting in America's history at that moment in time (CNN 2016). The terror attack according to Trump was "just the beginning," words that once more instilled fear within his followers. Trump declares his superior insight as he lauds himself with the words "I called it and asked for the ban." (It is important to note that the perpetrator

FIGURE 9.9 Tweet #8.

for the attack was a home-grown terrorist born in New York, therefore the ban would not have prevented his actions.)

According to Lal (2015), this style of xenophobia is ubiquitous throughout U.S. history, particularly with respect to Muslims. Indeed, the ban was incredibly popular. A poll completed by Morning Consult (Easley 2016) in the wake of the Brussels attack revealed that 50% of Americans supported it. If the Orlando attack is "just the beginning," as Trump says, the public are left to wonder what will be next? At what time and what place? Here, Trump once more drives home his proactive message of populism to the people, that *he* will be the one to solve the threat of Islamic terrorism.

Silence and seclusion

Throughout the primaries, Trump sought to portray himself as a "man's man," evident in his powerful political performances, and his timely, truculent tweets (Rosen 2016, np). Trump received much attention for misogyny and sexism during the campaign (Anderson 2017; Rosen 2016; Tumulty 2015). However, Trump is a master of evasion as seen in Tweet #9 (Figure 9.10). Trump deftly strikes both radical Islam and Clinton using the female body as a proxy. Pain (2010) discusses the intimate role between disempowerment, fear, and victimization, culminating in the restriction of agency. Trump, through this tweet, is attempting to cloud the experiences of terror on an international scale with the domestic, to soften the spatial boundaries between fear and its local effects. This correlates with Pain et al.'s (2010) espousal of embodiment and fear within the everyday.

The nickname "Crooked Hillary," alongside the others Trump used throughout the campaign, bore great significance for they reinforced within the subconscious of the followers a discourse of blame and suspicion following Clinton's e-mail scandal (BBC 2016b). A crucial way he did this was through his unique communication style on Twitter. During the U.S. election, negative tweets were

FIGURE 9.10 Tweet #9.

the most popular and Trump became synonymous with Twitter, creating sound bites such as these to spark discussion and enkindle fear (Gross and Johnson 2016; Ott 2017). The provocative question in this tweet regarding how much Clinton "cares" for women, seeks to challenge the imagination of the followers. Yet, despite the shackling of Trump to misogyny, Wang, Li, and Luo (2016) discovered that there was no gender discrepancy between Clinton followers and Trump followers on Twitter. Despite countless controversies, Trump was able to transcend such fetters through his unparalleled preoccupation with "America First."

Trump's "America First" foreign policy was perfectly clear in his acceptance speech at the end of the Republican National Convention three weeks later (Politico 2016). All throughout the campaign, Trump adopted the Reaganite adage of "Peace through strength," both militarily and economically, becoming known as the "Trump Doctrine" (Navarro 2016). Trump, through this statement, is thereby reassuring voters that *their* interests will take priority, that these horrific attacks cannot and will not occur on U.S. soil under a Trump administration. Foundational pillars to totalitarianism are law and order, pillars which Trump greatly admired, declaring himself as the president of law and order (Stanley 2016).

Conclusions: Politics rewritten

Donald Trump's performance in the Republican primaries, and the subsequent election, changed the face of politics for generations to come. This chapter has wrestled with Trump's pugnacious and truculent use of Twitter throughout the Republican primaries in constructing identity, fear, and emotion. To understand how a businessman with no prior experience of the political world rose to such heights requires much scholarship and attention concerning *how* such an improbable victory occurred. Though much scholarship of Trump's use of Twitter has been centered on quantitative methods, this study takes these authors' works one step further, by intricately analyzing the discursive construction of Trump's tweets throughout the campaign, adopting three research questions to steer the study.

Firstly, the chapter explored the role geographical themes played in shaping and serving the campaign. Geographically, the role of space and place helped situate his tweets contextually, building on the imaginative geographies of his followers, and reaffirming an American identity juxtaposed with an unknown and hostile "Other." Alongside this, Trump's use of scale was paramount, as local situations were translated into national threats. Secondly, the research enquired of *how* Trump constructed fear and identity regarding immigration and terror. Trump's contentious wall along the southern border was used materially and metaphorically on Twitter in relation to a fear of an exterior "Other" encroaching on U.S. soil, as well as a rejection of those who do not conform to (or perform) the identity of a true American patriot. Finally, the chapter questioned the role Twitter played in relation to how Trump performed politically, but also how the digital platform empowered the "silent majority." This denouement of Trump's dramaturgical performance embodied the espousal between identity and fear, with authoritarianism seeping into Trump's tweets in often lucid and lavish ways. The growing discrepancy between public retweets and private favorites revealed a growing support for Trump from the "silent majority" eager to support Trump in secret.

To conclude, the election of Donald Trump marked the beginning of the Age of Twitter, and the rise of the "silent majority" (Enli 2017). As Arendt (1973) observed, a leader is required for such a movement to exist, but who this is matters less than the organization itself. Indeed, if Taub (2016) is correct, Trump is just the beginning. Trump's campaign must be understood in the realm of the imagination. From "Make America Great Again" to "America First," Trump dared individuals to dream of a world that conceptually had yet to be realized. Through Twitter, Trump appealed to the anti-political storm that was brewing among the potential electorate, encouraging them to trust their instincts rather than the naysayers of the political elite and mainstream media (Giroux 2016). Trump performed on Twitter as he did on stage, a hybridity that breathed authenticity, anchored to and premised on a deeply rooted fear of the "Other" and a yearning to belong. Trump's tweets enkindled within the electorate an ardent flame of liberty, a medium through which they could find sympathy and solidarity among a rapidly changing and neoliberal world. Without Twitter, there would have been no such platform through which to appease the aching desires of millions of voters. Without Twitter, perhaps there would be no President Trump.

References

Alashri, S., S. Kandala, V. Bajaj, R. Ravi, K. Smith, and K. Desouza. 2016. An analysis of sentiments on Facebook during the 2016 US presidential election. *Advances in Social Networks Analysis and Mining (ASONAM), 2016 IEEE/ACM International Conference*: 795–802.

Anderson, B. 2017. "We will win again. We will win a lot": The affective styles of Donald Trump. *Environment and Planning D: Society & Space* (Feb.28). http://societyandspace.org/2017/02/28/we-will-win-again-we-will-win-a-lot-the-affective-styles-of-donald-trump/

Arendt, H. 1973. *The Origins of Totalitarianism*. San Diego: Houghton Mifflin Harcourt.

Attride-Stirling, J. 2001. Thematic networks: an analytic tool for qualitative research. *Qualitative Research* 1(3): 385–405.

Barrett, L., M. Tugade, and R. Engle. 2004. Individual differences in working memory capacity and dual-process theories of the mind. *Psychological Bulletin* 130(4): 553–573.

Baumgartner, J. C. 2016. Rejecting more of the same? The 2016 veepstakes. *PS: Political Science & Politics* 49(4): 775–781.

BBC. 2015. Paris attacks: As they happened. *BBC News* (Nov. 13). www.bbc.co.uk/news/live/world-europe-34815972

BBC. 2016a. Brussels explosions: What we know about the airport and metro attacks. *BBC News* (April 9). www.bbc.co.uk/news/world-europe-35869985

BBC. 2016b. Hillary Clinton emails – what's it all about. *BBC News* (Nov. 6). www.bbc.co.uk/news/world-us-canada-31806907

Benwell, M.C. 2019. Connecting ontological (in)securities and generation through the everyday and emotional geopolitics of Falkland Islanders. *Social and Cultural Geography* 20(4): 485–506.

Billig, M. 1995. *Banal Nationalism*. London: Sage.

Blankenship, C. 2019. President, wrestler, spectacle: An examination of Donald Trump's firing Tweets and the celebrity apprentice as response to Trump's media landscape. *Journal of Communication Inquiry*: 1–22.

Breitbart. 2015 (Nov. 18). Exclusive – Confirmed: 8 Syrians caught at Texas border in Laredo. www.breitbart.com/big-government/2015/11/18/report-8-syrians-caught-at-texas-border-in-laredo/

Burston, D. 2017. "It can't happen here": Trump, authoritarianism and American politics. *Psychotherapy and Politics International* 15(1): 1–9.

Chaudhry, I. 2015. #Hashtagging hate: Using Twitter to track racism online. *First Monday* 20(2). http://uncommonculture.org/ojs/index.php/fm/rt/printerFriendly/5450/4207#p3

Chomsky, N. 2016. Trump in the White House: An interview with Noam Chomsky. *Truthout* (April 12). www.truth-out.org/opinion/item/38360-trump-in-the-white-house-an-interview-with-noam-chomsky

Ciftci, S., and G. Tezcür. 2015. Soft power, religion, and anti-Americanism in the Middle East. *Foreign Policy Analysis* 12(3): 374–394.

CNN. 2015a (Nov. 15). Passport linked to terrorist complicates Syrian refugee crisis. https://edition.cnn.com/2015/11/15/europe/paris-attacks-passports/index.html

CNN. 2015b (Dec. 5). San Bernardino shooting investigated as "act of terrorism." http://edition.cnn.com/2015/12/04/us/san-bernardino-shooting/

CNN. 2016 (June 15). Orlando terror attack: What we know. http://edition.cnn.com/2016/06/12/us/orlando-shooting-what-we-know/

Cohen, M., D. Karol, H. Noel, and J. Zaller. 2016. Party versus faction in the reformed presidential nominating system. *PS: Political Science & Politics* 43(4): 1–8.

Coyne, B. 2016. How #Election2016 was Tweeted so far. *Twitter Blog* (Nov. 7). https://blog.twitter.com/2016/how-election2016-was-tweeted-so-far

Dalby, S. 1996. Writing critical geopolitics: Campbell, Ó Tuathail, Reynolds and dissident skepticism. *Political Geography* 15(6–7): 655–660.

Dirlik, A. 1999. Is there history after Eurocentrism?: Globalism, postcolonialism, and the disavowal of history. *Cultural Critique* 42: 1–34.

Dowler, L., and J. Sharp. 2001. A feminist geopolitics? *Space and Polity* 5(3): 165–176.

Easley, C. 2016. Half of voters back Muslim travel ban, patrols of Muslim neighbourhoods. *Morning Consult* (March 29). https://morningconsult.com/2016/03/29/polling-muslim-travel-ban-patrolling-muslim-neighborhood/

Enli, G. 2017. Twitter as arena for the authentic outsider: Exploring the social media campaigns of Trump and Clinton in the 2016 US presidential election. *European Journal of Communication* 32(1): 50–61.

Epstein, M. 2009. Transculture: A broad way between globalism and multiculturalism. *American Journal of Economics and Sociology* 68(1): 327–351.

Feldman, S., and K. Stenner. 1997. Perceived threat and authoritarianism. *Political Psychology* 18(4): 741–770.

Fisher, P. 2016. Definitely not moralistic: State political culture and support for Donald Trump in the race for the 2016 Republican presidential nomination. *PS: Political Science & Politics* 49(4): 743–747.

Flynn, T. 2007. Foucault among the geographers. In J. Crampton and S. Elden (eds.) *Space, Knowledge and Power.* pp. 59–64. London: Routledge.

Foucault, M. 2002. *The Archaeology of Knowledge.* (Trans. by S. Sheridan). Oxon: Routledge.

Gallagher, T. 2017. President-elect Trump: Is the past prologue? *Society* 54(1): 1–4

Gallup. 2015. Terrorism in the United States. *Gallup, In depth: Topics A to Z.* www.gallup.com/poll/4909/terrorism-united-states.aspx

Giroux, H. 2016. Political frauds, Donald Trump, and the ghost of totalitarianism. *Knowledge Cultures* 4(5): 95–108.

Gonawela, A., J. Pal, U. Thawani, E. van der Vlugt, W. Out, and P. Chandra. 2018. Speaking their mind: Populist style and antagonistic messaging in the Tweets of Donald Trump, Narendra Modi, Nigel Farage, and Geert Wilders. *Computer Supported Cooperative Work* 27: 293–326.

Gregory, D. 2004. *The Colonial Present.* London: Blackwell.

Gross, J., and K. Johnson. 2016. Twitter taunts and tirades: Negative campaigning in the age of Trump. *PS: Political Science & Politics* 49(4): 748–754.

Haraway, D. 1988. Situated knowledges: The science question in feminism and the privilege of partial perspective. *Feminist studies* 14(3): 575–599.

Hetherington, M., and E. Suhay. 2011. Authoritarianism, threat, and Americans' support for the war on terror. *American Journal of Political Science* 55(3): 546–560.

Huntington, S. 1993. The clash of civilizations? *Foreign Affairs* 72(3): 22–49.

Hyndman, J. 2001. Towards a feminist geopolitics. *Canadian Geographer* 45(2): 210–222.

Hyndman, J. 2004. Mind the gap: bridging feminist and political geography through geopolitics. *Political Geography* 23(3): 307–322.

Kjeldsen, L. 2016. Event-as-participation: Building a framework for the practice of "live-tweeting" during televised public events. *Media, Culture & Society* 38(7): 1064–1079.

Lacatus, C. 2019. Populism and the 2016 American election: Evidence from official press releases and Twitter. *PS: Political Science & Politics* April: 223–228.

Lal, V. 2015. Implications of American Islamophobia. *Economic & Political Weekly* 50(51):12–14.

Lalami, L. 2016. Donald Trump's hate-in. *Nation* 302(10): 10–11.

Lee, J., and Y.S. Lim. 2016. Gendered campaign tweets: The cases of Hillary Clinton and Donald Trump. *Public Relations Review* 42(5): 849–855.

Li, Q., and M. Brewer. 2004. What does it mean to be an American? Patriotism, nationalism, and American identity after 9/11. *Political Psychology* 25(5): 727–739.

Lieven, A. 2016. Clinton and Trump: Two faces of American nationalism. *Survival* 58(5): 7–22.

MacWilliams, M. 2016. Who decides when the party doesn't? Authoritarian voters and the rise of Donald Trump. *PS: Political Science & Politics* 49(4): 716–721.

McLevy, A. 2016. #ImWithHer demonstrates how pop culture (hash)tags its candidates. *A.V. Club* (July 11). www.avclub.com/article/imwithher-demonstrates-how-pop-culture-hashtags-it-238037

Mead, L. 2017. Trump's impact: The end of sameness. *Society* 54(1): 1–4.

Müller, M. 2008. Reconsidering the concept of discourse for the field of critical geopolitics: Towards discourse as language and practice. *Political Geography* 27(3): 322–338.

National Review. 2016 (Jan. 21). Conservatives should stand against him. www.nationalreview.com/article/430126/donald-trump-conservatives-oppose-nomination

Navarro, P. 2016 (March 31). The Trump Doctrine: Peace through Strength. *The National Interest* (March 31). http://nationalinterest.org/feature/the-trump-doctrine-peace-through-strength-15631

Nixon, R. 1969. Nixon's "Silent Majority" speech. November 3, 1969. http://watergate.info/1969/11/03/nixons-silent-majority-speech.html

Ó Tuathail, G. 1994. Critical geopolitics and development theory: Intensifying the dialogue. *Journal of the Royal Geographical Society* 19(2): 228–233.

Ó Tuathail, G., and J. Agnew. 1992. Geopolitics and discourse: Practical geopolitical reasoning in American foreign policy. *Political Geography Quarterly* 11(2): 190–204.

Ott, B. 2017. The age of Twitter: Donald J. Trump and the politics of debasement. *Critical Studies in Media Communication* 34(1): 59–68.

Pain, R. 2009. Globalized fear? Towards an emotional geopolitics. *Progress in Human Geography* 33(4): 466–486.

Pain, R. 2010. The new geopolitics of fear. *Geography Compass* 4(3): 226–240.

Pain, R., R. Panelli, S. Kindon, and J. Little. 2010. Moments in everyday/distant geopolitics: Young people's fears and hopes. *Geoforum* 41(6): 972–982.

Politico. 2016 (July 21). Full text: Donald Trump 2016 RNC draft speech transcript. www.politico.com/story/2016/07/full-transcript-donald-trump-nomination-acceptance-speech-at-rnc-225974

Purdy, J. 2016. A legacy highjacked. *Juncture* 23(3): 150–154.

RealClearPolitics. 2017. 2016 Republican presidential nomination. GOP delegate count. www.realclearpolitics.com/epolls/2016/president/us/2016_republican_presidential_nomination-3823.html

Rinke, E., L. Willnat, and T. Quandt. 2015. The Obama factor: Change and stability in cultural and political anti-Americanism. *International Journal of Communication* 9: 2954–2979.

Rosen, D. 2016. Donald Trump and the crisis of masculinity. *CounterPunch* (Feb. 26). www.counterpunch.org/2016/02/26/donald-trump-and-the-crisis-of-masculinity/

Said, E. 2003. *Orientalism.* London: Penguin.

Seitz, D. K. 2017. "Most damning of all … I think I can live with it": Captain Sisko, President Obama, and emotional geopolitics. *The Geographical Bulletin* 58(1): 19–28.

Segesten, A., and M. Bossetta. 2016. A typology of political participation online: How citizens used Twitter to mobilize during the 2015 British general elections. *Information, Communication & Society* 20(11): 1–19.

Šimunjak, M., and A. Caliandro. 2019. Twiplomacy in the age of Donald Trump: Is the diplomatic code changing? *The Information Society* 35(1): 13–25.

Stanley, J. 2016. Beyond lying: Donald Trump's authoritarian reality. *New York Times* (Nov. 4). www.nytimes.com/2016/11/05/opinion/beyond-lying-donald-trumps-authoritarian-reality.html

Taub, A. 2016. The rise of American authoritarianism. *Vox* (March 1). www.vox.com/2016/3/1/11127424/trump-authoritarianism

Time. 2015 (June 16). Here's Donald Trump's presidential announcement speech. http://time.com/3923128/donald-trump-announcement-speech/

Trump, D. 2015 (Dec. 7). Donald J. Trump statement on preventing Muslim immigration. www.donaldjtrump.com/press-releases/donald-j.-trump-statement-on-preventing-muslim-immigration

Tumulty, K. 2015. Trump's history of flippant misogyny. *Washington Post* (Aug. 8). www.washingtonpost.com/politics/trumps-history-of-flippant-misogyny/2015/08/08/891f1bec-3de4-11e5-9c2d-ed991d848c48_story.html?utm_term=.d4274973b69f

Tyner, J., and S. Henkin. 2014. Feminist geopolitics, everyday death, and the emotional geographies of Dang Thuy Tram. *Gender, Place & Culture* 22(2): 288–303.

Van Dijk, T. 1985. Introduction: Discourse analysis in (mass) communication research. In T. van Dijk (ed.) *Discourse and Communication*. pp. 1–9. Berlin: Walter de Gruyter.

Van Dijk, T. 1997. What is political discourse analysis. *Belgian Journal of Linguistics* 11(1): 11–52.

Van Dijk, T. 2008a. *Discourse and Context. A Sociocognitive Approach*. Cambridge: Cambridge University Press.

Van Dijk, T. 2008b. *Discourse and Power*. London: Palgrave Macmillan.

Wang, Y., Y. Li, and J. Luo. 2016. Deciphering the 2016 US Presidential campaign in the Twitter sphere: A comparison of the Trumpists and Clintonists. *ICWSM*. https://arxiv.org/pdf/1603.03097.pdf

Wang, Y., J. Luo, R. Niemi, Y. Li, and T. Hu. 2016. Catching fire via "likes": Inferring topic preferences of Trump followers on Twitter. *ICWSM*. https://arxiv.org/pdf/1603.03099.pdf

Watt, A., C. Carvill, R. House, J. Livingston, and J. Williams. 2017. Trump typhoon: A rhetorical analysis of the Donald's Twitter feed. *2017 IEEE International Professional Communication Conference*: 1–7.

Weiler, J., and M. MacWilliams. 2016. Authoritarianism, not social class, is the dividing line between supporting and opposing Donald Trump. *USApp–American Politics and Policy Blog*. http://bit.ly/1SmJ2ob

Wells, K. 2017. What does a Republican government with Donald Trump as president of the USA mean for children, youth and families? *Children's Geographies* 15(4): 491–497.

Wodak, R., and M. Meyer. 2009. Methods of critical discourse analysis. In R. Wodak and M. Meyer (eds.) *Critical Discourse Analysis: History, Agenda, Theory and Methodology*. pp. 1–33. London: Sage.

Zakaria, F. 2016. America would be Trump's banana republic. *Washington Post* (July 21). www.washingtonpost.com/opinions/america-would-be-trumps-banana-republic/2016/07/21/f652820a-4f57-11e6-a422-83ab49ed5e6a_story.html?utm_term=.2658fe53058e

Zook, M., M. Dodge, Y. Aoyama, and A. Townsend. 2004. New digital geographies: Information, communication, and place. In S. Brunn, S. Cutter, and J. Harrington (eds.) *Geography and Technology*. pp. 155-176. Dordrecht: Kluwer Academics Publishers.

10

DONALD TRUMP AND THE POTENCY OF HIS ASSEMBLAGE

Sam Page

"Each time there is an operation against the State – insubordination, rioting, guerrilla war machine, or revolution as an act – it can be said that a war machine has revived."

Deleuze and Guattari (2013, p. 45)

"I could stand in the middle of 5th Avenue and shoot somebody and I wouldn't lose any voters."

Donald Trump, Jan. 23, 2016 (Reilly 2016)

Donald Trump's campaign and presidency can be conceived not as a series of separate, unrelated points, but as a singular "flowing movement" (Colebrook 2002, p. 40), where it is "nothing other than its movement" (Colebrook 2002, p. 45). This is revealed by the difficulty in attempting to conceptualize a study of Donald Trump's political trajectory through any specific example, since the relentless flow of events presents the question of what exactly to focus on, exactly. I argue that no one "event" is representative of the Trump moment, and Trump's political presence provides a plethora of notable instances too numerous to point at any singular one as more or less an exemplar. It is more a case of repetition and difference as attention quickly moves from one thing to the next: for instance, the uproar around "Pussygate" in 2016 (the publication by *The Washington Post* of a 2005 video where Trump can be heard saying "when you're a star, [women] let you do it, you can do anything … grab them by the pussy") was quickly followed by his first victory in the race to become the Republican presidential candidate; this, too, was quickly followed by something else. And while Pussygate is still in the air at the time of writing (as are other examples of Trump's misogyny), it reveals how Trump's steamrollers over any issue. In an article for *National Public Radio*,

McCammon (2016) observed that "Trump's astonishing rise to Republican nomination was marked by an aura of invincibility unlike any politician in memory." While other, perhaps more conventional, political figures would not think to survive, Trump ploughs on, barely acknowledging something of note has happened. This is partly because he denies conventional sources of information and sows distrust of these platforms through his presence and influence on social media (Chadwick and Stromer-Galley 2016; Boler and Davis 2018), and this flattening over issues seems to be part and parcel of his adult life. When Trump was performing as a real estate developer, Felix Guttari noted that "Trump [is] permitted to proliferate freely, like another species of algae ... he 'redevelops' by raising rents, thereby driving out tens of thousands of poor families ... becoming the equivalent of the dead fish of environmental ecology" (as quoted by Saldanha 2017, p. 157). Fast forward, and a month after his inauguration, Trump appeared to "put aside the stress of Washington governing and return to the campaign trail" (Baker 2017), suggesting the electoral victory and inauguration did not put a stop to his campaign. As such, Trump's political presence is always changing, always becoming; never to be pinned down by any one issue or moment, but always producing what seems to be a variation on a theme.

From a Deleuzian-informed ontological perspective, events are not necessarily those practiced, precise, planned moments that may be typically considered a political "event," such as the election count, the campaign rally, the televised debate. While these can be events, they are not necessarily so, as the Deleuzian event is defined by its effect. Beck and Gleyzon (2017, p. 329) explain that:

> Deleuzian events are rhizomatic and part of an ever-changing, on-going process ... [they] spur change; they reshape the conceptual and material fabric of connectivity, relationships, pathways and institutions ... events begin from the domain of affect and the virtual (temporal) but are only actualised in space.

In other words, an event can appear anywhere, between the paving cracks of official "moments" (think Pussygate), and its affects changes things. It is not the intentional, but rather the felt, that matters: Berardi (2017, p. 35) writes that "every event is untimely, as [it] does not correspond to a chain of causation." This description of events resembles the Donald Trump political moment *par excellence*, as it chaotically rampages through the social and political norms of the U.S. state, potentially changing the fabric of state and social politics and yet, struggles to pass any legislation despite Republicans being in control of much of the state mechanisms until 2018 as Doucette and Lee (2019) have noted. Thus, the contradiction is prominent: despite being president, despite the high-volume resonance and dissonance around his presidency, any striving for implementation of policy is frequently hampered.

The Deleuzo-Guattarian concept of the "war machine" (Deleuze and Guattari 2013), as I have argued elsewhere (Page 2019), may provide a way to

182 Sam Page

understand current populist moments around the world. From Jeremy Corbyn's rise and fall in the UK to Jair Bolsonaro's in Brazil, the war machine provides a conceptual framework to understand the relations between these movements, its supporters, the state, and the sense of disgust that these political moments are marked by for many, as well as the assemblage's potentials once they have reached some sort of relationship with the state. Thus, in what follows, I develop a reading of the Trumpian moment through the concept of the war machine. Buchanan (2017, p. 461) argues that the use of the concept of assemblage should ask the question: "given a specific situation, what kind of assemblage would be required to produce it?" He explains that "the assemblage is not a thing in the world – it is assemblages that explain the existence of things in the world" (Buchanan 2017, p. 463). This concept of a particular form of assemblage may help to explain the time and place of particular situations (Buchanan 2015). Moreover, while I rely on a heavy use of Deleuze and Guattari in this chapter, I regard the war machine as a tool in their "toolbox" approach, and I am not averse to using it somewhat heretically, as Grossberg (2014) suggests was their want. As such, this chapter asks the following questions: given the Trump presidency, what kind of assemblage would be required to produce it? And what might the future hold for that assemblage?

This chapter begins by grounding the concept of the state as its "other" by exploring how Trump has expressed the logic of his and his supporters' relationship. I then move onto looking at his support base in the 2016 U.S. general election, tracing it through the Bush and Obama administrations, and how it is echoed in populist movements around the world, finding that Franco Berardi's (2017) concept of "impotence" explains the racist desire for Trump. After this, I move onto a key point of my argument– for all the need to explain Trump, we frequently neglect the role of the state. In the concept of the war machine, the state always takes control of the war machine. The question for the conclusion is: what does this mean for either?

The logic of the war machine

The war machine has been variously explored in relation to political events, and has been claimed to take various guises, with several different social groups named. For the most part, it has been interpreted as something from below, frequently resembling some sort of grassroots left-wing movement. Nicholas Tampio (2009) has criticized perhaps the most famous application, conceived in Michael Hardt and Antonio Negri's influential book *Empire*, for marrying Marxist-Leninism to Deleuze and Guattari, and so "fabricating a concept of political subjectivity for postmodernity" by calling the war machine "the *multitude* ... combating the state apparatus, the composition of a joyful body" (Tampio 2009, p. 384). While he concedes that Hardt and Negri identify "a gap in Deleuze's philosophy: an adequate concept of political subjectivity," it is particularly Negri's "Marxist-Leninist assumptions" that Deleuze himself attempted to guard against (Tampio 2009, pp. 384–5). Indeed, the war machine is perhaps

Trump and the potency of his assemblage **183**

not as even as easily defined as a poststructuralist lumpenproletariat by Negri himself, who has argued that the war machine is "a particular way of occupying, taking up spacetime, or inventing new spacetimes: revolutionary movements … but artistic movements too, are war machines" (as quoted by Saldanha 2017, p. 35). Building on Tampio, I contend that the war machine is not necessarily exclusive to the left-wing revolutionary movement, but rather, that a prefascist right-wing libertarianism can somehow embody it, too. Or, at least, it can mimic the war machine to a haunting effect.

In trying to understand his appeal, Donald Trump himself has provided some guidance. In a speech at a campaign rally in Phoenix, Arizona in August 2017, termed a "rant" by *Time* magazine (Trump 2017), Trump declared himself simultaneously better than "the elite" and more approachable than them. He would have us believe that he and his supporters are not of "the elite." "The elite," in this case, becomes something of an "floating signifier," where the meaning of "the elite" is an "indeterminate between alternative equivalential frontiers," and its "meaning is 'suspended'" (Laclau 2018, p. 131), since Trump decides only moments later that he and his supporters, "we're the elites. They're not the elites" (Trump 2017). This is premised by the logic that not only did he have a better education, but he lives in a nicer apartment than "the elite" do. He is not of the same ilk as the elite, and neither are his supporters, thus he and his "honest, hard-working, taxpaying" supporters (Trump 2017) are the real elite.

However, this movable "elite" is more than an empty signifier or a rhetorical device. This discussion displays the concept of the "outsider" that Trump feels he embodies and appeals to, and the concept of the war machine reveals this appeal of logic of the assemblage that derives from outside the state mechanism. Trump is laid bare as his "feelings become uprooted from [his] interiority … projected violently outward into a milieu of pure exteriority … they are no longer feelings, but affects" (Deleuze and Guattari 2013, p. 415). There is no internal, consistent Trump, rather he is on show for all to see. Deleuze and Guattari (2013, p. 413) write that the war machine is "of another species, of another nature, of another origin" than the "state apparatus." It is, Widder (2017, p. 196) writes, "marked by its 'exteriority' to the State." The war machine's logic is not defined by the state's logic; Trump politics is not of a logic defined by previous political convention.

Although they are not to be held in binary, it is in comparison to a loosely abstracted "state" that the war machine is revealed. Put simply, the Deleuzo-Guattarian concept of the state is defined by the desire of "the perpetuation or conservation of organs of power. The concern of the State is to conserve" (Deleuze and Guattari 2013, p. 416). Any one state is not specific, and all are abstracted. As such, the state is not defined by any precise set of processes, mechanisms, or particular features; it is only defined by its survival instinct for itself. It is indiscriminate, and unconcerned with what it produces, only that it continues to produce itself in some way. By contrast, the war machine "exists in only in its own metamorphoses" (Deleuze and Guattari 2013, p. 418), defined by its continuously becoming, "a scientific, technological, industrial, commercial,

184 Sam Page

religious, or philosophical force that flees or punctures the containment of the state" (Tampio 2009, p. 391). The war machine is an extreme, a collective variation of Deleuze and Guattari's "schizo," in other words, "a way of thinking a life not governed by any fixed norm of image or self – a self in flux and becoming, rather than a self that has submitted to law" (Colebrook 2002, p. 6). "War" is not so much the act of violence, but rather a process of a constant state of attack on the state (Saldanha 2017), and is not defined by even its own survival instinct (if it has one), but defined by change and that its "organization … is directed against the State-form" (Deleuze and Guattari 2013, p. 418). It is the Trump campaign's rallying cry of "drain the swamp" that echos loudly here, revealing the position he tries to claim: through his independent wealth, lack of political experience, and embodiment of all that implies, he is poised to change the state.

Who is the war machine?

There has been much discussion of exactly who Trump's supporters and voters are. Many news articles frequently point fingers at the "white working class" (see Carnes and Lupu 2017), whereas Sioh (2018, p. 113) has argued that the Trump campaign found favor on the basis of "the rage" of white working and middle class men, fearful of "economic convergence with other racialized groups … [where] 'White masculinist identity' politics constructed legal gains domestically by minorities and women and economic gains internationally by emerging economies, crucially, in East Asia, as trauma." Thus, the Trumpian call to arms was not one of class, but one of the white race. A markedly similar demographic to the UK's vote to leave the EU (Antonucci, Horvath, and Krouwel 2017). Trump's war machine was an assemblage of some working class, but mostly non-college educated white middle class Americans.

This is not a particularly new assemblage within the U.S. electorate. William Connolly (2008, p. x) has written of the confounding mixture of the religious and capitalist that converged to elect President George W. Bush in 2000, dubbing it "the evangelical-capitalist resonance machine." Then, as now, the resonant material was not an ideology, but rather the "ethos of existential revenge" (Connolly 2008, p. 4). This was never made explicit (until perhaps recently, with support for Trump coming from the likes of neo-Nazis such as Richard Spencer), but "rather, it finds expression in punitive orientation to other faiths, states, and civilisations … in an extreme sense of entitlement for your constituency" (Connolly 2008, p. 4). Under Bush, this bought together "evangelical Christianity, cowboy capitalism, the electronic news media and Republican Party … these diverse elements *infiltrate* each other, metabolizing into a moving complex" (Connolly 2008, p. 39).

During the Obama administration, this assemblage transformed into the grassroots movement the Tea Party. This was shaped through the rhetoric of economic and social resentment, particularly in the wake of the 2008 economic crash. And despite some electoral sense by the Tea Party, it is quite easy to locate this ethos in Trump's support, which is thus part of a machine that has continued to change and morph, affecting the Republican Party in its wake.

Echoing Connolly and Sioh's arguments, Berardi (2017) has conceptualized the emergence of the populist likes of Trump through the theme of "impotence." This impotence is not so much the lack of physical virility of any individual, but rather the sensation of the inability to change things: if "power is based on the hypostatization of the existing relations of potency, on the surreptitious absolutization of the necessity implied in the existing rapport de force," then "impotence is the shape that potency takes in the age of technical and geopolitical hyper-complexity" (Berardi 2017, p. 60). In other words, the sensation of impotency stems from the inability to effect change on one's own situation and the wider world. This is a sense that has not only effected the resentful right, however, but was also evident in Barack Obama's second term, as "he attempted to demonstrate that reason and political skill have the potency to implement hope, and to heal the wounds of [U.S.] society and of the world. The final lesson of this experience, however, is impotence" (Berardi 2017, p. 59).

In the face of the re-emergence of the "dead dog" of financial capitalism after 2008, and the lack of political change, Berardi (2017, p. 60) argues that:

> the re-emerging cult of nation and ethnicity, as exposed through the ascent of Donald Trump and the proliferation of macho fascist dictators worldwide, is the backlash of impotence. Violence is replacing political mediation because political reason is determined to be devoid of potency.

This reminds us that Trump does not exist in isolation, and we would do well to locate him in a context beyond the immediate one in the U.S. (Bachmann and Sidaway 2016). For instance, since the 2008 crash, in the Alternative für Deutschland in Germany, The True Finns (now The Finns Party) in Finland, Brexit, Bolsonaro in Brazil, Duterte in the Philippines, Lega Nord in Italy, and so on. Berardi has written that the current emergence of the far right is not the disciplined extremism of the past, but that "the anthropological substance has deeply changed" (2019, p. 43) in that "the new brand of fascism arises not from juvenile futuristic euphoria but from a widespread sense of depression and an impotent will for revenge" (Berardi 2019, p. 45). However, the rise of support for the likes of Bernie Sanders, Jeremy Corbyn, Podemos in Spain, Syriza in Greece, and so on has grown, asserting that this sense of impotence is a choice. Trump context is both local and intranational, marked by a crisis at the "center" and a resurgence of both left and right, authoritarian and socialist.

The role of the leader

Any assemblage can change its components. As such, the war machine has no essential defining component, and different components attach themselves to the same machine at different times. This has applications for what it means to be the leader of the war machine, as well as making the assemblage appear as if it has emerged from nowhere, all of a sudden, whereas it may have been taking root all along.

Moreover, any relation with this assemblage is not a constant. Trump did not originate from the assemblage, nor it from him; and it will continue beyond him, in some form. In light of Connolly, Sioh, and Berardi, Trumps role echoes Deleuze and Guattari's (2013, p. 416) description of a war machine's chief

> who has no instituted weapon other than his prestige, no other means of persuasion, no other rule than his sense of the groups desires. The chief is more like a leader or a star than a man of power and is always in danger of being disavowed, abandoned by his people.

Trump and contemporaries "smell the opportunity to win power by embodying the white race's will to potency in the wake of its decline" (Berardi 2017). In light of this, Trump's position of support may appear precarious, powerful only so long as he might be granted it.

By contrast, the man of the state, Deleuze and Guattari (2013, pp. 409–10) write, has "two heads: the magician-king and the jurist-priest," who are part of a binary as "they function as a pair." These are archetypes, and we can witness their like in previous recent presidents – the magician-king, otherwise termed "the despot," might be read as George W. Bush; whereas the jurist-priest, otherwise termed "the organiser," could be Barack Obama. However much Bush was derided during his term, he and his administration had the veneer of a presidency: passing laws as a presidential administration, and waging war as a presidential administration.

Trump, however, "from the standpoint of the State … appears in a negative form: stupidity, deformity, madness, illegitimacy, usurpation, sin" (Deleuze and Guattari 2013, p. 412). Which of these terms, and more, have not been uttered in the same breath as Trump from both the left and right? A search for headlines in prominent publications in relation to these key words reveals that Trump is indeed all these things (Figures 10.1–10.6). As such, Trump, the man of war, is guilty of either "betraying everything […] or *of* understanding nothing" (Deleuze and Guattari 2013, p. 412).

Foreign Policy
Donald Trump Is Proving Too Stupid to be President
"You know, I'm like, a smart person." Uh huh.
By Max Boot
June 16, 2017, 2.31pm

FIGURE 10.1 "Stupid" (Boot 2017).

Source: Foreign Policy logo by Mindy Bricker – www.thetinybank.com/new-index/, Public Domain, https://commons.wikimedia.org/w/index.php?curid=58245127)

Trump and the potency of his assemblage **187**

Rolling Stone
Trump's Junk: Is It OK to Dick-Shame the President?
Excerpts from Stormy Daniels' tell-all memoir, 'Full Disclosure,' have too many people pondering the president's penis
By Lilly Dancyger
September 18, 2018

FIGURE 10.2 "Deformed" (Dancyger 2018).

Source: Rolling Stone logo by Rolling Stone – www.rollingstone.com/templates/rolling-stone-templates/theme/rstheme/images/rsLogo.png, Public Domain, https://commons.wikimedia.org/w/index.php?curid=10786564

The New European
Is Donald Trump mad? (Asks Britain's leading psychology writer)
By Louise Chunn
March 13, 2017

FIGURE 10.3 "Mad" (Chunn 2017).

Source: Logo use granted by copyright holder.

The Guardian
One year on, Donald Trump is still an illegitimate president
By Rebecca Solnit
November 8, 2017, 11.00am

FIGURE 10.4 "Illegitimate" (Solnit 2017).

Source: *The Guardian* logo by Asvensson – Own work, Public Domain, https://commons.wikimedia.org/w/index.php?curid=65527841

TIME

Time
This Is What Ancient Greeks Would Have Called Donald Trump
By Devin Singh
March 18, 2016

FIGURE 10.5 "Usurper" (Singh 2016).

Source: *Time* logo by Time Inc – www.time.com/time/, Public Domain, https://commons.wikimedia.org/w/index.php?curid=7468445

USA Today
Trump embodies every one of the Seven Deadly Sins
By Brian Klass
August 1, 2017

FIGURE 10.6 "Sin" (Klaas 2017).

Source: *USA Today* logo by USA Today – www.usatoday.com, Public Domain, https://commons.wikimedia.org/w/index.php?curid=76048437

The role of the state

Despite the importance of understanding his logic, the attraction to him for his supporters, and who they are, Trump did not become the president by winning the popular vote, although he legitimately became the Republican presidential nominee, and many of those in the Republican Party eventually (if not wholeheartedly) embraced him. There are two figures that reveal the issue. First, the electoral turnout was 55.7%; second, he lost the popular vote by 2.1% to Hilary Clinton. A similar moment was witnessed during the 2000 election, when George W. Bush became the president by winning the Electoral College, losing the popular vote by 0.5%. Again, the U.S. electoral system is not isolated, other systems are not immune to such moments, for instance the UK Labour Party lost the 1951 general election after winning the popular vote. Instead, both Trump and Bush won the Electoral College. His presidency is thus partly a result of a defect of the U.S. presidential voting system, and three years into his presidency, he continues to be one of the most, if not the most, unpopular presidents since polling began. Moreover, as Boler and Davis (2018) write, the involvement of Russians in the campaign also raises important questions over Trump's popular (and legal) legitimacy.

These issues reveal one of the most important insights of the concept of the war machine: while many have spent time trying to understand his supporters, it is equally important that we understand how the state deals with it. While the war machine may wage war, without the state, it has nothing to attack or resist. In the end, Trump legally became the president, invited in by the organs of state. Perhaps because of fear, perhaps because of incompetence, or perhaps because of desire. Others have noted, significantly, that Hitler's Nazi Party never won an election; it was invited in by caretakers of the state (Hobsbawm 1995). When looking at these figures, we must not point fingers simply at voters, but the system and its protectors.

The victory of the state

According to the conceptualization of the war machine, some kind of taking over the war machine by the state is an inevitability. The state does not recognize the temporary role of the war machine chief, instead anointing him/her as a point of power by producing "special institutions ... to enable a chief to become a man of State" (Deleuze and Guattari 2013, p. 416). They adopt the signatures and controls of the state: as every president does, Trump had his 100 days to try and reshape the state to what he desired. Thus, it is possible to conceive that the struggles Trump has had in implementing much has been a result of struggling against the state organs that focus on preservation. The state is caught in a contradiction: adopting the war machine and its chief, while trying to maintain a complex organization of bodies.

Becoming president does not mean the chief is cut off from the war machine. Rather, the war machine, too, can be adopted/ossified, as "*The State has no war machine of its own*; it can only appropriate one in the form of a military institution, one that will continually cause it problems" (Deleuze and Guattari 2013, p. 418, their italics). Thus, trust is never created between the two, and each are changed by it. This excitement of becoming part of the state is evidenced by the potency felt by Trump's far right supporters, and the rise in prominence of other "chiefs" – Richard Spencer, Steven Bannon, and others. It seems as if Trump's campaign, and then presidency, has given confidence to the American far right – that the state's machinery will do its bidding. To paraphrase the well-known saying: not everyone who voted for Trump was a racist, but all (voting) racists voted for Trump. So, the problem becomes that it creates the illusion that the war machine is larger than it is, it creates the illusion that the far right has a large base, when it may not. As has been well recorded in electoral geography: the voting system creates the voters the state organs see, but the voters do not create the electoral choices (Johnston and Pattie 2006).

However, while Deleuze and Guattari are vague when it comes to what happens once the war machine becomes part of the state, this machine cannot become or take over the state, since its "destiny" is either to be an (uneasy) *part* of the machinery, or "a double suicide machine for a solitary man or a solitary woman" (Deleuze and Guattari 2013, p. 415). To understand the implication of this statement, it needs reiterating that the state and the war machine are not binaries, they are not opposites: they are of different logics. The Deleuzo-Guattarian state does not emerge, it does not grow from a previous war machine, nor does it require Hobbes's suppression of natural law of war or Rouseau's social contract. Rather, Deleuze and Guattari (2013, p. 419) find themselves "compelled to say that there has always been a State, quite perfect, quite complete." By contrast, the war machine is their social "schizo": it is emergence, becoming, always a new line of flight. It is an extreme, one that does not ossify by itself, but does so once it becomes part of the state machine. The state will inevitably triumph, and it will change the war machine by doing so, but a state, in its detail, will also be changed.

There are some clues, however. The logic of the state is that of striating. When a war machine becomes part of the state, it changes and its components become part of the state apparatus. The logic of the state is forced onto the war machine, which becomes a tool in the sense that the state forces it into a mold through which it can try and understand and use. In other words, a free-flowing machine based on affect and intuition is forced to regularize itself, to conform to a different logic, as the state "only tolerates and appropriates stone cutting by means of *templates*" (Deleuze and Guattari 2013, p. 425). In other words, it becomes more organized – we saw this with the Tea Party, but as other Trumpians gain ground, they may express other ways of being.

The struggles between the war machine and state can be interpreted to reveal some of the issues that Trump has faced since becoming president; such as keeping staff, passing things through Congress, and even seeing them implemented. It is clear that his administration has struggled to follow precedents set by others. First, Tenpas (2018) has noted that "turnover within the senior level of White House staff members bumped up to 83 percent." In November 2018, *The Atlantic* reported that "almost half the top jobs in Trump's state department are still empty" (McManus 2018); the high turnover reportedly a result of the difficultly of working with Trump, as well as the difficulty in implementing anything.

Moreover, the U.S. state is supposed to have three legislative bodies, each supposedly having a moderating effect on the other.

This has worked, to an extent, since Trump's administration struggles to pass laws. Soon after coming into office, Trump signed Executive Order 13769. Commonly known as the Muslim Ban, this was aimed at preventing people from seven different Muslim-majority countries from entering the U.S. for 90 days. The day after it was issued, civil rights groups implemented challenges through various state and federal legal systems, resulting in several courts deeming the ban "unconstitutional" only days after its signing. Since then, it has gone through three different iterations, its third version reduced the focus on Muslims, and expanded to North Koreans and Venezuelans. This was (narrowly) deemed constitutional by the Supreme Court. This final version was significantly changed from the first iteration, less overt in its anti-Muslim bias, more state managed, more comprehensible. The history of this struggle shows the issues that Trump's administration has faced. The turnover of staff and the struggles to implement policy are signs of the uncomfortable relationship Trump's administration has with the logic of the state.

Moreover, the Mueller investigation into the Trump Administration also found that staff are reluctant to follow his orders, and several of them have been ignored (Alexander and Alper 2019). And if simply getting orders followed was not hard enough, their implementation has been made more so since the 2018 midterm elections awarded the Democrats the House of Congress. The immediate effect of this was the longest government shutdown in history, a standoff between Trump and the Democrats over a budget in which Trump's team had specified funding for one of his most prominent campaign pledges – to build a wall between the U.S. and Mexico. It should perhaps be noted that there are already significant parts of the border between the two states that already feature walls. Rather, as Saldanha (2017, p. 157) writes, this Trumpian wall has "once again demonstrated the affective and geopolitical impotence of the archaic figure of *walls*, belying everything liberal democracy is supposed to stand for."

This last point, perhaps, indicates a final complication in the war machine becoming part of the state. Trump's policies are not (necessarily) objectionable to many governing Republicans, and perhaps Democrats, because they are abhorrent, but because of the discourse Trump and his supporters produce. This machine is also a deterritorializing one, bringing fore affects akin to disgust in many, that also creates a rallying cry against him.

Conclusion and implications

To return directly to the question of what kind of assemblage is required to produce a Trump presidency, the war machine has an answer. Trump's assemblage consists not just of those wearing "Make America Great Again" caps, but also the mechanisms of state and those who maintain the state. The state, in this case, refers to an abstract that combines the political and economic, as it is hard to escape the hard reality of the U.S. market doing relatively well under Trump. This is not because it is particularly productive, but because those producing the financial economy are buoyed by Trump's presence.

The implications of the concept of the war machine thus tells us Trump will continue to struggle to implement policies, but he will have his successes. The state is not interested in the details of who is in power, it only cares that it, itself, is maintained: the organs of the state are not rigid, their role is to maintain it. It will find a way of making the outrages of the war machine acceptable, once the war machine has become part of it. One of the hopes of the rise of Trump was that his presence might instigate a reimagining of the divisions in U.S. political society (Page and Dittmer 2016). Instead, there is an uneasy alliance between many Republicans and Trump's position as president: they may not agree with what he says or how he does things, but he is a Republican president. It would seem that power means more than principle. It is not a productive administration, but a negative one, leaving a legacy through dismantling rather than building.

The state's relationship with the Trump war machine may still produce his end (in one way or another), and one that takes revenge on him afterwards. While his rise to political prominence has seemingly produced a feeling of virility in the far right in the U.S., the reaction by many of those who disagree with Trump is still disgust. While his presence in the White House does not seem to be creating a realignment, it is helping to produce an energy both in the center and on the left. This is not just true in the Democratic Party, but in society outside it. As with analyzing political or social movements, we should not look only at the immediate aftermath, but for its lingering mutations.

References

Alexander, D., and Alper, A. 2019. On staff following orders, Trump says – "Nobody disobeys me." *Reuters* (April 22). https://af.reuters.com/article/worldNews/idAFKCN1RY19J

Antonucci, L., L. Horvath, and A. Krouwel. 2017. Brexit was not the voice of the working class nor of the uneducated – it was of the squeezed middle. *British Politics and Policy.* https://blogs.lse.ac.uk/politicsandpolicy/brexit-and-the-squeezed-middle/

Bachmann, V., and J. Sidaway. 2016. Brexit geopolitics. *Geoforum* 77: 47–50.

Baker, P. 2017. Trump returns to the campaign trail after a month in office. *New York Times* (Feb. 18). www.nytimes.com/2017/02/18/us/politics/donald-trump-rally-melbourne-florida.html

Beck, C., and F.-X. Gleyzon. 2016. Deleuze and the event(s). *Journal for Cultural Research* 20(4): 329–33.

Berardi, F. 2017. *Futurability: The Age of Impotence and the Horizon of Possibility.* Brooklyn: Verso

Berardi, F. 2019. *The Second Coming.* Cambridge, MA: Polity Press..

Boler, M., and E. Davis. 2018. The affective politics of the "post-truth" era: Feeling rules and networked subjectivity. *Emotion, Space and Society* 27(May): 75–85.

Boot, M. 2017. Donald Trump is proving too stupid to be president. *Foreign Policy* (June 16). https://foreignpolicy.com/2017/06/16/donald-trump-is-proving-too-stupid-to-be-president/

Buchanan, I. 2015. Assemblage theory and its discontents. *Deleuze Studies* 9(3): 382–92.

Buchanan, I. 2017. Assemblage theory, or, the future of an illusion. *Deleuze Studies* 11(3): 457–74.

Carnes, N., and N. Lupu. 2017. It's time to bust the myth: Most Trump voters were not working class. *Washington Post* (June 5). www.washingtonpost.com/news/monkey-cage/wp/2017/06/05/its-time-to-bust-the-myth-most-trump-voters-were-not-working-class/

Chadwick, A., and J. Stromer-Galley. 2016. Digital media, power, and democracy in parties and election campaigns: Party decline or party renewal? *International Journal of Press/Politics* 21(3): 283–93.

192 Sam Page

Chunn, L. 2017. Is Donald Trump mad? (asks Britain's leading psychology writer). *The New European* (March 13). www.theneweuropean.co.uk/top-stories/is-donald-trump-mad-asks-britain-s-leading-psychology-writer-1-4928028

Colebrook, C. 2002. *Gilles Deleuze*. London and New York: Routledge.

Connolly, W. 2008. *Capitalism and Christianity, American Style*. Durham, NC: Duke University Press.

Dancyger, L. 2018. Trump's junk: Is it OK to dick-shame the president? *Rolling Stone* (Sept. 18). www.rollingstone.com/culture/culture-features/stormy-daniels-trump-penis-sex-725871/

Deleuze, G., and F. Guattari. 2013. *A Thousand Plateaus: Capitalism and Schizophrenia*. Trans. Brian Massumi. London: Bloomsbury.

Doucette, J., and S.-O. Lee. 2019. Trump, turbulence, territory. *Political Geography*, March.

Grossberg, L. 2014. Cultural studies and Deleuze-Guattari, Part 1. *Cultural Studies* 28(1): 1–28.

Hobsbawm, E. 1995. *The Age of Extremes: 1914-1991*. London, UK: Abacus.

Johnston, R., and C. Pattie. 2006. *Putting Voters in Their Place: Geography and Elections in Great Britain*. London and New York: Oxford University Press.

Klaas, B. 2017. Trump embodies every one of the seven deadly sins. *USA Today* (July 31). https://eu.usatoday.com/story/opinion/2017/07/31/how-trump-embodies-seven-deadly-sins-brian-klaas-column/523664001/

Laclau, E. 2018. *On Populist Reason*. New York: Verso.

McCammon, S. 2016. Donald Trump has brought on countless controversies in an unlikely campaign. *NPR* (Nov. 5). www.npr.org/2016/11/05/500782887/donald-trumps-road-to-election-day?t=1555342491360

McManus, D. 2018. Almost half the top jobs in Trump's State Department are still empty. [Blog] *The Atlantic* (Nov. 4). www.theatlantic.com/politics/archive/2018/11/state-department-empty-ambassador-to-australi/574831/

Page, S. 2019. Jeremy Corbyn and the war machine: Assemblage and affect in the 2015 UK Labour Party leadership contest. *Environment and Planning C: Politics and Space* (April). https://doi.org/10.1177/2399654419841385

Page, S., and J. Dittmer. 2016. Donald Trump and the white-male dissonance machine. *Political Geography* 54: 76–78.

Reilly, L. 2016. Donald Trump says he 'could shoot somebody' and not lose voters. *Time*. https://time.com/4191598/donald-trump-says-he-could-shoot-somebody-and-not-lose-voters/

Saldanha, A. 2017. *Space after Deleuze*. London, Oxford, New York, New Delhi, & Sydney: Bloomsbury Academic.

Singh, D. 2016. This is what ancient Greeks would have called Donald Trump. http://time.com/4261816/trump-ancient-greeks/

Sioh, M. 2018. The wound of whiteness: Conceptualizing economic convergence as trauma in the 2016 United States presidential election. *Geoforum* 95: 112–121.

Solnit, R. 2017. One year on, Donald Trump is still an illegitimate president. *The Guardian*. www.theguardian.com/commentisfree/2017/nov/08/donald-trump-illegitimate-president-rebecca-solnit

Tampio, N. 2009. Assemblage and the multitude: Deleuze, Hardt, Negri, and the postmodern left. *European Journal of Political Theory* 8: 383–400.

Tenpas, K. 2018. Record-setting White House staff turnover continues with news of Counsel's departure. *Brookings* (Oct. 19). www.brookings.edu/blog/fixgov/2018/10/19/record-setting-white-house-staff-turnover-continues-with-news-of-counsels-departure/

Trump, D. 2017. President Trump ranted for 77 minutes in Phoenix. Here's what he said. *Time*. http://time.com/4912055/donald-trump-phoenix-arizona-transcript/

Widder, Nathan. 2015. State philosophy and the war machine. In C. Lundy and D. Voss (eds.) *At the Edges of Thought: Deleuze and Post-Kantian Philosophy*. pp. 190–211. Edinburgh: Edinburgh University Press.

11

SMARKS, MARKS, AND THE ELECTORATE

Trump, wrestling rhetorics, and electoral politics

David Beard and John Heppen

Cartography by Matthew Millett

Donald Trump's political style has been explained as an outgrowth of American exceptionalism or American examples of demagoguery (Hinck 2018; Edwards 2018; McDonough 2018). This move locates Trump within the norm of the 200-year history of American politics. But we believe Trump is outside the norm. During his campaign, Trump derided his opponents with insults. Jeb Bush had low energy and Ted Cruz's father was linked to the Kennedy assassination. Trump denigrated his female opponent, Carly Fiorina, and called Hillary Clinton a nasty woman. This trash talk places Trump outside politics and within a different style of communication – one he learned working with Vince McMahon and World Wrestling Entertainment (WWE).

Trump uses rhetoric like that of a professional wrestler, but did these appeals give Trump the election? And does remaking presidential elections as wrestling contests have implications for our future? In this chapter we outline Trump's history with the WWE – the organization that taught Trump to use media to appeal to an audience. We illustrate the ways his political communication reflects the rhetorical style of pro wrestling. Then, we map enthusiasm for wrestling (as measured by attendance in comparison to population) against enthusiasm for Trump (as measured by voting), demonstrating a correlation. This indirect data points toward Trump's use of wrestling rhetoric as a cause of his electoral success and a challenge for approaching elections in the future.

A history of Trump's media apprenticeship with World Wrestling Entertainment

To understand Trump's relationship to wrestling, we describe the WWE, the organization that taught him to engage audiences. We sketch the character named "Donald Trump" who enters the ring with the other characters of the

WWE. Then, we outline his business and political relationship with Vince and Sharon McMahon.

The WWE began as the Worldwide Wrestling Federation (WWWF), founded in 1952 by Jess McMahon and Toots Mondt. Vincent J. McMahon took over for his father after his death in 1954 and Mondt was later bought out. The promotion became the WWWF in 1962. In 1982, third-generation Vincent K. McMahon bought his father out and led the WWF (later renamed the WWE) into national prominence by signing top talent away from other promotions and by beginning *WrestleMania* from Madison Square Garden in 1984 (Hornbaker 2018).

WWE sees itself as an entertainment company providing family-friendly content to hundreds of millions across the world via media, live events, merchandise, and its own television and movie studio; the WWE is "a publicly traded company … an integrated media organization and recognized leader in global entertainment [with] a portfolio of businesses that create and deliver original content 52 weeks a year to a global audience" (WWE Network 2020). The WWE streaming network has about two million subscribers paying $9.99 per month; the WWE broadcasts shows live every week on cable television and on the Fox broadcasting network. Overall, in 2017 WWE generated $801 million. Trump has related to the WWE inside and outside the ring.

Trump's history in professional wrestling: In the ring

Trump made appearances in WWE promotions as a character named "Donald Trump" who became part of the fictional world of the WWE. As Heather Bandenburg (2016) articulated, "Trump has always been essentially a wrestling gimmick embodied in a real life person." The blurring between the fiction and the reality of "Donald Trump" within the WWE media environment began on March 14, 2004, when Trump was interviewed by Jesse Ventura at ringside during *WrestleMania XX*. Ventura asked whether Trump would support Ventura if he ever got back into politics. Ventura ended the interview saying, "You know what? I think we may need a wrestler in the White House in 2008." While Ventura was referring to himself, in a way, Trump became the wrestler in the White House.

Three years later, the blurring continued as the real-life feud between Trump and Rosie O'Donnell would be played out within the ring. In December 2006, O'Donnell claimed that Trump was "not a self-made man" but a "snake-oil salesman." According to CNN, "she proceeded to slam his multiple marriages: '(He) left the first wife – had an affair. (He) had kids both times, but he's the moral compass for 20-year-olds in America. Donald, sit and spin, my friend'" (Zaru 2017). Trump responded by telling *People Magazine* that O'Donnell is "a real loser" and "a woman out of control." He declared an intention to sue for libel: "You can't make false statements. Rosie will rue the words she said," referencing her claims that he went bankrupt. "Rosie's a loser. A real loser. I look forward to taking lots of money from my nice fat little Rosie" (Zaru 2017).

Within weeks after the media feud began, on WWE *Raw*, January 8, 2007, actors playing O'Donnell and Trump took to the ring. The fictional "Rosie O'Donnell" on *Raw* was played by former NWA Women's Champion Kiley McLean. ROH wrestler Ace Steel played a toupeed "Trump," who defeated Rosie. More to the point, however, Season 6 of *The Apprentice* premiered in the same week as the match between the fictional Trump and O'Donnell; the event was cross-promotional.

Two weeks later, the fictionalized Trump, played by Ace Steel, would be replaced with a fictionalized Trump, played by himself, engaged in cartoonish plots typical of the WWE. Trump appeared on the "Jumbo-Tron" and dropped money in the arena on *Raw*, January 29, 2007. In further episodes of *Raw,* Trump became the voice of the common WWE fan, the millionaire who appreciates WWE fans more than WWE owner McMahon; this fiction "builds heat" for a contest at *WrestleMania XXIII*, the "Battle of the Billionaires Match" on April 1, 2007, an event recognized by *The Economist* as Trump's real education in media (*The Economist* 2019).

Trump was the main attraction for *WrestleMania XXIII*, in a showdown with McMahon. The loser would have his head shaved at Ford Field before over 80,000 spectators. Trump would face McMahon using surrogate wrestlers. Bobby Lashley was the stand-in for Trump; Umaga, a Samoan-American wrestler, was the stand-in for McMahon. The guest referee was retired wrestler "Stone Cold" Steve Austin. Lashley defeated Umaga, and Trump and Lashley shaved McMahon bald. In a surprise move, though, Trump took a stunner – Austin's finishing move – at the end of the match. The event had over 1.2 million pay-per-view buys (a record at the time) and took in over $32 million (Margolin 2017). Of course, the outcome of any pro wrestling match is predetermined. In that way, the contest, and its characters, are a fiction.

On June 15, 2009, Trump announced that he had purchased the TV program *Raw* from under McMahon's nose – also a fiction. As new owner, Trump declared that *Raw* would run ad-free. This did not work, financially, and Trump sold *Raw* back to McMahon on June 22, 2009.[1] This storyline cross-promoted *The Apprentice*, and Trump may have felt pressure for brand maintenance because Trump Entertainment Resorts filed for bankruptcy in spring 2009. Trump also lost a libel suit against Timothy O'Brien that year. The *New York Times* reported that "A judge in New Jersey dismissed on Wednesday a $5 billion defamation lawsuit filed by Donald J. Trump against an author whose book placed Mr. Trump's personal wealth far below his public estimates" (Goodman 2009). Trump wanted to create the illusion that he had enough financial resources to make money fall from the sky (Margolin 2017).

Whether promoting his media properties (*The Apprentice*) or sustaining the illusion of wealth in his personal brand, the Trump "character" in the WWE appears to the benefit of both Trump and the WWE. The fiction ignites the audience, and the fiction reinforces the public image of the real Trump. That mutually reinforcing relationship culminated in Trump's admission to the Hall of Fame the night before *Wrestlemania XXIX*. His induction was greeted with boos and chants of "you suck" by fans. Margolin (2017) interpreted the fan reaction as impatience at the length of the ceremony.

Trump learned from crowd reactions and crafted his presidential campaign with a storyline that placed him into the heroic position as the advocate for the common fan. We believe that Trump's rhetoric (decrying bad trade deals hurting the American worker, disparaging foreign elements both internal and external, portraying politicians as corrupt, and more) was honed by his work in the WWE. The WWE provided Trump with tools to attract a segment of American society that was vital in his campaign, a segment foreign to a man accustomed to real estate deals in one of the most expensive cities in the world. And, the WWE taught him to build an audience that encouraged cable and broadcast TV to cover his campaign. Francia (2018) argues that Trump's media coverage and Twitter use provided him with an advantage in 2016. Trump provided Twitter and cable and broadcast television news networks with content attracting viewers and advertisers, giving him $5 billion of free media (Stewart 2016). Arguably, McMahon taught Trump to use media.

Trump's history in professional wrestling: Backstage

As a business partner, Trump's first foray into wrestling was in Atlantic City in 1989. Trump paid a fee to host *WrestleMania IV* to boost attendance at his properties in Atlantic City (Margolin 2017). Trump was featured in the front row of the event, but he had nothing to do with the storyline. Trump hosted *WrestleMania V* in Atlantic City and was featured in an interview. Trump attended *WrestleMania VII* in Los Angeles where his future second wife, Marla Maples, was featured as a guest celebrity. Trump was interviewed during the event about returning *WrestleMania* to his Atlantic City properties but it never happened. (In the 1990s Trump's properties in Atlantic City went bankrupt; his last property in Atlantic City closed in 2016.) Trump's Trump Taj Mahal in Atlantic City was host to the 1991 World Bodybuilding Federation (WBF) Championship (owned by McMahon as well). The success of *WrestleMania* and so of the WWE was part of the success of Trump properties.

Reports from *Forbes* suggest that the WWE donated close to $4 million to the Trump Foundation in 2007. This contribution brought total donations to the foundation that year to $4.1 million – the McMahons were *the* major donor to the Foundation, and for the WWE, this was a significant expense. The donation equaled 8% of the WWE net profit that year.

The ties between the McMahons and Trump go beyond charity. Linda McMahon was appointed by Trump to serve as administrator of the Small Business Administration. She made two runs for the U.S. Senate from Connecticut where the WWE is headquartered and where the McMahons reside. She lost both times in 2010 and 2012. Trump contributed $5,000 for her first campaign. Linda McMahon is also an active contributor to the Republican Party. She contributed over $150,000 to the National Republican Committee and the National

Republican Senatorial Committee and, during the fall campaign, she contributed $6.5 million to Rebuilding America Now – a Political Action Committee which supported Trump (Margolin 2017). In summary, the links between Trump and the McMahons went beyond a business relationship into a political one as well.

Wrestling shapes Trump's political style

Critics have traced the influence of wrestling on Trump's campaign. Josh Dawsey traces the wrestling impulse in Trump's campaign through interviews with staffers: "'I would say to him, we're going to be the WWE of the primary with the smash-mouth adrenaline pumping,' said Sam Nunberg, a former campaign aide who met Trump for the first time at a wrestling match. 'He loved the sensationalism, the drama, the fantasy'" (Dawsey 2017). Similarly, Christopher Wilson (2016) tells us that the character of Trump at *Wrestlemania* addressed McMahon "in the same bullying way he went after Jeb Bush," with the same language. And, if *The Economist* (2019, p. 31) is to be believed, this is what audiences, what voters want: "Why choose Jeb Bush trying to be a pantomime bad-ass when you could have the real thing?"

Wrestling saturates contemporary political discourse. Migliore (1993, p. 68) tells us that "professional wrestling constructs, deconstructs, and reconstructs a particular image of reality," also a goal of political communication. Oliver Willis (2016) makes broad attempts to describe American politics in terms of "faces" and "heels," using the overarching narrative and soap operatic structure of the wrestling match as an analogy for elements of American political life. Heather Bandenburg (2016) tells us that "wrestling and politics both rely on over the top characters to clamor for popularity in outrageous PR stunts." Stodden and Hansen (2015) note that processes employed by politicians are similar to the creation of angles and storylines in wrestling.

For our purposes, we see three dimensions of wrestling rhetoric in Trump's political rhetoric: "By means of 'mic work,' the wrestlers boast and brag of their successes, denigrate their opponents, and coax or goad the audience" mediated by an announcer (Lipscomb 2005, p. 16). We will trace Trump's boasting and bragging, denigrating opponents, and coaxing or goading the audience, often mediated by right-wing media.

Trump's boasting and bragging become character

Trump is a self-aggrandizer who exaggerates his attributes and his achievements. Martin Montgomery (2017) collected a sample of his boasts:

> "Nobody knows the system better than me, which is why I alone can fix it." (July 2016)
> "I have made billions of dollars in business making deals – now I'm going to make our country rich again. I am going to turn our bad trade agreements into great ones." (July 2016)

198   David Beard and John Heppen

"People love me. And you know what, I have been very successful. Everybody loves me." (July 2015)

"I have had tremendous success. I'm, like, a really smart person." (July 2015, cited in Montgomery 2017, p. 625)

Montgomery (2017, p. 625) summarizes Trump's exaggeratory claims about himself: "Wealth, beauty, intelligence, popularity, business acumen and know-how, all of these attributes are claimed." Montgomery sees the origins of this boastfulness in the wrong sport: boxing, in Muhammad Ali's claims that "It's hard to be humble when you're as great as I am." In fact, both Ali and Trump derive their rhetorical style from the wrestling ring.

Braggadocio typifies wrestling performance; Gorgeous George, a wrestler from the 1950s who called himself "the sensation of the nation, the toast of the coast," inspired Ali (Lipscomb 2005, p.60). Randy "Macho Man" Savage claimed that "I am the greatest Intercontinental Heavyweight Champion that ever lived, and I'm the greatest professional wrestler that ever lived" (Young 2013). Booker T entered the ring proclaiming that he is "five-time, five-time, five-time world champion" (Lipscomb 2005, p. 112). A catalog of every wrestler claiming to be the greatest would go on forever.

Bragging is part of the job description, mandated by the WWE. At arena shows, print materials brag, too. Lipscomb (2005, p. 110) transcribes one brochure, in which wrestler Hardcore Holley is called "hardcore to the bone, having held numerous Hardcore Championships to prove his reputation. In addition, he's one of the most technically sound competitors ever. His drop-kick is considered by many to be the best in the business." Braggadocio is how the wrestlers build a brand. Trump learned these strategies as a character in the WWE, and he deploys them in rally speeches, the mass media, and on Twitter.

Trump's insults become votes and merchandise sales

Insult typifies Trump's political style. Ed Appel collects a list of the names Trump has called other politicians:

Kerry the "Disaster"; "Losers" George Will and a CNN panel; the "Nervous Mess" of a clergy- woman at a church in Flint, MI; "Lyin' Ted" Cruz; "Weak" Jeb Bush, who showed "no stamina"; "Little Marco" Rubio; the "Coward" Michael Bloomberg, afraid to run for president; an "Absolute Clown, Robert Gates"; "wacky," "crazy" Maureen Dowd, a "Neurotic Dope"; that "Bimbo" Megan Kelly of Fox News. (Appel 2018, p. 164)

Theye and Melling (2018, p. 329) add to the list: "According to Trump, Glenn Beck is a 'failing, crying, lost soul,' Mitt Romney 'was one of the dumbest and worst candidates in the history of Republican politics,' and the writer Harry Hurt is a 'dummy dope.'" This list is far from exhaustive.

Trump's demeaning and demonizing ways of talking about his political enemies are an integral part of what Enli (2017) calls his "social media style." Theye and Melling (2018, p. 328) cite numbers tabulated from tweets during the campaign: "he called his opponents 'stupid' (at least 30 times), 'horrible' (14 times), 'weak' (13 times) and other names." Theye and Melling (2018, p. 329) note that "since Trump announced his candidacy for president, he has managed to insult, as of this writing, 487 different things, places, and people on Twitter, as catalogued by *The New York Times*." Insult is his rhetorical style.

Hillary Clinton bore the brunt of this rhetorical style. Enli (2017, p. 58) points to tweets that insult ability, intelligence, and looks, like Trump's assertions that "Crooked Hillary has ZERO leadership ability." Others, especially women, suffered name calling and insults. Ott (2017, p. 64) cites Trump's tweet of August 28, 2012: "@ariannahuff is unattractive both inside and out." Montgomery (2017, p. 620) points to print interviews: "'Look at that face!' referring to Carly Fiorina, a rival for the Republican nomination. 'Would anyone vote for that? Can you imagine that, the face of our next president?!'" Insults characterize Trump's rhetorical style.

Insults also characterize communication in pro wrestling, primarily in trash talk, or "insulting comments about an opponent" (Yip, Schweitzer, and Nurmohamed 2018). Common tropes of wrestling trash talk include insulting the looks, ability, and intelligence of opponents. Bernthal and Medway (2005, p. 229) note that "insults and threats hurled back and forth between wrestlers are a staple of wrestling programming." In a study of verbal aggression typical in a wrestling show, Tamborini et al. (2008, p. 253) found that "character and competence attacks are among the three most common verbal aggression types in professional wrestling, behind swearing." Trump learned to insult his competition from McMahon.

Trash talk generates fan interest in the match. When preparing for the WWE "Battle of the Billionaires," Trump taunts McMahon with the assertion "You're a rich guy, I'm a richer guy" and tells him "You don't have guts" as he builds heat for *WrestleMania* (WWE Network 2014). The WWE is where Trump learned to make the crowd "pop."

Verbal aggression creates narrative and characterization for wrestlers. As Tamborini et al. (2008, p. 253) note, "character and competence attacks seem well suited here for narrative goals such as establishing character dispositions, advancing storylines, and adding humor." Trump builds heat against his political opponents in this way. As the narrative progresses, the heat turns into votes (and merchandise sales).

Trump works the media the way wrestlers worked with "Mean Gene"

An important trope in wrestling is the interview. Sehmby (2002) describes a wrestling show as "a news program in terms of its documentary style: presented live, like a news broadcast, the wrestling reporters interview wrestlers as though they are politicians arguing with other politicians." Interviewers like "Mean Gene" Okerlund worked for the WWE to build "heat" for future matches. As Spencer Hall (2019) notes, "Okerlund served as the level. He kept everything on balance, and gave the exact measure of real gravitas to a moment no matter how absurd that moment might be ... while never forgetting to mention that the show was at the National Guard Armory in Nashville this coming Saturday." Trump's understanding of the relationship between the media and the star was conditioned by his experience in the WWE.

Trump struggles to connect with the media, who see themselves as independent and can be antagonistic. He declares them "fake news" and, when individual reporters become antagonistic, he bans them from the White House. And yet, he calls in to Fox News regularly – arguably, we think, because Fox News personalities work Trump the way Okerlund worked the wrestlers. Okerlund was the wrestler's partner, not their interrogator, and Okerlund and the wrestler worked together to ignite the fans. With Fox reporters, the voters are ignited for Trump the same way that wrestling fans are ignited for the WWE.

The wrestling rhetoric appeals to Trump voters

A demographic that finds wrestling appealing may also find Trump's rhetoric, informed by his time in the WWE, appealing. We posit that by looking at electoral data and data on fans of wrestling, we can provide a link between the appeal of wrestling and an attraction to Trump. We will examine the percentage of the vote received by each candidate in the Census Bureau's metropolitan statistical area at the county level in 2016. The hypothesis is that Trump gained more votes in places where wrestling has high appeal. The appeal of wrestling will be measured by attendance and frequency of WWE events at places throughout the United States in 2015 and 2016.

Geographers (e.g., Archer and Taylor 1981) have used factor analysis and other spatial analytical means to place presidential elections in their spatial-temporal context. T-mode factor analysis reduces a series of elections into eras or time periods based on similar factor loadings (Shelley, Watrel, and Archer 2018). The method compares a series of elections by examining the likeness of results in sequences of consecutive elections (Shelley et al. 2018). Shelley et al. (2018) have studied presidential election results at the county level since 1872. (For more on T-mode factor analysis see Archer and Taylor 1981; Archer and Shelley 1986). We situate our work within this tradition and methodology.

Our analysis considers county or multi-county census statistical areas or metropolitan areas. (A wrestling show at the Target Center in Minneapolis, Hennepin County, Minnesota will draw most of its fans from the metropolitan region where the population is large enough to support a WWE show.) Electoral and social data attempting to measure a link between the WWE and Trump voting will be at that scale. We use voting data at the metropolitan region from the *Atlas of the 2016 Elections* (Watrel et al. 2018).

Our data includes attendance at WWE live events in 2015 and 2016, events in front of a live audience in an arena or similar venue – both televised and non-televised. Included are WWE's *Raw*, which is televised lived on Monday nights, *WrestleMania* and the Pay Per View (PPV) and WWE Network events (like *Money in the Bank* and *NXT* events filmed in Florida, which are part of PPV and on the WWE Network). Attendance figures are estimates obtained from *Wrestling Observer Newsletter* (Harrington 2016). We present both the raw data and then a standardized measure of attendance since 10,000 fans in Milwaukee, Wisconsin as standardized for population is not the same as 10,000 fans in Los Angeles.

For each location (such as Minneapolis, MN) we created a ratio of the attendance at the arena to the population of the Minneapolis-St. Paul Metropolitan statistical area. We use the Census Bureau's estimates for metropolitan areas for 2016. For each metropolitan area that hosted a live WWE event in 2015 and 2016, we created a standardized measure based on the attendance at the event in ratio to the population of the metropolitan area. By standardizing attendance, we are able to categorize metropolitan regions as having above or below average support for wrestling. We calculated the mean support for WWE events and identified metropolitan areas that were above one standard deviation of support for WWE. For metropolitan areas like New York and Los Angeles, where multiple arenas hosted events, we consolidated attendance for the entire region. For example, events in Brooklyn, New York and Newark, New Jersey for 2015 were added together to create the attendance figure used in calculating the ratio for the multi-state New York metropolitan area.

WWE live events 2015

The location, dates, and attendance estimates for 283 events in the United States were analyzed.[2] In 2015, the attendance estimates are from *Wrestling Observer* and announcements from WWE which do tend to be slightly exaggerated (Margolin 2017). The average attendance for WWE events was 5,266 spectators with a standard deviation of 5,925 spectators. The most attended event was *WrestleMania XXXI* in Santa Clara, California with an announced attendance of 76,976 by the WWE. The median number was 4,500 in 2015. Of note is that 24% of all shows held an attendance of less than 1,000. (Of the 65 events with less than 1,000 spectators, all were NXT events with over 90% of them filmed in Florida.) WWE hosts shows from markets as big as New York and as small as Moline, Illinois.

Attendance for 2015 were not distributed evenly in both absolute and relative terms. The next step in analysis of attendance for WWE events was to create a relative measure of attendance based on the ratio of people attending WWE

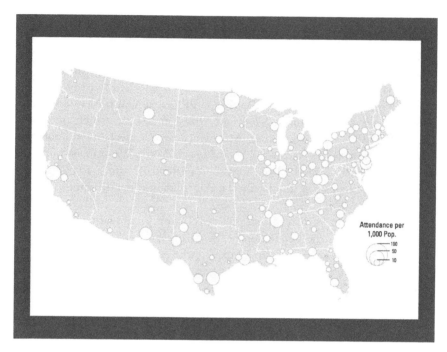

FIGURE 11.1 Wrestling attendance ratio, 2015.

events per 1,000 people in a metropolitan region. To calculate the ratios, we combined attendance in a metropolitan region for the entire year. For example, if a multi-county metropolitan region hosted two wrestling events in two different arenas at two different dates, we combined that into a total attendance for the metropolitan area. The ratios were mapped (Figure 11.1) and Tables 11.1 and 11.2 present the most over- and under-attended metropolitan areas. Some places in 2015 (like Beltrami County, Minnesota) are micropolitan places not big enough to meet the definition of a metropolitan place. Population of metropolitan and micropolitan places are based on counties.

An analysis reveals that places with the highest attendance per 1,000 people are generally smaller and mid-market places. Places like Danville, Illinois, Bemidji, Minnesota, Corpus Christi, Texas, Billings, Montana, Charleston, West Virginia, and Lake Charles, Louisiana are places where the attendance per 1,000 people are the highest. These and other places in the bottom quartile are mainly small to mid-market places. San Jose, California ranks high because *WrestleMania XXXI* was held in Santa Clara, California. The bottom end of the ratio is dominated by big market metropolitan places. Miami, Portland, Washington, D.C., Detroit, Houston, and Phoenix are in the lower quartile of attendance per 1,000. WWE shows in larger markets may not be as big of an event.

Smarks, marks, and the electorate 203

TABLE 11.1 Highest wrestling attendance ratios, 2015.

Area	Population 2015	Attendance	Attendance Ratio
Beltrami County, MN	44,442	2,500	56.25
San Jose-Sunnyvale-Santa Clara, CA Metro Area	1,968,578	98,576	50.07
Danville, IL Metro Area	78,990	3,500	44.31
Tupelo, MS Metro Area	82,910	3,500	42.21
Corpus Christi, TX Metro Area	452,735	18,500	40.86
Las Cruces, NM Metro Area	213,567	8,000	37.46
Ocean City, NJ Metro Area	94,843	3,100	32.69
Billings, MT Metro Area	168,164	5,000	29.73
Charleston, WV Metro Area	220,375	6,500	29.50
Lake Charles, LA Metro Area	205,495	6,000	29.20
Johnson City, TN Metro Area	200,607	5,500	27.42
Huntington-Ashland, WV-KY-OH Metro Area	361,357	9,200	25.46
Bradford County, FL	28,520	725	25.42
Odessa, TX Metro Area	159,689	4,000	25.05
Des Moines-West Des Moines, IA Metro Area	622,580	15,300	24.58
Casper, WY Metro Area	82,191	2,000	24.33
Erie, PA Metro Area	278,052	6,700	24.10
Laredo, TX Metro Area	268,929	6,100	22.68
Fargo, ND-MN Metro Area	233,642	5,000	21.40
Lubbock, TX Metro Area	310,688	6,500	20.92
Abilene, TX Metro Area	169,893	3,500	20.60
Charleston-North Charleston, SC Metro Area	744,603	14,700	19.74
Bangor, ME Metro Area	152,478	3,000	19.67
Cape Coral-Fort Myers, FL Metro Area	700,285	13,380	19.11
State College, PA Metro Area	160,491	3,000	18.69
Tallahassee, FL Metro Area	377,806	7,000	18.53
Green Bay, WI Metro Area	316,413	5,800	18.33
Atlantic City-Hammonton, NJ Metro Area	273,035	5,000	18.31
Terre Haute, IN Metro Area	170,754	3,000	17.57
Florence, SC Metro Area	206,341	3,500	16.96
Springfield, IL Metro Area	210,950	3,500	16.59

WWE live events 2016

We analyzed attendance for WWE events from January 1 to November 18, just after the election on November 8, 2016 – data from 308 events was obtained on average attendance. As in 2015, the attendance are estimates from *Wrestling Observer* and from the WWE. The average attendance was 4,301. The single largest event was *WrestleMania XXXII* in Dallas, with 101,763 people in attendance. As in 2015 a large number of events had fewer than 1,000; these events were in the WWE *NXT* program, but in 2016 more *NXT* events were held outside of Florida. There were approximately 90 events which had attendance of fewer than 1,000 fans. Almost one-third of WWE events in our sample took place before relatively small crowds.

204 David Beard and John Heppen

TABLE 11.2 Lowest wrestling attendance ratios, 2015.

Area	Population 2015	Attendance	Attendance Ratio
North Port-Sarasota-Bradenton, FL Metro Area	768,013	766	1.00
Palm Bay-Melbourne-Titusville, FL Metro Area	567,934	750	1.32
Portland-Vancouver-Hillsboro, OR-WA Metro Area	2,384,807	3,200	1.34
Gainesville, FL Metro Area	276,583	400	1.45
Miami-Fort Lauderdale-West Palm Beach, FL Metro Area	6,001,717	9,500	1.58
Virginia Beach-Norfolk-Newport News, VA-NC Metro Area	1,723,468	3,000	1.74
Grand Rapids-Wyoming, MI Metro Area	1,038,337	2,000	1.93
Charlotte-Concord-Gastonia, NC-SC Metro Area	2,424,643	5,200	2.14
Washington-Arlington-Alexandria, DC-VA-MD-WV Metro Area	6,078,469	16,400	2.70
Houston-The Woodlands-Sugar Land, TX Metro Area	6,647,465	20,969	3.15
Phoenix-Mesa-Scottsdale, AZ Metro Area	4,567,857	14,500	3.17
Stockton-Lodi, CA Metro Area	723,496	2,500	3.46
Detroit-Warren-Dearborn, MI Metro Area	4,297,538	15,000	3.49
Fort Wayne, IN Metro Area	429,372	1,500	3.49
San Antonio-New Braunfels, TX Metro Area	2,381,703	8,500	3.57
Seattle-Tacoma-Bellevue, WA Metro Area	3,727,097	14,000	3.76
Portland-South Portland, ME Metro Area	526,795	2,000	3.80
Salisbury, MD-DE Metro Area	394,521	1,500	3.80
St. Louis, MO-IL Metro Area	2,808,330	11,000	3.92
Providence-Warwick, RI-MA Metro Area	1,612,574	7,000	4.34
Minneapolis-St. Paul-Bloomington, MN-WI Metro Area	3,518,252	15,500	4.41
Milwaukee-Waukesha-West Allis, WI Metro Area	1,574,349	7,000	4.45
Jacksonville, FL Metro Area	1,448,016	6,450	4.45
Dallas-Fort Worth-Arlington, TX Metro Area	7,089,888	32,000	4.51
Indianapolis-Carmel-Anderson, IN Metro Area	1,986,542	9,000	4.53
Las Vegas-Henderson-Paradise, NV Metro Area	2,109,289	9,700	4.60
Raleigh, NC Metro Area	1,271,381	6,000	4.72
Atlanta-Sandy Springs-Roswell, GA Metro Area	5,699,050	26,981	4.73
Chicago-Naperville-Elgin, IL-IN-WI Metro Area	9,532,569	46,697	4.90
Richmond, VA Metro Area	1,270,414	6,300	4.96
Lexington-Fayette, KY Metro Area	500,663	2,500	4.99

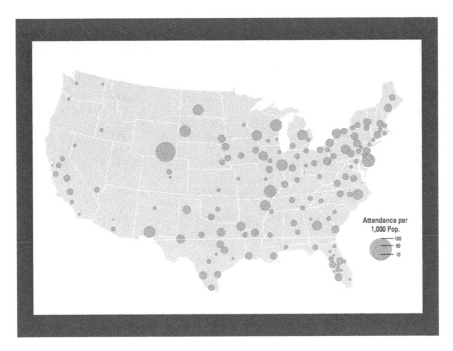

FIGURE 11.2 Wrestling attendance ratio, 2016.

As in 2015 events were not evenly distributed across the country. We calculated a ratio based on population once again. The results are presented in Figure 11.2, and Tables 11.3 and 11.4 show over-and under-represented places in 2016. Places of smaller and medium-sized markets once again dominate in a more standardized analysis. Laramie, Wyoming with a metro population of about 31,000 had an estimated attendance of 2,500 with a ratio of 80 people per 1,000 attending a wrestling show. Other communities include Pike County, Cape Girardeau, Green Bay, Las Cruces, Rapid City, Danville, Jonesboro, Bismarck, Saginaw, La Crosse, and Greenville. The lower end of the ratio includes major markets like Cincinnati, Phoenix, Miami, San Diego, San Francisco, Atlanta, Houston, Milwaukee, and Portland. The largest metro areas of New York, Los Angeles, and Chicago ranged from 3.8 to 4.6 fans per thousand attending WWE events.

Hypotheses explaining higher attendance per 1,000 people in small communities include higher energy for an unusual event: the WWE is the NFL or Major League of wrestling, and the fan base reacts enthusiastically to the opportunity to see the biggest stars.

Hypotheses explaining lower ratios in major cities include the size of venue; Madison Square Garden, when sold out, cannot approach the ratios in smaller

206 David Beard and John Heppen

TABLE 11.3 Lowest wrestling attendance ratios, 2016.

Area	Population 2016	Attendance	Attendance Ratio
Riverside-San Bernardino-Ontario, CA Metro Area	4,527,837	1,000	0.22
Virginia Beach-Norfolk-Newport News, VA-NC Metro Area	1,726,907	1,000	0.58
Cincinnati, OH-KY-IN Metro Area	2,165,139	1,500	0.69
Phoenix-Mesa-Scottsdale, AZ Metro Area	4,661,537	6,000	1.29
North Port-Sarasota-Bradenton, FL Metro Area	788,457	1,250	1.59
Miami-Fort Lauderdale-West Palm Beach, FL Metro Area	6,066,387	10,000	1.65
San Francisco-Oakland-Hayward, CA Metro Area	4,679,166	8,000	1.71
Ocala, FL Metro Area	349,020	600	1.72
Spokane-Spokane Valley, WA Metro Area	556,634	1,000	1.80
San Diego-Carlsbad, CA Metro Area	3,317,749	6,000	1.81
Austin-Round Rock, TX Metro Area	2,056,405	4,000	1.95
Sebring, FL Metro Area	100,917	200	1.98
Atlanta-Sandy Springs-Roswell, GA Metro Area	5,789,700	11,580	2.00
Gainesville, FL Metro Area	280,708	600	2.14
Houston-The Woodlands-Sugar Land, TX Metro Area	6,772,470	15,900	2.35
Palm Bay-Melbourne-Titusville, FL Metro Area	579,130	1,450	2.50
Milwaukee-Waukesha-West Allis, WI Metro Area	1,572,482	4,000	2.54
Colorado Springs, CO Metro Area	712,327	2,000	2.81
Portland-Vancouver-Hillsboro, OR-WA Metro Area	2,424,955	7,500	3.09

communities. Possibly, many fans cannot obtain tickets. Local Pay Per View data and television ratings might enrich future analysis.

Analysis of Trump support and WWE fandom

The next part of the analysis examined the relationship between WWE fandom and support for Trump and Clinton in the metropolitan areas that hosted WWE wrestling events in 2015 and in 2016 until November. To match the multiple county CBSA level of analysis used to create our wrestling fandom attendance ratio, we aggregated the vote for the Democratic and Republican candidates for president to the metropolitan CBSA level. We summed the total vote for candidates for the counties in each metropolitan area. For example, since we created the attendance ratio for Minneapolis-Saint Paul by using the attendance at WWE events and the population of 16 county metropolitan

Smarks, marks, and the electorate **207**

TABLE 11.4 Highest wrestling attendance ratios, 2016.

Area	Population 2016	Attendance	Attendance Ratio
Laramie, WY	30,816	2,500	81.13
Pike County, Kentucky, USA	65,024	4,400	67.67
Ocean City, NJ Metro Area	94,430	3,700	39.18
Cape Girardeau, MO-IL Metro Area	97,443	3,500	35.92
Green Bay, WI Metro Area	318,236	11,000	34.57
Las Cruces, NM Metro Area	214,207	6,800	31.74
Rapid City, SD Metro Area	145,661	4,500	30.89
Danville, IL Metro Area	78,111	2,400	30.73
Jonesboro, AR Metro Area	129,858	3,500	26.95
Bismarck, ND Metro Area	131,635	3,500	26.59
Greenville, NC Metro Area	177,220	4,600	25.96
La Crosse-Onalaska, WI-MN Metro Area	136,936	3,500	25.56
Saginaw, MI Metro Area	192,326	4,800	24.96
Macon-Bibb County, GA Metro Area	229,182	5,000	21.82
State College, PA Metro Area	161,464	3,500	21.68
Saline County, Kansas	55,606	1,200	21.58
Davenport-Moline-Rock Island, IA-IL Metro Area	382,268	8,200	21.45
Buffalo-Cheektowaga-Niagara Falls, NY Metro Area	1,132,804	24,000	21.19
Texarkana, TX-AR Metro Area	150,098	3,000	19.99
Odessa, TX Metro Area	157,462	3,000	19.05
Dallas-Fort Worth-Arlington, TX Metro Area	7,233,323	131,853	18.23
Wheeling, WV-OH Metro Area	142,982	2,500	17.48
Amarillo, TX Metro Area	263,342	4,500	17.09
Monroe, LA Metro Area	179,470	3,000	16.72
Laredo, TX Metro Area	271,193	4,500	16.59
Augusta, Maine	121,581	2,000	16.45
Erie, PA Metro Area	276,207	4,500	16.29

regions, we summed the vote totals for the candidates for the same 16 county metropolitan regions.

First, the vote for Trump and Clinton is presented for each of the metropolitan areas that hosted a wrestling event during 2015 and 2016 (Figures 11.3 and 11.4). Metropolitan areas in the South and Midwest generally showed greater support for Trump than Clinton. But across all regions, the larger the metropolitan region, the stronger the support was for Hillary Clinton. Our thesis is that places that showed a higher ratio of WWE fandom will be positively correlated with support for Trump in 2016.

Second, a bivariate regression analysis was conducted with the Trump vote in each of the metropolitan areas as the dependent variable and the wrestling ratio as the independent variable. There were 132 metropolitan places that hosted a WWE event in 2015. In the 2016 regression analysis there were 145 metropolitan places that held a WWE event before the election. The attendance ratio for 2015

208 David Beard and John Heppen

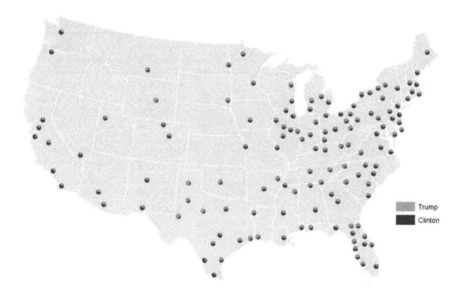

FIGURE 11.3 2016 presidential election results at 2015 WWE event sites.

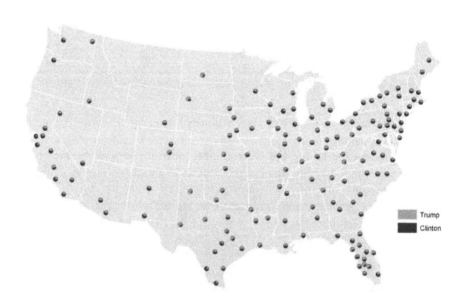

FIGURE 11.4 2016 presidential election results at 2016 WWE event sites.

TABLE 11.5 Regression analysis results Trump vote and attendance ratio.

Independent Variable	R^2	Adjusted R^2	F	Sig.	B	Std. Error	Beta	t	Sig.
Attendance Ratio 2015	0.066	0.067	9.235	0.003	0.289	0.095	0.258	3.039	0.003
Attendance Ratio 2016	0.093	0.087	14.691	0.000	0.329	0.086	0.305	3.833	0.000

Dependent Variable is the Trump Vote

has a positive relationship with the Trump vote as does the attendance ratio for 2016 (Table 11.5). The model presents evidence of a relationship between enthusiasm for WWE wrestling and voting for Donald Trump. Though in 2015 and 2016 the ratio is explaining a small percentage of the variation in the Trump vote the coefficient is significant with an acceptable T-statistic.

The residuals were analyzed as well with a standard deviation of approximately 11 for both years and mapped (Figures 11.5 and 11.6). The metropolitan areas were categorized into cities where the model poorly under and overperformed. The next step was to identify metropolitan areas where the residual or error term was within one-half of a standard deviation above and below the mean of zero. An analysis of the maps of residuals for 2015 and 2016 show that larger metropolitan areas on the East and West Coasts offered the poorest prediction. The best predicted metro areas in 2015 and 2016 were in the South and what can

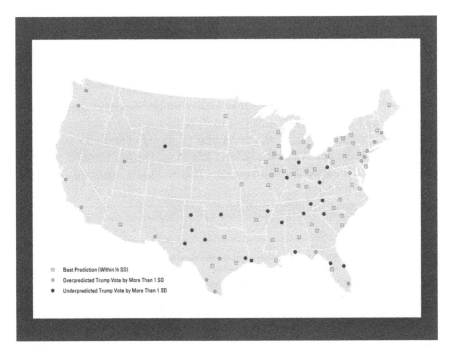

FIGURE 11.5 Trump vote prediction, 2015.

FIGURE 11.6 Trump vote prediction, 2016.

be called Rust Belt areas of medium to small-sized markets of the Midwest and Industrial Northeast. Though the overall model is weak we do find places where the model works best and sheds some light on Trump's appeal to working class voters in places where the old industrial economy has faded.

In 2015, 54 metropolitan areas that were within those strict parameters of between one-half of a standard deviation were then subject to another regression analysis (Figure 11.5). With the 54 best predicted metropolitan areas, the model was run again with better results (Table 11.6). The better model shows an improvement in R squared predicting up to 30% of the variance in 2015. The same regression model of the 52 the best predicted metro areas for 2016 was run again showing a similar improvement.

TABLE 11.6 Regression analysis results using best predicted metro areas.

Independent Variable	R^2	Adjusted R^2	F	Sig.	B	Std. Error	Beta	t	Sig.
Attendance Ratio 2015	0.302	0.289	22.97	0.00	0.265	0.55	.550	4.8	0.00
Attendance Ratio 2016	.301	.287	21.97	.000	.270	.058	.549	4.69	0.00

Dependent Variable is the % Trump Vote

Conclusion

For the record: 65,853,516 people voted for Trump in the presidential election. We are not claiming that fans of pro wrestling gave Trump the election. The appeal of a wrestling rhetoric may be wider than we might think, but the election also, to be clear, fell within expectations set by research in political geography. Despite the history making election and unprecedented historical political times the Trump presidency represents his election has not marked an unusually different pattern from what we have witnessed in a spatial-temporal pattern. An analysis of Moran's I at the state level revealed that the Democratic vote for president has been in a similar pattern of spatial autocorrelation since 2004 (Heppen 2018). Even with the loss of key states of Florida, Michigan, Pennsylvania, and Wisconsin the margin of election in those states was close enough resulting in a similar global pattern. Though, by other measures, Johnston, Manley, and Jones (2016) found evidence of sorting by counties by tracking landslide counties by regions in a non-spatial method which suggests voter polarization occurring without spatial polarization, meaning Republican counties are becoming more Republican with the same phenomenon happening in Democratic counties. In summary, the election of 2016 behaved temporally and spatially in a similar pattern to the previous elections in the century. The fact that only about 77,000 votes in Pennsylvania, Michigan, and Wisconsin decided the election speaks to the continuity of the election, though debates on the fairness of the electoral college vis-à-vis the popular vote have been studied by electoral geographers finding no bias in favor of either party from 1960 to 2012 (Pattie and Johnston 2014).

Still, we think, the correlation between Trump's political style, the popularity of wrestling, and his popularity among communities that value wrestling raises key questions, if not for the 2016 election, for the future. Typically, the process of seeing politics through the lens of wrestling reduces politics to a polarized contest. Migliore (1993) believes that when one sees politics through the lens of wrestling, opponents are "presented as extreme positions with no middle ground," a description apt to describe Republican and Democratic politicians in contemporary politics since the 2016 election. When campaigns take on an agonistic form that resembles a *WrestleMania*, the electorate becomes engaged. That might be a good thing. For Trump, getting votes is like getting pops from the audience, like ratings and Pay Per View buys. To Trump being president means attacking his rivals rhetorically in the most savage and meanest terms – and we must ask what the future of American elections might be within this paradigm.

Notes

1 For a fuller, opinionated account, see "Donald Trump Buys Raw" by Art O'Donnell on *WrestleCrap*, July 2, 2017, available online at http://wrestlecrap.com/inductions/donald-trump-buys-raw-dropped-almost-as-fast-as-wwes-stock/

2 Trump announced his campaign on June 16, 2015. We use the data from the entire year since there was speculation about Trump running for president from at least February of that year when he did not renew his contract with NBC for his program *The Apprentice* (Feely 2015).

References

Appel, E.C. 2018. Burlesque, tragedy, and a (potentially) "yuuuge" "breaking of a frame": Donald Trump's rhetoric as "early warning." *Communication Quarterly* 66(2): 157–175.

Archer, J.C., and F. Shelley. 1986. *American Electoral Mosaics.* Washington, D.C.: Association of American Geographers.

Archer, J.C., and P. Taylor. 1981. *Section and Party: A Political Geography of American Presidential Elections, from Andrew Jackson to Ronald Reagan.* Chichester, UK: Wiley.

Bandenburg, H. 2016. Did the WWE and wrestling help get Donald Trump elected? *The Independent* (Nov. 16). www.independent.co.uk/sport/general/wwe-mma-wrestling/donald-trump-wwe-wrestling-us-election-latest-policies-president-elect-a7416901.html

Bernthal, M., and F. Medway. 2005. An initial exploration into the psychological implications of adolescents' involvement with professional wrestling. *School Psychology International* 26(2): 224–242.

Dawsey, J. 2017. Trump's obsession with *WrestleMania* and fake drama. *Politico* (Jan. 1). www.politico.com/story/2017/01/trump-wrestlemania-fake-233615

Edwards, J. 2018. Make America great again: Donald Trump and redefining the U.S. role in the world. *Communication Quarterly* 66(2): 176–195.

Enli, G. 2017. Twitter as arena for the authentic outsider: Exploring the social media campaigns of Trump and Clinton in the 2016 US presidential election. *European Journal of Communication* 32(1): 50–61.

Feely, P. 2015. Trump won't renew *"Apprentice"* so that he might focus on a presidential run. *New Hampshire Union Leader* (Feb. 27). www.unionleader.com/apps/pbcs.dll/article?AID=/20150227/NEWS0605/150229334/1010/Art

Francia, P. 2018. Free media and Twitter in the 2016 presidential election: The unconventional campaign of Donald Trump. *Social Science Computer Review* 36(4): 440–455.

Goodman, P. 2009. Trump suit claiming defamation is dismissed. *New York Times* (July 15). www.nytimes.com/2009/07/16/business/media/16trump.html

Hall, S. 2019. "Mean" Gene Okerlund took wrestling seriously, so we could too. *SB Nation* (Jan. 2). www.sbnation.com/wrestling/2019/1/2/18165293/mean-gene-okerlund-wwe-interviews-took-wrestling-seriously-so-we-could-too

Harrington, C. 2016. WWE attendance by city 2008–2016. *Indeed Wrestling* https://sites.google.com/site/chrisharrington/mookieghana-prowrestlingstatistics/wwe-attendance-by-city-2008-2016

Heppen, J. 2018. Spatial analysis of the 2016 election. In R. Watrel, R. Weichelt, F. Davidson, J. Heppen, E. Fouberg, J. Archer, R. Morrill, F. Shelley, and K. Martis. 2018. *Atlas of the 2016 Elections.* pp. 89–92. Lanham, MD: Rowman & Littlefield.

Hinck, E. 2018. 2016: Not a normal campaign. *Communication Quarterly* 66(2): 214–221.

Hornbaker, T. 2018. *Death of the Territories: Expansion, Betrayal and the War that Changed Pro Wrestling Forever.* Toronto: ECW Press.

Johnston, R., D. Manley, and K. Jones. 2016. Spatial polarization of presidential voting in the United States, 1992–2012: The "Big Sort" revisited. *Annals of the American Association of Geographers* 106(5): 1047–1062.

Lipscomb, W. 2005. *The Operation Aesthetic in the Performance of Professional Wrestling.* Ph.D. Diss. Baton Rouge: Louisiana State University.

Margolin, L. 2017. *TrumpMania: Vince McMahon, WWE and the Making of America's 45th President.* H. Delilah Business & Career Press

McDonough, M. 2018. The evolution of demagoguery: An updated understanding of demagogic rhetoric as interactive and ongoing. *Communication Quarterly* 66(2): 138–156.

Migliore, S. 1993. Professional wrestling: Moral commentary through ritual metaphor. *Journal of Ritual Studies* 7(1): 65–84.

Montgomery, M. 2017. Post-truth politics? Authenticity, populism and the electoral discourses of Donald Trump. *Journal of Language and Politics* 16(4): 619–639.

Ott, B. 2017. The age of Twitter: Donald J. Trump and the politics of debasement. *Critical Studies in Media Communication* 34(1): 59–68.

Pattie, C., and R. Johnston. 2014. "The electors shall meet in their respective states": Bias and the US presidential electoral college, 1960-2012. *Political Geography* 40: 35–45.

Sehmby, D. 2002. Wrestling and popular culture. *CLCWeb: Comparative Literature and Culture* 4(1). https://doi.org/10.7771/1481-4374.1144

Shelley, F., R. Watrel, and J.C. Archer. 2018. Statistical analysis of the 2016 election in historical perspective. In R. Watrel, R. Weichelt, F. Davidson, J. Heppen, E. Fouberg, J. Archer, R. Morrill, F. Shelley, and K. Martis (eds.) *Atlas of the 2016 Elections.* pp. 79–88. Lanham, MD: Rowman & Littlefield.

Stewart, E. 2016. Donald Trump rode $5 billion in free media to the White House. *The Street* (Nov. 20). www.thestreet.com/story/13896916/1/donald-trump-rode-5-billion-in-free-media-to-the-white-house.html

Stodden, W., and J. Hansen. 2015. Politics by KayFabe: Professional wrestling and the creation of public opinion. In B. Lang (ed.) *The Sociology of Sports.* San Diego: Cognella.

Tamborini R., L. Chory, D. Westerman, and P. Skalski. 2008. Talking smack: Verbal aggression in professional wrestling. *Communication Studies* 59(3): 242–258.

The Economist (April 13). 2019. TrumpMania. p. 32.

Theye, K., and S. Melling. 2018. Total losers and bad hombres: The political incorrectness and perceived authenticity of Donald J. Trump. *Southern Communication Journal* 83(5): 322–337.

Watrel, R., R. Weichelt, F. Davidson, J. Heppen, E.H Fouberg, J.C. Archer, R. Morrill, F. Shelley, and K. Martis (eds.). 2018. *Atlas of the 2016 Elections. Lanham*, MD: Rowman & Littlefield.

Willis, O. 2016. How professional wrestling explains American politics (especially Donald Trump). *The Medium (*March 2). https://medium.com/@owillis/how-professional-wrestling-explains-american-politics-especially-donald-trump-5449df1db9de

Wilson, C. 2016. Donald Trump's presidential training ground? The WWE. *Yahoo News* (March 17). www.yahoo.com/entertainment/wwe-donald-trump-193147594.html

Wrestling Observer. www.f4wonline.com

WWE Network. 2014 (Jan. 6). Mr. McMahon and Donald Trump announce the Battle of the Billionaires. www.youtube.com/watch?v=dVxVDDYwNvU

WWE Network. 2020. Compony overview. https://corporate.wwe.com/who-we-are/company-overview

Yip, J., M. Schweitzer, and S. Nurmohamed. 2018. Trash-talking: Competitive incivility motivates rivalry, performance, and unethical behavior. *Organizational Behavior and Human Decision Processes* 144: 125–144.

Young, M. 2013. Wrestling the English language. Transcribing a macho man Randy Savage promo. *Bacon Sports* [Blog] (Oct. 21). www.baconsports.com/macho-man-randy-savage-interview/

Zaru, D. 2017. The Donald Trump-Rosie O'Donnell feud: A timeline. *CNN.com* (Aug. 14). www.cnn.com/2015/08/07/politics/donald-trump-rosie-odonnell-feud/index.html

12

PRESIDENTIAL LIES AND POST-TRUTH GEOGRAPHIES

Barney Warf

> "When I can, I tell the truth."
>
> Donald Trump (quoted in Wagner 2018)

Among the greatest of Donald Trump's numerous flaws is his persistent, chronic, and habitual mendacity. Trump lies more than any other figure in American history, perhaps in the history of the world. Donald Trump is the most mendacious person ever to occupy the White House, and one of the greatest liars in human history. The volume of his lies has no precedent. Trump lies so frequently that if he tells the truth, it is by accident. Trump has even admitted to lying: in *The Art of the Deal*, he referred to the practice as "truthful hyperbole." As Waldman (2019a) puts it:

> Trump is blessed with a preternatural shamelessness; while ordinary people would ask themselves, "What will happen if I get caught in this lie?" Trump never seems to. He simply updates the old lie with a new one, and when that one is exposed, he offers up yet another.

Other observers have made the point similarly: As Gerson (2020 puts it,

> The president is a bold, intentional liar, by any moral definition. A habitual liar. A blatant liar. An instinctual liar. A reckless liar. An ignorant liar. A pathological liar. A hopeless liar. A gratuitous liar. A malevolent liar.

Similarly, Bruni (2020) notes

> He lies because he grew up among liars. He lies because hyperbole and hooey buoy his fragile ego. He lies because he is practiced at it, is habituated to it and never seems to pay much of a price for it.

Trump's constant, incessant lying has given him a reputation as a habitual abuser of the truth, reinforcing stereotypes about his intelligence, and deeply undermining his credibility. Indeed, in late 2018 the U.N. Special Rapporteur on Freedom of Expression and Opinion, Daniel Kaye, called Trump "the worst perpetrator of false information in the United States" (*Policy Times* 2018).

This chapter explores Trump's multitudinous lies in several steps. It opens with a review of the president's addiction to prevarication and dissimilation. Next it turns to the geographies embedded in such claims, including the fantastical landscapes that Trump pulls out of thin air and how his lies have affected policies on immigration, refugees, climate change, and international trade. Finally, it views Trump as a philosopher, contrasting his nihilistic view of truth with those of philosophers Jürgen Habermas and Michel Foucault.

A penchant for prevarication

Donald Trump's proclivity to exaggerate, misstate the truth, make unfounded claims, and assert flat-out falsehoods has been widely documented. Trump pulls figures out of thin air, rewrites history, and contradicts his own past statements. He lied more than 20,000 times in his first 1,267 days in office, an average of roughly 12 per day and sometimes up to 40 per day (Figure 12.1) (Kessler et al. 2020). The *Washington Post*'s fact checker crew even published a book about Trump's assault on the truth (Kessler et al. 2020). His rate of lying fluctuates over time, varying from roughly 200 per month during relatively quiet times and soaring to 1,200

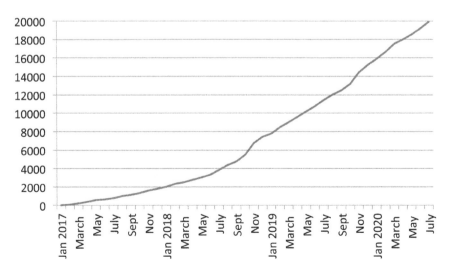

FIGURE 12.1 Cumulative number of lies told by Donald Trump, Jan. 2017–July 2020.

Source: author, using data from *Washington Post*, www.washingtonpost.com/graphics/politics/trump-claims-database/

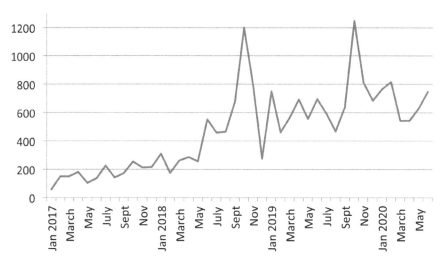

FIGURE 12.2 Average number of lies told per month by Donald Trump, Jan. 2017–May 2020.

Source: author, using data from *Washington Post*, www.washingtonpost.com/graphics/politics/trump-claims-database/

per month around the 2018 midterm elections (Figure 12.2). What was once considered to be shocking presidential behavior has become normalized, or mere background noise.

Trump has a long history of lying. His carefully groomed public image of the self-made billionaire businessman was built on a foundation of lies. His "birtherist" stance on President Obama's birthplace was filled with racist innuendo, an attempt to delegitimize his predecessor. He claimed that five young men imprisoned for a rape in Central Part were guilty even after they were exonerated by DNA evidence, asserting "They admitted they were guilty" (Waxman 2016). In 2014 he tweeted that "I am being proven right about massive vaccinations – the doctors lied" (Blake 2017). Trump has lied about his wealth; the cost of membership in his golf clubs; how many condos he has sold; how much debt he owes; whether he associated with members of organized crime; that he had opposed the Iraq war when he had not; and who had endorsed his presidential bid (O'Brien 2017). Trump has lied about the ratings of news outlets he does not like, like CNN; the rate of taxation in the U.S. relative to other countries; that Immigration and Customs Enforcement and the Border Patrol endorsed him; and that Obama's policies created ISIS. He has lied about U.S. contributions to NATO and falsely claimed dozens of times that Democrats colluded with Russia in the 2016 presidential election. He told evangelicals that he had ended the Johnson Amendment, which prohibits religious groups from endorsing or financially supporting political candidates, when in fact he had not.

Lies and post-truth geographies 217

Perhaps the most frequent lie Trump tells is the claim that the wall on the U.S.-Mexican border is already under construction. He also claimed that Middle Eastern terrorists have sought to enter the U.S. through the border with Mexico, and at times claimed they carried Ebola. He falsely claimed that the GOP tax cut bill signed in December 2017 was the largest in history, which it was not. Some of Trump's lies are infamous whoppers. He made his first press secretary, Sean Spicer, lie about the size of his inauguration crowd when he claimed "This was the largest audience to ever witness an inauguration – period – both in person and around the globe" (Kessler 2017). The claim was easily disproven by data on ridership on mass transit, eyewitness testimony, independent crowd counts, and Nielsen television ratings. Trump also falsely claimed to have written his own inauguration speech. Incensed that he lost the popular vote in 2016 to Hillary Clinton, Trump claimed that "Between 3 million and 5 million illegal votes caused me to lose the popular vote" (Phillip and DeBonis 2017). Later, he argued "Terrible! Just found out that Obama had my 'wires tapped' in Trump Tower just before the victory. Nothing found. This is McCarthyism!" (Nussbaum 2017). He lied about attending the famous June 9, 2016 meeting in Trump Tower to discuss cooperation with the Russians, then lied about writing the reason it was held (allegedly to discuss adoptions), then lied about personally dictating the public response to media scrutiny about it.

Trump also lies about matters of less significance. Leonhardt and Thompson (2017) compiled a long, helpful list, although it grows daily. He claimed that Trump Tower is 68 stories high when it is only 58. He bragged that the Trump winery is the "largest winery on the East Coast" (Gorman 2016) when it is not even among the 10 largest in Virginia. Before the 2018 midterm elections he claimed that work on a middle class tax cut was underway. In a visit to troops in Iraq in December, 2018, he invented a magical 10% pay raise for service members, "the first in ten years." He claimed windmills cause cancer (Bump 2019b), which they most assuredly do not. These are not simply careless errors; Trump tells these lies knowing fully that they are false.

Trump lies so much that the *Washington Post* invented a new category, the Bottomless Pinocchio, for false claims that he repeated more than 20 times. Kessler (2018a) notes "That dubious distinction will be awarded to politicians who repeat a false claim so many times that they are, in effect, engaging in campaigns of disinformation." Some lies Trump has told more than 100 times. Most politicians dread the *Post*'s rating, and stop telling lies when caught. Not Trump. Kessler (2018a) notes:

> The president's most-repeated falsehoods fall into a handful of broad categories – claiming credit for promises he has not fulfilled; false assertions that provide a rationale for his agenda; and political weaponry against perceived enemies such as Democrats or special counsel Robert S. Mueller III.

218 Barney Warf

TABLE 12.1 Lies Trump has told most frequently, as of May 2019.

Border wall	160
U.S. trade deficits	147
Trump's tax cut	143
U.S. economy	134
NATO spending	102
Drug trafficking	91
Immigration laws	63
Mueller's team's bias	61
Diversity visa lottery	55
Democrats' collusion	50
MS-13 deportations	50
McCain healthcare vote	42
Middle East wars	41
U.S. Steel	39
Saudi Arabia deal	35
Payment to Iran	35
Sanctuary cities	35
Trade tariffs	29
Open borders	29
Illegal immigration	22

Source: Kessler and Fox (2019).

The types of lies Trump has told most frequently are found in Table 12.1, led by the border wall, trade deficits, the Republican tax cut, and the health of the U.S. economy.

Trump is such an incorrigible liar that his own lawyers refused to let him be deposed by the Robert Mueller investigation on the grounds that their client was incapable of telling the truth. As Schmidt and Haberman (2018) note, "His lawyers are concerned that the president, who has a history of making false statements and contradicting himself, could be charged with lying to investigators." Trump even lies about lying. After he accused President George W. Bush of lying about weapons of mass destruction in Iraq, he said "I didn't say lie. I said he may have lied" (Lavender 2016). In reality, he did say that Bush lied, with no qualifiers (Kiely 2016).

Trump lies as if everyone simply believes him, or takes him at face value. This is a sign of pathological narcissism. He is so important that we must accept whatever he says is true; no one else is capable of detecting the falsehood. His lies are thus a function of his narcissism, which produces a self-imagined reality, a delusional fantasy in which he is at the center of everything. This worldview reflects a sense of entitlement in which he can say anything he wants to anyone, and never pay for consequences. Indeed, Trump has never paid a penalty for the whoppers he repeats year after year. Without a cost to his lies, Trump has no incentive to stop issuing them.

Whether Trump believes his own lies has been the subject of much debate. "When he lies, does he know he is lying, or does he believe his own lies?"

(Kessler and Lee 2017, p. 7). If Trump does realize he is lying, then his behavior constitutes a classic case of "gaslighting," a deliberate attempt to convince others that the proposed reality is more real than what they experience in daily life. The tactic is commonly used by pathological narcissists. As Schwartz (2017, p. 71) puts it, "His aim is never accuracy, it's domination."

Even worse, much of the public tolerates or even adores Trump's lies, as Carpenter (2018) notes in *Gaslighting America*. She argues that his lying is methodical, following a consistent, strategic pattern: first he makes an outrageous claim; next he denies it, while simultaneously advancing it; third, he claims more information is coming; fourth, he attacks those who accuse him of lying; and fifth, he declares victory under any and all circumstances regardless of the evidence. She makes a prescient point (pp. 7–8):

> He learned that people actually love it when he lies. ... We want to think his crazy lies are his greatest weakness when they are, in fact, the source of his strength. ... The conventional wisdom currently says that when Trump tweets something laughably incorrect, the fact-checkers will reveal the truth, the public will turn against him, and his political allies will desert him. This is has not borne out.

Trump's lies are necessary for his political success, to ward off opponents, and keep his base in line. Blow (2019) points out, "He lies to brag. He lies to deflect. He lies to inflate. He lies to defame. He lies to praise. He sometimes seems to lie just for the sport of it." Trump uses mendacity to attack his critics, demean the press, and advance his political agenda. For example, in 2019 he claimed that "The Democrat [sic] position on abortion is now so extreme that they don't mind executing babies AFTER birth" (Grady 2019). In April 2019 he stated that Democrats approve of situations in which "The baby is born. The mother meets the doctor, they take care of the baby, they wrap the baby beautifully, and then the doctor and the mother determine whether or not they will execute the baby" (Cameron 2019). He claimed "The Democrats want to invite caravan after caravan of illegal aliens into our country. And they want to sign them up for free health care, free welfare, free education, and for the right to vote" (Valverde 2018). He added that Democrats wanted to purchase a new car for all undocumented immigrants (Jacobson 2018).

The news media have been complicit, spreading Trump's falsehoods repeatedly. Trump knows that his lies will be broadcast by the very channels he denounces as "fake news." "Fake news," in this reading, does not mean false reporting, but anything that criticizes Trump. Of course, any other politician would have long ceased to have a career after being exposed as a liar at any level approaching Trump's, but given the depth of the personality cult that surrounds him, Trump has political Teflon like no other, and seems impervious to the repeated demonstrations of his falsehoods. His fans believe him more than the truth.

220 Barney Warf

Trump both publicizes the conspiratorial views of the extreme right, such as Alex Jones and Fox News. He has retweeted theories of far right activists, such as the claim that Obama and Clinton founded ISIS, that the media covered up terrorist attacks, and that Mexican cartels carry bags of drugs across the Rio Grande. He thus makes those views part of the "mainstream," first by circulating them among alt-right political circles, and then the gullible viewers of Fox News, where Sean Hannity and Tucker Carlson bring them into the mainstream as truth. Trump's lies have also been spread far and wide by an army of online trolls.

An unfortunate byproduct of Trump's habitual lying is that it is contagious, and other members of his administration have followed suit (*New York Times* 2018). Some lie to support their boss, others to justify administration policies, yet others regard honesty as a handicap. Examples include Brock Long, head of the Federal Emergency Management Agency, who lied about the deaths from Hurricane Maria; Wilbur Ross, Secretary of Commerce, who lied about attempts to insert a citizenship question in the national census; Kirstjen Nielsen, Secretary of Homeland Security, who lied about Russian interference in the 2016 presidential election; and Sarah Huckabee Sanders, the White House press secretary, who lied about African American unemployment rates. A vast cadre of Trump fans, sycophants, aides, and surrogates back up his lies on television talk shows and op-ed pieces, deliberately overlooking the most extravagant falsehoods and attempting to shore them up when possible.

Trump succeeds in lying in part because his base and Republican Party leaders will accept anything he says or does without question. This issue is aptly summed up by Waldman (2019b), who notes:

> There is no volume of lies he could tell, no extent of his corruption that could be revealed, no amount of bigotry he could spread, no number of family members he could appoint to high positions in government, no degree of profiteering off the presidency, no amount of admiration he could express for authoritarian dictators, no obstruction of justice he could engage in, no assault on the integrity of his office too appalling for them not to enthusiastically defend him.

Trump's post-truth geographies

Geography has always been poised between matter and meaning, between the material and immaterial worlds. As a discourse (of sorts), Trump's lies thus have very real material effects on people, landscapes, and social relations. Many of Trump's lies have a profoundly geographic dimension. For example, he frequently claimed, with no evidence, that U.S. Steel is "opening six new plants" (Tobias 2018) (sometimes seven, eight, or nine). He also claimed Californians were rioting "to get out of their sanctuary cities" (Bump 2018).

Trump has lied in many ways about immigrants, arguing that more undocumented people are crossing the border than ever, even though apprehensions at the border dropped from 1.6 million in 2000 to 304,000 in 2017. He argued that "Over the years, thousands of Americans have been brutally killed by those who illegally entered our country and thousands more lives will be lost if we don't act right now" (Nakamura 2019). However, statistically, undocumented immigrants commit far fewer crimes than do American citizens. During the 2016 campaign, he argued that undocumented immigrants were bringing "tremendous" amounts of disease into the U.S. The World Health Organization notes that "Nicaragua, Costa Rica and Mexico all have higher average vaccination rates than the United States, making people from those countries on average less likely to transmit diseases like tuberculosis, diphtheria and hepatitis B" (Rizzo, Kessler, and Kelly 2019). Trump also claimed "The drugs are pouring into this country. They don't go through the ports of entry" (Lewis 2017), which is simply not true, according to the Drug Enforcement Administration, which reports that the most common trafficking technique by transnational criminal organizations is to hide drugs in passenger vehicles or tractor-trailers as they drive into the U.S. though entry ports. The wall will do nothing to stop the influx of drugs. Trump also claimed that terrorists often cross the U.S.-Mexico border, which has no basis in reality (Bergen 2018). In 2017, the Department of Homeland Security apprehended 3,755 suspected terrorists trying to enter the U.S. through all points of entry; 2,170 of these attempted entry through airports. Trump's own State Department noted in 2017 that "there was no credible evidence indicating that international terrorist groups have established bases in Mexico, worked with Mexican drug cartels, or sent operatives via Mexico into the United States" (Bump 2019a).

If anything demonstrates the fictitious geographies that Trump calls into being, it is the famed border wall with Mexico, a central feature of his 2016 election campaign. He has claimed more than 134 times that the wall on the U.S.-Mexico border is under construction, which is simply not true. In 2018 Trump claimed "We started building our Wall. I'm so proud of it. We started. We started. We have $1.6 billion, and we've already started" (Kessler 2018b). In fact, the $1.6 billion was explicitly not for a wall. The 2006 Secure Fence Act resulted in about 1,050 kilometers of border barrier, but under Trump no part of the wall has been started, and perhaps never will be. Trump's lies create geographies where none existed beforehand. The wall with Mexico, for example, is simply dreamed into existence by sheer force of rhetoric. Trump repeatedly claimed Mexico would pay for it, then forced the longest government shutdown in American history over Congress's refusal to appropriate funds. When that tactic failed, he declared a national "emergency" where none existed, with the backing of an obsequious Republican Party (which showed some resistance when the Senate condemned the measure as executive overreach). He also claimed that a reworking of the North American Free Trade Agreement (NAFTA) will earn enough money for pay for the wall (Kessler 2019), which reveals a lack of understanding of basic economics. Similarly, Trump told the Spanish Foreign Minister to build a wall across the Sahara Desert to stop immigrants (Meixler 2018).

Nor do refugees get any better treatment from Trump, who has called them "the ultimate Trojan horse" (Kopan 2015). Indeed, his lies about them have served to restrict the movement of desperate people fleeing poverty, crime, and violence. He argued that "Refugees are pouring into our great country from Syria. We don't even know who they are. They could be ISIS. They could be anybody," adding that there are many "who are definitely, in many cases, ISIS-aligned" (Byrnes 2015). Trump has threatened to deport the roughly 12,000 Syrian refugees currently living in the U.S. These lies and actions are part of the broader Islamophobia that pervades his administration. Following the collapse of the World Trade Center in 2001, Trump claimed that "I watched when the World Trade Center came tumbling down. And I watched in Jersey City, New Jersey, where thousands and thousands of people were cheering as that building was coming down. Thousands of people were cheering" (Kessler 2015). These lies are simply not true (Kessler 2015). His hatred of Muslims, and use of Islamophobia for political ends, culminated in the so-called "Muslim ban" that sought to restrict immigration from several Muslim-majority countries (it was rejected by the courts until finally approved in a limited manner by the Supreme Court).

Trump also invents fictitious geographies about sanctuary cities. Angry that many have refused to turn undocumented immigrants over to the federal government, he boasted to his supporters that he was "dumping" refugees on these places. The claim, however, is simply untrue, and lacks any legal basis for doing so.

Trump also lies about the environment. On climate change, he argued that climate scientists "have a very big political agenda" (Samenow 2018). He tweeted in 2012 that "The concept of global warming was created by and for the Chinese in order to make U.S. manufacturing non-competitive" (Wong 2016). Whenever the U.S. is faced with a cold front during the winter, he uses it as evidence that climate change is not real. Regarding the vast majority of climate scientists who insist that anthropogenic climate change is real, he said "It's a hoax. I mean, it's a money-making industry, okay? It's a hoax, a lot of it" (Jacobson 2016). Later he added "Look, scientists also have a political agenda" (Rubin 2018). When he withdrew the U.S. from the Paris Climate Accord, he claimed that it would cost the country 2.5 million jobs, even though most experts hold that it would save far more money than it cost (Kessler and Lee 2017). Trump's stance has left the U.S. essentially alone in denying the greatest existential threat to the planet. Trump's own National Climate Assessment contradicted his false claims (Jay et al. 2018). Even the victims of climate change are denied empathy by his lies: when Hurricane Maria devastated Puerto Rico in 2017, Trump claimed "3,000 people did not die" (Klein and Vazquez 2018), and that the statistic was manufactured by Democrats desperate to make him "look as bad as possible" (Qiu 2018). When California was devastated by forest fires in 2018, he argued "There is no reason for these massive, deadly and costly forest fires in California except that forest management is so poor" (Pierre-Louis 2018).

Lies and post-truth geographies **223**

International trade is another domain in which Trump lies frequently. Trump lied to Canadian Prime Minister Justin Trudeau about the U.S.-Canada balance of trade, and later bragged at a fundraising speech that he had made up facts during the meeting (Dawsey, Paletta, and Werner 2018). Although the U.S. has a trade surplus with Canada, Trump claimed it was a deficit. He claimed "There's a tremendous tax that we pay when we [American businesses] go into China, whereas when China sells to us there's no tax" (Greenberg 2016). China's tariffs are higher than those imposed by the United States.

Given both Trump's innumerable lies, the environment in which they flourish, and the very real social and spatial consequences, it is worth asking about the nature of truth. The section that follows addresses that issue.

Habermas, Foucault, Trump

> "Truth isn't truth."
>
> Rudy Giuliani (quoted in Morin and Cohen 2018)

Social scientists have long been concerned with epistemological debates over the nature of truth. There are, of course, multiple theories about truth, including the correspondence theory (the truth is what fits the facts); the consensus theory (truth is the product of common agreement); and the pragmatist theory (truth is what works), which owes much to the works of John Dewey and particularly William James (1907), in which "truth" is determined and confirmed by its utility and effectiveness in application, i.e., from its consequences. Thus, "the 'true' is only the expedient in our way of thinking, just as the 'right' is only the expedient in our way of behaving" (James 1907, p. 2). To appreciate the relation between Trump and the truth, it is helpful to take a brief detour to explore two major perspectives, those offered by Jürgen Habermas and Michel Foucault.

The German philosopher Jürgen Habermas is often regarded as the last defender of the Enlightenment. Habermas (1991) famously argued that communications are central to the social process of truth construction, through which individuals and communities of interest partake in the public, discursive interpretation of reality (cf. Calhoun 1992). Habermas's "ideal speech situation" consisting of unfettered discourse is central to the "public sphere" in which social life is reproduced and through which truth is constructed in the absence of barriers to communication. Truth in this reading is inseparable from lived experience, intent, and social practice, leading to the consensus rather than correspondence theory of truth. In this reading, all participants in a debate would theoretically have equal rights and abilities to make their views known and to challenge any other view; when all power relations have been removed from the freedom to engage in discourse, the only criteria for resolving contesting claims is their truth value. And, importantly, "the participants in an ideal speech situation [must] be motivated solely by the desire to reach a consensus about the truth of statements and the validity of norms" (Bernstein 1995, p. 50).

224 Barney Warf

Michel Foucault offered a powerful notion of truth grounded in historical reality, i.e., truth as a social construction. For Foucault, knowledge and truth are intimately linked to power. He famously stated that

> Truth is a thing of this world: it is produced only by virtue of multiple forms of constraint. And it induces regular effects of power. Each society has its regime of truth, its "general politics" of truth: that is, the types of discourse which it accepts and makes function as true; the mechanisms and instances which enable one to distinguish true and false statements, the means by which each is sanctioned; the techniques and procedures accorded value in the acquisition of truth; the status of those who are charged with saying what counts as true. (quoted in Rabinow 1991)

Power in this conception is not simply imposed from above, but woven into the fabric of everyday life. Power as ideology is a way of producing subjects, of disciplining them, including their bodies via the microphysics of biopolitics (e.g., schools, hospitals, asylums). Foucault's suturing of truth and power deeply shaped his views of mental illness in *Madness and Civilization* (1965), the history of power in *The Archaeology of Knowledge* (1969), and the production of ideas in *The Order of Things* (1966). Social discourses and epistemes do not simply reflect the world, but constitute people (hence Foucault was an anti-humanist). Thus, Foucault socialized the notion of truth, noting that what is held to be truth varies historically (and geographically). Every claim to truth is a claim to power, linked to an interest; the claim to universal truth is a claim to universal power. If for Habermas truth is the product of reasoned debate unfettered by power, for Foucault it is all about power and the ability to produce subjects that imbibe discourse as truth.

In contrast to Habermas and Foucault, Trump's view is that truth – and that of the right-wing mediasphere more generally – is whatever benefits Trump and friends, not facts (or as Kellyanne Conway called them, "alternative facts"). More radically, one might say that Trump's view of truth is decisively nihilist: there is no truth. This line of thought is perhaps the ultimate apotheosis of postmodernism, of the "anything goes" view. Trump's epistemology is not grounded in philosophical debate or historical reality: in this view, truth is simply a means to an end, a self-serving tool. Call it the "opportunistic theory of truth." Trump often repeats falsehoods over and over, until they become "alternative facts" for his base and Fox News. Fact checker Kessler (2018a) argues that

> The president keeps going long after the facts are clear, in what appears to be a deliberate effort to replace the truth with his own, far more favorable, version of it. He is not merely making gaffes or misstating things, he is purposely injecting false information into the national conversation.

In this sense, Trump eerily resembles the Newspeak of George Orwell's famous dystopian novel *1984*. Trump told his followers "What you're seeing and what you're reading is not what's happening" (Kwong 2018). Orwell (1948, p. 88) noted that "The party told you to reject the evidence of your eyes and ears. It was their final, most essential command." Such a line of thought essentially blurs the boundaries between truth and falsehood altogether. Bruni (2019) offers a biting summary of Trump's cavalier attitude toward the truth: "a man who wouldn't know the truth if it raced toward him with sirens blaring, ran over him, then backed up and did it again." This view of truth appears at the historical moment when political tribalism in the U.S. reigns supreme, when truth is seen as a political weapon and little more. Smith (2016), in an essay entitled "Truth after Trump," argues that "He is a mere bullshitter, and what comes out of his mouth has more to do with pathologies of personality than with any real vision of how the world, or America, ought to be brought into line with some super-empirical truth to which he alone has access." Following this line of thought, Kakutani (2018) notes that the Trump Administration ordered the Centers for Disease Control and Prevention to avoid using the terms "science-based" and "evidence-based."

Of course, Trump did not invent this view of the world, which has long been popular with dictators and autocrats. It was long established within the Republican Party, including its war on science (Mooney 2006). Thus, under George W. Bush, a senior advisor (widely believed to be Karl Rove) told Ron Suskind (2004) of the *New York Times*:

> We're an empire now, and when we act, we create our own reality. And while you're studying that reality – judiciously, as you will – we'll act again, creating other new realities, which you can study too, and that's how things will sort out. We're history's actors ... and you, all of you, will be left to just study what we do.

For such actors, truth is simply too inconvenient, such as the truth about climate change. The explosion of right-wing media has created a vast echo chamber in which vast numbers of people willfully subscribe to the falsehoods perpetuated by professional political liars, fakes, and frauds. Telling lies has been a frequent tactic among many types of politicians, but recently the denial of objectivity and the manipulation of facts and scientific data for political purposes appear to have become a monopoly of the political right (Fuller 2018). Famed right-wing radio commentator Rush Limbaugh has repeatedly said "The Four Corners of Deceit are government, academia, science, and the media" (Waldman 2020). Indeed, the tribalism of truth reflects the intense political polarization of American society, in which winning has become more important than learning (Fisher et al. 2018). The effects are deeper than systemic anti-intellectualism, because as Stephens (2019) points out:

> it is further poisoning a society in which the idea of truth was already being Balkanized (*our* truth), personalized (*my* truth), problematized (*whose* truth), and trivialized (*your* truth) – all before Trump came along and defined truth as whatever he can get away with.

Ironically, this shift mimics the academic debates about postmodernism in the 1990s, with roots that can be traced back to Nietzsche's perspectivism. It finds its most explicit statement in the deconstruction of Jacques Derrida, in which all truths are held to be social constructions, partial, and reflect embodied interests. In this way, postmodernism played a very real role in the rise of the post-truth society (Boler and Davis 2018). Trump's ability to blur the boundaries between fiction and reality also calls to mind Baudrillard's (1994) famous notion of the simulacrum, in which hyperreal entities like Disneyworld become more real than reality itself. Indeed, in the fevered minds of the far right, the geographies imagined by Trump exist even though they bear no relation to any reality whatsoever. A widespread distrust of expertise cultivates a climate in which any opinion is as good as any other (Nichols 2017). Truth simply becomes a matter of perspective. When the decline in objectivity becomes normalized, emotions and affect rise to the fore (Boler and Davis 2019). As waves of fake news and fake science (e.g., climate change denial, anti-vaccination discourses, creationism) wash over the country, it has suffered from what the Rand Corporation has called "truth decay." The very notion of objectivity has come under question and challenged the Enlightenment notion of reason.

Trump's lies reflect the culmination of a long-standing, and increasingly virulent, form of American anti-intellectualism (Gore 2007; Jacoby 2008). This phenomenon has been taken to new heights by the Republican Party. Starting in the 1990s, a vast web of conservative media outlets and websites has emerged, anchored by Fox News, but also including *The Washington Times*, Breibart, the Drudge Report, Sinclair Broadcasting, Infowars, World Net Daily, the Blaze, Red State, and Daily Caller. This interlocking set of channels has created a vast echo chamber in which pre-existing prejudices are reaffirmed and no dissenting ideas creep in, leading viewers to become impervious to facts. Amplified by filter bubbles, many conservatives have fallen into an information abyss. Sometimes it takes the form of bizarre conspiracy theories, such as the famous "Pizzagate" story that held Hillary Clinton operated a child sex ring out of a pizza shop in Maryland. Other times it is broader and less overt. Wehner (2019) argues that:

> for a significant number of Americans – including many people on the right who long defended the concept of objective truth and repeatedly rang the alarm bell about the rise of relativism – truth is viewed as relative rather than objective, malleable rather than solid; as instrumental, as a means to an end, as a weapon in our intense political war.

Thus, two-thirds of Trump supporters believe that President Obama is a Muslim not born in the U.S. (Gangitano 2016) and most Republicans believe that Trump won the popular vote in 2016 (Oliver and Wood 2016). Others assert that millions of immigrants voted illegally in the election. Conservative commentator and never-Trumper Charlie Sykes (2017) lamented how this mediasphere created an alternative reality that empowers the most reckless elements of the far right.

Concluding thoughts

The avalanche of lies that Trump has promulgated are the inevitable result of having a con man and huckster in the White House. With little credibility, his falsehoods make many wonder what else he has lied about. Trump's lies subvert democracy and make a reality-based dialogue impossible. Trump's lies do more than keep the fact checkers working overtime. They undermine confidence in the government, and in truth more generally. They perpetuate a political climate in which telling outright falsehoods becomes acceptable, muting the possibility of reasoned debate. They degrade the presidency, fuel cynicism, and make evidence-based political discussion difficult. *Washington Post* Eugene Robinson (2018) believes that Trump's war on the truth is worse than simple self-aggrandizement. "When Trump insists on his own invented 'facts,'" he wrote, "he makes reality-based political dialogue impossible. His utter disregard for truth is a subversion of our democracy and a dereliction of his duty as president." Trump's mendacity has been widely interpreted as an attack on the truth itself, part of an austere neoliberal refashioning of the state. As Wehner (2019) puts it:

> Many politicians are guilty of not telling the full truth of events. A significant number shade the truth from time to time. A few fall into the category of consistent, outright liars. But only very few – and only the most dangerous – are committed to destroying the very idea of truth itself. That is what we have in Donald Trump, along with many of his aides and courtiers.

Many have become inured to Trump's lies, or numbed to them. By relentlessly spreading a nihilist view of truth, Trump has decisively blurred the boundaries between reality and fantasy. Geographically, this process takes the form of conjuring nonexistent threats from immigrants and terrorists and using them to justify a needless wall with Mexico, a monument to white supremacy, and to promote the rollback of environmental legislation that benefits the donor class. Epistemic nihilism and neoliberalism thus go hand in hand with one another.

References

Baudrillard, J. 1994. *Simulacra and Simulation*. Ann Arbor, MI: University of Michigan Press.
Bergen, P. 2018. Trump's terrorism argument for border wall is bogus. *CNN* (Dec. 13). www.cnn.com/2018/12/11/opinions/trump-southern-border-terrorists-opinion-bergen/index.html
Bernstein, J. 1995. *Recovering Ethical Life: Jürgen Habermas and the Future of Critical Theory* New York: Routledge.

Blake, A. 2017. Donald Trump is rekindling one of his favorite conspiracy theories: Vaccine safety. *Washington Post* (Jan. 10). www.washingtonpost.com/news/the-fix/wp/2017/01/10/donald-trump-is-rekindling-one-of-his-favorite-conspiracy-theories-vaccine-safety/

Blow, C. 2019. An ode to "Desperate Don." *New York Times* (May 20). www.nytimes.com/2019/05/19/opinion/donald-trump-lies.html

Boler, M., and E. Davis. 2018. The affective politics of the "post-truth" era: Feeling rules and networked subjectivity. *Emotion, Space and Society* 27: 75–85.

Bruni, F. 2019. Donald Trump's phony America. *New York Times* (March 2). www.nytimes.com/2019/03/02/opinion/sunday/trump-cohen-theranos-fraud.html

Bruni, F. 2020. Donald Trump is the best ever president in the history of the cosmos. *New York Times* (July 25). www.nytimes.com/2020/07/25/opinion/sunday/trump-lies.html

Bump, P. 2018. Trump has a new go-to political foil: An imaginary version of California. *Washington Post* (Oct. 23). www.washingtonpost.com/politics/2018/10/23/trump-has-new-go-to-political-foil-an-imaginary-version-california/

Bump, P. 2019a. Key parts of the Trump administration's border rhetoric are wrong, according to the Trump administration. *Washington Post* (Jan. 8). www.washingtonpost.com/politics/2019/01/08/key-parts-trump-administrations-border-rhetoric-are-wrong-according-trump-administration/

Bump, P. 2019b. Trump claims that wind farms cause cancer for very Trumpian reasons. *Washington Post* (April 3). www.washingtonpost.com/politics/2019/04/03/trump-claims-that-wind-farms-cause-cancer-very-trumpian-reasons/

Byrnes, J. 2015. Trump: Refugees "pouring into" US could be ISIS. *The Hill* (Nov. 17). https://thehill.com/blogs/blog-briefing-room/news-campaigns-presidential-campaigns/260420-trump-refugees-pouring-into-us

Calhoun, C. 1992. *Habermas and the Public Sphere*. Cambridge, MA: MIT Press.

Cameron, C. 2019. Trump repeats a false claim that doctors "execute" newborns. *New York Times* (April 28). www.nytimes.com/2019/04/28/us/politics/trump-abortion-fact-check.html

Carpenter, A. 2018. *Gaslighting America: Why We Love It When Trump Lies to Us*. New York: Broadside Books.

Dawsey, J., D. Paletta, and E. Werner. 2018. In fundraising speech, Trump says he made up trade claim in meeting with Justin Trudeau. *Washington Post* (March 15). www.washingtonpost.com/news/post-politics/wp/2018/03/14/in-fundraising-speech-trump-says-he-made-up-facts-in-meeting-with-justin-trudeau/

Fisher, M., J. Knobe, B. Strickland, and F. Keil. 2018. The tribalism of truth. *Scientific American* 318(2): 50–53.

Foucault, M. 1965/1988. *Madness and Civilization: A History of Insanity in the Age of Reason*. New York: Vintage Books.

Foucault, M. 1966/2002. *The Order of Things: An Archaeology of the Humans Sciences*. London: Routledge.

Foucault, M. 1969. *The Archaeology of Knowledge*. London: Tavistock.

Fuller, S. 2018. *Post-Truth: Knowledge as a Power Game*. London: Anthem Press.

Gangitano, A. 2016. Poll: Two-thirds of Trump backers think Obama is Muslim. *Roll Call* (May 10). www.rollcall.com/news/politics/poll-two-thirds-trump-supporters-think-obama-muslim

Gerson, M. 2020. Trump is the king of lies. *New York Times* (July 23). www.washingtonpost.com/opinions/trump-is-the-king-of-lies/2020/07/23/b9a52fb0-cd02-11ea-91f1-28aca4d833a0_story.html

Gore, A. 2007. *The Assault on Reason*. New York: Penguin Books.

Gorman, S. 2016. Donald Trump incorrectly says Virginia winery is the largest on East Coast. *Politifact* (March 21). www.politifact.com/factchecks/2016/mar/21/donald-trump/donald-trump-says-virginia-winery-largest-east-coa/

Grady, D. 2019. "Executing babies": Here are the facts behind Trump's misleading abortion tweet. *New York Times* (Feb. 26). www.nytimes.com/2019/02/26/health/abortion-bill-trump.html

Greenberg, J. 2016. Trump miscasts impact on trade of Chinese taxes. *Politifact* (March 30). www.politifact.com/factchecks/2016/mar/30/donald-trump/trump-miscasts-impact-trade-chinese-taxes/

Habermas, J. 1991. *The Structural Transformation of the Public Sphere: An Inquiry into a Category of Bourgeois Society*. Cambridge, MA: MIT Press.

Jacobson, L. 2016. Yes, Donald Trump did call climate change a Chinese hoax. *Politifact* (June 3). www.politifact.com/factchecks/2016/jun/03/hillary-clinton/yes-donald-trump-did-call-climate-change-chinese-h/

Jacobson, L. 2018. Donald Trump says Democrats want to give cars to undocumented immigrants. Nope. *Politifact* (Oct. 22). www.politifact.com/factchecks/2018/oct/22/donald-trump/donald-trump-says-democrats-want-give-cars-undocum/

Jacoby, S. 2008. *The Age of Unreason in a Culture of Lies*. New York: Vintage.

James, W. 1907/1978. *Pragmatism and the Theory of Truth*. Cambridge, MA: Harvard University Press.

Jay, A., D. Reidmiller, C. Avery, D. Barrie, B. DeAngelo, A. Dave, M. Dzaugis, M. Kolian, K. Lewis, K. Reeves, and D. Winne. 2018. Overview. In D. Reidmiller, C. Avery, D. Easterling, K. Kunkel, K. Lewis, T. Maycock, and B. Stewart (eds.) *Impacts, Risks, and Adaptation in the United States: Fourth National Climate Assessment, Volume II*. Washington, D.C.: U.S. Global Change Research Program. https://nca2018.globalchange.gov/chapter/1/

Kakutani, M. 2018. *The Death of Truth: Notes on Falsehood in the Age of Trump*. New York: Crown Publishing.

Kessler, G. 2015. Trump's outrageous claim that "thousands" of New Jersey Muslims celebrated the 9/11 attacks. *Washington Post* (Nov. 22). www.washingtonpost.com/news/fact-checker/wp/2015/11/22/donald-trumps-outrageous-claim-that-thousands-of-new-jersey-muslims-celebrated-the-911-attacks/

Kessler, G. 2017. Spicer earns four Pinocchios for false claims on inauguration crowd size. *Washington Post* (Jan. 22). www.washingtonpost.com/news/fact-checker/wp/2017/01/22/spicer-earns-four-pinocchios-for-a-series-of-false-claims-on-inauguration-crowd-size/

Kessler, G. 2018a. Meet the Bottomless Pinocchio, a new rating for a false claim repeated over and over again. *Washington Post* (Dec. 10). www.washingtonpost.com/politics/2018/12/10/meet-bottomless-pinocchio-new-rating-false-claim-repeated-over-over-again/

Kessler, G. 2018b. President Trump says his "beautiful wall" is being built. Nope. *Washington Post* (April 5). www.washingtonpost.com/news/fact-checker/wp/2018/04/05/president-trump-says-his-beautiful-wall-is-being-built-nope/

Kessler, G. 2019. The trade deal does not pay for the wall. *Washington Post* (Jan. 8). www.washingtonpost.com/politics/2019/live-updates/trump-white-house/live-fact-checking-and-analysis-of-president-trumps-immigration-speech/the-trade-deal-does-not-pay-for-the-wall/

Kessler G., and J. Fox. 2019. The false claims that Trump keeps repeating. *Washington Post* (March 17). www.washingtonpost.com/graphics/politics/fact-checker-most-repeated-disinformation/

230 Barney Warf

Kessler, G., and M. Lee. 2017. Fact-checking President Trump's claims on the Paris climate change deal. *Washington Post* (June 1). www.washingtonpost.com/news/fact-checker/wp/2017/06/01/fact-checking-president-trumps-claims-on-the-paris-climate-change-deal/

Kessler, G., S. Rizzo, and M. Kelly. 2020. *Donald Trump and His Assault on Truth: The President's Falsehoods, Misleading Claims and Flat-Out Lies.* New York: Scribner.

Kiely, E. 2016. Yes, Trump said Bush "lied." *FactCheck.org.* (March 17). www.factcheck.org/2016/03/yes-trump-said-bush-lied/

Klein, B., and M. Vazquez. 2018. Trump falsely claims nearly 3,000 Americans in Puerto Rico "did not die." *CNN* (Sept. 14). www.cnn.com/2018/09/13/politics/trump-puerto-rico-death-toll/index.html

Kopan, T. 2015. Donald Trump: Syrian refugees a "Trojan horse." *CNN* (Nov. 16). www.cnn.com/2015/11/16/politics/donald-trump-syrian-refugees/index.html

Kwong, J. 2018. "Truth isn't truth": Here are all the ways Trump's administration has claimed facts are no longer real. *Newsweek* (Aug. 20). www.newsweek.com/truth-isnt-truth-here-are-all-ways-trumps-administration-has-claimed-facts-1081618

Lavender, P. 2016. Donald Trump totally accused George W. Bush of lying. *Huffington Post* (March 17). www.huffpost.com/entry/donald-trump-george-w-bush_n_56eb1707e4b03a640a6a0147

Leonhardt, D., and S. Thompson. 2017. Trump's lies. *New York Times* (Dec. 14). www.nytimes.com/interactive/2017/06/23/opinion/trumps-lies.html

Lewis, N. 2017. President Trump's claim that a wall will "stop much of the drugs from pouring into this country." *Washington Post* (Sept. 11). www.washingtonpost.com/news/fact-checker/wp/2017/09/11/president-trumps-claim-that-a-wall-will-stop-much-of-the-drugs-from-pouring-into-this-country/

Meixler, E. 2018. President Trump suggested Spain build its own border wall across the Sahara. *Time* (Sept. 20). https://time.com/5401489/donald-trump-spain-sahara-border-wall/

Mooney, C. 2006. *The Republican War on Science.* New York: Basic Books.

Morin, R., and D. Cohen. 2018. Giuliani: "Truth isn't truth." *Politico* (Aug. 19). www.politico.com/story/2018/08/19/giuliani-truth-todd-trump-788161

Nakamura, D. 2019. Amid warnings of dangerous immigrants, Trump paints an incomplete and misleading picture. *Washington Post* (Jan. 8). www.washingtonpost.com/politics/amid-warnings-of-dangerous-immigrants-trump-paints-an-incomplete-and-misleading-picture/2019/01/08/2ecb909a-13b9-11e9-b6ad-9cfd62dbb0a8_story.html

New York Times. 2018 (Sept. 23). Presidential lying is contagious. www.nytimes.com/2018/09/23/opinion/trump-lies-white-house-dishonesty.html

Nichols, T. 2017. *The Death of Expertise: The Campaign against Established Knowledge and Why it Matters.* Oxford: Oxford University Press.

Nussbaum, M. 2017. Justice Department: No evidence Obama wiretapped Trump Tower. *Politico* (Sept. 2). www.politico.com/story/2017/09/02/obama-trump-tower-wiretap-no-evidence-242284

O'Brien, T. 2017. My lawyers got Trump to admit 30 lies under oath. *Bloomberg Opinion* (June 12). www.bloomberg.com/opinion/articles/2017-06-12/trump-s-history-of-lies-according-to-biographer-timothy-o-brien

Oliver, E., and T. Wood. 2016. A new poll shows 52% of Republicans actually think Trump won the popular vote. *Washington Post* (Dec. 18). www.washingtonpost.com/news/monkey-cage/wp/2016/12/18/a-new-poll-shows-an-astonishing-52-of-republicans-think-trump-won-the-popular-vote/

Orwell, G. 1948/2014. *1984.* New York: Harper.

Phillip, A., and M. DeBonis. 2017. Without evidence, Trump tells lawmakers 3 million to 5 million illegal ballots cost him the popular vote. *Washington Post* (Jan. 23). www.washingtonpost.com/news/post-politics/wp/2017/01/23/at-white-house-trump-tells-congressional-leaders-3-5-million-illegal-ballots-cost-him-the-popular-vote/

Pierre-Louis, K. 2018. Trump's misleading claims about California's fire "mismanagement." *New York Times* (Nov. 12). www.nytimes.com/2018/11/12/us/politics/fact-check-trump-california-fire-tweet.html

Policy Times. 2018 (Dec. 27). Trump worst perpetrator of fake news: David Kaye. https://thepolicytimes.com/trump-worst-perpetrator-of-fake-news-david-kaye/

Qiu, L. 2018. Trump's false claims rejecting Puerto Rico's death toll from Hurricane Maria. *New York Times* (Sept. 13). www.nytimes.com/2018/09/13/us/politics/trump-fact-check-hurricane.html

Rabinow, P. (ed.) 1991. *The Foucault Reader*. New York: Penguin.

Rizzo, S., G. Kessler and M. Kelly. 2019. Your fact-checking cheat sheet for Trump's immigration address. *The Washington Post* (Jan. 8). www.washingtonpost.com/politics/2019/01/08/your-fact-checking-cheat-sheet-trumps-immigration-address/

Robinson, E. 2018. Trump subverts our democracy with his lies. *Washington Post* (Oct. 15). www.washingtonpost.com/opinions/trump-subverts-our-democracy-with-his-lies/2018/10/15/46afae02-d0ad-11e8-8c22-fa2ef74bd6d6_story.html

Rubin, J. 2018. Trump shows the rank dishonesty of climate-change deniers. *Washington Post* (Oct. 15). www.washingtonpost.com/news/opinions/wp/2018/10/15/trump-shows-the-rank-dishonesty-of-climate-change-deniers/

Samenow, J. 2018. Trump's claim about climate scientists is "misleading and very damaging," weather group says. *Washington Post* (Oct. 17). www.washingtonpost.com/weather/2018/10/17/trumps-claim-about-climate-scientists-is-misleading-very-dangerous-leading-weather-group-says/

Schmidt, M., and M. Haberman. 2018. In Russia inquiry, lawyers tell Trump to refuse Mueller interview. *New York Times* (Feb. 5). www.nytimes.com/2018/02/05/us/politics/trump-lawyers-special-counsel-interview.html

Schwartz, T. 2017. I wrote *The Art of the Deal* with Donald Trump. In B. Lee (ed.) 2017. *The Dangerous Case of Donald Trump*. pp. 69–74. New York: St. Martin's Press.

Smith, J. 2016. Truth after Trump. *Chronicle of Higher Education* (Oct. 30). www.chronicle.com/article/Truth-After-Trump/238174

Stephens, B. 2019. What "Chernobyl" teaches about Trump. *New York Times* (June 20). www.nytimes.com/2019/06/20/opinion/chernobyl-hbo-lies-trump.html

Suskind, R. 2004. Faith, certainty and the presidency of George W. Bush. *New York Times Magazine* (Oct. 17). www.nytimes.com/2004/10/17/magazine/faith-certainty-and-the-presidency-of-george-w-bush.html

Sykes, C. 2017. *How the Right Lost its Mind*. New York: St. Martin's Press.

Tobias, M. 2018. No, U.S. Steel is not opening six new mills as Donald Trump said. *Politifact* (Aug.2). www.politifact.com/factchecks/2018/aug/02/donald-trump/us-steel-not-opening-six-new-mills-donald-trump/

Valverde, M. 2018. Donald Trump falsely says Democrats invite migrant caravans. *Politifact* (Nov. 1). www.politifact.com/factchecks/2018/nov/01/donald-trump/donald-trump-falsely-says-democrats-invite-migrant/

Wagner, J. 2018. "When I can, I tell the truth": Trump pushes back against his peddling of falsehoods. *Washington Post* (Nov. 1). www.washingtonpost.com/politics/when-i-can-i-tell-the-truth-trump-pushes-back-against-his-peddling-of-falsehoods/2018/11/01/e8278d68-ddbe-11e8-85df-7a6b4d25cfbb_story.html

Waldman, P. 2019a. Trump's corruption keeps getting more obvious. *Washington Post* (Jan. 21). www.washingtonpost.com/opinions/2019/01/21/trumps-corruption-keeps-getting-more-obvious/

Waldman, P. 2019b. Trump may have degraded U.S. politics for a generation to come. *Washington Post* (April 29). www.washingtonpost.com/opinions/2019/04/29/trump-may-have-degraded-us-politics-generation-come/

Waldman, P. 2020. How Rush Limbaugh made the Trump presidency possible. *Washington Post* (Feb. 5). www.washingtonpost.com/opinions/2020/02/05/how-rush-limbaugh-made-trump-presidency-possible/

Waxman, O. 2016. Donald Trump says Central Park Five "admitted they were guilty." Here's what to know about the case. *Time* (Oct. 7). https://time.com/4523257/donald-trump-central-park-five/

Wehner, P. 2019. Trump's sinister assault on truth. *The Atlantic* (June 18). www.theatlantic.com/ideas/archive/2019/06/donald-trumps-sinister-assault-truth/591925/

Wong, E. 2016. Trump has called climate change a Chinese hoax. Beijing says it is anything but. *New York Times* (Nov. 18). www.nytimes.com/2016/11/19/world/asia/china-trump-climate-change.html

PART III

The geopolitics of the Trump administration

13

WITH FRIENDS LIKE THESE

Trump's Middle East geopolitics as the space of exception

Carl T. Dahlman and Nathan S. French

Of sovereignty and shitholes

The presidency of Donald Trump departs from the practice of past administrations in many respects. In both domestic and foreign policy his administration has cast aside understood policy formulas and institutional norms. As a candidate and as a president, he derided and then abandoned long-standing commitments of the U.S. government in favor of "renewing this founding principle of sovereignty," which runs close to his campaign slogan to "Make America Great Again" by "putting America first" (Trump 2017e). In fomenting populist animus toward not just immigration policy but Muslim and Latino immigrants themselves, he has conjoined domestic and foreign policies that meet in the vision of a wall to separate the United States from a world it once claimed to lead. As America's lead diplomat, he has withdrawn from multilateral arrangements the U.S. helped design, spoken of his love for autocrats, wined and dined adversaries, and disparaged poor countries, notoriously referring to Haiti, El Salvador, and African countries as "shitholes" (Dawsey 2018).

Trump's foreign policy has generated intense criticism from most corners of the foreign policy community, both in the United States and globally. The primary complaints about Trump's foreign policy mostly focus on his reckless confrontational style with adversaries and his disengagement with traditional allies, such as threatening to withdraw from the North Atlantic Treaty Organization, as well as abandoning negotiated agreements with adversaries, such as the Iran nuclear deal, or the Joint Comprehensive Plan of Action, discussed below. Some commentators complain about his style, some suggest that he is cognitively impaired, others think that he is simply stupid, including those who work for him (Morin 2018). The default interpretation, however, is that Trump is transactional, pursuing short-term "deals" that enhance his political reputation at the expense of alliances and international standing that served American interests for decades (Rubin 2018; Hadar 2017).

In this chapter, we suspend our judgement regarding Trump's theatrics and his cognitive abilities to focus instead on what his words and actions tell us about his foreign policy (as of June 2019). As regional specialists in the Middle East and Islamic world, we are narrowing our examination of the 45th president's tweets, speeches, and actual policy choices in the countries of the region we know best. We take seriously Trump's former deputy national security advisor and speechwriter, Michael Anton, who, along with others, argues that the president does have a consistent foreign policy, often referred to as "principled realism" (Anton 2018; Schaefer 2018; Schweller 2018; Yoshitani 2018). Despite widespread doubt as to whether the Trump administration consistently sets policy based on any such "Trump Doctrine," we can nonetheless outline its basic dimensions as follows: long-standing international multilateral institutions and alliances are exhausted and must be abandoned or renegotiated because they unfairly cost, constrain, or "punish" the United States. In the next section we differentiate this approach from preceding U.S. foreign policy based on international liberalism and compare it to both Jacksonian and fascist geopolitical thought before moving on to examine whether a putative Trump Doctrine is at work in the Middle East.

Mapping Trump's geopolitics

In the normal course of foreign policy, U.S. presidents over the last century have tended to position themselves as leading the world in the cause of international liberalism, a world of democracies engaged in peaceful trade. This vision has had long-standing bipartisan support as a model of world affairs that reflects U.S. interests even when presidents followed specific policies that seemed to contradict the basic tenets of liberalism in the short term. Since Wilson, the leadership of the United States in promoting this vision among the world's nations, whether through building international institutions like the United Nations and the Bretton Woods agreement, or through interventions meant to combat liberalism's enemies – whether fascism, "totalitarianism," or terrorism – tended to produce several forms of U.S. foreign policy that nonetheless upheld liberalism as fundamental to U.S. interests.

On one side of U.S. foreign policy were idealists who championed international cooperation and institutions that would further American hegemony by appealing to the needs of smaller states. On the other side were realists who thought that foreign policy goals should be driven by more narrow U.S. interests expressed in terms of security and economics but who nonetheless accepted political and economic liberalism as assumptions that framed their calculations. Cutting across these groups were those more inclined toward hawkish uses of force to achieve foreign policy goals and those that gave more room for diplomatic resolutions. In truth, the differences among any of these camps were often slight, perhaps distinguished only by tone. For them, the old bromide from Senator Vandenburg would suffice, "politics stops at the water's edge."

As critics of U.S. foreign policy have long noted, there is a wide gap between America's liberal presuppositions and its actual practice. Stripped of its establishment pretensions, U.S. foreign policy may well be nothing more than the geopolitics that lie beneath it, a crude instrumentalization of complex political questions that turn world order into a tool of statecraft, minus the craft. But even geopolitics claims an intellectual provenance, a supposedly scientific model of how world power works. This vision of a natural science (geo) of power (politics) imagines territories, peoples, and resources as the primary factors shaping states' "natural" interests, returning us again to the gritty gambit of Hobbesian realism that without a decisive sovereign, life is solitary, poor, nasty, brutish, and short. In the imperial style of its progenitors, geopolitics could justify expansionist wars, racial hierarchies, and global circuits of wealth extraction.

Twentieth century liberalism, which ended European imperialism, owed much to the same geopolitical assumptions, i.e., that territorial security, identity, and economic interests dictate human affairs. What distinguished Wilsonian liberalism was an effort to ameliorate the worst impulses of states through international institutions that promoted peace and shared prosperity: the United Nations; the European Union; and the Bretton Woods agencies, among others. While liberalism survived the Second World War and the Cold War it has struggled to confront the crises of the last two decades: ethnic war; terrorism; migration; and environmental devastation. The past two decades of growing "crisis mentality" have certainly ripened the populist appeal of Trump's attacks on all things foreign. In contrast to the Wilsonian liberalism of the last century, some have described Trump's politics as Jacksonian in their nativist populism, militarism, xenophobia, and isolationist impulses (Cha 2016). Yet Trump's retreat from multilateral liberal internationalism is not actually isolationist but rather an assertive and narrow self-interest that aligns his foreign policy with core conservative values on national identity and economic gain.

The Trump Doctrine, according to its interpreters, begins by first insisting on a sovereign equality among all nations. While sovereignty does, in fact, impart an international legal equivalence among states, it does so only in the international institutions that the Trump Doctrine seeks to abandon or collapse. In its place is the realist's imagination of states competing in an anarchic global space – all against all. This creates the conditions for the second goal of the Trump Doctrine, to establish new bilateral relations in which the United States can maximally leverage its economic and military strength for U.S. trade and security interests while minimizing its costs and exposure (Anton 2018; Schweller 2018). Abandoning multilateral arrangements decreases security for weaker allies and increases systemic uncertainty. The remedy, according to the Trump Doctrine, is that the United States will narrow its focus on its primary adversaries – Russia and China – while contracting powerful regional allies to police rough neighborhoods.

Trump's Jacksonian appeal at home is not unrelated to his foreign policy. As Anton argues, they are conjoined aspects of how nations pursue their own interests in a Hobbesian state of nature. "America First," he continues, is nothing more than national "self-preservation and perpetuation" of a "homogenous" people (Anton 2018, p. 42). This ontological form of nationalism and "national sovereignty" is "intrinsic to human nature" (p. 45). This formulation of the Trump Doctrine is, we argue, a return to a criticism of international liberalism developed in the 1930s by Carl Schmitt, a conservative German legal scholar and member of the Nazi party. Schmitt's analyses of parliamentary democracy and international institutions are perhaps some of the most clearly written critiques of modern liberalism and are organized around several key ideas, all present in the Trump Doctrine (Schmitt 1923; 1932; 1954).

First, Schmitt's core assumption is that the state is the fundamental expression of how a people distinguish themselves from others, what Schmitt calls "the political." Religion, culture, economy, law, and science are wrongly considered outside the political in his formulation – everything can be weaponized. The Trump administration's politicization of what were once apolitical aspects of social life are actually an assault on liberal institutions such as the press and science. Second, for Schmitt, all political action and meaning center on the distinction between friend and enemy. As Anton imagines, and evident in Trump's xenophobia, every political entity is based on the distinction between "insiders and outsiders, between those who belong and those who do not, between citizens or subjects and foreigners" (Anton 2018, p. 43). Third, the state's self-preservation in the face of its enemies means that the sovereign is whoever can decide upon the exceptions to the rules (Schmitt 1923, p. 43; 1954, pp. 5–15). Similarly, Anton argues that "there is no higher law" or superseding authority than that of national self-preservation or "national sovereignty." Trump echoes Schmitt when he critiques multilateralism as the weak ensnaring the strong. In what follows we develop our interpretation of Trump's foreign policy in the Middle East based on another Schmittian concept, that of sovereign exception, which allows the United States to geopolitically organize its friends and enemies into spaces of transactional alliance and extreme violence.

Spaces of an exceptional enemy

For those who herald the inaugural addresses of U.S. presidents as moments of consensus-building, the inaugural address of Donald J. Trump must have felt bewildering. Shortly after thanking the outgoing administration, Trump traced a series of injustices perpetrated against Americans by their own government, politicians, and the broader establishment. Touring a series of American sufferings – impoverished inner-city families, failing educational systems, crumbling infrastructure, and criminal elements run rampant – Trump declared an "American carnage" that his predecessors allowed to fester for far too long (Trump 2017a). The speech painted an image of Middle America as the rusted-out shell of a

General Motors car left to decay in a yard while foreign neighbors cruised down U.S.-built roads in clean, modern models – all constructed at the expense of American ingenuity and commerce. Over the first year of his administration, Trump extended these domestic themes of lawlessness, carnage, and savagery outward in his foreign policy rhetoric regarding America's international woes.

Promising to clean up the most egregious of these violations, Trump turned his attention to the rest of the world, putting it on notice that all prior relationships and treaties were open to renegotiation or cancellation. First signaling this shift in his speech to a Joint Session of Congress – referring to extinguishing the "lawless savagery" of the Islamic State of Iraq and al-Sham (ISIS) from the planet – Trump applied such language as a frame for understanding U.S. policy toward the Middle East when he gave his first foreign policy remarks abroad at the "Arab Islamic American Summit" on May 21, 2017 in Riyadh (Trump 2017c; 2017d). The title of the summit was revelatory. The summit tied national identity (American) to ethnic identity (Arab) and religious identity (Islamic) revealing an intersectionality to the geography of the administration's policy objectives. For the first time in his tenure, Trump tied nation-states in the region to specific territories wherein his administration advanced contractual sovereignty as a key determinant to a Schmittian dichotomy of friend and enemy. This framework of patron and client demonstrated how Trump would seek to preserve American foreign policy objectives while emphasizing local sovereignties.

Such an approach to the Middle East is by no means revolutionary. Contractual relations between Arab, Iranian, and other Middle Eastern leaders with U.S. presidents characterized much of 20th century U.S. foreign policy in the region. As the Trump administration's approach to the Middle East unfolded, however, the renegotiation over the conditions by which it would distinguish friend from enemy revealed that its decision-making framed the pursuit of a contractual sovereignty. Those who would be friends of the United States, signaled by their willingness to align the sovereign interests of their nations with the Trump administration's foreign policy objectives, would be considered "friends" and authorized to affect violence within specific spaces. Such spaces, whose populations Trump often classified in civilizational and cultural terms, would be defined by the exceptional suspension of the norms of international and national law by both the United States and its chosen interlocutors, an affirmation of "the right of all nations to put their own interests first" (Trump 2017a). The central goal of this new policy would require "old alliances" and "new ones" to eradicate shared enemies. Months later, Trump sharpened this vision. Turning to "friends and allies," Trump promised the specific extermination of the "network of lawless savages" of ISIS while also promising to impose new sanctions on the Iranian ballistic missile program (Trump 2017c).

The list of territories that the administration has since framed as new spaces of exception reflects a tour of ongoing conflicts in the region. The writings of Sebastian Gorka (a one-time Deputy Assistant to the President) and Michael Flynn (briefly Trump's National Security Adviser) and Trump's tweets during

240 Carl T. Dahlman and Nathan S. French

the campaign reveal a common geographical focus: Afghanistan, Iran, Iraq, Libya, Syria, Russia, the West Bank (and Gaza), and Yemen (Gorka 2016; Flynn and Ledeen 2016; Trump 2016). All represent spaces wherein the Trump administration sought exceptional friends to further U.S. policy. In his speech in Saudi Arabia, Trump connected U.S. transactions – specifically weapons sales – with the persistence of "friendship," "peace," "security," and "prosperity" predicated on shared goals (Trump 2017d). The future of the region, he stipulated, would only be preserved through a declaration of the enemy followed by a purification of territory. On this point, Trump became emphatic:

> Drive. Them. Out. DRIVE THEM OUT of your places of worship. DRIVE THEM OUT of your communities. DRIVE THEM OUT of your holy land, and DRIVE THEM OUT OF THIS EARTH ... The first task in this joint effort is for your nations to deny all territory to the foot soldiers of evil. Every country in the region has an absolute duty to ensure that terrorists find no sanctuary on their soil (Trump 2017d, emphasis in the original).

As Trump continued, he listed off the exceptional friends now contracted to exterminate enemies. Eastern Syria and northern Iraq were being tamed by a coalition effort that included the Kingdom of Jordan. The Lebanese army pursued ISIS crossing its borders. Saudi Arabia was identified as the friend pursuing Houthi enemies in Yemen, joined by the armed forces of the United Arab Emirates – whom Trump also identified as assisting in the fight against ISIS and enemies of the Afghan national government. Kurdish forces were recognized for their essential assistance in the fight in Iraq and Syria. In each example, Trump identified war-torn territories – wealthy with economic resources, sharing a common culture, but impoverished by conflict – and the actors there who would work as America's friends to defeat a shared enemy.

In each space, Trump declared the right of local friends to represent U.S. interests in exceptional territories. As Schmitt observes in his *Political Theology* (1922), "the authority to suspend valid law – be it in general or in a specific case – is so much the mark of actual sovereignty" (Schmitt 1922, p. 9). Law emerges in the Trumpian order as open to contractual sovereign renegotiation. A few months after his Saudi visit, Trump observed that defeating ISIS demanded the renewal of the extraordinary legal architecture of "unlawful enemy combatants" crafted under the George W. Bush administration (Trump 2018a). With an extrajudicial suspension of international legal norms and treaties, Trump argued that the executive branch would be able to exercise its sovereign duty to identify and defeat enemies of the United States. All of this was part, he noted, of serving America's friends and "restoring clarity about our enemies" (Trump 2018a). It also expanded Trump's pursuit of American sovereignty through contractual relations.

Such clarity is a reflection of an exercise of sovereign decision-making. Spaces of exception emerge out of the negotiation of the Trump administration's distinction between friend and foe. Such spaces are areas where the administration's friends engage in the construction of sovereignty as a form of transaction. Even during the campaign, Trump boasted of the extraordinary abilities of the human and technological achievements of the U.S. armed forces while remaining reserved about his desire to extend the boot-print of those same forces across the globe. The Trump administration's approach to the Middle East resembles Schmitt's understanding that all law is situational wherein a true sovereign "produces and guarantees the situation in its entirety" (Schmitt 1922, p. 13). By pursuing what it considers the actual interests of the United States, the Trump administration authorizes local powers to pursue their own sovereign interests. Where those sovereign interests overlap with U.S. foreign policy objectives, the administration greets those governments warmly as friends and, by proclaiming them as such, extends the reach of American sovereignty within what the administration considers a realist order of foreign policy.

States of exceptional friendship

Friendly states are also those that assist with the advancement of the Trump administration's domestic objectives while helping to advance U.S. claims to proclaim friends and eliminate foes across the globe. Following his inauguration, Trump and his vice president, Mike Pence, proclaimed their protection of religious freedom through their campaign promise of a "total and complete shutdown" of immigrants from Muslim-majority countries. Executive Order 13769 called for the suspension of the issuance of visas and immigration benefits for nationals from Iran, Iraq, Libya, Somalia, Sudan, Syria, and Yemen for at least 90 days (Taylor 2015; Trump 2017b). Following court litigation and a successive series of Executive Orders hoping to clarify the constitutionality of the restrictions, the total number of Syrian refugees admitted to the U.S. declined to 62 in 2018 from 12,587 in 2016 (Zezima 2019). The decline of refugees entering the U.S. certainly does not imply their disappearance from migration numbers. After all, Turkey, Iraq, Lebanon, and Jordan absorbed around 5.3 million refugees as of 2018 – nearly one-quarter of Syria's pre-war population (Connor 2018).

Those nations deemed to have accepted their fair share of refugees are frequent recipients of Trump's gratitude. In his Saudi speech, Trump praised Jordan, Turkey, and Lebanon for hosing the refugees from the Syrian conflict. Such praise reflects the client/patronage model of contractual sovereignty in practice. Trump frames refugees as possessing a common cultural inheritance with regional neighbors and therefore of best benefit to their home countries. For Middle Eastern economies, he suggested, refugees represent a form of human capital that would "build stable societies and economies … [giving] young people hope for a brighter future in their home nations and regions" (Trump 2017d). Nations understanding the benefit of containing the flow of refugees and keeping displaced persons near to their own cultures are those whom the administration includes as exceptional friends – permitted to flaunt international norms and laws in pursuit of goals shared with the United States.

The pursuit of contractual sovereignty by the Trump administration, which we identify as a component of principled realism, locates friends who are permitted by the administration to pursue their own suspensions of the law in pursuit of their own – and America's – enemies. Such states are promised U.S. support – in the form of weapons, technology, and preferential economic treatment – for their cooperation. Perhaps just as important, however, is the explicit promise made by the administration that the United States will shelter allies from the pressures of international observers seeking to uphold the liberal order of international legal norms. The Trump administration's pursuit of what we term "exceptional friends" does demonstrate a departure from prior contractual relations with Middle Eastern governments, which upheld at least a symbolic respect for international laws and human rights.

One of the more prominent examples of this rupture appeared in the resignation of Secretary James Mattis from the Department of Defense. In his letter dated December 20, 2018, Mattis wrote:

> My views on treating allies with respect and also being clear-eyed about both malign actors and strategic competitors are strongly held … We must do everything possible to advance an international order that is most conducive to our security, prosperity and values, and we are strengthened in this effort by the solidarity of our alliances. (Mattis 2018)

Here, Mattis signaled that the Trump administration's friend-enemy distinction departed from an international order, however eroded, that secured American interests. In the days prior to Mattis's resignation, Trump signaled his intent to withdraw U.S. forces from Syria following a conversation with Turkish President Recep Tayyib Erdogan in which the latter assured Trump that Turkish forces could handle any remaining militants (DeYoung et al. 2018). For Trump, the Turkish assurances completed what was arguably a contractual negotiation between the Trump administration and Erdogan. When Mattis and other advisers raised objections to the withdrawal, Trump swept them aside, condemning the cost to U.S. taxpayers and affirming that friends could handle all fighting on behalf of the United States.

The public affirmation of Erdogan's capabilities also link Trump's domestic and foreign policies. In April 2018, Trump tweeted his support of Andrew Bunson, a U.S. pastor whom the Turkish government arrested on charges of espionage in 2016 (Trump 2018b). Three months later, the U.S. Treasury Department placed sanctions on Turkish officials (Wilhelm and Toosi 2018). Those sanctions were followed in August by Trump's announcement of a doubling of steel and aluminum tariffs on the Turkish economy and a proclamation that U.S. relations with Turkey were "not good!" (Trump 2018d). By October, however, the mood shifted. With the release of Brunson by Turkish authorities, Trump tweeted that relations would again become "good" if not "great" (Trump 2018e). Although Trump proclaimed on Twitter that there was "NO DEAL" with Turkey to provide any economic relief as a result of Brunson's release, in May 2019 the tariffs placed against Turkey were halved from 50% to 25% – their original August 2018 level (Pamuk and Beech 2019).

Turkey proved itself a possible exceptional friend with the release of Brunson. Trump tested this exceptionality with his withdrawal proclamation. Erdogan attempted to publicly confirm his willingness to handle this role noting that Turkey was one of the closest friends and allies of the United States and NATO in the region while both saw ISIS as an enemy in common with "Islam and Muslims." It was ISIS, Erdogan argued, that presented a threat to Syria's territorial integrity (Erdogan 2019). Yet, Erdogan's language reflected his own understanding of contractual sovereignty. Addressing the question of the Kurdish PKK, Erdogan maintained Turkey's right to police its borders and Syrian terrain for PKK elements to identify and eliminate. Trump signaled his willingness to accept these terms, provided Turkey would agree to a "20 mile safe zone" separating those Kurdish groups with which the U.S. enjoyed friendly relations from Erdogan's proclaimed foes (Trump 2019a).

As the drama with Turkey unfolded, the Trump administration continued its careful cultivation of ties with the Kingdom of Saudi Arabia. In the summer of 2018, Trump tweeted his praise that Saudi Arabia would assist with Syrian rebuilding efforts while also agreeing to help offset any benefits to the Iranian and Venezuelan economies that would accrue from the sale of oil (Trump 2018c). The relationship shared by the three would be brought into question in October 2018 with the disappearance of Jamal Khashoggi from a Saudi consulate in Turkey and accusations of murder leveled against close associates of Saudi Crown Prince Muhammad bin Salman. In his public statements after the disappearance, Erdogan worked to craft pressure against Muhammad bin Salman (without naming him directly) while seeking concessions from his friends in the Trump administration. This led, in part, to the Trump administration considering the extradition of Fethullah Gulen, a long-time foe of the Erdogan government (Lee, Ainsley, and Kube 2018). The attempt by Erdogan failed.

Both Secretary of State Mike Pompeo and Trump affirmed their public support for the Kingdom of Saudi Arabia's efforts to investigate and bring to justice those responsible for Khashoggi's death. In a public statement issued on November 20, 2018, Trump recognized that the Saudi monarchy considered Khashoggi "an enemy of the state" and that the circumstances of his death would remain unknown (Trump 2018f). As friends, however, the Saudis aided the fight against the Iranians and Hizbullah in the region. It was this service provided by Saudi Arabia, Trump argued, that underwrote Saudi as an exceptional friend deserving of American forbearance, not to mention U.S. military hardware. Any diplomatic crises from Khashoggi's death were nullified by Trump's decisive public proclamation. Turkey, on the other hand, received little to no concessions over its declarations of Saudi violations of its sovereignty. Apparently, in the contractual sovereignty of the Trump administration, friendship has a hierarchy.

The pattern of permitting exceptional friends to pursue their enemies by any means necessary extends to the UAE and Egypt as well. While the administration sided with the Saudis and Emiratis against Qatar in their embargo and noted their continued support – along with the other Arab nations – in standing against Iran while at the summit in Saudi Arabia, the Trump administration never condemned the UAE on the imprisonment and death sentence delivered to Christopher Hedges, a UK citizen and academic (Parveen and Wintour 2018). Instead, the administration – this time through an op-ed by the Trump-appointed Ambassador to the Vatican, Callista L. Gingrich – praised the UAE for its "advancement of religious freedom and tolerance" following its invitation of Pope Francis to Abu Dhabi (Gingrich 2019). In Egypt, Trump has repeatedly praised President Sisi's fight against the acts of "extremism" conducted in the Sinai by terrorists – going so far as to call him a "fucking killer" – while quietly and softly muting critiques of Sisi's human rights record against Egyptian political dissidents (Trump 2017f; Woodward 2018, p. 324). Sisi agreed to review Egypt's promotion of religious freedom, women's freedoms, and human rights in exchange for U.S. support for his continued governance and his campaigns in the Sinai (Talev 2019). Exceptional friends, in this framework, signal their friendship through economic ties and a willingness to proclaim the objectives of the administration with an understanding that friendship brings the administration as sovereign power to recognize exceptional enemies and the spaces within which they are to be fought.

Yemen, throughout the first three years of the administration, exemplifies this approach. Although numerous humanitarian organizations expressed concern about the Saudi and Emirati campaigns in Yemen, the Trump administration continues to provide active support to the armed forces of both nations. When Congress attempted to cut funding for the Trump administration's support of the Saudis and Emiratis, Trump issued a veto – his first usage of the constitutional power – stating that "this resolution is an unnecessary, dangerous attempt to weaken my constitutional authorities" (Edmondson 2019; Trump 2019b). Such weakened authorities, he concluded, would erode his sovereign ability to both foster bilateral relationships with U.S. allies while negatively affecting U.S. attempts to "prevent the spread of terrorist organizations such as al-Qaʻida in the Arabian Peninsula and ISIS, and embolden Iran's malign activities in Yemen" (Trump 2019b). The U.S. Congress, in the administration's estimation, had no constitutional right to limit the president's bilateral contractual ability to decide upon those friends who could exercise authority upon spaces of exceptional violence.

What of Iran amid this analysis of Trump's transactions? Certainly, the withdrawal from the Joint Comprehensive Plan of Action (JCPOA), negotiated by the Obama administration and its European allies to limit Iranian access to fissile material and limit Iranian nuclear pursuits, signaled that the Trump administration considered Iran an enemy. Yet, the territory of Iran remains just outside the category of exceptional space such as that filled by eastern Syria and Yemen. Recent rhetoric from the administration signals the possibility of a decisive change in this status. Some legal scholars fear the administration will stretch the 2001 U.S. Authorization for Use of Military Force to permit war on Iran (Chesney 2018). In his own Cairo speech, structured as a refutation of Barack Obama's speech at Cairo University in 2009, Pompeo addressed the crowd at the American University of Cairo wherein he identified a list of U.S. enemies – ISIS, "radical Islamism," Bashar al-Assad, and Iran. "The ayatollahs and their henchmen murdered, jailed, and intimated freedom-loving Iranians," Pompeo argued, and now "the regime spread its cancerous influence to Yemen, to Iraq, to Syria, and still further into Lebanon" (Pompeo 2019). Recognizing the friendly support of Bahrain, Egypt, Jordan, Kuwait, Oman, Saudi Arabia, and the UAE, Pompeo concluded: "Our aim is to partner with friends and vigorously oppose our enemies, because a strong, secure, and economically viable Middle East is in our national interest, and it's in yours as well."

A will to exceptionality in a time of shit

In their public statements, cabinet members of the Trump administration maintain a careful balance between a projection of American power through bellicosity and a promise that the president does not wish to repeat the adventurous wars of his predecessors. While National Security Advisor John Bolton might issue a statement projecting American power – "The United States is deploying [military forces] ... to send a clear an unmistakable message to the Iranian regime" – in that same statement, he cautions, "The United States is not seeking a war with the Iranian regime, but we are fully prepared to respond to any attack" (Bolton 2019). In a longer essay, Pompeo echoed Bolton's balance noting that declaration of Iran as an "outlaw regime," and the subsequent U.S. strategy of economic pressure and deterrence, would cease if Iran would only relent to the sovereign desires of the U.S. and its regional friends for meaningful negotiations (Pompeo 2018). Such a balance is often framed as a corrective to failed Obama administration policies. Matthew Kroenig (2017) argues that the central failure of the Obama administration – reflected in the perceived failure of the JCPOA to end Iranian nuclear interests once and for all – endangered friends and "emboldened enemies." The Trump administration, Kroenig concludes, will reemphasize the importance of our friends – in the case of Iran, Saudi Arabia, and Israel – against all enemies.

The negotiation of friend and enemy and the identification of contractual friendships meant to police exceptional spaces characterizes the Schmittian foundations of the emerging Trumpian foreign policy in the Middle East. Yet, for commentators such as Kroenig, a strong foreign policy must support a strong domestic policy as well. The exercise of these Schmittian friendships by the administration, which we explain as a contractual exchange in recognition of a hierarchical sovereignty that extends U.S. foreign policy objectives, supplants the traditional constitutional role of the U.S. Congress to consult with the office of the president to form treaty relationships. Instead, the administration's pursuit of friendly surrogates in spaces of exception expands the singular powers of the office of the president to declare friend and enemy out of an imminent concern for the national interest. This suggests that the "unitary executive theory" reported upon by Charles Savage and others may now become an institutionalized element of American domestic and foreign statecraft (Savage 2007). In the pursuit of the sovereign authority to proclaim friendship and enmity at home and abroad, the president of the United States with a wink, a nudge, a handshake, or a phone call, does not shred the foundations of democracy – as many suggest – but instead reveals the demand of self-interested polities to secure a leader with the will to balance and contain spaces of enmity through partnership with truly exceptional friends.

References

Anton, M. 2018. The Trump Doctrine. *Foreign Policy* (April 20). https://foreignpolicy.com/2019/04/20/the-trump-doctrine-big-think-america-first-nationalism/

Bolton, J. 2019. Statement from the National Security Advisor Ambassador John Bolton. *The White House* (May 5). www.whitehouse.gov/briefings-statements/statement-national-security-advisor-ambassador-john-bolton-2/

Cha, T. 2016. The return of Jacksonianism: The international implications of the Trump phenomenon. *The Washington Quarterly* 39(4): 83–97.

Chesney, R. 2018. Does the Corker-Kaine AUMF bill really open the door to war with North Korea and Iran? *Lawfare* (April 25). www.lawfareblog.com/does-corker-kaine-aumf-bill-really-open-door-war-north-korea-and-iran

Connor, P. 2018. Where Syrian refugees have resettled worldwide. *Pew Research Center* (Jan. 29). www.pewresearch.org/fact-tank/2018/01/29/where-displaced-syrians-have-resettled/

Dawsey, J. 2018. Trump derides protections for immigrants from "shithole" countries. *Washington Post* (Jan. 12). www.washingtonpost.com/politics/trump-attacks-protections-for-immigrants-from-shithole-countries-in-oval-office-meeting/2018/01/11/bfc0725c-f711-11e7-91af-31ac729add94_story.html

DeYoung, K., M. Ryan, J. Dawsey, and G. Jaffe. 2018. A tumultuous week began with a phone call between Trump and the Turkish president. *Washington Post* (Jan. 21). www.washingtonpost.com/world/national-security/a-tumultuous-week-began-with-a-phone-call-between-trump-and-the-turkish-president/2018/12/21/8f49b562-0542-11e9-9122-82e98f91ee6f_story.html

Edmondson, C. 2019. Senate votes again to end aid to Saudi war in Yemen, defying Trump. *New York Times* (March 13). www.nytimes.com/2019/03/13/us/politics/yemen-saudi-war-senate.html

Erdogan, R. 2019. Trump is right on Syria. Turkey can get the job done. *New York Times* (Jan. 7). www.nytimes.com/2019/01/07/opinion/erdogan-turkey-syria.html

Flynn, M., and M. Ledeen. 2016. *The Field of Fight: How We Can Win the Global War Against Radical Islam and Its Allies*. New York: St. Martin's Press.

Gingrich, C. 2019. US Vatican Ambassador: Pope's historic UAE visit advances religious freedom and tolerance. *Fox News* (Feb. 9).

Gorka, S. 2016. *Defeating Jihad: The Winnable War*. New York: Regnery Publishing.

Hadar, L. 2017. The limits of Trump's transactional foreign policy. *The National Interest* (Jan. 2). https://nationalinterest.org/feature/the-limits-trumps-transactional-foreign-policy-18898

Kroenig, M. 2017. The case for Trump's foreign policy: The right people, the right positions. *Foreign Affairs* (May/June). www.foreignaffairs.com/articles/world/2017-04-17/case-trump-s-foreign-policy

Lee, C., J. Ainsley, and C. Kube. 2018. To ease Turkish pressure on Saudis over killing, White House weighs expelling Erdogan foe. *NBC News* (Nov. 15). www.nbcnews.com/politics/national-security/white-house-weighs-booting-erdogan-foe-u-s-appease-turkey-n933996

Mattis, J. 2018. James Mattis' resignation letter. *CNN News* (Jan. 21). www.cnn.com/2018/12/20/politics/james-mattis-resignation-letter-doc/index.html

Morin, R. 2018. "Idiot," "dope," "moron": How Trump's aides have insulted the boss. *Politico* (Sept. 4). https://politi.co/2Q6fK3W

Pamuk, H., and E. Beech. 2019. U.S. terminates Turkey's preferential trade agreement, reduces tariffs on steel. *Reuters* (May 17). www.reuters.com/article/us-usa-trade-turkey/us-terminates-turkeys-preferential-trade-agreement-reduces-tariffs-on-steel-idUSK-CN1SN01Z

Parveen, N., and P. Wintour. 2018. Matthew Hedges: British academic accused of spying jailed for life in UAE. *The Guardian* (Nov. 21). www.theguardian.com/world/2018/nov/21/british-academic-matthew-hedges-accused-of-spying-jailed-for-life-in-uae

Pompeo, M. 2018. Confronting Iran: The Trump administration's strategy. *Foreign Affairs* (Dec.) www.foreignaffairs.com/articles/middle-east/2018-10-15/michael-pompeo-secretary-of-state-on-confronting-iran

Pompeo, M. 2019. A force for Good: America reinvigorated in the Middle East. *U.S. Department of State* (Jan. 10). www.state.gov/a-force-for-good-america-reinvigorated-in-the-middle-east/

Rubin, J. 2018. Why transactional foreign policy is destined to fail. *Washington Post* (Oct. 19). www.washingtonpost.com/news/opinions/wp/2018/10/19/why-transactional-foreign-policy-is-destined-to-fail/

Savage, C. 2007. *Takeover: The Return of the Imperial Presidency and the Subversion of American Democracy*. New York: Back Bay Books.

Schaefer, B. 2018. President Trump at the UN: An unapologetic defense of "principled realism." *The Heritage Foundation* (Sept. 28). www.heritage.org/global-politics/commentary/president-trump-the-un-unapologetic-defense-principled-realism

Schmitt, C. 1922/1985. *Political Theology: Four Chapters on the Concept of Sovereignty*. Chicago: University of Chicago Press.

Schmitt, C. 1923/1996. *The Crisis of Parliamentary Democracy*. Cambridge, Mass.: MIT Press.

Schmitt, C. 1932/2008. *The Concept of the Political: Expanded Edition*. Chicago: University of Chicago Press.

Schmitt, C. 1954/2006. *The Nomos of the Earth in the International Law of the Jus Publicum Europaeum*. Candor, NY: Telos Press.

Schweller, R. 2018. Three cheers for Trump's foreign policy: What the establishment misses. *Foreign Affairs* (Oct.). www.foreignaffairs.com/articles/world/2018-08-13/three-cheers-trumps-foreign-policy

Talev, M. 2019. Trump praises Egypt's El-Sisi amid efforts to extend rule. *Bloomberg* (April 9). www.bloomberg.com/news/articles/2019-04-09/trump-says-he-doesn-t-oppose-el-sisi-s-effort-to-extend-his-rule

Taylor, J. 2015. Trump calls for "total and complete shutdown of Muslims entering" U.S. *NPR.Org* (Dec. 7). www.npr.org/2015/12/07/458836388/trump-calls-for-total-and-complete-shutdown-of-muslims-entering-u-s

Trump, D. 2016. Hillary Clinton failed… [tweet]. *@realDonaldTrump* (Sept. 26). https://twitter.com/realDonaldTrump/status/780594362862362624

Trump, D. 2017a. The inaugural address. *The White House* (Jan. 20). www.whitehouse.gov/briefings-statements/the-inaugural-address/

Trump, D. 2017b. Executive Order Protecting the Nation from Foreign Terrorist Entry into the United States. *The White House* (Jan. 27). www.whitehouse.gov/presidential-actions/executive-order-protecting-nation-foreign-terrorist-entry-united-states/

Trump, D. 2017c. Remarks by President Trump in joint address to Congress. *The White House* (Feb. 28). www.whitehouse.gov/briefings-statements/remarks-president-trump-joint-address-congress/

Trump, D. 2017d. President Trump's speech to the Arab Islamic American Summit. *The White House* (May 21). www.whitehouse.gov/briefings-statements/president-trumps-speech-arab-islamic-american-summit/

Trump, D. 2017e. *Speech by President Trump.* Presented at the 72nd Session of the United Nations General Assembly, New York, Sept. 19.

Trump, D. 2017f. Horrible and cowardly… [tweet]. *@realDonaldTrump* (Nov. 24). https://twitter.com/realDonaldTrump/status/934080974773776384

Trump, D. 2018a. President Donald J. Trump's State of the Union Address. *The White House* (Jan. 30). www.whitehouse.gov/briefings-statements/president-donald-j-trumps-state-union-address/

Trump, D. 2018b. Pastor Andrew Brunson… [tweet]. *@realDonaldTrump* (April 17). https://twitter.com/realDonaldTrump/status/986432143189512192

Trump, D. 2018c. Just spoke to King Salman… [tweet]. *@realdonaldtrump* (June 30). https://twitter.com/realdonaldtrump/status/1013023608040513537

Trump, D. 2018d. I have just authorized… [tweet]. *@realDonaldTrump* (Aug. 10). https://twitter.com/realDonaldTrump/status/1027899286586109955

Trump, D. 2018e. There was NO DEAL… [tweet]. *@realDonaldTrump* (Oct. 13). https://twitter.com/realDonaldTrump/status/1051114825391239169

Trump, D. 2018f. Statement from President Donald J. Trump on standing with Saudi Arabia. *The White House* (Nov. 20). www.whitehouse.gov/briefings-statements/statement-president-donald-j-trump-standing-saudi-arabia/

Trump, D. 2019a. Starting the long overdue pullout… [tweet]. *@realDonaldTrump* (Jan. 13). https://twitter.com/realDonaldTrump/status/1084584259510304768

Trump, D. 2019b. Presidential veto message to the Senate to accompany S.J. Res. 7. *The White House* (April 16). www.whitehouse.gov/presidential-actions/presidential-veto-message-senate-accompany-s-j-res-7/

Wilhelm, C., and N. Toosi. 2018. U.S. sanctions Turkish officials over detained pastor. *Politico* (Aug. 1). www.politico.com/story/2018/08/01/trump-administration-to-sanction-turkish-officials-over-imprisonment-of-american-pastor-756896

Woodward, B. 2018. *Fear: Trump in the White House.* New York: Simon and Schuster.

Yoshitani, G. 2018. Jeane Kirkpatrick and the roots of principled realism. *War on the Rocks* (Oct. 9). https://warontherocks.com

Zezima, K. 2019. The U.S. has slashed its refugee intake. Syrians fleeing war are most affected. *Washington Post* (May 7). www.washingtonpost.com/immigration/the-us-has-slashed-its-refugee-intake-syrians-fleeing-war-are-most-affected/2019/05/07/f764e57c-678f-11e9-a1b6-b29b90efa879_story.html

14

TRUMP IN THE TROPICS

Territorialities and the misdirection of U.S. foreign policy toward Cuba[1]

Richard N. Gioioso and Lisa A. Baglione

> "To justify its policy of normalizing relations with Cuba, President Obama said Cuba quote 'poses no genuine threat.' Tell that to the American diplomats who were attacked in Havana. Tell that to the terrorized people of Venezuela. The reality is that the Obama government sought to normalize relations with a tyrannical dictatorship…. [The Trump policy is designed to reject] the disastrous Obama-era policies, and finally end the glamorization of socialism and communism."
>
> John Bolton, U.S. National Security Advisor, April 19, 2019[2]

In 2017, the Trump Administration began reversing Obama-era policies of opening U.S.-Cuban relations. Trump's efforts were a return to long-standing coercive U.S. approaches since the Cuban Revolution[3] in 1959. The change appears to be based on the neoconservative contention that pressure and isolation will destabilize a repressive (and anti-American) regime, enabling the many ready and willing opponents to rise up and topple the state. The opposition will then replace the system with a relatively well-functioning, American-style market economy and a government that is friendly to the United States. Leaving aside previous visible and costly failures of this logic, this policy is particularly unsuited to Cuba because of the thorough and resilient territoriality of the Cuban state and the Communist Party of Cuba (*Partido Comunista de Cuba*, PCC). This territoriality means first that alternative political leaders or institutions do not exist to contest the pervasive roles of the PCC in the state and society. Second, over nearly 60 years the Cuban government has cultivated a political culture that allows the PCC to exert hegemonic power over the imaginations of most Cuban people.

Ethnographic data of interactions with young Havanans, ages 20–40, collected over five years, reveal their great frustration with the politics and economy that the PCC has constructed, but not a sense that transforming the system is possible.[4-5] Instead, these individuals are overwhelmingly apolitical, apathetic, and demoralized citizens. They do not believe in their own agency as political or civic actors who can bring about the kinds of changes American policymakers envision. The respondents understand and have internalized the high cost of participating in such activities and prefer to avoid the ensuing surveillance and possible repercussions (physical and otherwise).

Thus, the logic that the regime will collapse and individuals will be ready to govern is highly questionable. Instead of pursuing a coercive approach toward the island, the U.S. would be better served to restart its policy of engagement. In the few years it was tried, the enhanced connections between the United States and Cuba began a process of opening minds to and developing habits of entrepreneurship and individual efficacy. These efforts began empowering citizens and encouraging the regime to accommodate popular demands for more access to consumer goods and global culture.

The centrality of territoriality in analyzing the U.S.-Cuban relationship

Political geography and the key concept of territoriality are essential to understanding how and why U.S. attempts at creating change within Cuba have largely failed. Territoriality refers to a state's effective governance of both *physical* and *ideological spaces* within and between territories. In the *material* sense, states work to demarcate and impose the physical limits of their power, turning blurred boundaries into precisely delineated ones.[6] In the *non-material* sense, territoriality refers to the state's efforts to diffuse the ideas, norms, and practices that it employs in governing and ruling its population.[7] Territoriality can thus be applied to domestic, internal spaces (e.g., subnational divisions, voting districts), as well as to international spaces, especially regarding the establishment and defense of sovereignty between and among states.[8] A related term that emphasizes the agency of state actors, territorialization is the process of marrying the bounding of spaces using borders and the ideas that justify the political, social, economic, and legal institutions implemented in these places.

As Nevins (2010) showed in his analysis of the U.S.-Mexico border in the 19th century,[9] *demarcation, domination, and establishment of governance* of the physical spaces are the essence of territoriality and the processes of territorialization. These efforts are not simply material, but are ideational and social. In the 19th century, the U.S. remade the border on the ground, established physical control over the territory, and constituted a consensus on both national ownership in the minds of citizens on both sides and the rules governing relations between the states. With respect to Cuba, over the last almost 60 years, the PCC has succeeded in an analogous project of physical, social, and mental territoriality which empowers the state to resist the United States' efforts to attain American foreign policy objectives, that is, to turn Cubans against the regime so that they will overthrow it. The U.S.'s physical and ideological goals have failed because the PCC's achievement of territoriality in Cuba has been and overwhelming remains complete. The domination of the Cuban state and official political, economic, and social apparatuses, e.g., the PCC, are the status quo, and Cubans on the island have thoroughly internalized the norms, rules, practices, and political culture (including acceptable political and civic behaviors).[10] Thus, Cuba's territoriality again (as it did prior to 2013) trumps American attempts to deterritorialize this state.

America's Cuba policy prior to Trump

In 2013, the Obama Administration began reversing the decades-long approach to Cuba.[11] Previously, the goal had been to isolate this troublesome communist state in the hemisphere and to overthrow the regime. After 1960, Cuba represented an ideological and strategic challenge to the U.S. Its existence demonstrated that a communist-style system could work in the Western hemisphere, and its close relationship with Moscow provided the potential for a base for the Soviet military and an ally in that country's revolutionary activities. While the Cuban Missile Crisis thwarted Soviet attempts to have land-based nuclear capability 90 miles off the coast of Florida, the success of the Cuban Revolution meant that it served as a beacon to leftists in Latin America and elsewhere.[12] Moreover, Cubans were enthusiastic in supporting revolutionary efforts in Central America and parts of Africa during the 1970s and 1980s (Domínguez 1989).

With the fall of the USSR in 1991, many Americans (and Cubans too) believed the days of the communist Castro regime where numbered, because the financial and moral support of the Soviets had been so important to Cuba's communist survival. Thus, U.S. pressure remained firm, but, contrary to those expectations, Castro and communism remained, aging and weakening (Castro finally dying in 2016). Still, the system carried on, as did American hostility to it.[13]

In this way, the U.S., even in its post-Cold War phase of seeking integration and connection across societies, economies, and peoples throughout the world, continued to view Cuba as an anomaly, as a state to be isolated. The U.S., therefore, continued its policies of coercion, hoping Cuba's collapse was near. Particularly in the Clinton years, the Cuba policy seemed contradictory (perhaps reflecting domestic political hopes of winning Florida for the Democrats in presidential races), although the approach of George W. Bush was consistent not only with the past, but with the preferences of his base (Ambrose and Brinkley 2011).

Thus, Obama's reversal was both shocking because it ended this long-standing (nearly 60-year) policy, but also overdue. America's Cuba policy was out of step with its general approach to foreign policy in the era of globalization, and more in line with the sentiments of public opinion in the post-Iraq War and post-Arab Spring America (Bacevich 2016; Ricks 2009). Forcible regime change didn't seem to work, and the pernicious actors in these long-lived systems appeared to have a staying power that popular uprisings couldn't break (McFaul 2018). Obama's policy reinstated diplomatic ties and encouraged people-to-people interactions, allowing Americans to travel to the island and promoting various kinds of relationships between citizens and organizations in both societies.

252 Richard N. Gioioso and Lisa A. Baglione

Many Americans (including Cuban-Americans) and Cubans greeted these changes positively (NORC 2016), although clearly, in the U.S., there was an age and partisan split. Those Americans who viewed the new policy negatively were overwhelmingly older and Republican.[14] In Cuba, the vast majority saw the new openness as an important lifeline to economic possibilities and more social freedom. For most, their hopes were not grand, but they believed that the new relationship would give them opportunities for a better existence and some happiness. Our Cuban young adult research participants unanimously (n = 35) favored President Obama's policies of openness toward Cuba. Their agreement with facilitating engagement was, again, unanimously accompanied by enthusiasm about the economic opportunities and resulting life changes that American tourism would bring. As is often the case in our data, however, their hope existed alongside skepticism about whether détente would continue. Respondents tended to believe that both the American and Cuban governments were unpredictable and were able to reverse such policies without serious consequences for either. Of course, they knew such reversals would have great impacts on their lives.

A specific example of the joy and the hopes for increased contacts comes from Andy. Having migrated from the western province of Pinar del Río with his mother as a boy and attended one of the best high schools in Havana, he earned his degree in the humanities at the University of Havana. With the announcement of re-engagement by both President Obama and Cuban President Raúl Castro in December 2014, Andy immediately and elatedly began writing to his friends in the United States expressing his approval, which included sentiments of incredulity that such a step was possible. "Is this for real?", he wrote. "What does this mean? Will more *yumas*[15] really be able to come to Cuba? I can't believe it. So when are you coming to Havana again? Come now, and bring friends!"[16] Andy later explained that he hoped to meet new people to expand his horizons, and he'd be happy to help with any tourist-oriented activities he could. "*No me voy a aprovechar de ellos ni nada*, I don't want to take advantage of them [tourists] or anything, but *comisiones* are a part of almost anything that a *yuma* does in Cuba, and every little bit counts [for his income]."[17]

For Katia, too, the news of the opening was both welcome and a relief. Originally from the Havana countryside, she had lived in that city for ten years, leaving her hometown to take advantage of the many opportunities the capital offers. She, too, attended the University of Havana, but received a degree in education, and worked in the school system for two years after graduation. In early 2013, however, she began a project of renovating her aunt's apartment in El Vedado, the "modern downtown" in Havana, equipping it to rent out to tourists. By 2014 the apartment was ready to rent, but the only means she had to promote it were friends and family abroad, and by circulating information among her networks in Havana. Although these networks resulted in occasional rentals before the normalization process began, by early 2016 her guestbook was mostly full with few days free each month. Her local and international word-of-mouth approach began to bear more fruit, as more

Americans were able to travel to Cuba, and booking through Airbnb became available. In August 2016, she said:

> ¿*Viste*? See? This is why I spent all that time and effort in preparing the apartment. It's been tough. My aunt is living with my mother, and I'm living between their apartment and staying with my boyfriend and his family, but it's worth it ...Why do you think it took so long for this [normalization between the two countries] to happen? Who cares about all those problems from way back when? Politicians are stupid and selfish. They keep fighting while we're the ones who suffer. I'm just glad that things have started to change. I'm actually working on another apartment to rent right now. I hope to have it ready within a month or so. But let's see how long it [opening between U.S. and Cuba] lasts.

These two examples are indicative of many others in the data. Young Cubans were thrilled with the opening as a chance for access to new people, ideas, and, of course, economic opportunities. Notice what they aren't discussing, however: there's no talk of political action or even hints about the possibility of system change.

Trump's Cuba policy: A return to neoconservative foreign policy with Cuba

While awareness of citizens' sentiments would seem to be important for any policy predicated on the Cuban people rising up and throwing off their government, American officials in charge of Cuba policy today seem unaware of or at least indifferent to popular sentiments on the island. Instead, they have reversed Obama's Cuba policy and called for increased isolation and pressure (Bolton 2018; PBS Newshour 2019).

That the approach to Cuba would be dramatically changed was not really surprising. Given Trump's campaign rhetoric, observers expected American foreign policy *in toto* to take a new tact. Many feared the administration would undo the partisan consensus on the U.S. role in the world and break apart a world order that had been both the product and instrument of U.S. power.[18] Since World War II, previous American administrations had been united in their vision of the U.S. as a leader of the market democracies. They had perceived the global economic and alliance systems built in the postwar era as central to maintaining, securing, and projecting American power (Ambrose and Brinkley 2011; McFaul 2018). While there were certainly previous discussions about how to make the global economy work more favorably for the United States and intra-alliance spats over burden-sharing, no postwar president had formulated the U.S. position as this one did in the December 2017 National Security Strategy:

> During my first year in office, you have witnessed my *America First* foreign policy in action. We are prioritizing the interests of our citizens and *protecting our sovereign rights as a nation* ... Unfair trade practices had weakened

254 Richard N. Gioioso and Lisa A. Baglione

our economy and exported our jobs overseas. Unfair burden-sharing with our allies and inadequate investment in our own defense had invited danger from those who wish us harm. Too many Americans had lost trust in our government, faith in our future, and confidence in our values ...We will pursue this beautiful [strategic] vision – a world of *strong, sovereign, and independent nations, each with its own cultures and dreams*, thriving side-by-side in prosperity, freedom, and peace.[19]

While this language and many of Trump's policies were certainly inconsistent with the neoconservativism of the George W. Bush era, the administration embraced key precepts in its approach toward Cuba.[20] According to Arturo Lopez-Levy:

Now [with new steps in spring 2019], the Trump Administration is doubling down on a failed strategy of hostility, reducing engagement with Cuba, and returning to the 1996 Helms-Burton law, one of the most repudiated pieces of "trade" legislation in the world. Trump's decision to restore the grip of Cold War-era policy to the Strait of Florida caters not to the interests of the Cuban people, but to a small group of voters between Little Havana and Doral – the new Little Caracas – in South Florida.[21]

Here, Lopez-Levy notes the continuation with the past consensus, but he also suggests the importance of domestic politics, as well as a neoconservative mindset. His mention of Venezuelan Floridians highlights the renewed danger this administration perceives emanating from Cuba: its role as an agitator for and supporter of anti-American regimes like Venezuela that challenge American values and the U.S. geopolitical system.

In fact, by resorting to pressure and pushing for regime change, Trump's Cuba policy seeks to achieve desirable outcomes by overpowering and outlasting an opponent. Joseph S. Nye (2004) has famously called these "hard power" approaches, and he has acknowledged that coercive policies have their roles in foreign affairs. Scholars and analysts have also noted, however, that to accomplish foreign policy objectives in today's world, states often benefit from other means of exerting influence. Nye, himself, has discussed the value of "soft power," the influence and behavior-changing tool that states employ (sometimes purposefully and sometimes without intent) by being an attractive role model with respect to good governance, a healthy economy, stable society, and appealing culture. The exercise of soft power, without coercion, can give individuals around the world both the desire to emulate behaviors and practices of another place and a sense of empowerment that they can achieve similar outcomes. In that way, soft power transforms peoples, societies, and ultimately states without any violence or threats. Then these social, economic, and even political refashionings provide opportunities for positive joint endeavors between individuals, businesses, societies, and states. The idea of soft power is inherently and necessarily not territorializing in nature, and the Trump Administration appears to give it no currency.[22] In fact, in its view, soft power is part of the failed (or rather, "disastrous") Obama-era approach.[23]

Challenging Cuban territoriality

The Trump Administration's abandonment of an engagement strategy is based on assumptions about the Cuban state and the nature of regime change[24] which, unfortunately, American administrations have used before and have been terribly flawed. Arguably, the perspective is rooted in Jeane Kirkpatrick's (1979) famous dictum that authoritarian states can fall to democrats, but that totalitarians never do.[25] Despite the ultimate collapse of the Soviet Union and the transformation of China from a totalitarian to an authoritarian and mixed state-run and capitalist regime, some policymakers, particularly of the neoconservative variant, have been particularly unwilling to deal with those they deem totalitarian. Perhaps most famously is the George W. Bush Administration's approach to Iraq. In 2002–2003, neoconservatives argued that Saddam had to be overthrown (ostensibly because of his weapons of mass destruction or potential to develop them) and that once the regime collapsed, a new "democratic" Iraq would be easy to build. In fact, it would be so easy to create that all of the former important institutions of that state (the Ba'ath Party, the military) could be disbanded and the improved regime would emerge relatively easily, with just some simple oversight from an American administrator and support from U.S. troops for about a year or so. Moreover, the collapse of Saddam's Iraq would create a "reverse domino" effect, leading to the democratization of the Middle East and potentially spreading to other parts of the world.[26]

While many outstanding works have been written to explain the failure of this logic in Iraq (Bacevich 2016; Ricks 2006; 2009), the problems in applying the argument to Cuba are both similar in some ways, but also exhibit unique Cuba-specific characteristics. The starting issue is that the new revolutionary state, as it developed after the overthrow of the government of Fulgencio Batista, effectively territorialized the country. As a domestic characteristic, this feat had two key elements. First, the PCC, founded in 1965, permeated the island and came to dominate every aspect of the Cuban polity, economy, and society.[27] It was embedded in all elements of control and governance and, in essence, spread its tentacles throughout the territory. Second, because of its ubiquity and its seemingly endless hold on the island, Cuban citizens had long ago acquiesced to the idea that they were stuck with the PCC and the Castros, or those who came after the Castros who would carry on their ideas. Again, the reach of the party-state had effectively seeped into the minds of so many, closing off their abilities to imagine a life without it.

An excellent example from our data of the pervasiveness of and disdain for the party, yet acquiescence to its continued domination comes from Adrián. Originally from the Marianao section of Havana, Adrián grew up in a household with parents who were born and raised after the "triumph of the Revolution,"[28] and spent their careers working in state-owned industries. They always proudly

256 Richard N. Gioioso and Lisa A. Baglione

considered themselves part and parcel of the party and good Cuban citizens. In raising their son, they inculcated similar values and beliefs. He was a member of the *Unión de Jóvenes Comunistas* (also referred to as the *UJC* or *la Juventud*), after which he went on to join *el Partido*. Membership in the PCC was frowned upon and rejected by almost all our young adults, although for someone like Adrián, a college professor, it is not unusual. Over the course of the past three years, however, his attitudes have changed regarding the government, notably shifting after his first trip out of Cuba for a two-month-long trip to Europe and the United States. Prior to traveling abroad, Adrián spoke passionately about the virtues of the Cuban government and Cuban society, and was a proponent of some kinds of political reforms, always and only within the currently existing system and managed by the PCC, *dentro de la Revolución*, within the revolution. After returning from abroad, his attitude regarding the Cuban political system and aspects of society that result from it, e.g., state-owned and run (censored) media, became much more critical. But, perhaps surprisingly from an American vantage, despite his disgust, Adrián was pessimistic about the likelihood of any significant changes to the system. His beliefs, like those of the vast majority of our Cuban young adults, are that both power and money have been accumulated and retained at the top echelons of the government and the military. These officials and their offspring have little desire to release their grip on the system that guarantees their privileges; thus, the system is stably corrupt, rigged, and authoritarian. In spite of developing this critical and pessimistic view of the party-state, Adrián still votes and participates in its organs. Unlike before, however, he now refers to Fidel with sarcasm and some amount of frustration as *el dueño*, the owner, of everything in the country.

Cuban state's territoriality over imaginations

Adrián's sentiments and behavior are not unique. Among the relatively privileged Cubans in our sample, people choose to cohabit with the regime, but take advantage of it as much as possible. In this system where citizens understand that the party-state is pervasive, they play along while looking for opportunities for entrepreneurship and consumption. Increased openness that came with the 2013 American policy reversal gave these young people new perspectives on their society. Their conclusions about the Cuban system, derived from the opportunities to engage and interact with others, especially Americans, were highly negative. Still, these adverse opinions have not translated into political action in favor of regime change.

The success of the system in inhabiting the minds of young Cubans stems from the early and all-encompassing ideological training that began when they were youngsters and continued through adulthood. All our research participants were educated in the state-run educational system, which is compulsory for Cuban nationals. Students, also known as *pioneros y pioneras* (pioneers), are inculcated with national values and patriotism, with an emphasis on fidelity to *la Revolución*. Every morning, to start the day, students gather together to perform the morning salute, *el matutino,* singing the national anthem as the flag is raised, and culminating in the slogan: ¡*Pioneros por el Comunismo, seremos como el Che!* (Pioneers for Communism, we'll be like el Che [Guevara]!). By their late teen years, most of our research participants had begun to laugh off their participation in such ideologically oriented activities as silly and childish, but membership or affiliation with official organs, like the *Federación Estudiantil Universitaria,* is seriously encouraged or required through college. This phenomenon – joining and retaining membership for professional advancement – is referred to as careerism, an occurrence that was also common in the Soviet bloc after 1968.[29] Alayn, for example, is a 26-year-old with a bachelor's degree in the social sciences who has become an entrepreneur in the private sector of the economy, opening his own *cafetería.* Through his network of friends and acquaintances in Cuba, he also became a driver of a private car for tourists, and later a tour guide. He felt somewhat discouraged and angry as he thought back to his participation in such groups, but his exposure to foreigners, including many Americans, began to open his mind and change his opinion:

> *La Juventud* was basically a waste of time. Now as I think back on it, it was a joke. In middle school, they fooled us by telling us that only the best students would get into *La Juventud,* and if we didn't join, then we wouldn't be accepted into the best high schools. They were just telling us that just so we would join. These groups were a way of committing you to the "principles" of the *Revolución.* And when you're a kid, you believe whatever they tell you. I didn't begin to question anything until now, even during college I did all the parades and marches that they made us do. It's all I knew. I kind of see things differently now. I never really met people from other countries, but with all these *yumas* here now, I'm getting to see how different other people can be, and how different we Cubans are. Things are really messed up here [in Cuba], but maybe they're starting to change for the better. We'll see. I'm hopeful, a lot of us are, but you never how things will go. Without an enemy [the U.S. government] to blame for the problems any more, the government is terrified.

Like Adrián and Alayn, most of the Cuban young adults in our study were thoroughly inculcated in the regime's values but have recently – as a result of the opportunities derived from travel and interactions with tourists – developed disdain for the system. Still, despite these shifts in attitude regarding the Cuban state and aspects of society, our subjects have never doubted the system's ubiquity, resilience, and continuity.

Perhaps the most striking example of newfound disdain comes from Verónica, a descendant of "*históricos,*" those who participated in the fight for the Revolution during the late 1950s, and were personally acquainted with Fidel for decades. They were faithful and ardent supporters of the *Revolución,* its ideology, and the political, economic, and social systems that sprung from it. Verónica, now 27 years old, was born in Havana and has lived her entire life in the family home, which was gifted to her grandparents as a reward for their participation and loyalty.

258 Richard N. Gioioso and Lisa A. Baglione

At first, Verónica, like her grandparents and parents, was, in her own words, "100% with the *Revolución*." Having already finished a degree at a technical academy three years ago, she is currently studying for her bachelor's degree in the humanities through the "night school" program at the University of Havana. Meanwhile, she also maintains an official job at a state agency. Verónica has become increasingly dissatisfied with life in Cuba, the scarcity, the low salaries, the transportation problems, in short, aspects of daily life that "always stay the same, or get even worse." Her aspirations for a higher standard of living have caused her to get "*harta ya*, fed up" with the system that does not permit her to achieve this. Like Adrián, Verónica, tapping her right shoulder twice with her index and middle finger, in the gesture that refers to the military, thinks "they keep it all for themselves." But also like Adrián, Verónica can't imagine life without the party, and she knows that she owes much of her privilege and opportunities to her own family connections.

Prior to the normalization of U.S.-Cuban relations in 2013, economic opportunities were few and survival was a challenge, even for the young, educated, and entrepreneurial. Citizens did their best to take from the system and look for additional opportunities. In essence, the party-state was like the omnipresent mosquitos of the tropics that people need to swipe away, never eliminating them from daily life, but necessary for the ecosystem. With the 2013 opening, however, opportunities for eluding the reach of authorities grew, as did possibilities for economic and social advancement.[30] Citizens, particularly those with some privilege – education, geographic location, and youth – had new chances to live a better life, one marked by the consumption of higher quality and more desirable goods, opportunities to travel, and access to Western culture that was reaching the island via improved cyber connections, cruise ships, and airlines.

Raúl, now 37 years old, is the main provider of his household, which consists of his mother and elderly grandmother. An athlete on one of Cuba's national sports teams, Raúl studied sports science at university and has lived outside of the country on two occasions, once in Panamá and another in El Salvador. He now has an official state job related to athletics, but his assignment to a facility that is defunct means that there is nothing for him to do. Nevertheless, he happily derives a monthly salary, albeit small, what he would call "a pittance." Given these circumstances, Raúl has had time to develop a clientele for personal training and massage therapy, and many of his clients are tourists or members of the international elite in Havana (e.g., from the diplomatic corps). Although these new opportunities have improved his standard of living and allowed him to provide some modicum of comfort to his mother and grandmother, his frustration with the Cuban government and the system is palpable:

> What kind of business could you possibly do in this country if nothing is reliable, nor consistent in any way? This [country] is for crazy people. And now with Trump, things are getting even worse here. There are blackouts sometimes, and I have to go all around Havana just to pick up basic food stuffs. I went to get chicken the other day and there was a mob scene.

It was insane ... But what are you going to do? I will leave them [officials, authorities] alone, just as long as they leave me alone. I look like a fool carrying my massage bed around with me all over the city, and with the heat [it] is suffocating. But I just need to make my money. That's all I can do.

Although the above quotes represent a small sample of our Cuban young adult research participants, their stories and opinions illustrate a consensus. The Cuban state is fully embedded and has very thoroughly territorialized both the land and citizens' minds. Among our sample, no one believes that any change in or challenge to the political status quo is possible.

Why Cuban territoriality trumps U.S. neoconservative efforts at deterritorialization

In sum, while American policymakers like to emphasize the failures of the Cuban state to provide the freedom and robust economy that its citizens deserve, our research emphasizes an important success: The PCC has territorialized its control over the land, the governance, and the people, *despite its failures*. Cuban young adults' attitudes toward their government, especially regarding the management of the economy – and the many rules, laws, and informal practices by authorities that restrict economic advance – are negative, very negative. Moreover, these citizens could provide a long list of their grievances. They are frustrated, fed up, and exhausted by the amount of work they have to put into navigating the complexities, inefficiencies, bureaucracies, and authorities. One of their main complaints is the uncertainty that the Cuban government and economy produce in their lives. Prominently, they express frustration at the constraints that the Cuban economic system, despite the steps that have been taken to liberalize some of its aspects, puts on their earning potential, which directly limits them from accessing the kinds of goods and services that they aspire to have thanks to the influences of globalization.

Yet, these citizens are apolitical. Since college (when participation was implicitly or explicitly mandatory), they have distanced themselves from political and even civic activity. Non-participation in and apathy toward political and civic life are the norm, in large part because they do not believe that being active would result in any kind of change at all. For example, on a walk along the Malecón seawall in the capital, Mayito, a 25-year-old graduate from the University of Havana, within an hour or so of knowing him, blurted out: "This is a dictatorship. Period. This is a dictatorship. There's no freedom here." He cut himself off suddenly though, as he realized that he was talking opening and loudly about such a topic. "*Se me fue la mano*, my passions got the best of me." He looked around to see if anyone was close by on the streets, as well as upwards for video cameras that could be filming and recording passersby.

If general political interest and participation are scant, what about the kind of participation sought after by American foreign policy, inspired, augmented, and nurtured by and through American foreign policy approaches to U.S.-Cuba

260 Richard N. Gioioso and Lisa A. Baglione

foreign policy? Activist, change-oriented demands, practiced through formalized institutions or informal networks labeled as oppositional and therefore dissident by Cuban authorities would lead to surveillance or incarceration. So where are our young adults on getting involved, embarking on actions that would put them on the radar of authorities as disruptors and negatively affect their upward socioeconomic trajectory within Cuba (or their outward trajectory from Cuba)?

Nowhere. Absolutely not interested. Zero consideration of such steps.

In short, at least in the case of these Cuban young adults living and working in Havana, any notion of political activism outside of official channels is out of the question. Despite their discontent, frustration, anger, or despair, they universally refuse any such activity because of the repercussions it would bring.

Thus, American attempts at deterritorializing the Cuban state by reversing the policy of openness and stepping up the pressure are doomed to fail, at least among this subset of Cuban young adults. Trump Administration's policies are confronted and rebuffed by both the material and ideological aspects of territoriality. That is, the Cuban state, and its companion *Partido Comunista de Cuba*, dominate the physical space of the island as the bedrock and go unchallenged as the norm in Cuban society. Reversion to pressure politics as a way of destroying the Cuban state is misdirected and destined to fail.

Instead, openness had begun a transformation of citizens' minds. Cracks had started to form in the picture that the PCC offered its Cuba (Havel 1978; Thomas 2001). While our respondents are still effectively quelled, the potential that increased and more extensive connections leads to empowerment is there. The Cuban state will respond to American pressure with more repression and stronger ideological propagandizing, thus reterritorializing itself. The promise of change comes from the erosion that is likely to result from the daily discrediting of the Cuban system and the cracking of the edifices that the PCC has constructed both on the ground and in the minds of Cubans.

Notes

1 This chapter is based on research supported by Saint Joseph's University College of Arts and Sciences Faculty Summer Development Grant, and the American Political Science Association's Small Research Grant. Any opinions, findings, and conclusions or recommendations expressed in this publication are those of the authors and do not necessarily reflect the views of Saint Joseph's University or the American Political Science Association. The authors wish to thank all of the Cuban young adults who have participated in research in Havana, and elsewhere, over the years. Their willingness to share their lives has allowed us to advance the understanding of U.S.-Cuba relations.

2 See *Miami Herald* (2019). Questions have emerged regarding whether the diplomats were targeted or whether they sustained their injuries because of stress, the noise of insects, other factors, or some combination. Currently, there is much disagreement in the scientific community with a sizeable number rejecting the idea that the U.S. officials were attacked and criticizing the quality of the initial diagnoses. See NPR (2019).

3 When referring to the Cuban Revolution as a series of events that resulted in the overthrow of the government of Fulgenico Batista culminating on January 1, 1959, we capitalize Revolution. In Cuba, *Revolución* is also used to refer to a political-economic-social

Trump in the tropics **261**

phenomenon that permeates society, the continuous process of development that falls within the accepted principles, ideas, and practices established since the overthrow of the previous government, led by the Castros and the PCC. The authors follow this usage throughout the chapter.

4 In this paper we draw from Gioioso's ongoing research project aimed at examining how Cuban young adults between the ages of 20–40 maneuver the realities they face within the context of ongoing (albeit slow, unreliable, and inconsistent) economic, political, and social reforms on the island. This age group is notable because they were born and/or grew up during the so-called *Período Especial* (the Special Period) of the 1990s, a particularly harsh time of economic downturn and scarcity after the fall of the Soviet Union and socialist bloc countries. Not only was Cuba cast adrift economically, but it also lost its primary ideological ally in the promotion and development of communism and the one-party state. Thus began a process of adjusting to a different geopolitical order and internal economic restructuring, very different than the previous generation. For more on the *Período Especial*, see Hernandez-Reguant (2009).

Beginning in June 2014, Gioioso has conducted in-depth interviews using a snowball recruitment technique and a semi-structured interview guide with residents in the target age range in the capital city, Havana. He has maintained contact with the vast majority of these research participants through telephone calls, email, social media, and in-person meetings both in Cuba and (when possible) outside of Cuba. In large part due to the snowball technique employed, most research participants could be characterized as college-educated Cubans, many internal migrants originally from other provinces on the island, who have managed to successfully navigate the educational system and economic reforms, and have been able to take advantage of Cuba's increasing openness to the world (including with North Americans, thanks to the policies of normalization under the Obama Administration) and the developing internal private sector economy on the island. They have raised their standards of living and social statuses, and in some cases levels of professional success. They are, in short, members of the upwardly mobile Cuban middle and upper-middle class.

Cubans of all ages tend to be very skeptical and cautious when it comes to participating in formal research projects with foreigners, especially with North Americans. The reality of U.S. directed or backed interventions is well known, and there could be ramifications to participants if their contact with Americans is interpreted by Cuban authorities as suspicious or a possible threat. Thus, a snowball sample, through recommendations by friends and family members, was the best way to meet and initially interact with research participants, because such personal endorsements inspire *confianza* – trust. Continued contact with participants over time has allowed for the collection of longitudinal qualitative data, and a much more detailed and complete picture of the lives of Cuban young adults. Note that names have been changed to protect the identities of research participants. The authors include details to illustrate various aspects of their lives, but are sensitive to not disclose too much identifying information.

5 Unfortunately, too few book-length works on Cuban youth or young adults have been written. See, however, Blum (2011) for an examination of the education of the "new socialist citizen" in Cuba.

6 See Prescott (1965) for an early analysis of the U.S. federal state and Mexico; See Calvocoressi (1991) re: Chinese territorial demarcation.

7 See Sack (1983) regarding territoriality and the ideological basis of state power.

8 Often used as key concept in analyzing sovereignty between countries and within them. See Agnew (2018).

9 In his excellent analysis, Nevins (2010) argues that American politicians created the notion of "illegal" Mexican immigrants through the use of the media. These officials were seeking to prevent demographic diversification by classifying Mexican immigrants as dangerous and illegal, justifying deportation and/or exclusion, and disrupting the status quo in which non-Hispanic white Americans were largely in control of setting political, economic, and social practices, rules, and norms. American *domination* of the physical space (through security forces and governance mechanisms) and *normalization* of

U.S. rule (in the minds and practices of citizens and state officials on both sides) were central to identifying Mexican immigrants as "illegal" when they crossed newly created borders in the American Southwest and Western states.

10 Although our data reveal that most research participants are very unhappy with some aspects of Cuba, e.g., the centralized economy, all are proud of certain achievements of the Revolution, e.g., universal socialized medicine and education.

11 Recent edited volumes published on U.S. policy toward Cuba and U.S.-Cuba relations include Hershberg and LeoGrande (2016) and Domínguez, Hernández, and Barbería (2017). For more insight into U.S.-Cuba relations through the decades, see LeoGrande (1982) and Domínguez (1997).

12 For a good, basic discussion of Cuba's importance to the U.S. during the Cold War, see Ambrose and Brinkley (2011), especially pp. 171–189.

13 See Centeno (2004) on the "return" of Cuba as part of Latin America.

14 The Cuban Research Institute at Florida International University has conducted a periodic poll of the opinions of Cuban-Americans in South Florida since 1991. It is the longest-running and most comprehensive source of such data, and pays special attention to attitudes regarding U.S. foreign policy toward Cuba. See Grenier and Gladwyn (2018).

15 The most commonly used, informal way to refer to U.S. citizens in Cuba, alternatively *norteamericanos* (North Americans) is used.

16 This and all other quotes in the chapter are translations by Gioioso.

17 Personal communication with Gioioso, December 19, 2014.

18 See, for example, Haass (2017) and Nye (2017). Note that both men have been part of the foreign policy establishment for decades, with Nye serving Democrats and Haas working for Republicans.

19 See Trump (2017, pp. i–ii). Emphasis added to highlight the unique language.

20 See Thomas Wright's (2019) explanation that in the first year the foreign policy officials surrounding Trump, "The Axis of Adults," saw their role as one of restraining the president from breaking from this consensus. Their influence can be found in parts of the National Security Statement that make commitments to NATO and to the liberal order clear. After that first year, however, Trump was looking to follow his instincts, and over time, there was turnover (some fired, some resigned) in his top national security advisors. This allowed John Bolton, an avowed neoconservative, into the inner sanctum as National Security Advisor. For a time, Bolton exerted great control, particularly by eliminating the meetings in which Defense, State, and CIA officials convened with the NSC and the president to make key decisions. See Wright (2019). Bolton has been particularly vociferous in his opposition to Cuba. See Bolton (2018) and PBS Newshour (2019).

21 See Lopez-Levy (2019).

22 Although the 2017 National Security Strategy (NSS) gives some nods to U.S. values and its example, the document stresses the role of force, the importance of serving U.S. interests, and understanding that world politics is a zero-sum game. Perhaps nowhere was Trump's commitment to these ideas clearer than at the NATO summit in the summer of 2018 and his follow-on meeting with Vladimir Putin in Helsinki. There, Trump scolded the alliance and praised his Russian counterpart, seeming to abandon any understanding of the purpose and values of the alliance and celebrating the accomplishments of his authoritarian interlocutor. See Wright et al. (2018).

23 Trump (2017, p. 61) and PBS Newshour (2019).

24 See, for instance, Sherman (2009).

25 For a contemporary refutation of this argument, see Kagan (2019).

26 For discussions of U.S. policy toward Iraq and the Middle East in this era, see Bacevich (2016) and Ricks (2006; 2009). The George W. Bush National Security Strategy (Bush 2006) is also quite instructive.

27 See Farber (2006) for compelling analysis of the origins of the Cuban Revolution. See Fernández (2000) for discussion of the importance of personal ties and networks, what he calls *lo informal*, in circumventing officialized aspects of life in Cuba.

28 In official state language and in common parlance on the island, Cubans use *triunfo de la Revolución*. The authors follow this local usage throughout the chapter, acknowledging that for those who oppose the Cuban government, either on the island or in its diaspora, might find the term problematic.

29 Because nominal party membership was necessary for economic and social advancement, ambitious and talented people joined in order to get ahead and have interesting work, but they were not true believers. Careerism became much more common from 1968 on (until the late 1980s) when economic inadequacies and the crushing of the Prague Spring showed that liberalization would not be tolerated despite the system's economic and moral bankruptcy.

30 An NORC (2016) opinion study carried out in late 2016 funded by the University of Chicago shows a majority of Cuban respondents (55%) believing that normalization of U.S.-Cuban relations is "mostly good" for Cuba, with only 3% saying it is "mostly bad" and 26% asserting normalization will have no impact. Regarding the economy, 30% believe that in three years, conditions will be better, and 47% said they will be about the same. The survey did not ask overtly political questions. See pages 4 and 8, respectively.

References

Agnew, J. 2018. *Globalization and Sovereignty: Beyond the Territorial Trap*, 2nd edition. Lanham: Rowman & Littlefield.

Ambrose, S., and Brinkley, D. 2011. *Rise to Globalism: American Foreign Policy since 1938*. New York: Penguin Press.

Bacevich, A. 2016. *America's War for the Greater Middle East: A Military History*. New York: Random House.

Blum, D. 2011. *Cuban Youth and Revolutionary Values: Educating the New Socialist Citizen*, Austin: University of Texas Press.

Bolton, J. 2018. Remarks of the National Security Advisor, Ambassador John R. Bolton on the administration's policies in Latin America. *White House* (Nov. 2). www.whitehouse.gov/briefings-statements/remarks-national-security-advisor-ambassador-john-r-bolton-administrations-policies-latin-america/

Bush, G.W. 2006. *National Security Strategy of the United States*. www.state.gov/documents/organization/64884.pdf

Calvocoressi, P. 1991. *World Politics Since 1945*. London: Longman.

Centeno, M. 2004. The return of Cuba to Latin America: The end of Cuban exceptionalism? *Bulletin of Latin American Research* 23(4): 403–413.

Dominguez, J. 1989. *To Make the World Safe for Revolution: Cuba's Foreign Policy*. Cambridge, MA: Center for International Affairs, Harvard University.

Domínguez, J. 1997. U.S.-Cuban Relations: From the Cold War to the Colder War. *Journal of Interamerican Studies and World Affairs* 39(3): 49–75.

Domínguez, J., R. Hernández, and L. Barbería. 2017. *Debating U.S.-Cuba Relations: How Should We Now Play Ball?* New York: Routledge.

Farber, S. 2006. *The Origins of the Cuban Revolution Reconsidered*. Chapel Hill: UNC Press.

Fernández, D. 2000. *Cuba and the Politics of Passion*. Austin: University of Texas Press.

Grenier, G., and H. Gladwin. 2018. FIU Cuba Poll. https://cri.fiu.edu/research/cuba-poll/

Haass, R. 2017. America's great abdication. *Atlantic* (Dec. 28). www.theatlantic.com/international/archive/2017/12/america-abdcation-trump-foreign-policy/549296/

Havel, V. 1978. Power of the powerless. *International Journal of Politics*. www.nonviolent-conflict.org/wp-content/uploads/1979/01/the-power-of-the-powerless.pdf

Hernandez-Reguant, A. (ed.). 2009. *Cuba in the Special Period: Culture and Ideology in the 1990s*. New York: Palgrave Macmillan.

Hershberg, E., and W. LeoGrande (eds.). 2016. *A New Chapter in US-Cuba Relations: Social, Political, and Economic Implications*. Cham: Palgrave Macmillan.

Kagan, R. 2019. The Strongmen Strike Back. *Brookings Report*. www.brookings.edu/research/the-strongmen-strike-back/

Kirkpatrick, J. 1979. Dictatorships and double standards. *Commentary* 68(5): 34–45.

LeoGrande, W. 1982. Cuba policy recycled. *Foreign Policy* 46: 105–119.

Lopez-Levy, A. 2019. Why Trump's Cuba policy is so wrong. *NACLA* (May 29). https://nacla.org/news/2019/05/27/why-trump%E2%80%99s-cuba-policy-so-wrong

McFaul, M. 2018. *From Cold War to Hot Peace: An American Ambassador in Putin's Russia*. New York: Houghton Mifflin Harcourt.

Miami Herald. 2019 (April 7). U.S. restricts travel, remittances to Cuba as part of a new policy under Trump. www.miamiherald.com/news/nation-world/world/americas/cuba/article229341009.html

Nevins, J. 2010. *Operation Gatekeeper and Beyond: The War On "Illegals" and the Remaking of the U.S. Mexico Boundary*. New York: Routledge.

NORC. 2016. *A Rare Look Inside Cuban Society: A New Survey of Cuban Public Opinion*. Chicago: University of Chicago Press. www.norc.org/PDFs/Survey%20of%20Cuban%20Opinion/Cuba%20Topline_FINAL.pdf

NPR. 2019 (March 25). Doubts rise about evidence that U.S. diplomats in Cuba were attacked. www.npr.org/sections/health-shots/2019/03/25/704903613/doubts-rise-about-evidence-that-u-s-diplomats-in-cuba-were-attacked

Nye, Jr., J. 2004. *Soft Power: The Means to Success in World Politics*. New York: Public Affairs.

Nye, Jr., J. 2017. Will the liberal order survive? *Foreign Affairs* 96(1): 10–16.

PBS Newshour. 2019 (April 17). WATCH: Bolton announces new crackdown on Cuba, Nicaragua and Venezuela. www.pbs.org/newshour/politics/watch-live-bolton-to-address-trump-administrations-cuba-policy-shift

Prescott, J. 1965. *The Geography of Frontiers and Boundaries*. London: Hutchinson.

Ricks, T. 2006. *Fiasco: The American Military Adventure in Iraq, 2003 to 2005*. New York: Penguin Press.

Ricks, T. 2009. *The Gamble: General Petraeus and the American Military Adventure in Iraq*. New York: Penguin Press.

Sack, R. 1983. Human territoriality: A theory. *Annals of the Association of American Geographers* 73: 55–74.

Sherman, A. 2009. Trump travel restrictions continue rollback of Obama's Cuba policy. *Politifact* (June 7). www.politifact.com/truth-o-meter/promises/trumpometer/promise/1378/reverse-barack-obamas-cuba-policy/

Thomas, D. 2001. *The Helsinki Effect: International Norms, Human Rights, and the Demise of Communism*. Princeton: Princeton University Press.

Trump, D. 2017. *The National Security Strategy of the United States*. www.whitehouse.gov/wp-content/uploads/2017/12/NSS-Final-12-18-2017-0905.pdf

Wright, T. 2019. Trump couldn't ignore the contradictions of his foreign policy any longer. *Order from Chaos* [blog] (July 6). Brookings Institution. www.brookings.edu/blog/order-from-chaos/2019/07/06/trump-couldnt-ignore-the-contradictions-of-his-foreign-policy-any-longer/

Wright, T., A. Polyakova, C. Stelzenmüller, S. Pifer, P.K. Baev, A. Sloat, C. Belin, K. Kirişci, and T. Chhabra. 2018. Around the halls: Brookings experts react to the Trump-Putin Meeting and the NATO Summit. *Order from Chaos* [blog] (July 16). Brookings Institution. www.brookings.edu/blog/order-from-chaos/2018/07/16/around-the-halls-brookings-experts-react-to-the-trump-putin-meeting-and-nato-summit/

15

PEACE FOR PROSPERITY? THE GEOPOLITICS OF THE KOREAN PEACE PROCESS

Steven M. Radil and Jin-Soo Lee

In the summer of 2018, Singapore hosted the first ever bilateral meeting between a sitting U.S. president and the leader of North Korea. On the day of the summit (June 12), President Donald Trump and North Korean leader Kim Jong-Un initially met privately and then again later with expanded delegations with an aim to reach agreement on issues concerning U.S.-North Korea relations, the North's relations with South Korea and, most centrally from the U.S. point of view, the North's nuclear weapon and ballistic missile programs. Although South Korean officials were not officially part of the summit, the South played a significant role in making the summit a reality, acting as a go-between to deliver an invitation to the White House just weeks earlier. During the summit, Trump and Kim signed a joint statement "to build a lasting and stable peace regime on the Korean Peninsula … [and] to work towards the complete denuclearization of the Korean Peninsula" (White House 2018). The next day, Trump proclaimed that the summit was a success, tweeting that "there is no longer a Nuclear Threat from North Korea" (Sullivan 2018).

Trump's claims about the denuclearization were later contradicted by other U.S. government officials and other parties and a second summit in Vietnam in February 2019 failed to produce any additional agreements about denuclearization. Even so, the Singapore summit was remarkable for several reasons. First, no other similar meeting had ever been arranged over the course of the nearly 70-year history of U.S. involvement in Korean politics. Second, just seven months before, North Korea had successfully launched a new ballistic missile estimated to be able to reach the west coast of the U.S. and much of Europe. Third, during the period of the North's missile test, Trump had engaged in an extraordinary series of threats toward Kim. In short order, Trump threatened to rain "fire and fury" down on the North, belittled Kim as "Little Rocket Man," and stated that North Korean leaders "won't be around much longer" in a series of remarks throughout 2017 (Keneally 2018). In sum, U.S. and North Korean interests seemed completely incompatible in late 2017 and yet, just a few short months later, the Trump administration had its first and, to date perhaps only, foreign policy success.

Although the Trump administration's foreign policy has received considerable media attention relative to North Korea, scholarly engagement with the specifics of U.S.-Korea relations under Trump has lagged. And where scholars have considered the issue, it has largely yielded a focus on the bilateral relations between the U.S. and North Korea, neglecting the South's role in this process. To help fill these gaps, we consider the how the issues connected to the Singapore summit and the broader inter-Korean peace process were represented within the South Korean news media. We do this from the perspective of critical geopolitics, examining the popular political discourses circulating in the South Korean news media concerning the U.S., Trump, the summits, and South-North relations. We find that traditional geopolitical discourses concerned with the territorial security of South Korea are competing with alternative discourses about the potential for economic growth and cooperation with the North.

Our argument unfolds as follows. First, we describe the recent history of the politics of the Korean peninsula, with an eye for moments that have characterized the overall context of South-North relations. We then describe our theoretical framework and apply it to interrogate the popular discourses circulating about the peace process in South Korea. We discuss the shifting concerns associated with the process, particularly how they varied by alignment with partisan politics. Lastly, we conclude with a discussion of the implications of our findings for the peace process and the geopolitics of the peninsula.

Overview of the peace process

The politically divided Korean peninsula has been described as the setting of the final echoes of the Cold War (Armstrong 2014). The two Koreas share a common history, language, and culture, and yet politically, one is an internationally isolated nuclear-armed Marxist-Leninist regime while the other is a liberal democracy with an advanced capitalist economy and a long-standing military alliance with the United States. As such, the Korean people exist in parallel but territorially separated political and economic worlds. Nevertheless, over the past 40-plus years, both states have ostensibly yet slowly moved to put an end to the Korean Cold War and to normalize relations with each other. Important first diplomatic steps toward a peaceful peninsula were the 1972 South-North Korea Joint Statement and the 1991 Inter-Korean Basic Agreement, both of which created opportunities for cooperation and exchanges between South and North (Levin and Han 2002).

Following the end of the Cold War elsewhere, relations between the Koreas have repeatedly vacillated between periods of relative cooperation punctuated by moments of open conflict. Most notably, the Kim Dae-Jung administration in South Korea (1998–2002) advanced its so-called "Sunshine Policy" to lay groundwork for peace and, eventually, reunification. The high point during this period was a summit in 2000 between President Kim and his Northern counterpart Kim Jong-Il. This meeting, the first Inter-Korean Summit, yielded an agreement to "assure [the] peaceful coexistence between the two Koreas on their way to the formation of a completely unified Korea" (Ministry of Unification 2019). The process also led to several tangible examples of cooperation between the two governments, such as allowing Southern tourists to visit the Mt. Kumgang cultural site in North Korea, establishing exchange visits for separated families, connecting separated railway lines, and most notably, establishing the Kaesong Industrial Complex (KIC) as a joint economic venture between the two Koreas (Son 2006). The South's pursuit of peace continued through the Roh Moo-Hyun administration (2003-2007) and in 2007, President Roh and Kim Jong-Il held a second Inter-Korean Summit in Pyongyang, signing a declaration calling for the formal end of the Korean War (Kim 2008).

These efforts at cooperation have been juxtaposed with moments of intense conflict (Michishita 2009). Although there are too many events to detail here, notable acts of aggression by the North prior to the Sunshine Policy period included the attempted assassinations of Presidents Park Chung-Hee (1968 and 1974) and Chun Doo-Hwan (1983), the 1978 kidnappings of a prominent movie actress and film director, and the 1987 bombing of a South Korean airline in 1987. Numerous other hostile acts occurred during the Sunshine Policy period, including repeated incursions by Northern soldiers across the Demilitarized Zone (DMZ) into South Korea, instances of sniper fire across the DMZ, and naval skirmishes along disputed maritime boundaries. A side effect of these repeated conflictual events was to erode the South Korean public's confidence in the potential for the Sunshine Policy to produce meaningful change and to strengthen the conviction within conservative circles in South Korea that military force was the only sensible political option to deal with the North (Levin and Han 2002).

The Sunshine Policy era reached a de facto end with the first successful test of a nuclear weapon by North Korea in late 2006. Then-U.S. President George Bush's infamous 2002 speech that labeled North Korea as part of a global "axis of evil" foreshadowed the breakdown of pursuit of peace. In 2003, North Korea withdrew from the Treaty on the Non-Proliferation of Nuclear Weapons (NPT), culminating in the 2006 test detonation (Perry 2006). During this period, the so-called "Six Party" talks began around North Korea's emerging nuclear program until negotiations finally collapsed in 2009, when North Korea conducted its second nuclear test (Buszynski 2013). In parallel with its push toward nuclear weapons, the North also advanced its missile capabilities during the Six Party talks period (Niksch 2014). From 2005 to 2009, the North conducted several missile tests in the region, including a failed satellite launch in 2009. Missile tests increased in frequency in the following years, with at least ten more tests occurring between 2012 and 2015. Although subject to numerous international economic sanctions since its withdrawal from the NPT, North Korea had managed to develop stable short and medium range missiles by the end of 2015. Over the same period, it also engaged in three additional nuclear weapons tests (one in 2013, two more in 2016).

The failure of the Sunshine Policy to produce tangible results also contributed to the election of the conservative Lee Myung-Bak (2008-2013) and Park Geun-Hye (2013–2017) governments in South Korea, who both advocated a harder approach to the North (Kim 2008). However, in late 2016, Park was impeached and later removed from office for her role in an influence-peddling scandal. New elections in 2017 returned progressive leadership to South Korea for the first time since the Sunshine Policy period and President Moon Jae-In quickly opened the possibility of normalized relations with the North. At nearly the same time, Donald Trump's election promised significant changes to U.S. foreign policy.

Since his election, President Moon insisted that North Korea could participate in international society (Heo and Yun 2019) despite yet another nuclear test by the North in late 2017. That test prompted Trump to state about Kim that "Rocket Man is on a suicide mission" (BBC 2017). Accordingly, Moon pressed forward with the idea of facilitating between the U.S. and North Korea and directly met with Kim Jong-Un three times in 2018 with another meeting planned for later in 2019. These meetings yielded several agreements, notably about reducing the military presence along the DMZ and restoring cooperation at the KIC (Heo and Yun 2019). At the same time, the Trump administration rapidly shifted away from his harsh "Rocket Man" rhetoric after the delivery of the North's summit invitation. Ahead of the summit, Trump famously described his detente with Kim this way: "And then we fell in love, okay? No, really – he wrote me beautiful letters, and they're great letters" (Rampton 2018).

The competing issues at stake ahead of the summit foreshadowed the complications awaiting each government. From the U.S. perspective, the core issue was the security threat posed by the North's combination of nuclear weapons with ballistic missiles. For the North, its weapons had led to an opportunity to break the stranglehold of economic sanctions. And for the South, the meeting was a chance to restart its economic and political programs with the North. Ultimately, the summit yielded only a statement to continue to work toward building "a lasting and stable peace regime on the Korean Peninsula" (White House 2018). The second summit, held in Hanoi in February 2019, failed to even reach this level of agreement as, in Trump's own words, the U.S. delegation "had to walk away" from the North's demands for economic relief. But each government has continued to pursue dialogue with each other as evidenced by Trump and Moon's impromptu meeting with Kim at Panmunjom in the DMZ in June 2019 (Figure 15.1).

Critical geopolitics and the peace process

In the broadest sense, critical geopolitics is concerned with how the foreign policy of states rest on a myriad of taken-for-granted assumptions about the

Peace for prosperity? **269**

FIGURE 15.1 The meeting in the DMZ in June 2019 between President Moon (right), Trump, and Kim Jong-Un (center) highlighted the different agendas underlying each government's pursuit of dialogue (Cheong Wa Dae 2019).

relationships between space and power in international politics. The applications of this concern vary widely, but a continuing theme has been the exploration of "how the world is [geographically] structured and acted on by political agents" (Agnew 2013, p. 29). By implication, critical geopoliticians have focused on an engagement with the language and analysis of "texts" to uncover these understandings and structures. "Texts" have a broad meaning in critical geopolitics and refer to any type of communicative event, written or spoken, including the visual aspects of communication: gestures, images, films, maps, and so on.

By way of example, consider Sparke's (2007) analysis of then-U.S. President George Bush's infamous 2002 "axis of evil" speech, which linked North Korea, Iran, and Iraq, stoking fears of cooperation between these very different geopolitical agents against a common enemy in the United States. The speech drew connections between these states based on shared enmity to the U.S., serving to erase the very real differences between them (such as the 1980–88 Iran-Iraq war, the lack of connections between North Korea and the others, and so on) to imagine a new space of opposition to the U.S. and its presumed role as a global leader in defending democracy. The speech simultaneously drew on discourses about a "new sense of insecurity after 9/11" and an "older Cold War geopolitical imagination of a nuclear-armed evil empire" to inform Bush's call for a new war (Sparke 2007, p. 341). The "text" reflected geopolitical discourse for a geopolitical purpose and contributed to the widespread public support for the U.S. Congress's subsequent declaration of war on Iraq later in 2002.

From its earliest inception, critical geopolitics has interrogated the foreign policy of states and the class of political elites involved in carrying them out. In this tradition, the texts to be examined are often speeches by government officials, governmental documents or reports, and so on. Over time, this concern has broadened to include what is called "popular geopolitics," or the processes by which understandings about world politics are expressed within and shaped by various forms of popular culture, including films, print magazines, music, and the like (Dodds 2007). An important subtheme that we leverage for our analysis is a concern for geopolitical discourses circulating within news organizations, which are often indivisible from the foreign policy of states enhancing, contesting, and sharing geopolitical events, claims, and ideas (Gruley and Duvall 2012). We use this understanding to focus our analysis on several key news organizations in South Korea as they are central to the dissemination and reproduction of important discourses regarding the Korean peace process.

One additional concern that informs our analysis that bears mentioning is the role of economics in geopolitical discourse. Critical geopoliticians have long argued that economic issues are part of larger "geo-strategic" discourses operating at various scales around the territorial state (Cowen and Smith 2009) and the economy is a self-evidently central theme of much statecraft and foreign policy. Luttwak (1990) coined the term "geoeconomics" to capture how economic power aids statecraft and it has been an important lens for geopoliticians. For example, Mercille (2008) explored the geoeconomic logics at the center of U.S. foreign policy during the Vietnam War, insisting that economic aspirations were one of the main motives for U.S. policymakers. Sparke (2007) proposed a dual framework of geopolitics and geoeconomics to show how fear about supposed Iraqi weapons of mass destruction on the one hand and hope about reconnecting Iraq to the global economy on the other both contributed to the U.S. invasion in 2002. Salient to the politics of Northeast Asia, Lee, Wainwright, and Glassman (2018) also presented a dialectical construction of geopolitics and geoeconomics as part of the hegemonic competition between the U.S. and China.

The distinction between geopolitics and geoeconomics merits explanation. As Sparke (2007, p. 340) states, geopolitical discourses are often fear-based and simplified "understandings of 'us' and 'them'" that are associated with politics that emphasize spatial strategies of state security. These politics involve not just the demonization of others, but the sundry territorial practices designed to partition, separate, isolate, or remove the source of such fear. The Trump administration's denouncement and jailing of immigrants at the U.S.-Mexico border is a reasonable example. In contrast, Sparke associates geoeconomics with hopeful imaginations of a world fully connected through a globalized and neoliberal free market economy. This yields a decidedly different form of politics, one focused on "networks not blocs, connections not walls, and transborder ties instead of national territories" (2007, p. 340).

Considering both geopolitical and geoeconomic discourses can be useful to examine the view about North Korea in South Korea. For example, Lee (2015) argued that South Korean conservatives have emphasized North Korea for "geo-political absorption" as it is too dangerous to exist as a separate political space while liberals have considered North Korea as a "geo-economic object" that holds opportunity to further the economic growth of South Korea. Furthermore, Doucette and Lee (2015) showed that the development of the KIC was based on simultaneously competing discourses of political antagonism and economic cooperation with North Korea. In other words, discourses of security and economics were the basic filters that influenced policymaking in South Korea. Moreover, the existence of North Korea has served as the primary and ongoing point of distinction between partisan (conservative and progressive) political identity in South Korea.

We obviously expect that fear-based geopolitical discourses about security are always present around the politics of the two Koreas. But we agree with Sparke's assessment that hope-based geoeconomic discourses are part of the issue and with Lee's assertion that the South has long seen the North as a space for economic expansion. Trump himself identified this dynamic in an exchange with reporters at the Singapore summit:

> They [North Korea] have great beaches. You see that whenever they're exploding their cannons into the ocean. I said, Boy, look at that view. Wouldn't that make a great condo? Instead of doing that you could have the best hotels in the world right there. Think of it from a real estate perspective, you have South Korea, you have China, and they own the land in the middle, how bad is that, right? It's great. (Lim 2018)

What this in mind, a fuller consideration of the geopolitics of the Korean peninsula would involve the politics of security and of economics.

Data and methods

Concerns about news organizations as political agents are often reflected in the debates about the political partisanship associated with U.S. news media organizations. Documenting and assessing the partisanship of the U.S. news media has been a long-standing theme in communication studies (e.g., Patterson and Donsbagh 1996) and the partisan alignment of news organizations is now a global phenomenon. The partisanship of privately owned news media in South Korea is well documented with several major newspapers consistently aligned with the conservative and progressive political parties (Ha and Shin 2016). The main two political parties in South Korea are the liberal Democratic Party of Korea (DPK) and the conservative Liberty Korea Party (LKP). The two parties comprise over 80% of the legislative seat in the National Assembly at the time of writing (242 out of 300 seats). Further, the issue of relations with North Korea is a clear partisan divide in South Korea, something often reflected in South Korea's news media (Kyu, Ryu, and Park 2015).

We consider the intermingling of geopolitical and geoeconomic themes in the partisan mass media of South Korea. Based on the literature, we expect that geopolitical discourses will focus on the danger posed by North Korea while geoeconomic discourses will focus on the potential benefits from economic cooperation with the North. In keeping with the partisan media divide and the association of liberal parties with the Sunshine Policy, we expect that fear-based or security-driven discourse will dominate in the conservative media while hope-based or economic-driven discourse will dominate in the liberal media.

To investigate this issue, we conducted a content analysis of news articles from the "big five" major newspapers (*Chosun Ilbo, Joongang Ilbo, Donga Ilbo, Kyunghyang Shinmun*, and *Hankyoreh*) in South Korea (see Kim and Johnson 2009). These media companies represent the largest conservative (*Chosun Ilbo, Joongang Ilbo*, and *Donga Ilbo*, also known collectively as "Chojoongdong") and progressive (*Kyunghyang Shinmun* and *Hankyoreh*) news outlets in the country. We sampled articles dated between 2016 and 2018 based on keyword searches (e.g., Kim 2014).[1] This yielded a body of 82 articles (34 published in progressive outlets and 48 in conservative ones) that provided the data for our analysis.

By sampling from news media organizations on both sides of the partisan divide, we allowed for the potential to identify key discourses about the peace process that either transcended the partisan split or that circulated separately but in parallel within partisan confines. We then coded the articles for emergent themes concerning South Korea-U.S. relations and issues connected to security and economics. We also coded for themes connected to Trump himself. As we discuss below, a primary finding from our analysis is a clear separation of geopolitical and geoeconomic themes between conservative and progressive media but also the noticeable growth of specific economic discourse following the summit.

Analysis

The 2017 election of Moon Jae-In reignited political debates in the Korean media about peacemaking and raised hopes of a major policy shift toward the North as the policies of the two preceding conservative administrations (2008–2017) had undermined the Sunshine Policy efforts of the two previous liberal administrations (1998–2007). In a July 2017 speech in Germany, Moon promised that he would actively lead on peacemaking with North Korea: "my country must sit in the driver's seat and lead Korean Peninsula-related issues based on cooperation with our neighbors" (Bae 2017). Although at time mocked by opponents in the media as not even in the "passenger's seat" during the North's provocations in 2017 (e.g., Hong 2017), the idea took hold, especially after the perceived diplomatic success of the joint South-North Olympic female hockey team fielded during the winter games in Pyeongchang in 2018. We refer to this as the "driver's seat" discourse (한반도운전자론) as it emphasizes the necessity for the South

Korean government to work directly and separately if necessary from the U.S. and others to craft a peaceful solution with the North.

The driver's seat discourse was the dominant theme present in the set of progressive articles, with nearly 60% of the articles referencing some version of the issue in a positive fashion (20 out of 34 articles). This mostly took the form of advocating for the Moon government to either actively facilitate dialogue between the U.S. and North Korea, or in a few minority examples, to press forward independently with North Korea no matter the U.S. position. A third of the articles pressed the discourse further, asserting that the U.S. was an unreliable partner or had entirely different interests that made following the U.S. untenable. In those versions, the U.S. was also usually described as overly aggressive or largely only interested in using South Korea as a pawn in a larger game with China for regional hegemony.

The driver's seat discourse was largely inverted in the conservative articles. A similar percentage addressed the theme (nearly 60% or 28 out of 48 articles) but in a critical fashion, with the clear majority arguing that any efforts to bypass the U.S. in negotiations with the North would ultimately put the South Korean-U.S. alliance at risk and that the South was too dependent on U.S. military might to go it alone. An interesting subtheme was connected to the need for nuclear balancing on the peninsula. Several articles referred to the necessity of the U.S. nuclear shield to protect the South while others raised the alarm of Chinese regional ascendancy if the South Korea-U.S. alliance was weakened. In all these versions, the South was presented as a naturally junior partner that could not go it alone in a difficult region.

In geopolitical terms, the driver's seat discourse is a simultaneously relational but inward-looking concern, casting the need for unilateral action by the South to build a new relationship with the North while raising anxieties of disrupting existing relations with the U.S. along the way. This perhaps helps to explain the absence of another discourse about Trump himself. Trump's personality, characteristics, and his relationship to the media are routine fare in U.S. news coverage but this was not routinely manifest in the South Korean coverage as Trump himself was infrequently discussed (less than 10% of the articles). However, when he was mentioned, he was usually framed as unpredictable or volatile, or as uninterested in Korea except to influence China or to resolve domestic political tensions in the US.

Security concerns for the South Korean state were at the heart of opposition to the driver's seat discourse, evoking the type of fears of foreign danger raised by Sparke (2007). While this most often focused on the risk of disrupting the South Korea-U.S. alliance and the potential loss of U.S. nuclear balancing against the North, a secondary concern that emerged after the September 2018 South-North summit was the prospect of the South's weakened conventional military posture. Both governments agreed to stop all kinds of hostilities, including beginning demining operations around the Joint Security Area (JSA) within the DMZ,

FIGURE 15.2 Destruction of a DMZ guard post – shown in a photo released by the South Korean government in December 2018 (*Kookbang Ilbo* 2018).

to disarm guards within the JSA, and to demolish several guard posts along the DMZ (Figure 15.2). The possibility of changes to such highly securitized spaces and the removal of obvious territorial markers of security was an open source of fear in the conservative media ahead of the agreement. For instance, an October 2018 article in *Chosen Ilbo* stated that this would herald a broader "collapse" in security for South Korea, limiting its ability to defend itself against future Northern aggression.

Conversely, an alternative narrative aligned with the driver's seat discourse was present in the progressive media. Rather than emphasizing security fears, economic opportunities for South Korea were offered as a rationale for better South-North relations. The shuttering of the Kaesong Industrial Complex (KIC) in 2016 by the Park government suspended the last meaningful form of cooperation between South and North remaining from the Sunshine era. The potential to reopen the KIC for the benefit of Southern commercial interests was a frequently offered defense for Moon's approach. And while the potential to reopen the KIC was the most discussed economic issue, a broader economic vision was present as well. An April 2018 article in *Hankyoreh* presented the possibility of a "new economic map" in which a peace deal with the North would end South Korea's economic territorial "isolation" in two ways. First, South Korea would connect to the rest of Asia through North Korea's rail and road networks. Second, and akin to Sparke's (2007) and Lee's (2015) arguments, North Korea itself could become a new space for investment for

FIGURE 15.3 A version of the "new economic map" from the South Korea government's Ministry of Unification (2018a).

Southern interests, promising development and capital extraction opportunities well beyond the narrow spatial confines of the KIC.

The new economic map discourse was announced in the media with numerous colorful and stylized maps. For example, the Ministry of Unification offered a basic version shown in Figure 15.3, in which a transformed DMZ would link rather than separate South Korea to the North and beyond. The map shows three economic "belts" that capture some of the spatial imaginations embedded in the discourse. The DMZ itself is described as a belt emphasizing environmental tourism based on pristine flora and fauna, a pan-Yellow Sea economic belt is labeled as emphasizing industry, logistics, and distribution/transportation around the Korean west coast connecting to China, and a pan-East Sea Economic belt proposes energy and resource transfers along the eastern coast connecting with Russia. Media organizations developed their own versions of these maps and

276 Steven M. Radil and Jin-Soo Lee

the associated term "new economic map for the Korean Peninsula" was coined to signal the optimism and hope associated with Moon's driver's seat approach. Interestingly, this economic optimism worked its way into some of the conservative media as well. Although the KIC was routinely discussed as an "economic giveaway" by the South that only served to support the Kim regime, some articles balanced criticism against the presumed weakening security situation with the promise for new development and investment opportunities.

Conclusion

The themes present in the articles cover some well-worn ground in Korean politics, especially the partisan debates about if and how to engage with the North, how the security of the South should be managed territorially along the DMZ, and the degree to which South Korea can or should pursue its foreign policy apart from U.S. interests. In this sense, our analysis reinforces the continued salience of the fears connected to these geopolitical issues so long as a formal peace between South and North remain elusive. It is possible that a focus on other types or forms of media might indicate alternative security discourses. However, even though we focus on conventional news media, our analysis reveals an underexplored side to the pursuit of peace which is the geoeconomic motives and imaginations at play and the hopes they have stimulated. Such hopes may help to explain what the Moon government believes is the destination that it is driving toward.

The politics of representing a space or region as *terra nullius*, an empty land, has been scrutinized by geopolitical scholars as a common rhetorical and cartographic strategy used to build support for territorial conquest and colonial exploitation (e.g., Gibson 1999). While not applicable to North Korea in the traditional sense, the new economic map rhetoric points to another interpretation, that of North Korea as an economic *terra nullius*, one of the last disconnected economic spaces for a global capitalist world economy. South Korean elites on both sides of the partisan divide are starting to craft an economic outline of tomorrow where the North Korean state is an economic void that they are best positioned to fill, invest in, and extract profit from. In this sense, the long-running *chaebol* governance system that fuses the South Korean state and its policies with the economic interests of its major corporations seems as vital and as bipartisan as ever.

But the new economic map discourse is about more than just the economic integration of the North Korean state. A largely understudied topic is the widely held notion among South Korean economic and political elites that the South Korean state functions as a geostrategic "island state" as the heavily militarized DMZ has effectively severed land connections (road and rail networks) between the South and the rest of Asia for decades. The imagination of South Korea as an island, severed not just from their fellow citizens but from the rest of the world by the trauma of the civil war is illuminated by a visit to Dorasan Station, the last passenger rail stop in South Korea on the way to Pyongyang. Emblazoned on the wall of the station is a map (Figure 15.4) that shows an integrated rail network

Peace for prosperity? 277

FIGURE 15.4 Dorasan Station map and sign – explaining the hoped-for outcomes of a lasting South-North peace.

Photo by Alexandra N. Stutzman.

that connects not just South to North but the entire Korean peninsula to the rest of Asia and Europe. An illuminated sign nearby fills in the story: once peace is achieved, the real connections begin.

The second Trump-Kim summit was largely dismissed as a failure and North Korea seems to have faded as a point of foreign policy emphasis for Trump, despite the recent seizure of a North Korean cargo ship by U.S. forces and additional missile tests by the North (Choe 2019). And yet, Moon drives on. Largely overshadowed by the September 2018 inter-Korean summit that has begun to slowly transform the DMZ was a preceding summit in April where both parties agreed to "adopt practical steps towards the connection and modernization of the railways and roads" (Ministry of Unification 2018b). This might be the exact destination that Moon had in mind when he declared himself in the driver's seat: a broader geoeconomic agenda that prefigures peace on the peninsula as but a first stop on the path to new opportunities for economic growth. To follow along with the driver's seat metaphor, geopolitical fear about Trump's capriciousness, U.S. regional policy, the South Korea-U.S. alliance, and any change in the territorial status quo in the DMZ are all in the back seat. For now, geoeconomic hope has a firm grasp on the wheel.

Notes

Authors' note: The views expressed in this article are those of the authors alone and do not reflect the official policy or position of the United States Air Force or the U.S. government.

1 Keywords included the closure of the Kaesong Industrial Complex (개성공단 폐쇄), the North's nuclear program (북한의 핵무력 완성), Kim's 2018 New Year's speech (김정은 신년사), the 2018 first and third inter-Korean summits (제1차 남북정상회담, 제3차 남북정상회담), the U.S.-North Korea summit (제1차 북미정상회담), and the inter-Korean military agreement (남북군사합의서). We reduced the initial list, excluding articles that only provided basic descriptions of an event.

References

Agnew, J. 2013. Origins of critical geopolitics. In K. Dodds, M. Kuus, and J. Sharp (eds.) *The Ashgate Research Companion to Critical Geopolitics*. pp. 19–32. Farnham: Ashgate.

Armstrong, C. 2013. *The Koreas*. New York: Routledge.

Bae, H-J. 2017. Full text of Moon's speech at the Korber Foundation. *The Korea Herald* (July 7). www.koreaherald.com/view.php?ud=20170707000032

BBC. 2017 (Sept. 19). Trump at UN: North Korea's "Rocket Man on suicide mission." www.bbc.com/news/av/world-us-canada-41324670/trump-at-un-north-korea-s-rocket-man-on-suicide-mission

Buszynski, L., 2013. *Negotiating with North Korea: The Six Party Talks and the Nuclear Issue*. London: Routledge.

Cheong Wa Dae. 2019. South, North and US leaders met at Panmunjom. https://www1.president.go.kr/articles/6730

Choe, S-H. 2019. North Korea demands return of cargo ship seized by U.S. *New York Times* (April 14). www.nytimes.com/2019/05/14/world/asia/north-korea-cargo-ship-usa.html

Cowen, D., and N. Smith. 2009, After geopolitics? From the geopolitical social to geoeconomics. *Antipode* 41(1): 22–48.

Dodds, K. 2007. *Geopolitics: A Very Short Introduction*. Oxford: Oxford University Press.

Doucette, J., and S.-O. Lee. 2015. Experimental territoriality: Assembling the Kaesong Industrial Complex in North Korea. *Political Geography* 47(1): 53–63.

Gibson, C. 1999. Cartographies of the colonial/capitalist state: A geopolitics of indigenous self-determination in Australia. *Antipode* 31(1): 45–79.

Gruley, J., and C. Duvall. 2012. The evolving narrative of the Darfur conflict as represented in *The New York Times* and *The Washington Post*, 2003–2009. *GeoJournal* 77(1): 29–46.

Ha, J-S., and D. Shin. 2016. Framing the Arab Spring: Partisanship in the news stories of Korean newspapers. *International Communication Gazette* 78(6): 536–556.

Heo, U., and S. Yun. 2019. South Korea in 2018: Summit meetings for the denuclearization of North Korea. *Asian Survey* 59(1): 54–62.

Hong, S-H. 2017. President not sitting in the driver's seat but sitting in the passenger's seat. *JoongAng Ilbo* (August 10). https://news.joins.com/article/21833455

Keneally, M. 2018. From "fire and fury" to "rocket man," the various barbs traded between Trump and Kim Jong Un. *ABC News* (June 12). https://abcnews.go.com/International/fire-fury-rocket-man-barbs-traded-trump-kim/story?id=53634996

Kim, D-K., and T. Johnson. 2009. A shift in media credibility: comparing internet and traditional news sources in South Korea. *International Communication Gazette*, 71(4): 283–302.

Kim, H-N. 2008. The Lee Myung-bak government's North Korea policy and the prospects for inter-Korean relations. *International Journal of Korean Studies* 12(1): 1–23.

Kim, K-H. 2014. Examining U.S. news media discourses about North Korea: A corpus-based critical discourse analysis. *Discourse & Society* 25(2): 221–244.

Kookbang Ilbo. 2018. Withdrawal of North and South GP, mutual verification enforcement. *Kookbang Ilbo* (July 14). http://kookbang.dema.mil.kr/newsWeb/20181218/10/BBSMSTR_000000100046/view.do

Kyu, S-H., S-J. Ryu, and S-J. Park. 2015. Fragmentation in the Twitter following of news outlets: The representation of South Korean users' ideological and generational cleavage. *Journalism & Mass Communication Quarterly* 92(1): 56–76.

Lee, S-O. 2015. A geo-economic object or an object of geo-political absorption? Competing visions of North Korea in South Korean politics. *Journal of Contemporary Asia* 45(4): 693–714.

Lee, S-O., J. Wainwright, and J. Glassman. 2018. Geopolitical economy and the production of territory: The case of US-China geopolitical-economic competition in Asia. *Environment and Planning A: Economy and Space* 50(2): 416–436.

Levin, N-D., and Y-S. Han. 2003. *Sunshine in Korea: The South Korean Debate over Policies toward North Korea*. Santa Monica, CA: Rand Corporation.

Lim, N. 2018. Trump muses about condos on North Korea's "great beaches." *Washington Examiner* (June 12). www.washingtonexaminer.com/news/trump-muses-about-condos-on-north-koreas-great-beaches

Luttwak, E. 1990. From geopolitics to geo-economics: logic of conflict, grammar of commerce. *The National Interest* 20(1): 17–23.

Mercille, J. 2008. The radical geopolitics of U.S. foreign policy: Geopolitical and geoeconomic logics of power. *Political Geography* 27(5): 570–586.

Ministry of Unification. 2018a. *Implementation of the Korean Peninsula New Economic Plan and Economic Unification*. www.unikorea.go.kr/unikorea/policy/project/task/precisionmap/

Ministry of Unification. 2018b. *Panmunjeom Declaration for Peace, Prosperity and Unification of the Korean Peninsula*. https://unikorea.go.kr/eng_unikorea/news/news/?boardId=bbs_0000000000000033&mode=view&cntId=54394&category=&pageIdx=

Ministry of Unification. 2019. *Progress, Significance and Future Prospects of Inter-Korean Summit*. www.unikorea.go.kr/eng_unikorea/news/speeches/?boardId=bbs_0000000000000036&mode=view&cntId=31926&category=&pageIdx=10

Michishita, N. 2009. *North Korea's Military-Diplomatic Campaigns, 1966–2008*. London: Routledge.

Niksch, L. 2014. North Korea's weapons of mass destruction. In Y.W. Kihl and HN. Kim (eds.) *North Korea: The Politics of Regime Survival*. pp. 109–129. London: Routledge.

Patterson, T., and W. Donsbagh. 1996. News decisions: Journalists as partisan actors. *Political Communication* 13(4): 455–468.

Perry, W. 2006. Proliferation on the peninsula: Five North Korean nuclear crises. *The Annals of the American Academy of Political and Social Science* 607(1): 78–86.

Rampton, R. 2018. "We fell in love": Trump swoons over letters from North Korea's Kim. *Reuters* (Sept. 30). www.reuters.com/article/us-northkorea-usa-trump/we-fell-in-love-trump-swoons-over-letters-from-north-koreas-kim-idUSKCN1MA03Q

Son, K-Y. 2006. *South Korean Engagement Policies and North Korea: Identities, Norms and the Sunshine Policy*. London: Routledge.

Sparke, M. 2007. Geopolitical fears, geoeconomic hopes, and the responsibilities of geography. *Annals of the Association of American Geographers* 97(2): 338–349.

Sullivan, E. 2018. Trump says "there is no longer a nuclear threat" after Kim Jong-un meeting. *New York Times* (June 13). www.nytimes.com/2018/06/13/us/politics/trump-north-korea-nuclear-threat-.html

White House. 2018. Joint Statement of President Donald J. Trump of the United States of America and Chairman Kim Jong Un of the Democratic People's Republic of Korea at the Singapore Summit. *The White House* (June 12). www.whitehouse.gov/briefings-statements/joint-statement-president-donald-j-trump-united-states-america-chairman-kim-jong-un-democratic-peoples-republic-korea-singapore-summit/

16

THE TRUMP EFFECT IN CHINA

Social aspects of the Sino-U.S. trade conflict and the pro-Trump group in China

Xiang Zhang

Since the inauguration of his presidency on January 20, 2017, Donald Trump (and the United States under his rule) seems to be traveling on a track that the world has never seen before. His words and views on the human rights of women, refugees, and undocumented immigrants challenge the social stability of the U.S. His desire to reduce military support for U.S. allies makes NATO members and East Asian countries uneasy due to the growing political risks represented by Russia, China, and North Korea. His attitude toward international trade and his ambition to bring production back to the U.S. threatens the existing global economic order and changes the role of the U.S. in the global market, and he has ordered the U.S. to withdraw from international agreements and organizations such as the Trans-Pacific Partnership (TPP) and the United Nations Educational, Scientific and Cultural Organization (UNESCO). These policy decisions raise a big question: Is the U.S. no longer willing to assume the dominant role in global affairs? Another question follows: What will be the world's new political order if America abandons that role?

Among Trump's attempts to "Make America Great Again" are the restriction of imports and withdrawal from global affairs, the most controversial and provocative of which is his attitude toward world trade and globalization, which fuels his trade wars against the European Union, Mexico, Canada, Japan, South Korea, and America's largest trade partner, China. Trade disputes are not simply a matter of imports and exports. In fact, they may have significant consequences due to trade's extensive connections to a variety of social matters, such as economic growth, unemployment, fiscal policy and investment, the migration of the labor force, political unrest, and environmental impacts (Glick and Taylor 2010).

This chapter examines the spatial pattern of U.S.-related trade in China and analyzes the social impact of the trade dispute. It first reviews the Sino-U.S. trade dispute to demonstrate regional vulnerability and risks toward trade disputes.

The second part of the chapter describes the spatial pattern of trade and considers the trade dispute's potential threat within the economic geography of China. In the third section, I examine the social and political impacts of Trump's claims in the trade war against China by providing an ethnographic observation of a pro-Trump group in China and by investigating the impacts of Trump's presidency on Chinese society.

Geographical linkages in the Sino-U.S. trade dispute

On January 7, 2016, when the U.S. presidential primaries roiled the country, Donald Trump, then a candidate for the Republican nomination, launched his first bomb on the topic of trade in Sino-U.S. relations. Commenting on the trade deficit and the imbalance in the U.S. economy, he promised to enact a 45% tariff on Chinese exports to the U.S. (Haberman 2016). His campaign slogan, "Make America Great Again," signaled the retreat of the U.S. from the global market and posed a threat to the world's existing economic integration, which was built on decades of efforts toward globalization by countries around the globe.

In fact, this would not be the first time that the world's largest economy had confronted the world's largest developing country with trade conflicts and an import tariff. In 1996, the U.S. government initiated its first investigation against Chinese business to protect intellectual property rights and to protest unfair subsidies from the Chinese government (Bown 2010).

Twenty years later, when a trade conflict again erupted between China and the U.S., the power structure of world politics and the integration of economic activity had been totally rewritten by the two countries' divergent growth trajectories. China has become the world's second largest economic power and America's largest trade partner, not only providing daily necessities to stores such as Walmart, Target, and Kroger but also making the largest contribution to the market share and profits of a large number of U.S. companies, from automobile producers to semiconductor companies. This time, the Sino-U.S. trade conflict played out in a more globalized, dynamic, and interdependent era of social and economic relations (Che et al. 2016). With more diverse and powerful channels and media available for communication and the diffusion of information, the new version of the Sino-U.S. trade war has not been limited to the theatre of international business and economics. Moreover, public attitudes in China toward the trade dispute and its social impact are moving far beyond general concerns about the potential damage of economic development and the effects on business expansion for Chinese stakeholders, but to political and social affairs that limit political freedom and human rights (Mingst, McKibben, and Arreguin-Toft 2018). The isolation of the U.S. from the world market raises other concerns, as China's export-oriented economy has shaped its economic geography into a well-known spatial pattern, with special industrial zones being regularly planned by administrative powers to stimulate economic development.

In the contemporary history of Chinese economic development, special economic zones and designated industrial campuses have been critical elements of growth, as such places grew from clusters of factories and assembly lines to well-planned industrial zones each featuring a comprehensive supply chain for a specialized product (Farole and Akinci 2011). Well-known examples of towns and cities that specialize in manufacturing a single product are spread across the country, particularly in the coastal provinces such as Guangdong, Zhejiang, Fujian, and Jiangsu. For instance, the town of Guzhen in Guangdong produces over 90% of the lamps and bulbs in the world market, and more than 50% of the entire economic output of the city of Jinjiang in Fujian province comes from the production of sporting shoes and clothes (Bellandi and Di Tommaso 2005; Fujian Statistical Bureau 2018). On the one hand, the growth of these industrial zones provides a well-established infrastructure that attracts capital and investment for the producers; while, on the other, such zones bring the risks inherent in economic monocultures, a fact that has been recognized by both government agencies and professional researchers (Wei 2015; Zhong 2015). Moving toward a more diverse economy would take a long time, however, and some towns and cities are still dependent on the revenue generated from the production of one particular product.

These specialized industrial towns and cities also change the demographic structure of China. Since exports began to dominate China's growth, the high demand for labor in these towns has radically changed the country's migration pattern (Ciżkowicz et al. 2016). Since the 1980s, hundreds of millions of peasants from rural areas have moved to these coastal areas to earn more money and improve their living standards. Nowadays, more than 100 million rural workers migrate like birds between their homelands and China's industrial zones. These factories and assembly lines have provided millions of job opportunities for Chinese workers, particularly in labor-intensive sectors such as electronics manufacturing, the production of light industrial products, and related logistical and transportation jobs.

For the above reasons, a potential halt in China's trade relationship or export production to the U.S. means much more to the country's government than the loss of economic profit and a decline in GDP. Should the export industry be hit by the trade dispute, millions of factory jobs would be lost due to diminishing orders from the world's largest market. It would also affect the supply chains in China, from the collection of raw materials to transportation and warehousing, as well as the associated services for workers in the industrial areas, ranging from catering to barbering, from general retail to the real estate market (Ansar et al. 2016).

When projecting from a Chinese perspective the possible outcome of a trade dispute with the U.S., therefore, one must consider more than its potential scale and the economic shock to the world's second-largest economy and the market with world's greatest number of consumers. Once a trade war is ignited, a research framework with at least three components must be considered. First,

The Trump effect in China **283**

the direct damage to the economies of the involved countries must be examined. Second, the countries' related social problems should be considered. Finally, the problems in one country caused by interactions with problems in the counter party must not be ignored.

Geography of U.S. trade with China

This section examines from a geographical perspective the trade dispute's potential damage to the Chinese economy. By illustrating the spatial pattern of exports to the U.S. in the Chinese economy, it identifies the regions most vulnerable to the dispute's economic impact and notes its potential social ramifications by considering the unique geographical features of those regions.

The discussion begins with a brief description of China's exports to the U.S. and the trade connection between the two countries. A spatial analysis of Sino-U.S. trade in the Chinese context must first be presented to provide a comprehensive analysis of the social and political geography of the trade war's impact in China. As China is the world's largest exporter of manufactured goods, foreign trade has played a critical role in the country's economic growth since the opening and reform in the 1980s. According to official statistics, the value of the trade of goods in China increased from U.S. $20.6 billion in 1980 to U.S. $4.1 trillion in 2017 (National Bureau of Statistics 2018). Moreover, services are becoming an increasingly important part of China's trade with its worldwide partners, having grown from U.S. $4.7 billion in 1982 to U.S. $695.7 billion in 2016.

In the meantime, U.S. companies are among the most active investors in building factories and branches in China, as there is a consensus among scholars that the emerging Chinese market will be the world's largest market for goods and services in the near future (Berger, Hasan, and Zhou 2009; Nolan 2012; Stiglitz 2015). American companies are also involved in a number of joint venture investments with Chinese companies or state-owned enterprises, particularly in the automotive sector. Both Ford and General Motors have cooperated with state-owned Chinese automotive firms to produce U.S.-branded cars.

Following the industrialization of China, the country's exports and imports of goods in the world market were transformed due to its role shifting from a major producer of light industrial products (such as textiles and home appliances) to a global supplier of all industrial products, including industrial machinery, electrical machinery and equipment, information and communication technology (ICT) goods, and more.

Figures 16.1 and 16.2 summarize the contemporary structure of Chinese exports. A dominant trend – the rising share of skill-required machinery and electronic production – can be observed in Figure 16.1. Currently, most smartphones sold in the world market are assembled by a Chinese factory. In the case of the U.S., Apple has contracted with several companies to produce its electronic devices, most of which are assembled in mainland China. As the world's

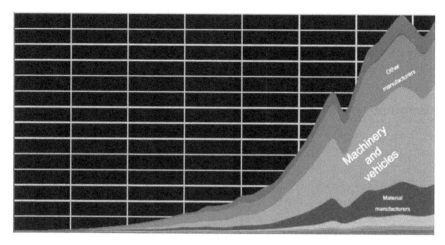

FIGURE 16.1 Total trade value and components of U.S.-China Trade, 1980–2016.
Source: Center of International Development.

largest consumer of electronic devices, the U.S. market may suffer from involuntary price increases if a tariff is imposed, and the cost of the tariff will be passed to consumers, as most U.S. wholesalers will consider the tariff a cost of the buying process and add it to the retail price.

With the growth of the Chinese economy in recent decades, international trade to and from China has also changed. China has moved from being an exporter to the world, with few imports, to being a more balanced trade player

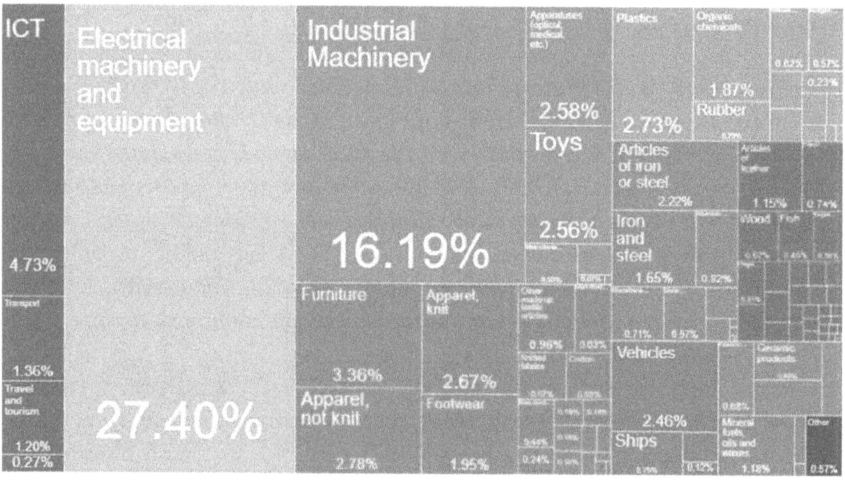

FIGURE 16.2 Percentage of China's exports by sector, 2016.
Source: Center of International Development.

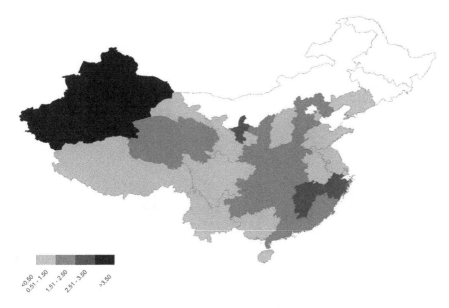

FIGURE 16.3 Export-to-import ratio in mainland China, 2017.

Source: Author, using data from National Bureau of Statistics 2018.

in the world market. Figure 16.3 shows the export-to-import ratios of Chinese provinces, which illustrate the dependency of local economies on the world market. Most regions in China have already established a fairly balanced trade account, with only a few, such as Xinjiang, Ningxia, and Zhejiang, still having a highly export-oriented economic structure in which exports are more than double imports.

If we focus only on Sino-U.S. trade, however, the story changes. China is the world's largest exporter and the largest trading partner of the United States, so trade with the U.S. is an important component of its economy. As sellers, Chinese exporters take advantage of relatively cheap labor and provide inexpensive, good-quality products to the U.S. market. On the Chinese side, U.S. investors and products from the U.S. are also increasingly significant in the Chinese economy. For electronics, Chinese companies must buy many kinds of integrated circuits from American companies. As the Chinese economy grows rapidly, the rising demands of its citizens also call for reliable supplies of food and agricultural products, which are among the more important U.S. imports in the Chinese market. Figure 16.4 presents the export-to-import ratio of Chinese provinces in 2016. It shows that over half of Chinese provinces export more to the U.S. than they import from the U.S., which implies that the Chinese market is more dependent on the U.S. market than vice versa and thus more vulnerable to possible trade restrictions from Washington.

According to Figure 16.5, several provinces are heavily reliant on exports to the U.S. in their international trade patterns, particularly several inland ones.

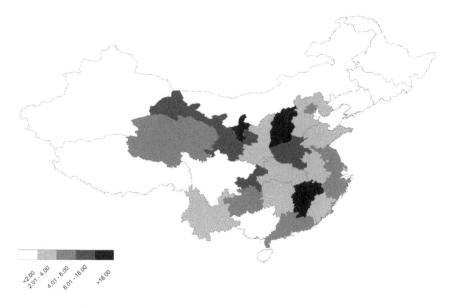

FIGURE 16.4 Export-to-import ratio of U.S.-Sino trade among Chinese provinces, 2017.

Source: Author, using data from National Bureau of Statistics, 2018; China Customs, 2018.

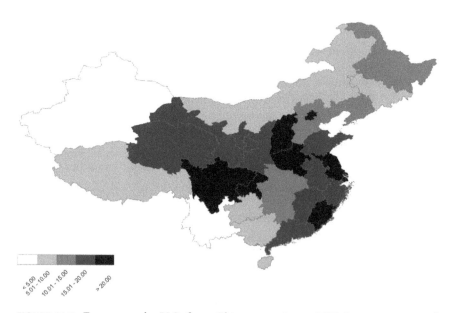

FIGURE 16.5 Exports to the U.S. from Chinese provinces, 2017 (as a percentage of total exports).

Source: Author, using data from National Bureau of Statistics, 2018; China Customs, 2018.

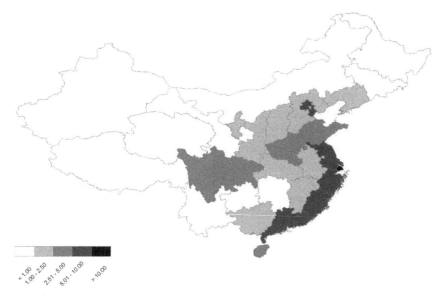

FIGURE 16.6 Exports to the U.S. from Chinese provinces, 2017 (as a percentage of GDP).

Source: Author, using data from National Bureau of Statistics, 2018; China Customs, 2018.

In fact, the leading exporters or industrial sectors in these provinces have been highly specialized in producing products demanded by the U.S. market or have received foreign direct investment for building joint venture factories with U.S. investors, making the U.S. a major destination for their products. One of the leading industries in this paradigm is the assembly and export of electronic products, which is dominated by several Taiwanese contract manufacturing (CM) companies, such as Foxconn, Compal, Quanta Computer, Wistron, and Inventec. These CM companies have invested in several giant factories and industrial campuses across China, using China for the final assembly of laptops, smartphones, tablets, and other popular products for consumers around the world, particularly in the U.S., the European Union, Japan, and Australasia. For example, Foxconn, which has 32 factories and manufacturing facilities in China, has become the leading exporter of goods in Henan, Shanxi, and Sichuan provinces. The Henan location is the major campus for the assembly of smartphones, the Shanxi factory produces a variety of digital electronics (including auto electronics, monitors, and other portable electronic devices), and the Sichuan site produces most tablets in the U.S. market. Quanta Computer, which makes laptops for U.S. brands such as Dell, Apple MacBook, and Hewlett-Packard as well the popular Apple Watch, has dominated the export of goods in Chongqing since it opened one of the largest factories in Asia in 2010.

Examining the exports to the U.S. in both total trade and GDP terms, there are several Chinese provinces that have a strong dependency on the U.S. market. If the trade dispute escalates and tariffs are added to the prices of products produced in these regions, it would be inevitable that those foreign contractor manufacturers may consider moving their plants and assembly lines to other countries in the world such as Vietnam, Thailand, Malaysia, and India, where they still can get cheap labor to produce the product (Li et al. 2012). However, such a move will cause several problems to the local societies in these Chinese provinces. As these contractors are highly labor intensive, their withdrawal would result in a huge amount of unemployment (Chan et al. 2016). Large-scale precipitous unemployment would threaten the entire Chinese society, not only for the provinces where these factories are located, but also the provinces where their workers come from. In this sense, the hit by the trade dispute would no longer be an economic problem, but a complicated social problem requiring more precautious handling from the government and local business due to the scale and multiplicity of issues that would result for China.

Basic information about the pro-Trump online group

Before becoming a candidate for the presidency, Donald Trump was known to the Chinese as a real estate businessman, media celebrity, and frequent filer for bankruptcy. His reality television program, *The Apprentice*, was quite popular on a number of Chinese streaming websites. His name was also closely associated with the American beauty pageant Miss USA, as was reported even by the website of the Communist Party's official newspaper, the *People's Daily*.

Trump's reputation in China as a conservative and nationalist figure grew with the coverage of the 2016 presidential campaign by Chinese media. The state-run Xinhua News Agency (2016a) designed a special website to report major events during the campaign from the viewpoint of the Chinese government. Labels attached to Trump by official Chinese media ranged from "an internet celebrity" (Guancha 2017) to "a gender discriminant" (Xinhua News Agency 2016b). The figure of Trump has also been used by China's authoritarian regime to attack the democratic system, as the election of Trump has been labeled "tyranny's victory."

At the same time, several social problems have been brewing in Chinese society in recent years. Concerns about the government's supervision of social stability – concerns that are anathema to the highly centralized authoritarian regime – have arisen in response to an increasingly restricted press, extensively censored internet, repressive reactions against assemblies and protections, and a stagnating economy marked by a surplus of unwanted products. International nongovernmental organizations and human rights activists have noted that control over social media, the internet, and the press has been further tightened by the Chinese government to maintain its control of social matters and economic growth (Singh 2016).

Although newspapers, television stations, and websites are strictly controlled and all public information is closely censored, social media users keep developing new ways to express their criticism and sarcasm toward the government's violations of the already limited freedom of press and speech in Chinese cyberspace (Chu and Ruthrof 2017). Common strategies of internet users include picturizing a text to thwart the textual filter system, devising various homophonic words to describe censored information, and using arcane metaphors from Chinese literature to challenge the censorship system. During this period of deteriorating freedom on Chinese social media platforms in regard to the potential social damage wrought by Trump's trade policy, one group of pro-Trump Chinese internet users has been a non-mainstream phenomenon since 2016.

The most common venue for these pro-Trump netizens to discuss social and political issues is the social media platform Baidu Tieba, provided by Baidu, China's largest search engine. Baidu has attracted a large group of users, ranging from the grassroots class to millionaires, as it monopolizes the search engine market. Baidu Tieba, a large discussion forum for diverse topics, allows users to create a specific discussion board, called a *ba* (literally "bar" in Chinese), which attracts users who are interested in the topic. The board for Trump was initially created in 2008, and older threads on this board focus mostly on his book *The Art of the Deal*, his media presence on *The Apprentice*, and his business strategies and bankruptcy stories. According to the timeline of posts, fewer than 50 posts were created every week before the declaration of his presidential campaign in May 2015.

With the commencement of his presidential campaign and the dissemination of his political stances on immigration, Chinese trade, globalization, religion, and terrorism, Trump's words attracted the attention of many Chinese netizens. The numbers of posts on the Trump discussion board exploded. Many users and commentators expressed their support for Trump's controversial views, and some began to allude to social problems implicit in Trump's language, which transformed a discussion board about a business celebrity into a special subcultural group that opaquely discussed political issues in China. By the time of the presidential election in 2016, the discussion board had already archived over 10,000 distinct threads and more than 80,000 posts, with the number of daily active discussants increasing from fewer than 50 in 2014 to more than 1,000. The trend continued after Trump moved into the White House. By the end of 2017, the discussion board had recorded over 200,000 posts and had 10,000 daily discussants, making it the largest gathering of pro-Trumpers in Chinese social media. Table 16.1 shows the recorded number of registered users on this pro-Trump discussion board since 2008. An exponential increase of discussants and participants happened between 2015 and 2017, during which the number of users grew over 40 times.

During the growth of this pro-Trump discussion board, several important dates saw explosions of daily active users and newly posted threads. On December 7, 2015, Trump first mentioned a possible ban on travel from Muslim countries should he be elected, which ignited a heated debate on the discussion board of China's Muslim policy, marking the first wave of new threads related to Trump's political stances. On May 3, 2016, when Trump sealed his candidacy by winning

TABLE 16.1 Numbers of registered users of the Baidu Trump discussion board.

End of Year	No. of Registered Users
2008	35
2009	50
2010	57
2011	59
2012	60
2013	68
2014	76
2015	339
2016	3,784
2017	15,132

Source: Baidu.com and author's calculation.

the Republican presidential primaries, a group of discussants began to reflect his political viewpoints from a Chinese perspective and declared themselves supporters of his stances on Muslims, white supremacy, and illegal immigration from Latin America. On January 23, 2017, the third day of his presidency, Trump withdrew the U.S. from the Trans-Pacific Partnership and declared that he would rethink the trade relationship between China and the U.S., starting a new wave of posts and discussions on the board and attracting a surprisingly large number of Chinese supporters online.

Reading the pro-Trump online group

Trump's popularity in China, particularly on the internet, seems like a strange phenomenon. In the history of the Sino-U.S. relationship, strong anti-U.S. sentiment and actions are expected in China whenever Washington expresses hostility towards Beijing. Past examples, including the Yinhe incident in 1993, the NATO bombing of the Chinese embassy in Belgrade in 1999, and the mid-air collision of military aircraft in 2001, were all followed by a huge wave of anti-U.S. protests in Chinese cities (Ross 2016).

When it comes to the Sino-U.S. trade dispute of the Trump presidency, however, China's social perception of the potential trade conflict becomes mixed. On the one hand, no spontaneous anti-U.S. protest was reported in any Chinese city. On the other hand, opinions that diverged from the official stance of objecting to Trump's policy spread, specifically among a group of pro-American individuals that has grown rapidly since 2000, when Sino-U.S. communication skyrocketed thanks to scholarly, commercial, and cultural interactions. A major idea promulgated by the pro-American faction is that the trade dispute and potential tariffs from Trump's government would force Chinese companies and sectors to accelerate China's structural change and its economic transformation from traditional manufacturing to sustainable growth.

The online pro-Trump group follows the precedent of the pro-America group, arguing that new U.S. trade restrictions could positively affect the existing economic structure in China by forcing the government to revise its development planning and abandon its outward orientation in favor of the domestic market, socially benefiting local people by increasing the profitability of local fiscal accounts related to international trade (Applebaum 2005). Both groups argue that the trade conflict would hurt those with a vested interest in the export-oriented Chinese economy, including high-ranking officials in state-owned enterprises, government servants with business interests in local areas, and workers in sectors receiving government subsidies (Noland, Robinson, and Moran 2016).

The explosion of posts and comments about the Trump's policy towards China and increasing number of participants on this discussion board make this online place a cluster for pro-Trump and pro-American opinions explicitly; it later become a place to implicitly criticize the government policy and ongoing social problems in China. Popular topics on this discussion board include the daily update of Trump's Twitter and reposted news about Trump's public activities from U.S. sources, and sometimes the information and knowledge about the political system in the U.S. For example, there was a popular thread posted in November 2016, where some Chinese-Americans used this online platform to broadcast their voting process. The thread received over 100 replies and comments on voting day. Initially people expressed their support and admiral for a process where an individual can make his or her voice heard. Then the discussion proceeded to another tone that criticized the Chinese system and the Communist Party implicitly by quoting historical comments from the Communist Party during the civil war in the late 1940s against the nationalist Kuomintang. Similarly, when Trump signed his executive order instituting a Muslim Ban in January 2017, the discussion board had hundreds of posts and comments supporting the discriminative policy and criticizing the Chinese government's attitude towards Muslims, as they thought that Muslims in China received favorable policies. One of the most controversial policies is that Muslim candidates are entitled to ten bonus points for the National College Entrance Exam, which was believed to be an unequal policy towards the majority Han Chinese.

Trump's trade policy and related comments on the claimed unfair competition from China ignited another wave of posts and comments on the economic issues and problems in China. Given the growing inequality and unconvincing statistical data from the government, people are more concerned about the economy as they experience it. Netizens express their disappointment in the government as they face pressure to sustain their lives and family in three major areas: housing, healthcare, and education. Trump's criticism of unfair competition and government subsidies to the state-owned enterprises in China has found favor with lots of discussants on this board.

Recent developments and the increasing popularity of discussions and threads have made this discussion board a place not only to show the group's embrace of American politics and positive aspects of Trump's China policy. Observing the contextual features of the vocabulary and discussions shows that it has already become a place for people to express their discontent over the Chinese government and the one-party regime. Most discussions start from one specific feature of American politics or Trump's policy, and then expand to netizens' disapproval over the socioeconomic policy designed by the Beijing government. On the recent Constitution Amendment in China, which allows literally a lifelong presidency, thousands of posts and comments appeared in implicit and metaphorical words to criticize this political backlash in China, stemming from an initial appraisal of the election system in the U.S. where everyone can make a voice. Towards the recent trade dispute between two countries, Trump's claims on the overuse of government subsidy and support to some big companies, particularly state-owned enterprises (SOEs), are among the most quoted arguments on the discussion boards. The associated comments and posts are deemed to criticize the unfair market competition between private companies and SOEs in the Chinese domestic market. Further development of this discussion evolved to an attack on the inequality of wealth distribution and the hierarchical crony system in the state-owned economy of China. Some discussants also used this stage to complain about the absence of political opposition and oversight of the Chinese government, which is considered a traditional feature of a democratic system.

However, these topics are taboo to the Chinese government and strictly censored by different devices in cyberspace. Therefore, discussants and participants on this board applied several ways to create neologisms to make their voices heard. Table 16.2 shows a list of frequently used neologisms and slang on the pro-Trump discussion broad after a simple crowdsourced analysis of their usage frequency. Among these frequently used slang terms, most address the public's discontent with the Chinese government and current social problems. From the threads and posts on the board, discussants and participants use Trump's claims against China as a way to illustrate domestic problems. They think that Trump's trade policy will hurt the SOEs and government-subsidized industries most, and the trade war and heavy tariffs will force the government to find another way to operate the Chinese economy; this is described as a "forced reform" to benefit the general public in China. During this process, the interests of the elite class may be affected significantly, which is hoped for by the general public due to the growth of the "miso-affluence" mentality or hatred towards the elite class. As the Chinese government claimed that it would pay more attention to the domestic market and the social welfare system, some people credited these concessions to Trump's tough attitude towards China.

Besides the concerns over social inequality and power distribution, another explicit label associated with the pro-Trump group is the racist and discriminative attitude towards Muslims as well as African workers in China. In the forum, most people use the racist analogy to describe Muslims as well as the government's affirmative policy for minority groups in China. According to the ethnicity classification in China, Chinese Muslims converted to Islam as early as the Ming Dynasty between the 14th and 16th centuries. Members in the pro-Trump

The Trump effect in China **293**

TABLE 16.2 Frequently used neologisms on the pro-Trump discussion board.

Neologism	Refers To	Explanation
"巴西" Baxi, "Brazil"	China	There are five stars on both the jersey of the Brazilian National Soccer Team and the National Flag of China. It also implies the corruption in the party system, which is comparable to that in the Brazilian government.
"后清" Houqing, "Post-Qing Dynasty"	The communist regime in China	A satire against the cultural blockade and affirmative policy of the communist regime.
庆丰 Qingfeng	Xi Jinping	Xi visited a famous restaurant in Beijing, the Qingfeng Bun Shop, in 2013, which was later promoted by the official media to illustrate Xi's close relationship to the public.
白左 Baizuo, "White-left"	Democrats and their supporters	Originated from the criticism of regressive liberalists on holding paradoxical, reactionary views due to their tolerance of illiberal principles and ideologies.
赵家 Zhaojia, "Zhao family"	CCP bureaucrats and elite class	Originated in Lu Xun's novel, *The True Story of Ah Q*, where the Zhao family is the biggest landlord in the village. Netizens use this word to describe the rich and the bureaucrats in China, particularly for those who are connected to the party.
绿教 Lvjiao, "Green religion"	Islam and related issues	A racist term for Islam and related affairs. Originated from the association between the color green and paradise in the Quran. Netizens use "green" to describe anything related to Islam and Muslims.
中必赢 Zhongbiying, "China will win"	Sarcasm against the Chinese government's foreign policy	Originated from its frequent usage by official media to show China's determination to win diplomatic disputes with foreign countries, particularly during the island dispute in the South China Sea.
屁民 Pimin	Powerless people, "shitizens"	Refers to the powerlessness of the general public in terms of political rights as the public voice is seldom heard.
毛左 Maozuo, "Maoist leftists"	The Chinese far-left pro-communists	Refers to Chinese leftists' pro-Maoist view against the Open and Reform neoliberalization. They are against the existing social structure and claim that the far-left Maoist society is ideal for China.
撒币 Sabi, "Throw money"	Xi's diplomatic policy	Refers to the "Renminbi" diplomacy used by the government. A homophonic from the Chinese slang "Shabi," meaning idiots.

Source: Author.

group claim that there are three hierarchies from the top to the bottom in China: foreigners, minorities, and the majority Han Chinese, and include themselves as victims of reverse discrimination from the government. They also attack Muslims for their daily religious customs such as food and drink restrictions.

African immigrants and workers living in China are another group receiving racist and discriminative attacks from the pro-Trump group. Since the early 1990s, as China expanded its market and business with African countries, more and more African workers, businessmen, and students moved to China, particularly to the city of Guangzhou. According to the official statistics, there were 15,000 lawful foreign residents living in Guangzhou by 2016. However, according to the 2014 air traffic statistics, nearly 100,000 Africans arrived in the Guangzhou area in just five months. According to the data from a third-party nongovernmental organization, there are about 500,000 illegal African immigrants living in the Guangzhou area. Gangs and gang crimes between different groups within the African immigrants and workers have already become a social problem in Guangzhou. Therefore, Trump's view on illegal immigrants has found favor with the racist Chinese view on blocking other minorities and Africans from the country and has frequently appeared in their posts and threads on the discussion board.

In order to track the origin and spatiality of discussants and members in this group, IP address tracking for posts and threads with pro-Trump viewpoints was conducted. Though only a limited number of posts make their IP address and location available to readers, it is still useful to track these given locations for a primary picturing of the spatiality of these pro-Trump views and conservative ideas. As the usage of virtual private networks is a common practice among Chinese netizens, IP addresses showing foreign locations are not considered in this research. Only IP addresses with the service provider's endorsement have been used in this calculation. Table 16.3 shows the statistics of geographical

TABLE 16.3 IP address based locations of frequent discussants on the pro-Trump discussion board.

Provinces	No. of Records
Guangdong	426
Jiangsu	339
Zhejiang	267
Shanghai	251
Fujian	183
Sichuan	169
Henan	135
Shandong	112
Shaanxi	109
Hubei	103

Source: Author.

The Trump effect in China **295**

locations of frequent visitors to this pro-Trump discussion board. It is not surprising to see that major export-oriented provinces, such as Guangdong, Jiangsu, and Zhejiang, have dominated this list. There are also many clicks on the discussion board from inland provinces which implies that the concerns over social problems and the appraisal of conservative ideas are not geographically concentrated to one specific region in China, but are becoming a nationwide phenomenon.

Discussion and concluding notes

The above discussion visualizes the geography of the U.S. trade in China and outlines the social problems and implications reflected by the growth of the pro-Trump online group in China's largest discussion thread platform. By inspecting the geography of trade in China, it demonstrates that a possible trade war may hit the manufacturing industry in China unequally as the level of dependency to U.S. trade varies across different regions. For the coastal region with more trade connections to the rest of the world, it also exposes limited risk to the potential loss of the U.S. market, and may recover from the first hit of tariff or embargo quickly by shifting its market to other markets such as the European Union, Africa, the Middle East, Southeast Asia, etc. However, for some inland provinces, where the economic transformation has recently brought in some export-oriented manufacturing, such as the new Foxconn assembly lines in Henan and Sichuan provinces, they will need more attention from the public and the government to help them cope with potential hit from the trade dispute. These inland provinces have high ratios of dependency on U.S. exports and related trade, and should be the places where the public focuses attention on creating new job opportunities and finding new markets across the world.

Besides a geography of potential impacts caused by the trade dispute, Trump's words also echo the growth of a group of fans on the Chinese internet. Among these discussants and participants of the online threads, some of them use Trump's political views to allude to concerns about social problems happening in China, such as the unequal distribution of wealth, the growing power of the rich and the bureaucrats, the lack of political freedoms and human rights, etc. However, his words and arguments also attract racists to attack Muslims and African immigrants in China. In this sense, the influence of American politics on China via the internet media does not only allow enlightenment on democracy and freedom, but also impacts on controversial issues that may deepen the existing social conflicts between different ethnic groups in China.

After examining the links between Trump's trade policy and his ideas, it is critical to acknowledge that Trump's presidency does not only symbolize a series of new trends and changes in American politics. More importantly, the spread of his ideas and opinions to different parts of the world results in deviations and explanations based on the context of local politics and social systems. His comments and arguments have worsened the humanitarian problems of refugees and immigrants, and fueled the fire of nationalism and racism across the world. If his ideas could do a little bit help to navigate the world towards a path of freeing and loosening restrictions for its people and society, it could be positive consequence of his words – though this a frail hope.

References

Ansar, A., B. Flyvbjerg, A. Budzier, and D. Lunn. 2016. Does infrastructure investment lead to economic growth or economic fragility? Evidence from China. *Oxford Review of Economic Policy* 32(3): 360–390.

Applebaum, A. 2005. In search of pro Americanism. *Foreign Policy* 149: 32–41. www.anneapplebaum.com/2005/07/18/in-search-of-pro-americanism/

Bellandi, M., and M. Di Tommaso. 2005. The case of specialized towns in Guangdong, China. *European Planning Studies* 13(5): 707–729.

Berger, A., I. Hasan, and M. Zhou. 2009. Bank ownership and efficiency in China: What will happen in the world's largest nation? *Journal of Banking & Finance* 33(1): 113–130.

Bown, C. 2010. China's WTO entry: Antidumping, safeguards, and dispute settlement. In S.J. Wei and R. Feenstra (eds.) *China's Growing Role in World Trade*. pp. 281–337. Chicago: University of Chicago Press.

Chan, J., N. Pun, and M. Selden. 2016. *Apple, Foxconn, and China's New Working Class*. Ithaca, NY: Cornell University Press.

Che, Y., Y. Lu, J. Pierce, P. Schott, and Z. Tao. 2016. *Does Trade Liberalization with China Influence US Elections?* (No. 22178). Washington, D.C.: National Bureau of Economic Research.

Chu, Y., and H. Ruthrof. 2017. The social semiotic of homophone phrase substitution in Chinese netizen discourse. *Social Semiotics* 27(5): 640–655.

Ciżkowicz, P., M. Ciżkowicz-Pękała, P. Pękała, and A. Rzońca. 2016. The effects of special economic zones on employment and investment: a spatial panel modeling perspective. *Journal of Economic Geography* 17(3): 571–605.

Farole, T., and G. Akinci. 2011. *Special Economic Zones: Progress, Emerging Challenges, and Future Directions*. Washington, D.C.: World Bank.

Fujian Statistical Bureau. 2018. Fujian Statistical Yearbook 2018. http://tjj.fujian.gov.cn/tongjinianjian/dz2018/index-cn.htm

Glick, R., and A. Taylor. 2010. Collateral damage: Trade disruption and the economic impact of war. *The Review of Economics and Statistics* 92(1): 102–127.

Guancha. 2017. Yǔzhòu wǎng hóng"tè lǎng pǔ 2018 gāoguāng shíkè láile: Zìchēng Ají zǒngtǒng [The glorious moment of a super internet celebrity in 2018: Self-claimed A+-rated president, Donald Trump is coming] [in Chinese]. https://news.163.com/18/1220/16/E3FVSCPC0001875O.html

Haberman, M. 2016. Donald Trump says he favors big tariffs on Chinese exports. *New York Times* (Jan. 7). www.nytimes.com/politics/first-draft/2016/01/07/donald-trump-says-he-favors-big-tariffs-on-chinese-exports/

Li, H., L. Li, B. Wu, and Y. Xiong. 2012. The end of cheap Chinese labor. *Journal of Economic Perspectives* 26(4): 57–74.

Mingst, K., H. McKibben, I. and Arreguin-Toft. 2018. *Essentials of International Relations*. New York: WW Norton.

National Bureau of Statistics. 2018. *China Statistical Yearbook 2016* [in Chinese]. Beijing: China Statistics Press.

Nolan, P. 2012. Is China buying the world? *Challenge* 55(2): 108–118.

Noland, M., S. Robinson, and T. Moran. 2016. Impact of Clinton's and Trump's trade proposals. *Assessing Trade Agendas in the US Presidential Campaign*. Washington, DC: Peterson Institute for International Economics.

Ross, R. 2016. *After the Cold War: Domestic Factors and US-China Relations: Domestic Factors and US-China Relations*. New York: Routledge.

Singh, G. 2016. Mass media in Xi's China: Markets versus control. *Strategic Analysis* 40(5): 379–385.

Stiglitz, J. 2015. The Chinese century. *Vanity Fair* (January). www.vanityfair.com/news/2015/01/china-worlds-largest-economy

Wei, Y. D. 2015. Zone fever, project fever: Development policy, economic transition, and urban expansion in China. *Geographical Review* 105(2): 156–177.

Xinhua News Agency. 2016a (Sept. 11). Trump won the 2016 US presidential election [in Chinese]. www.xinhuanet.com/world/2016-11/09/c_1119882518.htm

Xinhua News Agency. 2016b (May 16). Tè lǎng pǔ bèi méitǐ fān jiùzhàng pī zhǐzé wǔrǔ qíshì nǚxìng [Trump's dark history: His discrimination and insultation against women] [in Chinese]. www.xinhuanet.com/world/2016-05/16/c_128983999.htm

Zhong, Y. 2015. *Local Government and Politics in China: Challenges from Below*. New York: Routledge.

17

TANGIER ISLAND FOR TRUMP

A geographic reconfiguring of visibilities in American climate change displacement discourse

Victoria Herrmann

On early summer mornings, the first rays of light cascade over the wooden piers and tall grass on the Eastern Shore and blanket the landscape in a rich golden hue. Beyond the muddied coastline of Maryland, the murky waters of Chesapeake Bay are cloaked in a veil of persistent fog. The mist obscures the Bay's tumulus confluence of waters, its estuary ecosystem below the surface and its scatterplot geography of islands above. The two dozen islands embody the Bay's dynamism, each a layered landmass of cultures, histories, and peoples that simultaneously rely upon and will eventually succumb to the waters that surround them. Though moored by the formidable anchors of unique dialects, waterman livelihoods, and family ties, the centuries-old islands of the Chesapeake now face the relentless and eventually fatal rising tide of global climate change. It is perhaps this disquieting parallel of a long-forgotten but sanguine American heritage alongside the ever-present sorrow of climate loss and damage that attracts dozens of journalists each year to one vanishing Bay island in particular – Tangier.

To get to Tangier Island as a visitor takes a 90-minute ferry ride departing from Crisfield, Maryland in good weather. The ferry is piled high with incoming mail, packages, and a haphazard assortment of furniture, with passengers squeezing in between the inanimate commuters. Eighty minutes into the ride, the shadows of crab shacks begin to appear though the fog, and, finally, the island itself. On May 12, 2016, my research partner Eli Keene and I took the Crisfield ferry to Tangier Island. We had traveled some 100 miles from Washington, D.C. as part of a research and storytelling project titled *America's Eroding Edges*. The project was meant to identify and document the challenges of adapting American coastal communities to the impacts of climate change, and, after considering countless news articles, magazine features, and television broadcast segments about the sinking island at the edge of the Chesapeake Bay, we decided to visit the island ourselves to see and interview Tangier's community leaders about their experience. When we landed on Tangier in the heat of the 2016 presidential election, it was clear for which candidate the island was voting. Make American Great Again bumper stickers were slapped onto every golf cart (the island has no cars) and a large red Trump flag waved proudly overhead. When I sat down to interview residents, remarks about Trump were common, as were jokes about building his wall around their town.

Unbeknown to us in 2016, the visual politics we were experiencing on the island were a harbinger of a changing national narrative for Tangier. Where news coverage in or before 2016 positioned Tangier as an apolitical historic island crumbling into the sea, reporting from 2017 onwards has framed Tangier's disappearance in reference to its Trump-supporting Republican residents' denial of manmade climate change. This shift in the geographies of media reporting on Tangier Island, and the aforementioned 2016 research trip to Tangier Island, is the inspiration for the chapter to follow. It examines how President Donald Trump's personal actions and environmental policies have reconfigured media geographies of climate change reporting along America's eroding shorelines through the case study of Tangier Island. The chapter first provides a foundation of current scholarship on American media landscapes of climate change reporting, and the ways in which these landscapes have intersected, and been interdependent, with the political landscape. It then offers a multimodal discourse analysis of select American mass media publications on Tangier Island and climate change, comparing materials published during the Obama Administration (2008–2016) and the first two-and-a-half years of Trump's presidency (2017–2019). In doing so, it explores how the geographies of America's "first climate refuges" have shifted in line with the two presidents' rhetoric on domestic climate change displacement. The chapter traces the reshaping of media narratives of a white community in the Chesapeake Bay that voted 87% for Trump and does not believe in manmade climate change. In doing so, the case study of Tangier Island creates the foundation upon which to analyze the media geographies that create points of connection and of disassociation, of empathy and of apathy between Trump voters affected by climate change impacts and primarily liberal, climate-conscious readers. In all, the chapter offers an opportunity to consider the repercussions of these spatial transformations on the framing and empathy imbued in domestic climate impacts under President Trump.

Going under: The anchoring of Tangier Island as American

Tangier Island's estuarine wetlands and sandy upland ridges support a shrinking population of 460 people. Located in the middle of the Chesapeake Bay, the Virginia island is located in the middle of the Chesapeake Bay's blue crab fishery. Traditionally used as a summer camp by the Pocomoke Indians, Tangier has been continuously inhabited by European white settlers since the 18th century, with most of its current resident families arriving in the 1770s as farmers. Today, the town is a tight-knit community bound by a shared island dialect, culture,

300 Victoria Herrmann

history, belief system, and waterman livelihood. Islanders are heavily reliant on crabbing, with oystering and tourism supplementing the more prominent crabbing business. Since 1850, 66.75% of the island's landmass has been lost from one of the highest local land subsidence rates in the mid-Atlantic region, while much of Tangier's upload has already been converted to tidal marshes, as sea level rise.

Constructing familiarity: Shared histories, cultures, and nostalgia

For American journalists, and their readers, Tangier Island offers a captivatingly rare geography for climate change reporting – a layered landscape of domestic familiarity and exotic otherness. Islanders, white middle class families neighboring the nation's capital, are recognizable visual subjects. Though their skin is tanned from hours spent on the water and their attire of boots, camouflage, and baseball hats reflects their rural livelihood, media photographs of men in hardware stores and children playing basketball are unmistakably American. And yet, Tangier is also foreign to most Americans. It is an unknown island where people sound different and clutch close their way of life unchanged from the 18th century. This dichotomy of domesticity and *otherness* is perhaps best exemplified in a longform report published by Aljazeera America in May 2014 by Kate Kilpatrick, a writer, editor, and multimedia producer. Kilpatrick's article, "Treasure Island: The People of Tangier Fear Their Life, Land and Heritage Could Wash Away," includes three particularly narrative tropes that are repeatedly echoed by other articles, magazine features, and broadcast segments. These include: (1) a temporal and geographic positioning of Tangier Island in reference to identifiable American historic events, places, and cultural icons; (2) a temporal and cultural distancing of Tangier from America through its language, way of life, and landscape; and (3) a crisis narrative of current and future climate change impacts, displacement, and disappearance. Each of these narrative reference points is employed both before and after the election of President Trump. However, while the nexus of these three temporal, environmental, and cultural geographic themes are the dominant narrative of media publications in or prior to 2016, in 2017 a fourth political geographic theme supersedes these to become the dominant narrative.

"Most good journalists," Professor of Ethics at Pennsylvania State University Patrick Lee Plaisance writes in *Psychology Today* (2019), "want to connect with audiences through good storytelling that reveals the wider world. They hope, in many cases, to move audiences to empathy." As humans, our ability to understand and share the feelings of another increases with familiarity. The more similar the subject and salience of display in media stories to our own lived experiences, the more empathetic we feel towards the subject. In constructing Tangier as a space and place worthy of an audience's empathy, journalists position the island within familiar cultural, physical, and historical geographies of Americans, both real and imagined. In "Treasure Island," Kilpatrick (2014) roots Tangier's familiarity simultaneously in the past and in the present. Temporally she connects Tangier's history to a readily recognizable American historical figure, Captain John Smith, of Disney's *Pocahontas* fame, early in her article:

> Capt. John Smith discovered Tangier in 1608, naming it and other islands Russell's Isles, after the doctor aboard his ship. How it became known as Tangier in later decades remains a mystery. Pocomoke Indians are believed to have lived – or at least summered – on Tangier before that, and to this day Tangiermen (a label that includes women) find primitive tools, jugs, arrowheads and other artifacts.

These references act as a needle of familiarity, creating a line that orients the audience to connect their experience to that of Tangiermen that measures the degrees of similarity separation. Reference to the history of Captain John Smith's arrival on Tangier Island and its prominent position in American history continuously reappears: in a 2014 Slate article (Storm), a 2015 *Guardian* article (Milman), a 2017 *Washington Post* article (Portnoy), and *Politico Magazine* in 2018 (Swift), among many others. Connecting Tangiermen to one of America's founding exploration heroes provides an intimate similarity between audience and subject. A reader of Aljazeera in New York City was likely taught and knows the same national mythologies of America's time of discovery and settlement that were not only taught, but passed down as local history to the subjects about which she or he is reading.

Once the parallels between audience and subject are established, Tangier as a similar space is transformed into Tangier as an emotive, familiar space. In media reporting, Tangier's narrative not only has a component of shared history with other Americans; it is also captured as a place that holds onto and actively practices that history in a tangible way. Reporting on Tangier's language, livelihoods, and way of life performs a materialization of this shared past world into the present, so as to evoke a sense of American nostalgia. Tangier is anchored as a place that holds something valuable that the rest of America has lost, and in turn evokes a wistful longing for a bygone era. In multiple articles on climate impacts, Tangier is descried as taking a step back in time. In the 2015 *Guardian* article, living on Tangier is described as "stepping back in time. There is no reliable cellphone reception. The island is, officially, alcohol free. Most of the buildings were built before 1930. Doors are left unlocked" (Milman). And again in *Grist* in 2014, Tangier "still feels rooted in the old world: Cell service is unreliable. You can't buy alcohol. Most of the buildings were constructed before WWII" (Herzog). This romanticized version of the past protected and materialized in 21st century Tangier Island is also a key narrative facet of Aljazeera's feature:

> The island's vintage dialect – traced to its early settlers from Cornwall in southwest England – isn't the only thing that sets it apart. Here, families bury their loved ones in their front yards and townsmen meet for

coffee at the power plant every afternoon. Boys spend summers navigating the meandering creeks on their skiffs, and baby shower announcements are taped to public buildings, since the whole island is invited anyway. (Kilpatrick 2014)

Here, America is a missed, almost exoticized landscape; a geography where modern anxieties have no place and the rosy-colored nostalgic haze of innocence and rectitude persevere. As the rush of time has spilled over America's neighborhoods and inundated them with locked doors, national security threats, and modern technology-induced isolation, on Tangier, there is still a sense of community that has seemingly been lost on the mainland, where virtual communication has superseded neighborly friendships. Such a warm atmosphere echoes in stark contrast to the major news stories of 2014, when the threat of ISIS first emerged on the front pages of newspapers, the deadliest outbreak of Ebola had killed more than 6,000 people, and thousands poured into the streets of Ferguson, Missouri after a police officer fatally shot unarmed teenager Michael Brown. This is not to say, however, that Tangier's reproduction in media reporting has no connections to present-day America. This familiarity is carefully balanced between a nostalgia for the past and a shared cultural geography in the 21st century:

> Just about every home has a satellite dish, and on a long weekend in March, 16-year-old Nathan Bonniewell strolled around playing "Wrecking Ball" on his iPad, connected to a handheld speaker. While technology allows the residents to be well versed in life on the mainland, even Miley Cyrus can't expunge their distinctive language. (Kilpatrick 2014)

The temporal closeness constructed combines with a shared nostalgia for a forgotten America to buttress familiarity, and in turn create a pathway for empathy. The reader of Tangier's multimodal climate narrative shares the same cultural geography of modern-day America. Technology, music, and sports – like football, as seen in a photograph accompanying the Aljazeera feature wherein boys play a game on the airport tarmac – all draw a closer imagined connection between viewer and viewed. This present-day familiarity established extends from cultural to geopolitical, as nearly all coverage connects Tangier to its nearest large American city – Washington, D.C. The 2015 Guardian article references that Tangier is a "mere 91 miles from Washington DC," so close that, "Congressional delegations need not look far to witness the ravages of climate change" (Milman). The positioning of Tangier being geographically close to the center of U.S. power and yet still a neglected victim of climate change impacts is repeated in a number of articles in 2014, 2015, and 2016, including the 2015 *Grist* article: "Even though Tangier Island is just 90 miles from Washington, D.C., our leaders there seem happy to ignore it" (Herzog). And the Aljazeera feature uses Tangier's Mayor James "Ooker" Eskridge's own words:

But Ooker Eskridge, the mayor, sees it differently. "A lot of folks serve in the military from here. And they've gone all over the world," he said. "And now Tangier itself is in trouble. We're only a few miles from D.C., and we would like some help here." (Kilpatrick 2014)

Losing Tangier: Fear, guilt, compassion and climate change

As a recognizable American place, currently and historically, Tangier moves from the unknown to the known, capable of soliciting compassion from audiences. It is here in the narrative that climate change impacts are graphed onto this landscaped historic, cultural, and physical geographic familiarity. Pointedly stated in the 2014 *Guardian* article, the victims of climate change are in every American's backyard:

> You don't have to travel to a balmy Pacific island to hear the anguish of people whose land and culture is under threat from climate change. In Virginia's portion of the Chesapeake Bay, the idiosyncratic, and historic, community of Tangier Island is facing an uncertain future as the sea gnaws away at the land beneath them. (Milman)

"This is Trump Island"

Four years after "Treasure Island" was published in Aljazeera, the media outlet published a second feature on Tangier Island. Posted online on December 6, 2018 by reporter Heidi Zhou-Castro, the video "Can Tangier Island be First Climate Change Casualty in the US?" has a comparable beginning to its predecessor. Beginning with an aerial view of the island, the video references its sense of community, unique dialect, and 300-year history all within the first 30 seconds. It then shifts to the disappearance of the island from shoreline erosion, sea level rise, and climate change impacts. "Already," Zhou-Castro reports on a boat as she gestures towards the eroding shoreline, "entire neighborhoods have gone under." In an interview with Mayor Eskridge, the narrative harkens back to a time when a thriving community existed on the island, complete with an imagined visual of kids playing on land that no longer exists. But at 1:20 minutes into the video, a narrative turn is taken that unambiguously departs from news reports prior to 2016. After setting up a narrative of nostalgia and soliciting a sense of compassion and fear of losing the island entirely, reporter Zhou-Castro laments that Tangiermen "disagree with scientists who say that global warming is to blame." For the remainder of the video, the narrative focuses on Tangier's climate change denial, Republican conservatism, and love of President Donald Trump. While the narrative components detailed above are still present in post-2016 media stories on Tangier's fights with climate impacts, they are second to the island's relationship with the Trump Administration's climate inaction, Donald Trump's skepticism of science, and personal relationship with Trump.

304 Victoria Herrmann

Much of this can be traced to a June 9, 2017 CNN special report on Tangier Island's plight against sea level rise, wherein Mayor Ooker Eskridge recorded the message: "Donald Trump, whatever you can do, we welcome any help you can give us" (Gray). Three days later on Monday June 12, 2017 in response to the video, President Trump personally called Mayor Ooker to assure him that "Your island has been there for hundreds of years and I believe your island will be there for hundreds more" (D'Angelo 2017). In the November 2016 presidential election, 87% of Tangier Island voted for Trump, and few residents believe in human-made climate change. The 2017 call from the Oval Office redrew Tangier Island's reproduction in media reporting from a nostalgic, warmhearted American victim of climate change into a climate-denying, Trump-loving island of paradoxes. Where once media narrative elements constructed bridges of similarity, familiarity, and empathy between the reader and Tangier as subject, the introduction of a new, uncomfortable narrative introduces a complicated tension in the viewer/viewed relationship. "Here the love for Trump only comes second to the love for crabs," the 2018 Aljazeera feature concludes, "they say their beliefs simply run deeper than the tides rising around them" (Zhou-Castro).

In the immediate aftermath of President Trump's call to Mayor Eskridge in June 2017, dozens of media outlets covered Tangier Island's plight and climate change denial. The *Washington Post*, NBC, Forbes, Reuters, NPR, and CNN, among others, published shorter news items on the call itself, the science of Tangier's eroding shoreline, and the societal denial of that science. But throughout 2017 and especially 2018, major media outlets reported from, published on, and ultimately rewrote the narrative of Tangier Island' climate-doomed fate through in-depth multimedia coverage. On October 8, 2018 PBS dedicated a ten-minute segment to answer the question, "Will the traditions of tiny Tangier Island survive or sink?" Reporter John Yang traveled to Tangier to visually capture the historic livelihood of the island's watermen, following boats and zooming in on overflowing pots of Chesapeake Blue Crabs. Again here, PBS dedicates the first five minutes to introducing the standard narrative tropes of Tangier. As the camera pans over the cemetery, Yang notes that Tangier is "a place so isolated that virtually all residents are descended from the first settlers who arrived in 1778. The crowded cemeteries are filled with Parks, Pruitts and Crocketts" and the living Tangiermen echo the "speech of their ancestors who came from the Southwestern coast of England. The isolation has also fostered an unusually strong bond among its residents." The sense of community and foundation upon which a nostalgic empathy can be built is also provided through an interview with local author Earl Swift:

> I didn't understand how different the sense of community, the meaning of community is here. To reach the rest of America requires effort and time and, at certain times of the year, a certain amount of danger. (Yang 2018)

The narrative then turns to layer the new narrative of climate denial, a love of President Trump, and an uncertain future onto the existing foundation:

> **John Yang:** The debate has drawn national attention, largely because 87 percent of the island's voters went for President Trump, a climate change skeptic. That prompted CNN to visit last summer.
> **James "Ooker" Eskridge:** I love Trump as much as any family member I got.
> **John Yang:** After the broadcast, the president called Eskridge and told him the island would be around for hundreds of years more.

Reiterated in many forms, like a 2018 *National Geographic* article, "Tiny U.S. Island is Drowning. Residents Deny the Reason" (Worrall), and a 2018 *Politico Magazine* feature, "The Doomed Island that Loves Trump" (Swift), this new narrative frames Tangier as a less similar, though still knowable frame. It rewrites the points of connection earlier articles had made about the island, so that framings of a rural, conservative white American town that holds onto a foregone past exist in the same space as Make America Great Again.

A wall to empathy: Transforming Tangier's emotional geography

Prior to the 2016 election, Tangier Island and the U.S. mainland were grouped together in media narrations through a shared cultural, historic, and physical American geography that evoked tendencies to care about and help Tangier Island from unavoidable climate change impacts. The ingrouping of Tangier was a critical component for motivating an emotional response for readers to alleviate the suffering, loss, and damage from climate change documented on the island. Nonetheless, empathic responses are rare and fragile when a group or individual is an "other," an outgroup member that is known but not similar. "Failures of empathy are especially likely if the sufferer is socially distant, for example, a member of a different social or cultural group," psychologists Mina Cikara, Emile Bruneau, and Rebecca Saxe find in a 2011 survey of empathy research in psychological sciences (p. 4). "In fact, depending on the victim, we may feel secretly pleased about their misfortunes." A consumer of American news related to Tangier Island is less likely to detect and attend to their suffering when Tangier's victims are portrayed as distant in space, time, or kinship, or across racial, political, or social group boundaries (Batson and Ahmad 2009).

The 2016 election, buttressed by the 2017 call by President Trump to Tangier's mayor, redrew the emotional geographies of the island and recast its residents into an outgroup to many American audiences of mass media reporting. The powerful narrative presented to American audiences to care for and help fellow Americans living on Tangier Island was reconfigured, disrupting the perception of familiarity and similarity that in turn dampened empathetic responses and

306 Victoria Herrmann

led to indifference towards the suffering of the now-outgroup Tangiermen. This abrupt change is well documented by aforementioned local author Earl Swift in his 2018 *Politico Magazine* feature:

> But almost immediately CNN's Twitter account blew up with comments from viewers astounded that the island voted overwhelmingly for a man who derides the science behind sea-level rise. "I have NO sympathy for the people of Tangier Island," one wrote. "If they voted 87% for that IDIOT, they are getting what they ASKED FOR! GOOD LUCK." "Dear Tangier Island, Va: Be swallowed by the sea," another read. "You're all #Trump supporters and deserve what Nature gives you: submersion."
>
> So they went, screen after screen: "What do you call a sinking island of Trump supporters? A good start." And: "Hard to be empathetic for residents, who are objectively stupid and proud of it." And: "Hope they know how to swim." And this: "Tangier Island in MD?? Seriously. It's a test tube for inbreeding."

In part, the elevation of Tangier Island's support for President Trump, Republican conservatism, and climate change denial becomes the dominant narrative and subordinates the danger that sea level rise, erosion, and subsidence pose for the existence of the island. The grief of losing Tangier's unique culture, language, history, and social cohesion is lessened after its disappearing landscapes were renamed Trump Island. In this, author Swift notes, there is real sorrow on Tangier Island. "The islanders I spoke with, and those whose Facebook accounts I follow," Swift wrote in 2018 for *Politico Magazine*, "were dumbstruck by the ferocity of this invective from strangers, and confused – heartsick, disgusted, alarmed, even – that their support for Trump had moved fellow Americans to wish them dead." Most estimates give Tangier 50 years before its 500 residents will be forced to leave their homes behind in search of higher land. A major storm event could cause that abandonment to happen sooner. Despite its ruinous future, the once sympathetic narratives of the island written and reported by journalists have disappeared, replaced by ambivalence, contempt, and a dose of schadenfreude.

Climate change reporting in Trump's America

Since the 2016 election, Democratic voters from across the country have wrestled with questions of finding empathy for Trump supporters. On November 9, 2016, *The Atlantic* published a reader's note titled "Empathizing with Trump Supporters Right Now", which argued for understanding and empathy for American neighbors who may have been politically out-grouped by voting for Donald Trump (Bodenne). So too did the *New York Times* in their Opinion publication, "Stop Shaming Trump Supporters" (Lerner 2016), and WBUR with the commentary "I Keep Trying to Understand Trump Voters, But I keep

Failing" (Schlack 2018). The media's role, in one sense, is to make the unknown known. It is to illuminate human and physical geographies that still lay beyond their readers' lived experiences. Journalism is to shed light upon the underbelly of society's ills, to bring distant cultures and landscapes into focus. In 2016, journalists in all mediums explored the unknowns of Trump country. Through pen and lens, reporters tried to make the unknown known by publishing extensive profiles on Trump's poor, rural white base. In President Trump's first year in office, *The New Yorker* published stories on rural West Virginian and Coloradan Trump voters, *The New York Times* on disgruntled poor white Americans in the Midwest and unemployed coal miners in Appalachia, and *The Washington Post* on Tennessee's jovial and warmhearted Trump-supporting towns. The Associated Press even has a special section of reporting titled Trump Country. Though this near-obsessive focus on the forgotten rural geographies of Trump's America spilled onto Tangier Island with the President's June 2017 phone call, it is one strand in a much larger tapestry of how audiences of American media come to know, make judgements about, and feel for Trump voters today.

Reporting of Tangier Island straddles the gap between sympathetic profile and contemptuous narration of a climate-denying community disappearing from climate impacts. News narratives still attempt to establish a sense of familiarity, but the wordsmithing of pre-2016 stories of a kindly community just off the coast of Virginia fall away to be replaced by Trump flags and bumper stickers. But Tangier is not alone in this valley between mountains of empathy and apathy. It is a shared geography with other Trump-voting regions at risk to climate change impacts. A 2019 Brookings Institute report found that:

> Many of the states with the most to lose from climate change voted heavily for Donald Trump in 2016, thereby electing a president who has disavowed his own government's National Climate Assessment – the most careful government evaluation of climate risks ever done – and has systematically moved to dismantle former-President Barack Obama's foreign policy and regulatory initiatives to reduce carbon emissions. (Muro, Victor, and Whiton)

Using data from Climate Impact Lab, Brookings analysts found that nine of the ten states contending with the highest losses of county income from climate change impacts voted for President Trump in 2016, including Florida, Mississippi, Louisiana, Arkansas, and Alabama. It concluded that "Fifteen of the 16 highest-harm states were also red" (Muro, Victor, and Whiton 2019). In Spring 2019, record rainfall prevented farmers from planting crops across the largely conservative central plains and historic river flooding cost more than $1 billion in damage from Iowa to Mississippi. These natural disasters, increased in frequency and intensity from global climate change, generated a flurry of Trump Country narratives of climate-denying, impact-affected communities. In a June 2019 NPR report titled, "'We All Owe Al Gore An Apology': More

308 Victoria Herrmann

People See Climate Change In Record Flooding," journalist Nathan Rott narrates the tension felt by nearly two dozen conservative people in Oklahoma and Arkansas who believe that the climate was changing but do not believe that it is human-made.

From Tangier to Iowa, Trump voters are facing the consequences of climate change; and from New York to San Francisco, readers of America's major news outlets are deciding whether conservative climate victims are worthy of sympathy. In an era inundated with negative news narratives, humans have become "cognitive and emotional 'misers,' calculating how much energy we're willing to spend connecting with others" (Koole 2009). When given a choice to empathize with those who do not belong in their immediate social, political, or cultural group, recent research shows that people avoid empathy because of its perceived cognitive effort. "When given the opportunity to share in the experiences of strangers, people chose to turn away" (Cameron et al. 2019, p. 11). As Tangier Island transforms into Trump Island – as its inhabitants move from familiar to other – American readers are turning away. And as tens of millions of Trump voters across red states face the unbridled catastrophe of a warming world, American readers will face their own choice of empathy or apathy.

In 2017 after President Trump called Mayor Ooker, I wrote a commentary for Huffington Post titled "Bringing The Climate Sceptics On Board." In it, I wrote:

> As a climate change researcher, I am no fan of Donald Trump, or the current Republican Party, or climate change deniers. When confronted with Trump-loving climate sceptics on Tangier Island, it was easy to choose apathy over empathy – to call islanders like Ooker ignorant instead of vulnerable.
>
> But reacting indifferently towards Trump supporters at-risk to climate change is dangerous. It negates our opportunity to demand federal support for the slow-onset natural disasters facing all Americans. If I left the island and instead focused my project exclusively on threatened communities that didn't make me uncomfortable, I would also have to stop my work in Dauphin Island, Alabama, in Terrebonne Parish, Louisiana, and with my own family on the Jersey Shore.
>
> If I have learned one thing from my travels across the US' eroding edges it is this: climate change is an American story. It is an issue that disrupts the lives of Americans across our country. And even if residents don't believe in climate change, they have an intimate, localized understanding of its effects and a vision for what adaptation strategies will work best for their hometowns.

Two years have passed since penning that commentary, two years of the Trump Administration's inaction on climate change, and two years of inaction on Trump's promise to build a wall for Tangier Island. Tangier is four feet above sea level. It is just over one square mile in size, and loses 16 feet of land yearly to subsidence and coastal erosion. News stories are, at their core, accounts of events unfolding around us told for entertainment. Their narratives hold the immense ability to bring groups together, or to create distance between them. In 2017, I ended my commentary with a call to action to remold our ingroup of familiarity to include Tangiermen – to extend our empathy to Trump Island. "If we are to truly build national momentum to address the impacts of climate change on America in its entirety, we need everyone to be part of the conversation today – Trump-loving, climate-sceptic Tangier Islanders included." Spending two years consuming narrations distancing the island's residents from my own lived experiences, I cannot be certain that my own conclusion still resonates with the new, reconfigured narrative graphed onto the once familiar geographies of Tangier.

References

Bodenne, C. 2018. Empathizing with Trump voters right now. *The Atlantic* (Nov. 9). www.theatlantic.com/notes/2016/11/empathizing-with-trump-supporters-right-now/507104/

Batson, C., and N. Ahmad. 2009. Using empathy to improve intergroup attitudes and relations. *Social Issues and Policy Review* 3(1): 141–177.

Cikara, M., E. Bruneau, and R. Saxe. 2011. Us and them: Intergroup failures of empathy. *Current Directions in Psychological Science* 20(3): 149–153.

Cameron, C., C. Hutcherson, A. Ferguson, J. Scheffer, E. Hadjiandreou, and M. Inzlicht. 2019. Empathy is hard work: People choose to avoid empathy because of its cognitive costs. *Journal of Experimental Psychology: General* 148(6): 962–976.

D'Angelo, C. 2017. Trump tells mayor of sinking U.S. island not to worry about climate change. *Huffington Post* (June 13). www.huffpost.com/entry/trump-tangier-island-mayor-climate-change_n_59406a8ce4b09ad4fbe3fa03

Gray, J. 2017. Reporter's Notebook: Visiting the disappearing Tangier Island. *CNN* (June 9). www.cnn.com/2017/06/09/us/weather-tangier-island/index.html

Herrmann, V. 2017. Bringing the climate sceptics on board. *Huffington Post* (June 19). www.huffingtonpost.co.uk/gates-cambridge-scholars/climate-change_b_17202040.html

Herzog, K. 2015 Climate change threatens to swamp historic Chesapeake island. *Grist* (Dec. 10). https://grist.org/climate-energy/climate-change-threatens-to-swamp-historic-chesapeake-island/

Kilpatrick, K. 2014. Treasure Island: The people of Tangier fear their life, land and heritage could wash away. *Aljazeera America* (May 11). http://projects.aljazeera.com/2014/tangier-island/

Koole, S. 2009. The psychology of emotion regulation: An integrative review. *Cognition and Emotion* 23(1): 4–41.

Lerner, M. 2016. Stop shaming Trump supporters. *New York Times* (Nov. 9). www.nytimes.com/interactive/projects/cp/opinion/election-night-2016

Milman, O. 2015. Climate change could leave Chesapeake Bay island uninhabitable in 50 years. *The Guardian* (Dec. 10). www.theguardian.com/environment/2015/dec/10/climate-change-chesapeake-bay-tangier-island

Muro, M., D. Victor, and J. Whiton. 2019. How the geography of climate damage could make the politics less polarizing. *The Brookings Institution* (Jan. 29). www.brookings.edu/research/how-the-geography-of-climate-damage-could-make-the-politics-less-polarizing/

Plaisance, P. 2019. The dilemma of empathy and the news. *Psychology Today* (May 9). www.psychologytoday.com/us/blog/virtue-in-the-media-world/201905/the-dilemma-empathy-and-the-news?amp

Portnoy, Jeana. 2017. Why Senator Kaine wants to save Trump Country from sinking into the Chesapeake. *Washington Post* (Sept. 2). www.washingtonpost.com/local/virginia-politics/why-sen-kaine-wants-to-save-trump-country-from-sinking-into-the-chesapeake/2017/09/02/906d0016-8695-11e7-961d-2f373b3977ee_story.html

Rott, N. 2019. 'We all owe Al Gore an apology': More people see climate change in record flooding. *NPR* (June 8). www.npr.org/2019/06/08/730456004/more-people-see-climate-change-in-record-floods-and-extreme-weather-will-that-me

Schlack, J. 2018. I keep trying to understand Trump voters, but I keep failing. *WBUR* (Aug. 8). www.wbur.org/cognoscenti/2018/08/08/trump-voters-julie-wittes-schlack

Storm, C. 2014. On Tangier, a disappearing island. *Slate.com* (Sept. 11). https://slate.com/business/2014/09/tangier-an-island-in-the-chesapeake-bay-is-disappearing-underwater-and-dying.html

Swift, E. 2018. The doomed island that loves Trump. *Politico* (Aug. 19). www.politico.com/magazine/story/2018/08/19/tangier-island-donald-trump-2016-219349

Worrall, S. 2018. Tiny U.S. island is drowning. Residents deny the reason. *National Geographic* (Sept.11).www.nationalgeographic.com.au/nature/tiny-us-island-is-drowning-residents-deny-the-reason.aspx

Yang, J. 2018. Will the traditions of tiny Tangier Island survive or sink? *PBS News Hour* (Oct. 8). www.pbs.org/newshour/show/will-the-traditions-of-tiny-tangier-island-survive-or-sink

Zhou-Castro, H. 2018. Can Tangier Island be first climate change casualty in the US? *Aljazeera* (Dec. 6). www.aljazeera.com/news/2018/12/tangier-island-climate-change-casualty-us-181206111501734.html

18

THE EMOTIONAL REGIME OF APATHY, TRUMP, AND CLIMATE INJUSTICE

Nino Antadze

On January 28, 2019, Donald Trump tweeted:

> In the beautiful Midwest, windchill temperatures are reaching minus 60 degrees, the coldest ever recorded. In coming days, expected to get even colder. People can't last outside even for minutes. What the hell is going on with Global Waming [sic]? Please come back fast, we need you! (Trump 2019)

The Canadian journalist Daniel Dale, while retweeting the above, commented "Trump's climate-trolling is such obvious outrage bait that you almost want to ignore it, but it's also self-provided evidence of one of the most significant ignorance crises of this presidency" (Dale 2019). This *ignorance crisis* implies that President Trump fully dismisses not only the dangers posed by anthropogenic climate change but also the very existence of the phenomenon. And thus, he ignores the fact that millions of people on the planet have already been negatively affected by climate change, and for many it has become an existential threat.

In this chapter I argue that Donald Trump not only exemplifies a personal apathy toward the past, present, and future human and non-human victims of climate change, but also that through his political platform as president he encourages and enables an institutionalized apathy – which I refer to as *the emotional regime of apathy* – via specific actions and decisions that disregard the suffering of those particularly vulnerable in the face of the unfolding climate crisis. Drawing on Norgaard's (2011) account of climate denial in Norway, I use the term *apathy* to mean ignorance, nonresponse, and nonaction in regard to climate change. However, unlike public apathy, the emotional regime of apathy entails the normalization of ignorance and nonresponse to others through various policy decisions. While discussing the connection between apathy, and more broadly

312 Nino Antadze

emotions, and political processes, I follow the lead of Berezin (2002, p. 37), who points out that "what is interesting from a social science perspective is not that we have emotions but the mechanisms that transpose these emotions into some sort of action or institutional arrangement." While the reasons behind the Trump administration's environmental agenda can be explored from various standpoints – the venue of research that has been burgeoning for the past couple of years (Pulido et al. 2019; Bomberg 2017; Selby 2019; Sparke and Bessner 2019; Hejny 2018) – the aim of this analysis is to discuss the dangers of institutionalized apathy in exacerbating climate injustice.

In what follows I first detail what the emotional regime of apathy implies in relation to climate change. Next, I discuss the aftermath of Hurricane Maria in Puerto Rico and the decision to withdraw from the Paris Climate Agreement to illustrate how the emotional regime of apathy has penetrated the Trump administration's political decision-making process.

The emotional regime of apathy and climate injustice

The view that emotions are an important ingredient "of all social actions and social relations" (Goodwin, Jasper, and Polletta 2001, p. 9) has been gaining momentum across the social sciences, including sociology (Collins 2005; Stets and Turner 2014), scholarship on social movements (Collins 2001; Goodwin et al. 2004; Jasper 2011), organization and management studies (Ashkanasy, Humphrey, and Huy 2017; Fan and Zietsma 2017; de Holan, Willi, and Fernández 2017; Voronov and Weber 2016), human geography (Davidson, Bondi, and Smith 2005; Graybill 2019), and political ecology (González-Hidalgo and Zografos 2020; Sultana 2015).

Historically in political science the interplay between emotions and politics has been a relatively unexplored domain (Redlawsk 2006; Clarke, Hoggett, and Thompson 2006c). Starting with the Aristotelian distinction between *pathos* and *logos*, Western thought has embraced the passion vs. reason or emotion vs. cognition duality (Mercer 2006). Political scientists have largely followed this logic and viewed emotions either as epiphenomenal or as a source of mistakes and irrational decisions (Mercer 2006). According to Redlawsk (2006, p. 3), "while it may not be completely fair to say that feeling has been ignored, emotion has often been conceptualized thinly as the outcome of a cognitive process, rather than as an integral part of decision making." However, this trend has been changing, and scholars have been probing into the connections between politics and emotions (Brader and Marcus 2013; Clarke, Hoggett, and Thompson 2006a). This interdisciplinary inquiry bridges insights from political psychology, cognitive and social psychology, sociology, and neurophysiology (Redlawsk 2006). In terms of the study of specific emotions and their role in political processes, political scientists have explored, among others, hope, joy, pride, fear, anxiety, anger, disgust, hatred, shame, guilt, compassion, and envy (Brader and Marcus 2013; Clarke, Hoggett, and Thompson 2006c). Scholars also note that some emotions may be

The emotional regime of apathy **313**

more likely to emerge or can be more relevant in a particular political setting than others, and thus have more profound political consequences (Berezin 2002). While this book chapter does not aim to contribute to political psychology, it underscores the importance that the above scholarship has assigned to emotions for understanding political processes. Of particular interest to this inquiry is how emotion "contributes to collective macro-level processes and outcomes" (Berezin 2002, p. 33), specifically the relationship between emotions and institutions of government (Clarke, Hoggett, and Thompson 2006b).

In order to encapsulate this collective orientation of the emotion-politics interplay, I draw on Reddy's (2001) notion of an "emotional regime" to discuss the dangers of institutionalized apathy in exacerbating climate injustice. "Emotional regime" implies a certain "normative order for emotions" (Reddy 2001, p. 124), that is, "dominant modes for acceptable emotional thought and expression as created and enforced by governments and societies" (Garrido and Davidson 2016, p. 65). "'Emotional regimes' refer to the discursive practices and power relations prescribing specific 'emotional rules', ideals, rituals and vocabularies" (Zembylas 2017, p. 501). Two aspects of this definition are noteworthy: first, there is a close connection between emotional regimes and political institutions; and second, emotional regimes are embedded in historical periods and cultural contexts (Reddy 2001; Garrido and Davidson 2016; Wettergren 2009).

Apathy toward others represents the cornerstone of the emotional regime enacted and mainstreamed by the Trump administration. In this analysis apathy is treated not only as a personal sentiment of Donald Trump but also as what Olson (2016, p. 5) calls "a political emotion," which can "move individuals and collectivities toward certain forms of moral action" and thus shape institutions. While expressed performatively and discursively by President Trump through his numerous tweets and public statements, apathy as a political emotion in relation to climate change is a widespread sentiment among the GOP leadership (Selby 2019; Hejny 2018) as well and is a representation of deeply rooted views and values (Selby 2019; Jotzo, Depledge, and Winkler 2018).

Therefore, the political landscapes of Donald Trump, the subject of this volume, have an emotional dimension, which should be acknowledged and analyzed. As González-Hidalgo and Zografos (2020, p. 241) note, "considering everyday emotions in political processes can help move beyond individualised understandings of emotions, towards considering them as part of constellations of wider individual and collective landscapes, tied to power geometries and permeated by class, gender, sexuality, and ethnicity." The latter point on power geometries and differentiating various groups in society is central to understanding the emotional regime of apathy of the Trump administration: apathy is selectively applied to "others." "Other" can be characterized by various signs of difference, such as race, ethnicity, religion, nationality, income, and location. It should be noted that the disregard towards "others" is not limited only to climate change-related decisions or the environmental agenda more generally, but rather is one of the key characteristics of the Trump presidency.

As a result, the emotional regime of apathy permeating the political land-scapes of Donald Trump is conditioned by difference and thus hinders the ability of those "'that do not count' to be counted, named, and recognised" (González-Hidalgo and Zografos 2019; Swyngedouw 2014, p. 129). Yet it is well estab-lished that those who are already marginalized and disadvantaged will suffer most from environmental degradation generally, and climate change-related impacts specifically (Agyeman et al. 2016). It has been widely acknowledged that the causes and impacts of climate change have distributive logic, and therefore the considerations of justice and equity are central to climate change–related decision-making processes. As Harlan et al. (2015) explain, climate change is fundamentally a justice issue because: 1) wealthier states and people emit sig-nificantly more greenhouse gasses; 2) poor and marginalized communities are particularly vulnerable to the impacts of climate change; and 3) climate change policies, including emission reduction and climate adaptation policies, have une-qual consequences for different people and communities. The emotional regime of apathy, therefore, implies not only the denouncement of the severity of cli-mate change as a problem but also the ignorance of the moral implications of climate change, specifically as they relate to the issues of justice and equity. By denouncing the connection between climate change and justice considerations, the emotional regime of apathy institutionalizes a disregard for those particularly vulnerable to the unfolding climate crisis.

In what follows I describe how the emotional regime of apathy manifests in specific actions and decisions made by the Trump administration using as examples the response to Hurricane Maria in Puerto Rico and the decision to withdraw from the Paris Climate Agreement.

The emotional regime of apathy and the response to Hurricane Maria in Puerto Rico

It is now acknowledged that the unusually powerful Atlantic hurricane season of 2017 can be attributed to climate change (Sneed 2017). As a small island experi-encing economic hardship, outdated infrastructure, outmigration, and weak and ever-shrinking social services, as well as hosting multiple Superfund sites, Puerto Rico was particularly vulnerable as it faced first Hurricane Irma and shortly afterward the even more powerful Hurricane Maria. As a result of Hurricane Maria and its aftermath, it is estimated that thousands of people lost their lives and more than 200,000 fled the island, the economic loss exceeded $90 billion, and almost the entire electric grid was destroyed (García-López 2018). It would be fair to say that those who, as a result of the 2017 Atlantic hurricane season, died in Puerto Rico, fled the island, or found themselves in a desperate situation are the victims of climate change. The injustice here is manifested in the increas-ing vulnerability of already disadvantaged people, who have contributed much less to causing climate change in the first place. Climate change can be seen "as simply another, if broader, environmental manifestation of social injustice"

(Schlosberg 2013, p. 46). Climate injustice, therefore, is an additional layer to the web of the political and historical processes creating and exacerbating inequality in Puerto Rico.

The historical processes that have unfolded in Puerto Rico and the policy decisions made by the U.S. government over the past century can be described as lacking compassion and genuine interest in the long-term wellbeing of the island (Cabán 2019; Cortés 2018; García-López 2018; Brown et al. 2018). Therefore, the emotional regime of apathy may not be a completely new phenomenon; rather it has been forged gradually and is deeply embedded in historical and cultural contexts. Yet the Trump administration's reaction to the aftermath of Hurricane Maria in Puerto Rico made the emotional regime of apathy ever more visible.

President Trump's lack of emotional response to the disaster victims was well illustrated by his remarks and tweets. While visiting the island on October 3, 2017, he praised the Federal Emergency Management Agency (FEMA), blamed the island for its debt and economic hardship, and said that there were far fewer deaths in Puerto Rico compared to Hurricane Katrina in New Orleans (Taylor 2017). The train of insensitive remarks continued and culminated in a now infamous scene in which President Trump tossed rolls of paper towels to the hurricane victims (Nakamura and Parker 2018). His rhetoric portrayed Puerto Ricans as wanting their problems solved by the U.S. without putting in any effort themselves. On September 30, 2017, Trump tweeted that Puerto Ricans "want everything done for them" (Lloréns 2018). In March 2019 Trump questioned the need to provide additional aid to Puerto Rico while claiming that "Puerto Rico has been taken care of better by Donald Trump than by any living human being and I think the people of Puerto Rico understand" (Acosta and Liptak 2019). Such an attitude toward the victims of Hurricane Maria was described as a manifestation of his "self-absorbed" (Nakamura and Parker 2018) and "self-centered" (Krugman 2018) leadership. San Juan Mayor Carmen Yulín Cruz Soto noted that "When faced with a devastating human crisis, Trump augmented it because he made it about himself, not about saving our lives" (Acosta and Liptak 2019).

The case of Hurricane Maria in Puerto Rico reveals not only President Trump's individual sentiment of apathy toward the hurricane victims but also how the emotional regime of apathy is upheld through specific policy actions and decisions, and gets embedded into institutions and their practices and routines. For example, in the aftermath of Hurricane Maria, the response of federal agencies to the disaster was widely criticized (Cabán 2019; García-López 2018). In an unusual move, Oxfam (2017) commented on the post-disaster response in Puerto Rico, stating:

> Oxfam has monitored the response in Puerto Rico closely, and we are outraged at the slow and inadequate response the US Government has mounted in Puerto Rico. Clean water, food, fuel, electricity, and health care are in desperately short supply and quickly dwindling, and we're

hearing excuses and criticism from the administration instead of a cohesive and compassionate response. The US has more than enough resources to mobilize an emergency response but has failed to do so in a swift and robust manner.

Similarly, in a report issued in December 2017, Refugees International concluded that "the response to the catastrophic disaster in Puerto Rico lacked the requisite leadership from the highest levels of the U.S. government necessary to support a more effective, timely response by FEMA" (Thomas 2017). FEMA was not the only part of the government that exhibited a delayed response to the disaster. President Trump held the first meeting in the Situation Room on September 26, six days after Hurricane Maria hit, and the Trump administration waived the Jones Act (Carey 2017) two days after that, on September 28 (Holmqvist 2018). Between September 20 and September 26 President Trump spent four days at his private golf club in New Jersey (Phillips et al. 2017).

The case of Hurricane Maria in Puerto Rico is a vivid example of the emotional regime of apathy and its effects on the victims of climate change. Certainly, not everyone who works in the U.S. federal government or FEMA is insensitive and ignorant to the suffering of others, and apathy is not the only reason why the response to Hurricane Maria was inadequate. But the emotional regime of apathy implies that the institutions of government are designed and run to display apathy; institutions are devoid of the human emotions that connect them to people, and as a result, they become ineffective in addressing their problems and concerns.

Whereas the response to Hurricane Maria in Puerto Rico shows how the emotional regime of apathy affected a certain group in a specific place and time, the next example, the decision to withdraw from the Paris Climate Agreement, shows that the emotional regime of apathy can expand much more widely.

The emotional regime of apathy and the decision to withdraw from the Paris Climate Agreement

In June 2017 President Trump announced that the U.S. would withdraw from the Paris Climate Agreement, claiming that "the Paris Accord would undermine our economy, hamstring our workers, weaken our sovereignty, impose unacceptable legal risks, and put us at a permanent disadvantage to the other countries of the world" (The White House 2017).

Despite its many shortcomings, the Paris Climate Agreement is a significant step forward in activating global climate action. Symbolically and politically it is an important milestone after years of unsuccessful attempts to find common ground in regard to addressing climate action. Although it may not have immediate tangible consequences (Selby 2019) and may pose "a seriously debilitating but not necessarily fatal blow" to global climate action (Bomberg 2017, p. 956), the decision to withdraw from the Paris Climate Agreement is likely to result in long-term and indirect political implications, especially for those who are and will be particularly vulnerable to climate change-related impacts (Selby 2019).

In his analysis, Selby (2019, p. 473) discusses how the Trump administration not only changes climate change policy but also further enhances "extant hierarchies and inequalities." Specifically, Selby (2019, p. 474) details four areas where the impact will be felt:

> the worldwide inadequacy of greenhouse gas (GHG) emissions reduction targets and implementation efforts; parallel to this, the inadequacy of contemporary climate financing; third, the deepening embrace between populist conservatism, nationalism, and opposition to action on climate change; and not least, the current boom in global oil and gas production which, crucially, is being led by the US.

Urpelainen and Van de Graaf (2018) note that particularly damaging to global climate action may be the Trump administration's refusal to contribute any further to the Green Climate Fund, a multilateral fund that provides financial assistance to developing countries for climate mitigation and adaptation (Saad 2018). The nationally determined contributions under the Paris Climate Agreement made by many developing countries are dependent on this financial assistance (Selby 2019). Retracting U.S. participation in climate change finance will have an immediate impact on countries with developing and emerging economies in their efforts to tackle and adapt to climate change, and may also decrease their ambition to lower emissions and thus jeopardize the pledge-and-review system of the Paris Climate Agreement (Urpelainen and Van de Graaf 2018). Long term, the U.S. decision to walk back climate finance commitments may hinder global climate cooperation by decreasing trust between industrialized countries and developing and emerging economies (Urpelainen and Van de Graaf 2018). The justice implication of the decision to withdraw from the Paris Climate Agreement and roll back U.S. climate change commitments can be illustrated by the recent finding by Chen et al. (2018, p. 852), who conclude that "without US participation, increased reduction efforts are required for the rest of the world, including developing countries, in order to achieve the 2°C goal, resulting in 18% higher global cumulative mitigation costs from 2015 to 2100."

Trump's decision to withdraw from the Paris Climate Agreement is a manifestation of the emotional regime of apathy – an apathy toward not only vulnerable communities, such as those in Puerto Rico, but also spatially and temporally distant others, such as generations not yet born and the non-human others whose bodies and lives have been changing due to human actions (Alaimo 2016). By disclaiming any responsibility for the U.S. to act on climate change, Trump has fully embraced the emotional regime of apathy. Saad (2018, p. 49) refers to this phenomenon as "a callous political worldview" and notes that "Trump's election to the highest political office has raised the prominence and legitimacy of this worldview in the mainstream."

318 Nino Antadze

Conclusion

In this chapter I argue that within the context of climate change, the political landscape of President Trump is characterized by the emotional regime of apathy in regard to those who are and will be most affected by the unfolding climate crisis. The chapter underlines that the major danger is not the personal sentiment of Donald Trump (although empathy is considered to be an important component of leadership (Goleman 2004)) but the fact that apathy becomes a political emotion, which penetrates institutions of government and decision-making processes. The Trump administration's response to Hurricane Maria in Puerto Rico and its decision to withdraw from the Paris Climate Agreement are discussed to illustrate how the emotional regime of apathy translates into specific actions and decisions.

More research needs to be done on how the emotional tone set by the Trump administration may affect climate change policy developments. An interesting question in this regard is about the long-term ramifications of the emotional regime of apathy of the Trump presidency; that is, how the emotional regime of apathy can influence what Williams (1977) calls "structures of feeling" or what Graybill (2019, p. 391) refers to as "a wider societal emotional schema" regarding climate change. (For a discussion of the "structures of feeling" in relation to politics see Clarke, Hoggett, and Thompson 2006c.) This work could respond to the recent calls to advance research about the connections between emotional geographies and political regimes, "especially where political choices and policy are related to resource governance and energy (in)justice" (Graybill 2019, p. 392).

Last, although the Trump administration provides a vivid example of what the emotional regime of apathy looks like, the phenomenon is not limited to the United States. Unfortunately, we can observe similar trends in other parts of the world, although the processes, actors, and contexts are different. The broader manifestation of the emotional regime of apathy creates a political-emotional context that exacerbates climate injustice – the political processes, actions, and decisions that are stripped from other caring sentiments cannot lead to just and transformative climate action. The Trump presidency should serve as an important warning to avoid this possibility.

References

Acosta, J., and K. Liptak. 2019. Exclusive: Puerto Rico governor warns White House over funding. *CNN* (March 28). www.cnn.com/2019/03/28/politics/ricardo-rossell-donald-trump-puerto-rico-funding/index.html

Agyeman, J., D. Schlosberg, L. Craven, and C. Matthews. 2016. Trends and directions in environmental justice: From inequity to everyday life, community, and just sustainabilities. *Annual Review of Environment and Resources* 41(1): 321–340.

Alaimo, S. 2016. *Exposed: Environmental Politics and Pleasures in Posthuman Times.* Minneapolis: University of Minnesota Press.

Ashkanasy, N., R. Humphrey, and Q. Huy. 2017. Integrating emotions and affect in theories of management. *Academy of Management Review* 42(2): 175–189.

Berezin, M. 2002. Secure states: Towards a political sociology of emotion. *Sociological Review* 50(2 suppl): 33–52.

Bomberg, E. 2017. Environmental politics in the Trump era: An early assessment. *Environmental Politics* 26(5): 956–963.

Brader, T., and G. Marcus. 2013. Emotion and political psychology. In L. Huddy, D. O. Sears, and J. Levy (eds.) *The Oxford Handbook of Political Psychology*. 2nd ed. pp. 165–204. Oxford, UK: Oxford University Press.

Brown, P., C. Vélez Vega, C. Murphy, M. Welton, H. Torres, Z. Rosario, A. Alshawabkeh, J. Cordero, I. Padilla, and J. Meeker. 2018. Hurricanes and the environmental justice island: Irma and Maria in Puerto Rico. *Environmental Justice* 11(4): 148–153.

Cabán, P. 2019. Hurricane Maria's aftermath: Redefining Puerto Rico's colonial status? *Current History* 118(805): 43–49.

Carey, T. 2017. The Jones Act, explained (and what waiving it means for Puerto Rico). *PBS NewsHour* (Sept. 29). www.pbs.org/newshour/nation/jones-act-explained-waiving-means-puerto-rico

Chen, H., L. Wang, W. Chen, Y. Luo, Y. Wang, and S. Zhou. 2018. The global impacts of US climate policy: A model simulation using GCAM-TU and MAGICC. *Climate Policy* 18(7): 852–862.

Clarke, S., P. Hoggett, and S. Thompson (eds.) 2006a. *Emotion, Politics and Society*. New York: Palgrave Macmillan.

Clarke, S., P. Hoggett, and S. Thompson. 2006b. Moving forward in the study of emotions: Some conclusions. In S. Clarke, P. Hoggett, and S. Thompson (eds.) *Emotion, Politics and Society*. pp. 162–175. New York: Palgrave Macmillan.

Clarke, S., P. Hoggett, and S. Thompson. 2006c. The study of emotion: An introduction. In S. Clarke, P. Hoggett, and S. Thompson (eds.) *Emotion, Politics and Society*. pp. 3–13. New York: Palgrave Macmillan.

Collins, R. 2001. Social movements and the focus on emotional attention. In J. Goodwin, J. Jasper, and F. Polletta (eds.) *Passionate Politics. Emotions and Social Movements*. pp. 27–44. Chicago: University of Chicago Press.

Collins, R. 2005. *Interaction Ritual Chains*. Princeton, NJ: Princeton University Press.

Cortés, J. 2018. Puerto Rico: Hurricane Maria and the promise of disposability. *Capitalism Nature Socialism* 29(3): 1–8.

Dale, D. 2019. Trump's climate-trolling is such obvious outrage bait that you almost want to ignore it, but it's also self-provided [tweet]. (Jan. 28). https://twitter.com/ddale8/status/1090081739152785409

Davidson, J., L. Bondi, and M. Smith (eds.) 2005. *Emotional Geographies*. Aldershot, UK and Burlington, VT: Ashgate.

Fan, G., and C. Zietsma. 2017. Constructing a shared governance logic: The role of emotions in enabling dually embedded agency. *Academy of Management Journal* 60(6): 2321–2351.

García-López, G. 2018. The multiple layers of environmental injustice in contexts of (un)natural disasters: The case of Puerto Rico post-Hurricane Maria. *Environmental Justice* 11(3): 101–108.

Garrido, S., and J. Davidson. 2016. Emotional regimes reflected in a popular ballad: Perspectives on gender, love and protest in "Scarborough Fair." *Musicology Australia* 38(1): 65–78.

Goleman, D. 2004. What makes a leader? *Harvard Business Review* 82(1): 82–91.

González-Hidalgo, M., and C. Zografos. 2020. Emotions, power, and environmental conflict: Expanding the "emotional turn" in political ecology. *Progress in Human Geography* 44(2): 235–255.

Goodwin, J., J. Jasper, and F. Polletta. 2001. Introduction: Why emotions matter. In J. Goodwin, J. Jasper, and F. Polletta (eds.) *Passionate Politics. Emotions and Social Movements*. pp. 1–26. Chicago: University of Chicago Press.

Goodwin, J., J. Jasper, F. Polletta, D. Snow, S. Soule, and H. Kriesi. 2004. Emotional dimensions of social movements. In D. Snow, S. Soule, and H. Kriesi (eds.) *The Blackwell Companion to Social Movements*. pp. 413–432. Malden, MA: Blackwell.

Graybill, J. 2019. Emotional environments of energy extraction in Russia. *Annals of the American Association of Geographers* 109(2): 382–394.

Harlan, S., D. Pellow, J. Roberts, S. Bell, W. Holt, and J. Nagel. 2015. Climate justice and inequality. In R. Dunlap and R. Brulle (eds.) *Climate Change and Society. Sociological Perspective*. New York: Oxford University Press.

Hejny, J. 2018. The Trump administration and environmental policy: Reagan redux? *Journal of Environmental Studies and Sciences* 8(2): 197–211.

Holmqvist, J. 2018. *Playing the Trump Card : A Qualitative Rhetorical Analysis of President Trump's Crisis Communication on Hurricane Maria*. Jönköping, Sweden: Jönköping University. http://hj.diva-portal.org/smash/record.jsf?pid=diva2%3A1220329&dswid=-315

Jasper, J. 2011. Emotions and social movements: Twenty years of theory and research. *Annual Review of Sociology* 37(1): 285–303.

Jotzo, F., J. Depledge, and H. Winkler. 2018. US and international climate policy under President Trump. *Climate Policy* 18(7): 813–817.

Krugman, P. 2018. Trump's deadly narcissism. *The New York Times* (Jan. 20). www.nytimes.com/2017/09/29/opinion/trumps-deadly-narcissism.html

Lloréns, H. 2018. Ruin nation: In Puerto Rico, Hurricane Maria laid bare the results of a long-term crisis created by dispossession, migration, and economic predation. *NACLA Report on the Americas* 50(2): 154–159.

Martin de Holan, P., A. Willi, and P. Fernández. 2017. Breaking the wall: Emotions and projective agency under extreme poverty. *Business & Society* 58(5): 919–962.

Mercer, J. 2006. Human nature and the first image: Emotion in international politics. *Journal of International Relations and Development* 9(3): 288–303.

Nakamura, D., and A. Parker. 2018. "It totally belittled the moment": Many look back in dismay at Trump's tossing of paper towels in Puerto Rico. *Washington Post* (Sept. 13). www.washingtonpost.com/politics/it-totally-belittled-the-moment-many-look-back-in-anger-at-trumps-tossing-of-paper-towels-in-puerto-rico/2018/09/13/8a3647d2-b77e-11e8-a2c5-3187f427e253_story.html

Norgaard, K. 2011. *Living in Denial: Climate Change, Emotions, and Everyday Life*. Cambridge, MA: MIT Press.

Olson, E. 2016. Geography and ethics II: Emotions and morality. *Progress in Human Geography* 40(6): 830–838.

Oxfam. 2017. Statement by Oxfam America President Abby Maxman regarding Puerto Rico Hurricane response. *Oxfam* (Oct. 2). www.oxfamamerica.org/press/statement-by-oxfam-america-president-abby-maxman-regarding-puerto-rico-hurricane-response/

Phillips, A., E. O'Keefe, N. Miroff, and D. Paletta. 2017. Lost weekend: How Trump's time at his golf club hurt the response to Maria. *Washington Post* (Sept. 29). www.washingtonpost.com/politics/lost-weekend-how-trumps-time-at-his-golf-club-hurt-the-response-to-maria/2017/09/29/ce92ed0a-a522-11e7-8c37-e1d99ad6aa22_story.html

Pulido, L., T. Bruno, C. Faiver-Serna, and C. Galentine. 2019. Environmental deregulation, spectacular racism, and white nationalism in the Trump era. *Annals of the American Association of Geographers* 109(2): 520–532.

Reddy, W. 2001. *The Navigation of Feeling : A Framework for the History of Emotions*. Cambridge, UK: Cambridge University Press.

Redlawsk, D. 2006. Feeling politics: New research into emotion and politics. In D. Redlawsk (ed.) *Feeling Politics – Emotion in Political Information Processing*. pp. 1–10. New York: Palgrave Macmillan.

Saad, A. 2018. Pathways of harm: The consequences of Trump's withdrawal from the Paris Climate Agreement. *Environmental Justice* 11(1): 47–51.

Schlosberg, D. 2013. Theorising environmental justice: The expanding sphere of a discourse. *Environmental Politics* 22(1): 37–55.

Selby, J. 2019. The Trump presidency, climate change, and the prospect of a disorderly energy transition. *Review of International Studies* 45(3): 471–490.

Sneed, A. 2017. Was the extreme 2017 hurricane season driven by climate change? *Scientific American* (Oct. 26). www.scientificamerican.com/article/was-the-extreme-2017-hurricane-season-driven-by-climate-change/

Sparke, M., and D. Bessner. 2019. Reaction, resilience, and the Trumpist behemoth: Environmental risk management from "hoax" to technique of domination. *Annals of the American Association of Geographers* 109(2): 533–544.

Stets, J., and J. Turner (eds.) 2014. *Handbook of the Sociology of Emotions. Volume 2*: Dordrecht: Springer.

Sultana, F. 2015. Emotional political ecology. In R. Bryant (ed.) *The International Handbook of Political Ecology*. pp. 633–645. Cheltenham, UK: Edward Elgar Publishing.

Swyngedouw, E. 2014. Where is the political? Insurgent mobilisations and the incipient "return of the political." *Space and Polity* 18(2): 122–136.

Taylor, J. 2017. Trump touts relief efforts In Puerto Rico: "We've saved a lot of lives." *NPR. Org* (Oct.3).www.npr.org/2017/10/03/555357192/trump-touts-relief-efforts-in-puerto-rico-we-ve-saved-a-lot-of-lives

The White House. 2017. Statement by President Trump on the Paris Climate Accord. (June 1). www.whitehouse.gov/briefings-statements/statement-president-trump-paris-climate-accord/

Thomas, A. 2017. Keeping faith with our fellow Americans. Meeting the urgent needs of Hurricane Maria survivors in Puerto Rico. *Refugees International*. https://static1. squarespace.com/static/506c8ea1e4b01d9450dd53f5/t/5a37d01bec212d3032461511/1513607203969/RI_Puerto+Rico_Advocacy+Report+R3.pdf

Trump, D. 2019. In the beautiful Midwest, windchill temperatures are reaching minus 60 degrees, the coldest ever recorded [tweet]. (Jan 28).https://twitter.com/realDonaldTrump/status/1090074254010404864

Urpelainen, J., and T. Van de Graaf. 2018. United States non-cooperation and the Paris Agreement. *Climate Policy* 18(7): 839–851.

Voronov, M., and K. Weber. 2016. The heart of institutions: Emotional competence and institutional actorhood. *Academy of Management Review* 41(3): 456–478.

Wettergren, Å. 2009. Fun and laughter: Culture jamming and the emotional regime of late capitalism. *Social Movement Studies* 8(1): 1–0.

Williams, R. 1977. *Marxism and Literature*. Oxford: Oxford University Press.

Zembylas, M. 2017. Willful ignorance and the emotional regime of schools. *British Journal of Educational Studies* 65(4): 499–515.

19

UNDOCUMENTED YOUTH AND THEIR UNEQUAL RIGHTS

State responses to Trump's immigration policies

Marie Price and Nicole Prchal Svajlenka

A central tenet of President Trump's campaign and presidency was stoking fear of immigrants, especially the undocumented. He campaigned to build a wall along the Mexican-U.S. border, to remove undocumented people, and even ban Muslims from the territorial state. As president, he has struggled to build a portion of his wall (even after shutting down the government for 35 days in a funding fight) but he has aggressively detained and separated immigrant children and families, rescinded Deferred Action for Childhood Arrivals (DACA)[1] and certain Temporary Protected Status (TPS) designations, and continued the aggressive deportation policies begun under the Obama administration (Chishti, Pierce, and O'Connor 2019; Miyares et al. 2019).

But while demonizing undocumented immigrants, his message towards DACA holders (undocumented youth who arrived in the U.S. as children) has been inconsistent. Shortly after his inauguration, Trump spoke of DACA recipients, saying "They shouldn't be very worried. They are here illegally. They shouldn't be very worried. I do have a big heart" (CBS News 2017). Yet eight months after Trump's inauguration, on September 5, 2017 Attorney General Jeff Sessions announced the rescission of DACA. Upon announcing its termination, the Trump administration gave DACA recipients with expirations in the next six months a one-month window to renew. The administration gave Congress six months to respond with legislation that would fix a problem it had not been able to solve since the first DREAM Act was introduced in 2001.

As we will discuss later in this paper, the rescinding of DACA was challenged and ultimately reached the U.S. Supreme Court in November 2019. In June 2020, in a five to four decision, the justices determined that the Trump administration did not provide a proper legal justification to terminate DACA. This offered a victory for DACA holders who have consistently renewed their protections, and possibly reopens the application process for Dreamers who were locked

Undocumented youth and unequal rights **323**

out of DACA since the September 2017 rescission. But the decision is a reprieve at best, and not a long-term solution.

Trump's anti-immigrant actions and rhetoric are contrasted with increasingly divergent interpretations by U.S. states (as well as other smaller jurisdictions such as cities, towns, and counties) about who belongs in the country, what rights they have, and how they should or should not be integrated into society. A 2019 survey by the Pew Research Center revealed that the clear majority of Americans (62%) say immigrants strengthen the country because of their hard work and talents; whereas only 28% saw immigrants as a burden (Jones 2019). A recent summary of Trump's immigration policies by the Migration Policy Institute noted "the administration's goals are being consistently stymied by court injunctions, existing laws and settlements, state and local government resistance, congressional pushback, and migration pressures that are beyond the government's ability to swiftly address" (Chishti, Pierce, and O'Connor 2019, p. 1).

Given these diverging trends, it is not surprising that there are policy differences across the country in the barriers and opportunities undocumented youth face. This is especially significant for nearly 700,000 DACA holders, many of whom arrived in the country as young children, know no other home, and often act and feel like they belong to the social fabric of the nation. This chapter will examine how, in particular, states within the U.S. influence the lives and rights of those with DACA, and undocumented youth in general. Depending on where an undocumented youth lives in the United States can directly impact the opportunity structures and barriers before them – or to make the geographical argument – place really does matter in determining access to driver's licenses, higher education, and reduced fear of deportation or removal (Staeheli et al. 2012; Walker and Leitner 2011; Walker 2014). Such divergent policies towards undocumented youth are dynamically remapping the terrain of rights and exclusions that undocumented youth experience.

To be clear, this decentralization and differentiation of policies towards the undocumented began in the early 2000s, as activists frustrated by repeated failures to pass a federal DREAM Act worked with state legislatures, boards of regents, and city governments, to improve the rights and protections for undocumented people, especially youth (Varsanyi 2010). From 2009 to 2017, these actions intensified during the Obama administration, as deportations increased to record levels (Price and Breese 2016). Yet the staunchly anti-immigrant stance of the Trump administration has intensified the differentiation of policies by states, leading to strikingly high levels of state activity regarding both exclusionary and inclusionary policies towards undocumented youth.

Part of this differentiation is driven by organized immigrant youth advocates, often called the DREAMers, and their allies (Nicholls 2013; Nicholls, Uitermark, and van Haperen 2020). Many DREAMers currently have DACA protections, but many others are not eligible. DREAMers have engaged with state and federal politicians to make policies that are favorable for those who arrived in the country as children and were educated in public schools. Their actions reflect an *insurgent citizenship* (Leitner and Strunk 2014a) or what Jose Antonio Vargas, an undocumented rights advocate, refers to as "radical transparency" (Vargas 2018, p. 177) that continues to drive integrative policies in states and cities. The rescinding of DACA in 2017, however, was a major political defeat for those with DACA and to those who would have been eligible for it. And it is indicative of a counter narrative of anti-immigrant sentiments that President Trump harnessed in his successful run for the White House and continues to employ in his re-election campaign.

Conceptually, the decentralization and differentiation of policies towards undocumented youth in the U.S. is best understood as a tension between practices of insurgent citizenship by the undocumented and their allies and the heightened precarity resulting from the actions of the Trump administration and states that insist on exclusionary measures. We argue that a complex political landscape has formed that defies any simple explanation of red and blue America in which the rights of the undocumented are profoundly unequal and contested.

What follows is a brief literature review that explores the concepts of insurgent citizenship and precarity as a means to understand competing legislative activities by states. We then focus on what states have done in response to the Trump administration's actions with regards to undocumented youth and the rescinding of DACA drawing upon data and reports from the National Conference of State Legislatures. Finally, we map how states confer and restrict the rights of the undocumented, especially undocumented youth. We begin by mapping where the DACA recipients reside by state. We then examine the response of states to DACA, highlighting which states sued to end the executive action. Two areas that states directly control, access to driver's licenses and access to higher public education and tuition equity, are contrasted as being inclusionary or exclusionary with regard to undocumented youth. We then discuss shifts in the inclusionary and exclusionary policies by states which lead to a variegated political landscape of rights and barriers facing the undocumented in the U.S. The profound inequality showcased in this analysis underscores both the precarity and the insurgent citizenship of the undocumented in the age of Trump.

Insurgent citizenship vs. heighted precarity of undocumented youth

The tension over the relative power of states' rights versus that of the federal government goes back to the founding of the country and even today there are numerous regulatory and legal issues where state policies differ (some examples include access to abortion, minimum wages, state taxes, climate change policies, and procurement of firearms). With regards to the variation in state policies towards the undocumented, differences have been growing for two decades in response to geographic, demographic, and political forces driving states and cities to act differently (Ellis 2006; Varsanyi 2010; Walker and Leitner 2011; Price 2015; Wong and Garcia 2016). The last major federal legislation that

Undocumented youth and unequal rights **325**

addressed the undocumented population in the U.S. was over three decades ago. The Immigration Reform and Control Act (IRCA) of 1986 signed during the Reagan administration eventually allowed for nearly 2.7 million undocumented people to regularize their status. More than three-quarters of the beneficiaries of this federal law were concentrated in three states: California, Texas, and New York (Enchautegui 2013).

Yet by the 1990s and 2000s the number of undocumented grew, peaking at over 12 million people in 2007. In coping with a large number of undocumented people spread out over many more states, state governments responded by creating policies that allowed access to services for this population, most notably in California. Other states, often with fewer undocumented people, tried more exclusionary approaches such as Georgia. Politically, states were hoping that the federal government would resolve the issue by either increased enforcement/ border security or by legislative changes that created a path to legal status.

The failure of the U.S. Congress over the last two decades to address the needs of a large undocumented population has led to heightened immigrant activism. This is especially true in places where the immigrant communities are large and immigrant youth who grew up in the United States claim a form of citizenry. Walter Nicholls argues that first proposed DREAM Act in 2001 was a "niche-opening" event in which high-achieving, promising, law-abiding undocumented youth who came to the United States "at no fault of their own" began to find their political voice (Nicholls 2013, p. 29). DREAMer-based organizations quickly multiplied and adopted a multiscalar approach in pushing for access and rights within universities, and with city, state, and federal legislatures. Sojo's (2016) research on the activism of undocumented youth also underscores a sophisticated use of social media for organizing; major Democratic presidential candidates in the 2016 added high-profile DREAMers to their campaign staffs.

We borrow from the work by Leitner and Strunk (2014a) in adopting the concept of *insurgent citizenship* to explain the diverse actors who have aligned in support of undocumented immigrants. This activism "involves actions that engage the state by making rights claims and demands to rectify injustices and inequalities" (Leitner and Strunk 2014b, p. 944). The creation of DACA is 2012 is a good example of insurgent citizenry at work. Immigrant activists frustrated by Congress's inability to create a path to citizenship persuaded the Obama administration to create a quasi-legal status via executive action that lasted until the Trump administration rescinded it.

DACA conferred two critical rights to undocumented youth who met the criteria for renewable two-year periods. First, a stay of deportation reduced the fear of removal from the country for non-criminal reasons. Secondly, DACA recipients were given legal work authorization; this allowed youth to transition from no employment or under-the-table employment to often higher paid jobs. An ancillary right, the ability to drive legally, stemmed from DACA recipients' ability to get a Social Security Number via their work authorization. Surveys of DACA recipients illustrate the benefits of program: researchers found that 96% of

326 Marie Price and Nicole Prchal Svajlenka

DACA recipients surveyed were enrolled in school or employed, that the average hourly wage for those with DACA increased by 78%, and 62% of respondents purchased their first cars (Wong et al. 2018).

In 2014, Obama again used executive action in an attempt to expand the pool of individuals eligible for DACA along with the creation of Deferred Action for Parents of Americans and Lawful Permanent Residents (DAPA), a program that would extend similar legal protections to the undocumented parents of American citizens and lawful permanent residents. However, the DACA expansion and DAPA never went into effect, as several states sued to block their implementation.

The complex synergies among immigrant activists, social media, federal action, and local reactions contribute to the heightened precarity that undocumented youth experience. Anderson describes this quality of immigrant precarity as preventing people "from anticipating the future" (2010, p. 304). There are, of course, pernicious consequences of large number of residents dubbed "illegal aliens" or undocumented living and working in a territorial state unauthorized for years, often in limbo (Butler 2012; Gonzalez 2015). Referred to as "un-citizens" (Nash 2009), even when they are able to obtain work, these migrants are often subjected to substandard working conditions, exploitation by employers, receive lower wages, as well as long and erratic work hours. Undocumented migrants are also more likely to be exposed to occupational hazards that have impacts on long-term mental and emotional health (Preibisch and Otero 2014).

Precarity varies across space and time for undocumented youth in the U.S. (Chacko and Price 2020). In terms of scale, an undocumented youth might feel secure in an immigrant neighborhood or in a state where they receive greater protections such as California. Similarly, specific time periods matter. Youth with DACA felt that they had secured a quasi-legal status and embraced it in 2013. Yet with the rescinding of DACA in 2017, their precarity was heightened. The precarious nature of DACA, and the possibility of current DACA holders losing their status, has economic, social, and psychological consequences. Losing DACA means loss of work authorization, no longer having a social security number or driver's license, and being blocked from various programs – in short, a return to the shadows and heightened fear of deportation. Research shows that undocumented youth are keenly aware of the psychological challenges of the mental stress of living with these fears on a daily basis (Roche et al. 2018). Precarity has economic, social, and emotional costs, especially extended over long periods of time. And the precarity of all undocumented youth has been exacerbated under Trump.

Trump and the rescinding of DACA

President Trump's campaign stoked fear of immigrants among voters, positioning the American Dream as a zero-sum game: if opportunity is growing for some, it must be declining for others. Among his many immigration-related

Undocumented youth and unequal rights **327**

FIGURE 19.1 DACA recipients by state.

Source: Created by authors using data from USCIS: www.uscis.gov/sites/default/files/USCIS/Resources/Reports%20and%20Studies/Immigration%20Forms%20Data/All%20Form%20Types/DACA/Approximate_Active_DACA_Recipients_Demographics_-_Apr_30_2019.pdf

pledges, Trump promised to end DACA immediately upon assuming office. Eight months after Trump's inauguration he made good on this promise. Several lawsuits resulted that challenged the manner by which the Trump administration terminated DACA, leaving DACA recipients eligible to renew their protections but locking out DREAMers who had not previously applied – including those waiting to age into eligibility – from doing so.

Figure 19.1 shows the residence of DACA holders by state. Two states, California and Texas, have nearly half of the 700,000 DACA holders. Thus, the policy decisions in these states are extremely impactful and strikingly divergent. These are also the states with the largest undocumented populations and the largest overall immigrant populations (10.5 million immigrants in California and 4.6 million in Texas) (United States Census Bureau ACS 2017 5-year estimates). In the next tier (with 20,000 to 40,000 DACA holders) are Arizona, Florida, Georgia, Illinois, New York, and North Carolina. This is an interesting mix of established immigrant destinations (New York, Florida, and Illinois) and relatively new destinations (Georgia and North Carolina). At the low end of DACA holders are states such as Louisiana, Mississippi, Montana, West Virginia, and Vermont. Yet every state does have DACA holders.

After DACA was rescinded, Congress attempted to pass comprehensive protections for DACA recipients but efforts failed in the summer of 2018. The impasse came when restoring DACA was tied to increased funding to build a border wall along the Mexican–U.S. border. Politically engaged DACA recipients, along with the broader DREAMer community, refused to trade their futures for wall funding. A standstill on Congressional funding for the wall ultimately led to the longest federal government shutdown in history during December 2018 and January 2019.

In March 2019, H.R. 6, the American Dream and Promise Act was introduced in the House of Representatives. The bill would extend a pathway to citizenship for many immigrants whose protected status was stripped by the

Trump administration. Some 2.5 million DREAMers and immigrants eligible for Temporary Protected Status and Deferred Enforced Departure would be eligible for protection under the bill. In June 2019, the House voted in favor of this law (237 to 187) with bi-partisan support. Despite DACA's tenuous future and the Trump administration's continued efforts to end it, the House bill has yet to, and may never, be taken up in the Senate. As of June 30, 2019, 660,880 DACA recipients remain without permanent protection.

State responses to the end of DACA

Just as states have responded to the needs and challenges of undocumented residents over the past two decades, so too have states reacted since the rescinding of DACA. Nearly half of the states sued the federal government over the manner in which DACA was terminated (Figure 19.2). They include California, Colorado, Connecticut, Delaware, the District of Columbia, Hawaii, Illinois, Iowa, Maine, Maryland, Massachusetts, Minnesota, New Mexico, New York, North Carolina, Oregon, Pennsylvania, Rhode Island, Vermont, Virginia, and Washington. Collectively, more than half of all DACA recipients live in states challenging the manner by which the Trump administration tried to end DACA. Additional lawsuits also came from localities like San Jose and Santa Clara, CA as well as immigrant and civil rights organizations along with institutes of higher learning. In January 2018, the first of several preliminary injunctions issued by federal judges reopened the DACA renewal process, but eligible undocumented immigrants remained unable to apply for an initial grant of DACA.

On the other hand, some states doubled down on their efforts to restrict protections afforded to DACA holders (see Figure 19.2), most notably in a lawsuit led by Texas, which includes Alabama, Arkansas, Kansas, Louisiana, Nebraska, South Carolina, and West Virginia. They argued that the benefits afforded to DACA-holders cost the states, and is therefore prejudicial. Buoyed by the large number of DACA recipients in Texas, 20% of all DACA recipients

FIGURE 19.2 State lawsuits with regard to DACA.

Sources: Created by authors using data from www.americanprogress.org/issues/immigration/news/2019/09/12/474422/know-daca-recipients-state/

live in states that sued the federal government over DACA. The federal judge in this case, Andrew Hanen of the Southern District of Texas, is the same judge who took down the Obama administration's efforts to expand DACA and extend similar protections to undocumented parents of U.S.-citizen children (DAPA) (Shear 2018).

In addition, some state legislatures reacted to the Trump administration's actions on immigration by pursuing policies to protect the undocumented that had stalled in previous years or even would not have been imaginable even two years earlier. For example, New York State debated a Dream Act back in 2013 that would extend financial aid to undocumented students. Ultimately, the bill was pushed over the finish line in 2019 by a Democratic majority legislature as a response to the heighted precarity for DREAMers living under the Trump administration (Goldbaum 2019). But these actions are not limited to states with progressive legislating bodies. Led by a bipartisan team of members and signed into law by its Republican governor, in 2019 Arkansas passed legislation extending in-state tuition to DACA recipients and other foreign-born residents. Additionally, Arkansas passed a bill that permits DACA recipients to obtain state nursing licenses (Hardy 2019). Other states have clarified that policies related to DACA recipients apply to DREAMers more broadly. This is especially meaningful as there are roughly 100,000 DREAMers graduating high school each year who were too young to apply for DACA before it was terminated (Zong and Batalova 2019).

In November 2019, the U.S. Supreme Court heard the case to determine if DACA was unlawfully terminated. Before the justices rendered their decision, Covid-19 had spread across the United States. In April a report by the Center for American Progress estimated that 29,000 DACA recipients were healthcare professionals and that across the United States some 200,000 DACA recipients were considered essential workers during the pandemic (Svajlenka 2020). In June of 2020 the Supreme Court determined that the Trump administration did not provide proper legal justification for ending the DACA program. Thus, DACA holders were spared from losing their status, a major, albeit temporary, victory.

Other rights conferred and restrictions placed on undocumented youth

Since the 2000s, states and localities have been asserting their rights to either discourage or integrate their undocumented residents. Competing legislative actions have led to a "variegated landscape" and "complex geographies of citizenship," with some states (and cities) being much more rights friendly than others (Walker and Leitner 2013, Staeheli et al. 2012).

The National Conference of State Legislatures (NCLS) tracks laws and resolutions passed by states related to immigration. Data show that the number of immigrant-related laws passed by states in 2016 compared to 2018 increased by 250% (70 laws in 2016 and 175 laws in 2018) (Morse 2019, p. 3). Interestingly,

2016 was a low point in state activity regarding immigration laws, perhaps due to anticipating a new presidential administration. The vast majority of these laws in 2018 are concerned with budgets, education, law enforcement, public benefits, employment, and ID/driver's licenses. Two policy areas where state actions diverge significantly are access to higher education and driver's licenses for the undocumented in general, and youth in particular.

Higher education

This is a policy area where states have both fostered and limited access for undocumented youth. The 1982 Supreme Court decision of *Plyler v. Doe* affirmed that all children in the U.S., regardless of legal status, are entitled to a public education through high school. Nearly half of the states permit undocumented immigrants who meet certain criteria, typically that they graduated from and were enrolled in high school in that state for several years, to pay in-state tuition at state institutions (Figure 19.3). The tuition equity landscape is varied. In many cases, it is conferred by the state's legislative body. In several states, the decision is made by the state's board of regents and applies only to certain state institutions. And in a small number of states, the Attorney General has set the standard.

But the landscape grows even more complicated beyond who sets the policy. Some states offer state-funded financial aid, while others have alternative funding

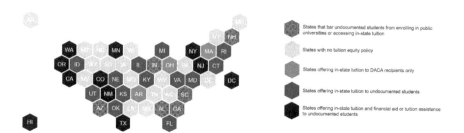

FIGURE 19.3 Undocumented youth and access to higher education by state.

Sources: Created by the authors using data from

CAP: www.americanprogress.org/issues/immigration/reports/2018/09/13/458008/daca-recipients-stand-lose-states-can/

uLEAD: https://uleadnet.org/

NILC: www.nilc.org/issues/education/basic-facts-instate/

NCSL: www.ncsl.org/research/education/undocumented-student-tuition-overview.aspx

Arkansas: www.thv11.com/article/news/politics/governor-hutchinson-signs-two-bills-in-support-of-daca-immigrants/91-1f3623e8-159f-4bc3-ae1b-3e4e5d014cd2

New York: https://chalkbeat.org/posts/ny/2019/07/10/as-dream-act-application-goes-live-for-ny-students-working-to-afford-college-advocates-turn-to-outreach-a-key-priority/

Colorado: www.denverpost.com/2019/05/13/colorado-undocumented-students-college-aid/

Illinois: https://today.uic.edu/pritzker-signs-laws-at-uic-helping-undocumented-trans-community

Utah: https://stepuputah.com/2017/09/paying-college-utahs-undocumented-students-need-know/

opportunities. In some states, in-state tuition applies to all undocumented students, in others it applies only to those students who hold DACA. And along the other end of the spectrum, some states expressly prohibit in-state tuition to undocumented students, while others go a step further and prohibit undocumented students from enrolling in some or all higher education institutions. Three states, Arizona, Georgia, and Indiana, have passed legislation that bans undocumented students from receiving in-state tuition, while New Hampshire implicitly bars undocumented students from in-state tuition by requiring them to sign an affidavit swearing their legal status. Alabama and South Carolina are even more restrictive, forbidding undocumented students from enrolling in any public post-secondary institutions (NCSL 2019a; 2019b; uLEAD 2019).

States that extend in-state tuition and even access to financial aid make the argument that they have invested in these residents' education, and extending the opportunity of accessing higher education to DACA recipients and the wider undocumented community helps retain these residents as they enter the workforce. In doing so, they assert the economic benefits of having highly skilled workers. Virginia Attorney General Mark Herring argued in 2014 that "We should welcome these smart, talented, hard-working young people into our economy and society rather than putting a stop sign at the end of 12th grade" (Vozzella and Constable 2014). Then in April 2020 the Governor of Virginia signed a tuition equity bill that allowed all undocumented youth who graduated from Virginia high schools access to in-state tuition if admitted to a public university or college in the state (Price and Mowry-Mora 2020). Beyond policies governing in-state tuition, ten states and the District of Columbia allow undocumented students to access state-funded financial aid. Federal Student Aid, accessed through completing the FAFSA form, is not accessible for undocumented youth with or without DACA. In addition, some states, such as Illinois and Utah, offer privately funded scholarships at public universities to undocumented youth.

The political paths and timing of in-state tuition and financial support of undocumented youth vary tremendously. Notably the states with the largest undocumented youth populations passed inclusive legislation in 2001. In Texas, Republican Governor Rick Perry signed a law with bipartisan support that granted in-state tuition to undocumented students who graduated from Texas high schools (or had a high school equivalency GED) and who had lived in Texas for at least three years. That same year, California allowed undocumented students to pay in-state tuition at public universities if they had graduated from California high schools. Ten years later, California passed a Dream Act that provided state funding to eligible undocumented youth (with and without DACA) admitted to public universities and community colleges. In Maryland voters passed a Dream Act, in 2012 that granted in-state tuition to undocumented immigrants at public four-year institutions, if they have attended high school in the state for three years and earned 60 credits, or an associate's degree at a community college.

Driver's licenses

Beginning in 2005 with Utah, by 2013 eight states and the District of Columbia permitted undocumented immigrants to apply for driver's licenses.[2] Especially in communities where public transportation is not available, undocumented immigrants must drive to accomplish daily tasks. These states recognize that licensing undocumented drivers is a beneficial policy because it requires drivers to demonstrate basic knowledge of the rules of the road and perhaps more importantly, to obtain insurance.

Given the ongoing uncertainty surrounding DACA and the undocumented population in general, some states have expanded access to driver's licenses for undocumented groups. Since DACA recipients receive a Social Security Number, they are permitted to apply for driver's licenses in all 50 states and the District of Columbia. Yet the wider community of undocumented immigrants is currently eligible to apply for licenses in 14 states and the District of Columbia (Figure 19.4). After DACA was rescinded in 2017, Rhode Island passed legislation to protect DACA recipients' facing uncertain futures, the state also extended driver's licenses to current and past DACA recipients.

As indicated in Figure 19.4, the vast majority of states have not granted access to driver's licenses for undocumented people. Texas, which has the second largest number of DACA recipients in the U.S. and grants in-state tuition to undocumented residents, does not allow undocumented people access to driver's licenses. This is especially prejudicial given the state's limited public transportation options. It is also an example of the heightened precarity undocumented people face in certain states. Being pulled over for driving without a license can easily result in deportation.

FIGURE 19.4 Undocumented authorization to drive by state.

Sources: Created by authors using data from

Pew: www.pewtrusts.org/en/research-and-analysis/articles/2016/11/22/drivers-licenses-for-unauthorized-immigrants-2016-highlights

CAP: www.americanprogress.org/issues/immigration/reports/2018/09/13/458008/daca-recipients-stand-lose-states-can/

NY: www.nytimes.com/2019/06/17/nyregion/undocumented-immigrants-drivers-licenses-ny.html

Oregon: www.ktvz.com/news/oregon-lawmakers-vote-to-extend-daca-protections/710834374

Rhode Island: www.ri.gov/press/view/33496

ACTIONS BY CITIES, TOWNS AND COUNTIES

While this chapter specifically focuses on states' immigration policies, the action does not stop at the state level. Smaller localities have also taken a role in dictating immigration policies. Beyond just a reaction to the federal government's inaction, these policies are sometimes taken in direct conflict with the policies of their states.

Before many states considered immigration-related policies in their legislatures, localities were taking it up as issues percolated. In smaller communities it is easier to mobilize and local governance can be very responsive to perceived issues.

On the restrictive front, small communities experiencing dramatic demographic shifts went on the defense. In the mid-2000s, places such as Hazelton, PA, Farmer's Branch, TX, and Fremont, NE instituted ordinances restricting day laborers and requiring proof of status on housing rental applications. These ordinances were largely challenged and deemed unconstitutional. Defending them in court proved to be a major financial burden for the localities.

Signing 287(g) agreements with Immigration and Customs Enforcement (ICE) that allow local law enforcement to take on certain roles and responsibilities of ICE were also popular among counties and localities where demographics shifted from white native-born to Latino foreign-born. For example, in Prince William County, VA, the county board not only agreed to cooperate with ICE but passed, without public hearing, ordinances in 2007 that banned access to business licenses and a variety of public services to undocumented immigrants (Singer, Wilson, DeRenzis 2009). In 2020, the county's jail board decided to let its 287(g) agreement expire. Some types of inclusionary policies are specific to the local level as well. Municipal identification cards were a widely touted way to protect undocumented residents. Cities such as New Haven, CT, New York City, Washington, D.C., Los Angeles, and San Francisco have all adopted municipal identification cards which provide access to city services and importantly, identification for undocumented residents when interacting with authorities such as the police.

Other places adopted broad, welcoming policy agendas with the help of organizations like Welcoming America. The original welcoming city, Dayton, OH, pursued what they called a "welcoming" platform to recognize the importance of all residents regardless of nativity, but also as a means to encourage population revitalization. And many mayors and local elected officials representing communities of all sizes have signed on to coalitions like Cities for Action, which pushes for pro-immigrant policy reforms at the federal level.

Discussion: Oscillating precarity and insurgent citizenship

States in the U.S. exhibit both inclusionary and restrictivist tendencies with regards to setting policies that directly impact the undocumented in their territories. These differences in rights, especially towards undocumented youth, are profound and shifting. Collectively, the data underscore how important place of residence is when assessing the overall precarity of this population. The figures presented also demonstrate that states can be both inclusionary, such as making in-state tuition available, and also exclusionary, suing to end DACA in the cases of Texas and Arkansas. That said, under the Trump administration the overall levels of precarity are increasing, especially with the rescinding of DACA. Even though the Supreme Court decided in 2020 that DACA was unlawfully suspended, the justices left the door open for the Trump administration to end the program permanently if proper legal justification is provided. With such uncertainty, some states have responded to protect undocumented youth in particular.

This patchwork of policies towards the undocumented did not begin with President Trump. Perhaps surprisingly, the modern immigrant restrictivist impulse by states began in California with its ballot initiative, Proposition 187, passed by voters in 1994. This was the first major state legislation targeting undocumented immigrants since the federal Immigration Reform and Control Act of 1986 was passed. Support for the initiative, which barred undocumented immigrants from accessing certain state services like education and non-emergency healthcare, stemmed from concern over a growing undocumented population and a perceived strain on the state budget. Proposition 187 was ultimately declared unconstitutional after a court challenge and is considered a motivating issue in turning California reliably Democratic (Nowrasteh 2016). Thirty years later, California is often hailed as one of the most welcoming states for undocumented residents, underscoring an extreme oscillation in attitudes and policies.

In 2013, California Governor Jerry Brown signed the Trust Act, limiting California's cooperation with federal immigration authorities and decoupling local police from engaging in the deportation of non-criminal undocumented migrants. The Trust Act was designed to protect civil rights, especially for the state's large Latino population, and ensure public safety. Similarly, states with much smaller immigrant and undocumented populations such as Vermont, Alaska, Montana, and Oregon, introduced state laws that asserted that immigration enforcement is the federal government's responsibility and that local agencies should not be involved (Garber and Marquez 2016).

After the Proposition 187 failure, states slowed down on passing immigration-related laws. However, with growing immigrant and Latino communities in new destinations scattered throughout the Southeast in the mid-2000s, there was a renewed interest in pursuing immigration policy at the local level. One such instance was under 287(g) agreements, by which states and localities could enter into partnership with Immigration and Customs Enforcement (ICE) to enforce immigration laws. Under the program, local law enforcement officers are deputized to check immigration status of individuals they come into contact with through their everyday responsibilities. While the majority of these agreements were between county sheriff's departments and ICE, Arizona, Colorado, Minnesota, Missouri, Tennessee, Alabama, Georgia, and Florida all had state agreements (Svajlenka 2018).

The early years of the Obama administration were also a period of notable examples by states to restrict immigrants living within their borders. Arizona's SB 1070 in 2010 and Alabama's HB 56 in 2011 were two extremely high-profile "Show Me Your Papers" laws that permitted police to check immigration status on anyone they suspected could be an undocumented immigrant. Beyond these provisions, the laws included many more attempts at hardline immigration policies. For example, HB 56 required Alabama school districts to report tallies of any suspected undocumented students and SB 1070 permitted residents to sue if they felt that any state government official was limiting ability to enforce immigration policy. These bills were largely deemed unconstitutional. Officials who pursued these policies claimed they targeted only undocumented immigrants, but research shows that they impact the wider foreign-born and Latino communities (Johnson 2012).

On the opposite end of the spectrum, many state legislatures have recognized the need to govern all residents, regardless of their nativity or legal status, and particularly young people who have grown up in their states and for all practical purposes know no other home. In this regard, many states – in both red and blue America – show a strong inclusionary impulse with regard to tuition equity for qualified undocumented students. Finally, the heightened level of state-based legislative activities in the last two years concerned with education, law enforcement, and IDs for undocumented people reflect the on-the-ground concerns within states of how to best deal with residents with no legal status but who are long-time residents, workers, homeowners, taxpayers, and business owners in their particular states.

While this research stresses the unequal patterns of rights afforded undocumented youth in the U.S., it must be emphasized that thousands of immigrant rights groups working at multiple political scales have pushed to make inclusionary changes happen. In particular, undocumented immigrant youth, collectively referred to as DREAMers, have exerted their rights in an act of insurgent citizenship that has led to an expansion of their rights and protections in several states. That said, the election of Donald Trump has led to heightened precarity for most immigrants, but especially undocumented ones. The resistance to the most exclusionary impulses of the Trump administration is being waged by states, immigrant rights organizations, and in the courts. What is certain in these precarious times, is the debate over who belongs in the United States and what rights they are entitled is robust and being decided at multiple political scales by a diverse set of actors.

Notes

1 DACA was created in 2012 by an Obama administration executive action, through which approved applicants receive a two-year stay of deportation and work authorization. To be eligible an immigrant youth must have arrived in the country before the age of 16 by June 2007 and be under the age of 31 on June 15, 2012. Successful applicants must have been 15, have earned a high school diploma or the equivalent, be enrolled in school, or an honorably discharged veteran, and meet specific requirements on a criminal record. The application fees are $495, and DACA recipients must apply for renewal every two years.

2 These are technically driver's privilege cards and are not federally recognized identification cards. DACA recipients can apply for actual driver's licenses.

References

Anderson, B. 2010. Migration, immigration controls and the fashioning of precarious workers. *Work, Employment and Society* 24(2): 300–317.

Butler, J. 2012. Precarious life, vulnerability and the ethics of cohabitation. *Journal of Speculative Philosophy* 26(2): 134–151.

Chacko, E., and M. Price. (2020). (Un)settled sojourners in cities: Exploring the scalar and temporal dimensions of temporary migrant precarity. *Journal of Ethnic and Migration Studies.* https://doi.org/10.1080/1369183X.2020.1731060

CBS News. 2017 (Feb. 2). "My life is made here": Undocumented students fear fate under Trump. www.cbsnews.com/news/undocumented-students-daca-immigrants-fears-under-trump/

Chishti, M., S. Pierce, and A. O'Connor. 2019. Despite Flurry of Actions, Trump Administration Faces Constraints in Achieving Its Immigration Agenda. *Policy Beat* (April 25). Migration Policy Institute, Washington, D.C. www.migrationpolicy.org/article/trump-administration-faces-constraints-achieving-immigration-agenda

Ellis, M. 2006. Unsettling immigrant geographies: US immigration and the politics of scale. *Tijdschrift voor Economische en Sociale Geografie* 97(1): 49–58.

Enchautegui, M. 2013. *A Comparison of Today's Unauthorized Immigrants and the IRCA Legalized: Implications for Immigration Reform.* Washington, D.C.: Urban Institute. www.urban.org/sites/default/files/publication/24311/412980-A-Comparison-of-Today-s-Unauthorized-Immigrants-and-the-IRCA-Legalized-Implications-for-Immigration-Reform.PDF

Garber, L., and N. Marquez. 2016. *Searching for Sanctuary: An Analysis of America's Counties and their Voluntary Assistance with Deportations.* San Francisco, CA: Immigrant Legal Resource Center. www.ilrc.org/sites/default/files/resources/sanctuary_report_final_1-min.pdf

Goldbaum, C. 2019. Dream Act is approved in N.Y. to aid undocumented students, in rebuke to Trump. *New York Times* (Jan. 23). www.nytimes.com/2019/01/23/nyregion/dream-act-bill-passed.html

Gonzalez, R. 2015. *Lives in Limbo: Undocumented and Coming of Age in America.* Berkeley: University of California Press.

Hardy, B. 2019. Arkansas Senate passes bill to let DACA students access in-state tuition rates. *Arkansas Times* (April 4). https://arktimes.com/arkansas-blog/2019/04/04/arkansas-senate-passes-bill-to-let-daca-students-access-in-state-tuition-rates

Johnson, K. 2012. A case study of color-blindness: The racially disparate impacts of Arizona's S.B. 1070 and a failure of comprehensive immigration reform. *University of California Irvine Law Review* 2: 313–358.

Jones, B. 2019. *Majority of Americans Continue to Say Immigrants Strengthen the US*. FactTank, News in the Numbers, Pew Research Center. www.pewresearch.org/fact-tank/2019/01/31/majority-of-americans-continue-to-say-immigrants-strengthen-the-u-s/

Leitner, H., and C. Strunk. 2014a. Spaces of immigrant advocacy and liberal democratic citizenship. *Annals of the Association of American Geographers* 104(2): 348–356.

Leitner, H., and C. Strunk. 2014b. Assembling insurgent citizenship: Immigrant advocacy struggles in the Washington DC metropolitan area. *Urban Geography* 35(7): 943–964.

Miyares, I., R. Wright, A. Mountz, and A. Bailey. 2019. Truncated transnationalism, the tenuousness of temporary protected status, and Trump. *Journal of Latin American Geography* 18(1): 210–216.

Morse, A. 2019. Immigrant Policy Project: Report on state immigration laws, 2018. *National Conference of State Legislatures*. www.ncsl.org/press-room/new-report-highlights-2018-state-immigration-legislation.aspx

Nash, K. 2009. Between citizenship and human rights. *Sociology* 43: 1067–1083.

NCSL (National Conference of State Legislatures). 2019a. *Undocumented Student Tuition: Overview*. www.ncsl.org/research/education/undocumented-student-tuition-overview.aspx

NCSL (National Conference of State Legislatures). 2019b. *Tuition Benefits for Immigrants*. www.ncsl.org/research/immigration/tuition-benefits-for-immigrants.aspx

Nicholls, W. 2013. *The DREAMers: How the Undocumented Youth Movement Transformed the Immigrant Rights Debate*. Stanford, CA: Stanford University Press.

Nicholls, W. J., J. Uitermark, and S. van Haperen. 2020. Going national: How the fight for immigrant rights became a national social movement. *Journal of Ethnic and Migration Studies* 46(4): 705–727. https://doi.org/10.1080/1369183X.2018.1556450

Nowrasteh, A. 2016. Proposition 187 Turned California Blue. *Cato at Liberty*. Washington, D.C.: Cato Institute. www.cato.org/blog/proposition-187-turned-california-blue

Preibisch, K., and G. Otero. 2014. Does citizenship status matter in Canadian agriculture? Workplace health and safety for migrant and immigrant laborers. *Rural Sociology* 79(2): 174–199.

Price, M. 2015. Cities welcoming immigrants: Local strategies to attract and retain immigrants in U.S. metropolitan areas. In *World Migration Report: Migrants and Cities: New Partnerships to Manage Mobility*. Geneva: International Organization for Migration.

Price, M., and D. Breese. 2016. Unintended return: U.S. deportations and the fractious politics of mobility for Latinos. *Annals of the Association of American Geographers* 106(2): 366–376.

Price, M., and I. Mowry-Mora. 2020. DACA and the differentiated landscape for college access: Experiences from a new destination state. *Geographical Review*. https://doi.org/10.1080/00167428.2020.1773267

Roche, K., E. Vaquera, R. White, and M. Rivera. 2018. Impacts of immigration actions and news and the psychological distress of U.S. Latino parents raising adolescents. *Journal of Adolescent Health* 62: 525–531.

Shear, M. 2019. Federal judge in Texas delivers unexpected victory in DACA program. *New York Times* (Aug. 31). www.nytimes.com/2018/08/31/us/politics/texas-judge-daca.html

Singer, A., J. Wilson, and B. DeRenzis. 2009. *Immigrants, Politics, and Local Response in Suburban Washington*. Survey Series for the Metropolitan Policy Program. Washington, D.C.: Brookings Institution.

Sojo, G. 2016. *The Diffusion of the Undocumented Youth Movement in United States: Dreamers' Networks and Strategies in Online and Public Spaces*. Unpublished Master's Thesis in Geography, George Washington University.

Staeheli, L., P. Ehrkamp, H. Leitner and C. Nagel. 2012. Dreaming the ordinary: Daily life and the complex geographies of citizenship. *Progress in Human Geography* 36(5): 628–644

Svajlenka, N. 2018. *What's at Stake: Immigrant Impacts in 287(g) Jurisdictions*. Washington, D.C.: Center for American Progress. www.americanprogress.org/issues/immigration/reports/2018/03/20/448172/whats-at-stake/

Svajlenka, N. Prchal. 2020. *A Demographic Profile of DACA Recipients on the Frontlines of the Coronavirus Response*. Washington DC: Center for American Progress. www.americanprogress.org/issues/immigration/news/2020/04/06/482708/demographic-profile-daca-recipients-frontlines-coronavirus-response/

uLEAD (University Leaders for Educational Access and Diversity). 2019. For information on access to higher education for the undocumented. https://uleadnet.org/

United States Census Bureau. 2017. American Community Survey 2017, 5-year estimates. Foreign born characteristics by state, S0506.

Vargas, J. 2018. *Dear America, Notes of an Undocumented Citizen*. New York: William Morrow.

Varsanyi, M. 2010. *Taking Local Control: Immigration Policy Activism in US Cities and States*. Stanford, CA: Stanford University Press.

Vozzella, L., and P. Constable. 2014. Virginia Attorney General declares "dreamers" eligible for in-state tuition. *Washington Post* (April 29).

Walker, K., and H. Leitner. 2011. The variegated landscape of local immigration policies in the US. *Urban Geography* 32(2):156–178

Walker, K. 2014. The role of geographic context in the local politics of US immigration. *Journal of Ethnic and Migration Studies* 40(7): 1040–1059.

Williamson, A. 2018. *Welcoming New Americans? Local Governments and Immigrant Incorporation*. Chicago: University of Chicago Press.

Wong, T., and A. Garcia. 2016. Does where I live affect whether I apply? The contextual determinants of applying for Deferred Action for Childhood Arrivals (DACA). *International Migration Review* 50(3): 159–173.

Wong, T., S. Abrar, T. Jawetz, I. Rodriguez Kmec, P. O'Shea, G. Martinez Rosas, and P. Wolgin. 2018. *Amid Legal and Political Uncertainty, DACA Remains More Important Than Ever*. Washington, D.C.: Center for American Progress. www.americanprogress.org/issues/immigration/news/2018/08/15/454731/amid-legal-political-uncertainty-daca-remains-important-ever/

Zong, J., and J. Batalova. 2019. How many unauthorized immigrants graduate from U.S. high schools annually? Migration Policy Institute Fact Sheet.

INDEX

2016 election 2, 4, 13, 14, 15, 17, 24, 30, 31, 33, 39, 69–90, 92–109, 112–125, 133, 140, 148–158, 161, 164, 173, 175, 182, 207–211, 221, 289, 299, 304, 305, 306, 317, 335

2018 midterm elections 34, 190, 216, 217

Abortion 17, 21, 153, 219, 324
Africa 19, 235, 251, 294, 295
African Americans 4, 60, 98, 147, 148, 150, 154, 156, 220
America First 2, 34, 111, 129, 162, 174, 175, 235, 238, 253

Base (Trump's) 1, 16, 17, 23, 25, 37, 79, 96, 131, 150, 182, 189, 219, 220, 224, 307
Birtherism 19
Brazil 27, 182, 185, 293
Breitbart News 16, 28, 131, 170

Canada 2, 11, 35, 223, 280
Children 7, 12, 21, 34, 35, 147, 300, 322, 323, 329
China 2, 6, 22, 35, 36, 37, 109, 223, 255, 270, 271, 273, 275, 280–296
Climate change 3, 6, 7, 22, 31, 32, 215, 222, 225, 226, 298–309, 311–318, 324
Clinton, Hillary 14, 15, 17, 19, 21, 25, 31, 70, 74, 89, 90, 94, 95, 98, 105, 108, 109, 131, 144, 145, 148, 151, 164, 167, 168, 173, 193, 199, 207, 226

Coal 14, 32, 307
Collusion 2, 3, 29, 30, 31, 218
Coronavirus 37, 38
Corruption 2, 3 11, 31, 32, 33, 34, 93, 95, 102, 144, 165, 220, 293
Cuba 4, 6, 249–260

DACA 7, 20, 322–335
Demagogue 2, 4, 161, 193
Democratic Party 15, 69, 87, 89, 191, 271
Deportation 171, 218, 322, 323, 325, 326, 332, 334

Electoral College 2, 4, 15, 70, 72, 74, 77, 79, 85–90, 96, 112, 144, 145, 149, 188, 211
Environmental Protection Agency 29, 32
Europe 2, 16, 35, 36, 38, 130, 147, 155, 237, 244, 256, 265, 277, 299
European Union 2, 35, 237, 280, 287, 295
Evangelicals 2, 4, 17, 75, 76, 77, 124, 149, 150, 152–154, 184, 216

Fascism 4, 130, 132, 133, 134, 138, 141, 145, 185, 236
FBI 18, 28, 29, 30, 39, 139
Fox News 16, 28, 37, 39, 93, 95, 200, 220

Geopolitics 2, 5, 162, 163, 170, 235, 237, 265, 266, 268–271
Globalization 1, 3, 14, 15, 16, 34, 80, 123, 125, 155, 251, 259, 280, 281, 289
Golf 12, 24, 33, 55, 216, 299, 316

340 Index

Immigration 2, 3, 5, 7, 11, 14, 15, 16, 26, 34, 35, 40, 56, 75, 103, 106, 107, 111, 117, 122, 131, 144, 146, 147, 148, 155, 162, 175, 215, 216, 218, 235, 241, 289, 290, 322–335

Impeachment 31, 36–37, 268

Iran 3, 6, 22, 28, 35, 218, 235, 239, 240, 241, 243, 244–245, 269

Iraq 6, 34, 216, 217, 218, 239, 240, 241, 245, 251, 255, 269, 270

Islamic State/ISIS 23, 25, 167, 170, 171, 216, 220, 222, 239, 240, 243, 244, 245, 302

Islamophobia 2, 11, 20, 26, 148, 167, 222

Jews 35, 146, 147, 153

Khashoggi, Jamal 36, 243

Kim Jong-Un 6, 27, 35, 265

Korea 3, 6, 22, 24, 26, 27, 28, 35, 36, 146, 190, 265–277, 280

Kushner, Jared 12, 30, 32

Latin America 2, 148, 251, 290

Latinos/Hispanics 19, 75, 80, 83, 84, 102, 150

Lies (Trump's) 5, 11, 17, 25, 39, 170, 214–223, 225–227

Make America Great Again 14, 94, 129, 161, 175, 235, 280, 281, 305

Mar-a-Lago 12

McCain, John 18, 24, 218

Merkel, Angela 24

Mexico 2, 3, 5, 14, 19, 25, 26, 28, 29, 34, 35, 36, 95, 106, 129, 150, 190, 217, 221, 227, 250, 270, 280

Michigan 2, 14, 38, 79, 84, 85, 90, 96, 98, 99, 109, 112, 113, 120, 123, 124, 125, 149, 211

Middle East 3, 5, 36, 167, 168, 217, 218, 235–246, 255, 295

Misogyny 1, 2, 3, 5, 11, 19, 20, 173, 180

Mueller investigation 2, 17, 25, 26, 29, 30, 31, 190, 217, 218

Muslim ban 109, 190, 222, 291

Muslims 5, 20, 25, 95, 11, 6, 141, 147, 158, 167, 172, 173, 190, 222, 243, 290, 291, 292, 294, 295, 322

NAFTA 2, 221

Native Americans 19, 147, 155

NATO 22, 23, 35, 216, 218, 243, 280, 290

Nazis 2, 19, 146, 184, 188, 238

Neoliberalism 1, 3, 4, 15, 125, 129, 130, 132, 133, 134, 136, 140, 141, 227

Nepotism 3, 11, 32

Never Trump 16

Obama, Barack 3, 6, 7, 19, 20, 25, 29, 32, 35, 70, 71, 75, 76, 80, 81, 83, 84, 90, 92, 93, 94, 96, 98, 105, 108, 111, 113, 119, 123, 125, 131, 148, 150, 151, 156, 157, 161, 164, 169, 171, 182, 184, 185, 186, 216, 217, 220, 226, 244, 245, 249, 251, 252, 255, 299, 307, 322, 323, 325, 329, 335

Paris Climate Accord 3, 22, 32, 36, 312, 314, 316, 317, 318

Pence, Mike 14, 241

Pennsylvania 2, 12, 14, 62, 79, 85, 90, 96, 99, 109, 112, 113, 125, 149, 211, 328

Philippines 12, 27, 185

Populism 5, 16, 93, 109, 111, 118, 129, 131, 132, 162, 168, 173, 237

Puerto Rico 7, 222, 312, 314–316, 318

Putin, Vladimir 3, 17, 18

Racism 1, 2, 3, 4, 11, 16, 17, 19, 20, 34, 121, 144, 296

Racism 1, 2, 3, 4, 11, 16, 17, 19, 20, 34, 121, 144, 296

Refugees 5, 6, 25, 107, 133, 170, 215, 222, 241, 280, 295

Republican Party 5, 16, 34, 69, 70, 87, 96, 105, 124, 161, 167, 168, 184, 188, 196, 220, 221, 225, 226, 308

Romney, Mitt 4, 37, 70–85, 88, 90, 92, 96, 97, 98, 108, 112, 113, 114, 115, 116, 119, 148, 151, 152, 154, 156, 157, 198

Rural voters 98, 100, 101, 107

Russia 2, 3, 17–18, 25, 26, 28, 29, 30, 31, 36, 39, 188, 216, 217, 220, 237, 240, 275, 280

Sexism 2, 17, 20, 82, 173

Shithole countries 19, 235

Swing states 69, 70, 71–79, 84, 85, 88, 90

Tariffs 2, 34, 109, 218, 223, 242, 243, 281, 284, 287, 290, 292, 295

Tea Party 14, 101, 184, 189

Terrorism 14, 26, 171, 172, 173, 236, 237

Trade wars 2, 3, 6, 35, 280, 281, 282, 283, 292, 295

Trans-Pacific Partnership 2, 35, 102, 280, 290

Trump Tower 12, 14, 24, 30, 33, 64, 65, 93, 95, 217
Trump University 13, 19, 32
Trump, Fred 3, 11, 13, 19, 58–62, 63, 64, 65
Trump, Friedrich 3, 11, 56–58, 62, 63
Trump, Ivanka 12, 26, 32, 33
Trump, Melania 12, 17, 33
Tweets 5, 19, 20, 21, 24, 26, 28, 31, 38, 39, 95, 161, 162, 164–175, 199, 216, 219, 222, 236, 239, 242, 243, 265, 311, 313, 315

United Nations 28, 236, 237, 280

Wall (border) 2, 3, 5, 14, 25, 26, 28, 29, 34, 95, 106, 107, 109, 158, 162, 171, 175, 190, 217, 218, 221, 222, 227, 235, 308, 323, 327
Wallace, George 39, 121, 124, 125, 131
Wikileaks 17, 31, 144
Wisconsin 4, 14, 84, 85, 90, 92–109, 112, 113, 120, 123, 124, 125, 126, 149, 201, 211
Working class 1, 2, 3, 4, 14, 15, 60, 79, 80, 112, 118, 134, 184, 210
Wrestling 5, 28, 193–211